William Mumford Baker

**Inside**

A Chronicle of Secession

William Mumford Baker

**Inside**
*A Chronicle of Secession*

ISBN/EAN: 9783337729646

Printed in Europe, USA, Canada, Australia, Japan

Cover: Foto ©ninafisch / pixelio.de

More available books at **www.hansebooks.com**

# INSIDE:

## CHRONICLE OF SECESSION.

BY GEORGE F. HARRINGTON.

WITH ILLUSTRATIONS BY THOMAS NAST.

NEW YORK:

HARPER & BROTHERS, PUBLISHERS,

FRANKLIN SQUARE.

1866.

# PREFACE.

THE AUTHOR BURYING HIS MANUSCRIPT.

NOT a Preface merely for preface' sake, but as few words as possible by way of explanation.

This book was written in one of the centres of Secession. Begun at the outset, it grew with the growth thereof, and closed with its ending. Owing to peculiar circumstances, the writer, never out of the pale of Secession during its continuance, had full time and opportunity for as careful a study of the period as he could wish. If he has cast the result in the form of a fiction his work is none the less as essentially true as the dryest history ever penned; and will be acknowledged to be by all who, by reason of occupying a like position during the war, are competent to speak. And it is as true, in most respects, for one region in the South as for any other, the Secessionist as a class in all its varieties, and the Union men as a class in all *its* varieties, being, in every village throughout the South, very much the same as in Somerville.

The form of a novel was adopted chiefly to make it impossible for any one to identify the place in which the scene is laid and the characters acting therein. And that for this reason: The period embraced in the story is one which will be, in all its aspects, a phenomenon interesting to men for generations to come. Other volumes will treat of other features of this most remarkable period; this book aims only to photograph the social aspect thereof from a point entirely within; and it is a period altogether too sublime, both in its evil and its good, for any thing so short-lived and insect-like as mere personalities, which, as they buzz and sting but during their brief moment, should perish also and be forgotten within the same. Yes, if there be one drop of gall, a least splinter of wormwood in these pages, the writer is ignorant of it.

Born at, and having spent almost his entire life in, the South, the writer's first affections are, by that nature which attaches every thing that breathes to its own home, with and for the South. At the very same time he entertains a love yet larger and stronger for the nation of which the South is but a part, and is powerless to refuse conviction, both of head and heart, to the truth that the whole is greater than part of the whole. Above all does he yield reverence and affection, still beyond this, to Truth, Right, Conscience, God. A love herein without the least conflict in its three degrees of positive, comparative, superlative. Toward no one, during Secession, has his hatred been even stirred. For many a one, during that time, has the writer's pity been excited—his deepest pity for the guiltiest as being the most infatuated: glad that justice, human justice perhaps, Divine justice certainly, is to be meted out; glad, also, that, save in these humble pages, to him is committed neither its determining nor the execution.

He claims no merit whatever above others, far better, mayhap, in every other respect than himself, for, being from his earliest memory, in every thought, emotion, word, deed, through all associations, oppositions, circumstances, whatever they were, a Union man—claims no merit for this, since it required no exertion on his part, he being such by a sort of nature, as a cedar-tree is not a cypress, and as an oak-tree is an oak. Conscious of many a shortcoming in other respects, he has nothing to reproach himself with in this, unless it be for excess of love to his country, which, perhaps, the times may excuse.

The very manuscript from which these lines are printed could tell a tale of its own, apart from that which it narrates, in confirmation of this. While writing it the author was perfectly aware that his life would have paid the forfeit had a written page been discovered. On more than one Sunday the wife of the writer has borne the manuscript to church concealed about her person, in terror of leaving it, like powder exposed to chance sparks, at home. However, as our story shows, that was but a small specimen of the totally new set of duties, unprovided for in the marriage ceremony, which wives had to perform for Union husbands during Secession. On two occasions the writer was obliged to bury his manuscript in the ground, thereby damaging it seriously. To *that* the printer whose misfortune it is to set up these pages will tearfully depone.

They say that even amidst rock and glacier, avalanche and tempest of Alpine regions, there spring flowers not unworthy the gathering. Who knows but it may be so with this volume, which has slowly and painfully matured its leaves under circumstances— But suppose we permit the book to speak for itself.

# INSIDE.

## A CHRONICLE OF SECESSION.

"HURRAH FOR LINCOLN AN' THE SOUF!"

### CHAPTER I.

"A LITTLE more powder and a little more shot
'll teach dem Yankees how to trot!"

"No, Amouse, no; that ain't the way; this
the way:

"Little more shot an' little powder
'll make them Yankees holler louder!"

"No, Bub, 'tain't; you an' Amouse bofe
wrong:

"Hurrah! hurrah! for the Yankee flag
That bears the stingle star!"

"Lor', Miss 'Ria, you better not sing dat—
not de Yankee flag—bonner blue flag—"

"You shut up, Amouse; hush, 'Ria."

"Hush your own mouth, Bub. Hurrah for
Lincoln an' Jeff Davis!"

"Oh, 'Ria, I'll tell Pa what you said! Hollered for old Lincoln; didn't she, Amouse? If
they don't hang you! Yonder's Pupper now,
just coming in the gate. Oh, Pupper, here's
'Ria been hollering all the morning for Abe
Lincoln! Ain't she a old Yankee?"

"Am a Yankee! Am a 'Bolitionist! Hate
old Davis! Hurrah for Lincoln an' the Souf!"

"Hush your racket, children; hush that, Maria!" and their father fastened the gate slowly
and carefully behind him.

"They know just about as much about it all
as most grown people," said, but strictly to himself, the father of 'Ria and Bub and the master
of Amos, about whose profession, as he walks toward the house, there is no necessity of informing you. That he is a doctor you can see by
the medical saddle-bags which he carries hung
over his left arm. A good, careful, conscientious doctor too, especially to nurse a patient
through a long illness. That you can read in
his mild, florid face, in the loiter of his very gait.

But, if you are a woman, and possess intuition, you can not help seeing also that this Dr.
Warner is not the man to make an eminent
surgeon. As you observe, following him with
your eyes toward the house, he has very light
hair and eyes—not the man to scoop a tumor
out of the bosom of one's screaming child—not
one you would care to call in if your leg had
suddenly to be taken out of its socket at the
thigh. When Nature has given a decided character to a man or woman she is very apt to hang
out some decided flag of it on the outer wall:
eyes of some definite color; hair red, black, or
very brown.

"But, Pupper," says Bub, calling after his
father, "oh, Pupper, please make 'Ria stop hollering out here for Lincoln; she's all the time
doing it. Joe Staples threw a rock at us yesterday; hit our Amouse plum on the head."

"You hear, Maria. Mind what Bub says.
Don't you let me hear of your hollering any
more," says the father, turning half around.
"Don't you know ladies never holler?"

"Oh, Pa, but yes they do!" exclaims his
daughter. "Don't you know how Sally Smithers waved her towel an' hollered that day the

soldiers marched?—all the ladies on the front porches—don't you 'member?"

"Handkerchief, child; but you are a little, little girl, not eight years old; you mustn't holler—"

"Yes I must, Pupper; have to holler. Amouse here, he hollers; Joe Staples hollers; Bub is always hollering; every body in Somerville is always hollering all the time."

"Well, Maria, if you must have something to holler—"

"'Bliged to," put in the little girl.

"Then holler for—Andrew Jackson;" and her prudent parent passed on into the house.

Ever mindful of the various poisons in his saddle-bags, Dr. Warner placed them on a small shelf made for the express purpose, in the hall beside the hat-stand, high out of reach of the children. Next he proceeded, with what might be styled a cautious step for a man in his own house, to the door leading into the breakfast-room.

"Ah, Sarah, breakfast over, I see," he said, first glancing in through the partly-opened door, and then venturing more boldly in, when he sees that no one is therein except the negro woman standing over the wrecks of the meal, washing up the cups and saucers.

Prey fairly in the trap, the trigger springs:

"Over, Dr. Warner? Of course it was, one good hour ago, and you knew it when you asked."

It was his wife who said it, following her voice into the breakfast-room as she spoke. She had been saying it over to herself ever since she heard the front gate click, and short and sharp enough were the tones in which she spoke.

"Gracious goodness! can't your patients fix it so we *can* have some little order about our meals? But it is all your fault, Dr. Warner. Why *can't* you just give them their physic, whatever it is, be done with it, and come home? Here's Sarah—why can't you get that coffee-pot, Sarah?—here's Sarah—and you haven't washed them plates up yet?—here's Sarah kept from her morning's work, and kept from and kept from it, and she a good six dozen washing to have done and hung out before the cows come up to-night. If I was you, Dr. Warner, I'd give up my practice; goodness knows you make little enough at it; you would make plenty if you would only collect. But precious little you'd make at any thing else!"

"It doesn't matter, Helen," ventured her spouse, whose somewhat bald head had fallen into an indescribable droop, as of one under a shower-bath, the instant his wife began. So saying, he drew his chair to the table while the servant was placing his breakfast thereon. "I have been up near all night," he continued, as he stirred his coffee; "haven't any warm hominy? Never mind, I have no appetite, any thing will do."

"That Mrs. Bowles, I suppose. Bring me my work here off the sewing-machine, and mind you wipe your wet hands clean before you do it, you Sarah;" and Mrs. Warner takes a seat at the other end of the table. "I would like to know when *she* settled last—such a lady as you always call her. And why haven't you told me what is the matter with the woman? They might have given you at least a cup of coffee."

"And so they did, Alice saw to that," says Dr. Warner, who never fails to speak the best he can of any and every one.

"Coffee! Yes, Confederate coffee, I'll bet," interposes his wife, threading her needle.

"Yes, but you couldn't have told the difference—at least, hardly;" for the Doctor is very truthful too.

"Stuff! Never tell me," breaks in his wife. "There's old Mrs. Juggins, she uses barley. You know you couldn't stand that, even the smell. Came to find out we had gone and ground it, while she used it so—only toasted. Tried not grinding, but it wouldn't do. There's sweet-potatoes, too, cut thin and browned. Mrs. Bowles's notion; you know what a sickly sort of sweet it was. Coffee! Rye, too, that is Mr. Neely's plan. Like a Yankee! Then there's Mr. Ferguson, okra seed's his Scotch scheme, as if one could get okra seed enough to last a week. Never tell me! A thing is either coffee or it ain't coffee. You are so polite you pretend you can't tell the difference—don't catch me."

"One dollar a pound," ventures her husband.

"What, gone up to a dollar? Oh, if I only was a man! If I didn't hang them. First thing you knew it was fifty cents. Next time I went in to the stores it was: 'Not one pound on hand, ma'am, sorry to say; hope to get some soon.' And when they did have some next time it was eighty cents. And all the time they were pretending to be out they had sacks and sacks of it piled away down in the cellar, or hidden under carpets and things way up in the loft. Oh, if I was only a man! Calicoes up to fifty cents; domestics, six bits; fifty cents for a tin cup; five pounds of sugar for a dollar; molasses, dollar and a quarter; shoes, eight dollars; flour, fifty dollars, or soon will be. I'd like to know what we are coming to! Mr. Barker was right—they are worse than Yankees! Our men gone off to fight the battles of their country, bleeding and dying somewhere, and they at home making money out of the poor wives, and widows, and orphans. Barker was right. Their stores ought to be just taken, the goods sold for them at the old prices. Hang them!" ejaculated Mrs. Warner, her wrath rising, as it ever did, at the sound of her own voice. "Yes, as brother Barker says, 'I could string them up with my own hands!'"

"Rather strong language for a preacher," interposed her husband, who was quietly eating his breakfast.

"As much as to say, if Mr. Barker oughtn't to say it because he is a preacher, I oughtn't to say it because I'm a woman."

Dr. Warner continues to breakfast. A little more, perhaps, of the shower-bath droop about the head. There is a pause of surprise in the eyes of his wife. She sits with suspended needle, looking at her husband. And while she is still an instant let us seize that rare instant to catch her photograph—if we can.

When Dr. Warner first settled in Somerville, years ago this 1862, Mrs. Warner was a tall, spare, shrill spinster. Other than being an exceedingly industrious and neat housekeeper Miss Helen Morris had only fourteen recommendations to a marrying man; and those fourteen had legs and could wield hoes, scrubbing-brushes, and washing-boards. Somehow or other the Doctor married her. Was it that the poor and patientless young Doctor wanted a home? Mrs. Warner very often afterward herself suggested that solution of the case. It was a special weapon in her arsenal in the worriment of her husband, which worriment was a large part of her housekeeping. Nor did she conceal her painful impression to that effect from chance company either; for it was a peculiarity of Mrs. Warner to express herself upon matters, pleasant and unpleasant, relating to herself openly, fully, and upon every occasion. Or it may be—most were of that opinion—that it was not the Doctor who married the lady, but the lady who married him. Good, easy, indolent man, he was no match for Miss Helen Morris—as natural a prey to such a woman as a mouse is to a cat.

Not that the Doctor did not have warning fair and sufficient. When he applied that day in the dirty county court office to Bob Withers, county clerk, for the marriage license, that gentleman did his best. Years after Bob prided himself upon that.

"To Miss Helen Morris—not the widow Morris—to Miss Helen Morris, did you say, Doc?" he asked, with an emphasis not complimentary.

Even when Bob Withers brought himself fairly to the task of filling up the blanks of a license he spoiled one form, and then another, with blunders, his mind evidently being on something else. And when he had dipped his pen in the ink to begin at the third it was only to stick it behind his ear, unlock the drawer in the desk at which he wrote, take out a pistol and lay it thereupon, the handle convenient to his friend. A frank and wholesome face, Bob's.

"Doc," he solemnly said, with hand resting upon the weapon, "I like you as much, by George! as any man I know. I haven't forgot that typhoid fever time. But look here, Doc. I know that Miss Helen Morris—gracious Heavens!" with considerable irritation, "who in Somerville don't know her?—and I just tell you as a friend, you see—no other possible interest in

the thing—but before you marry them black eyes and that awful tongue—you see I boarded with her once—you'd better take this Derringer and kill yourself, by George! and be done with it."

But the Doctor married her.

Early in life Miss Helen may have been a brunette and all the rest. But Mrs. Warner was now sallow—only sallow. The lips were still red, but very thin. And then her eyes? Once on a time the Reverend Edward Arthur had made a pretty long trip on a canal boat, and on his introduction to Mrs. Warner, when he first took charge of the Somerville church, he had been struck with a foolish fancy that her blackly-defined eyebrows resembled the lockgates on the canal when opening to let down the water. The fact is, the lady's eyes and eyebrows did have an oblique direction upward above the nose, giving her the appearance of being wide awake, becoming more and more oblique as she grew excited. Free as the air in the expression of herself; tough and elastic as gutta percha; electric from head to foot, the electricity quivering, as its nature is on every projecting point of the body charged, at the tips of her fingers, the corners of her eyes and mouth, in focus on the end of her tongue.

But let us be charitable. Perhaps if you, or even if I myself, had dipped snuff as long and as incessantly as she had, we too would have been as nervous as she was. But very little Bub, 'Ria, Amos, Sarah, and the rest had to endure it in comparison with the Doctor. Sharp and perpetual as were her eyes and tongue in regard to all within and without her household, the Doctor had by far the larger share thereof.

Because for him it was she cared most. Indolent, sensible, getting-to-be-corpulent, slovenly Dr. Warner! He has learned only to droop his head and take it. When it becomes too bad, and if Mrs. Warner pours her vial upon him when company—as she often does—is present, the Doctor, at the earliest possible moment, carries his drooped head out of the parlor and off the place. Yet, let us get at the eternal reason and meaning of things; for there is as solid a reason for the growth of a nettle as there is for the existence of a rose—as substantial a meaning in the existence of a mosquito as in the life of John Howard. As a needed spur—we will not call it thorn—in his side, this wife is a blessing to this husband. He married her, perhaps, with blind promptings—who knows?—from his physiological studies, because she was so unlike to himself. And she married him?—perhaps from some vague intuitions to the same effect.

If the stream of my story did not hurry me on so urgently I would like to turn out of its current for a moment and say just one word about that admirable provision of Nature, by which she preserves, in our species as in the planets, her own sacred balance. When it is not Parent, nor Pique, nor Mammon, nor any thing other than sweet Nature herself who weds you to your wife, you will find that she mates you two on the plan of a perfect compensation; that is, she makes up for the excess of any defect in one of you by an excess of the opposite virtue in the other. It was something other than Nature that made the match if you, a tall man, are wedded to any other than an undersized woman. Woe to you, Madam, if you, a blonde, are united to a fair-haired man! So of that inner nature of which the outer appearance is but the symbol. Alas for you, Sir, if you, a man of desponding temperament, are wedded to a wife of the same dismal hue of feeling! Though I believe, even in that case, Nature strives to make the best of a union in which she had no hand. I will not say how it will be if you are a man; but if you are a woman I am certain of this: however despondent you may yourself be, the instant you detect the slightest gloom in your husband's brow, or the least growl in his voice, you go instinctively to the other side of the tilting bark, and become as cheerful as possible. And the instant you give way to gloom notice how awkwardly, yet well meaningly, he, poor fellow! attempts at least to trim the tilting vessel by putting on at least an aspect of cheerfulness. Woe, then, had it been to Mrs. Warner if she had been united to some black-eyed, black-haired, black-bearded husband! Notice the union of two sable clouds in mid-air, if you would understand the result. So that when Mrs. Warner paused from her sewing and said,

"As much as to say, if brother Barker oughtn't to say it because he is a preacher, I oughtn't to say it because I'm a woman." The Doctor only helped himself in a sidelong and deprecatory manner to the butter.

"I do believe," said Mrs. Warner—"Sarah, step out and tell those children to hush that noise —I do believe," she continued in low, sepulchral tones, "that you, Dr. Warner, are a—Union man!"

Language can not set forth the awfulness of epithet implied in the charge, the canal gates opening wider and wider. "Yes, and I know now why the bells didn't ring last night! I was wondering, I know now!" said Mrs. Warner swiftly, and with a new light breaking all over her face. "Yes, and why you couldn't leave Mrs. Bowles. Worse, is she! Ha! Yes, I see it all." Canal gates open their widest.

Dr. Warner glanced up from his plate at his wife with a flash of admiration. "What an amazingly sharp woman!" he said to himself.

"Bells?" he said, however, at last. "Bells? I should think, Helen, you would have had enough of bells night before last. Every bell in town! There was the big Methodist bell; I lay

and counted no less than ten fresh hands in turn at that bell-rope before day. The first hand began as if he would break the bell to pieces, pulled until it was broken down; then you could notice the rope taken by another till he gave up exhausted; then by another, through the whole ten. I am not nervous, but I couldn't get a wink of sleep."

"Dr. Warner!" said Mrs. W. solemnly, needle, eyes, breath suspended.

"And you know I said at the time—or was it you yourself made the remark—"

"Dr. Warner!—Sarah, don't come here, stay in the kitchen till I call you."

"Well, it was one of us said it," continued the husband, very quietly sipping his coffee, looking over the top of his cup with unusual hardihood at his eager wife.

"You know I never said it!" broke in the wife. You know I never could have been such a traitor as to have said it. And if the paper that came last night says our soldiers have been whipped there in Tennessee, it's a lie! Didn't the papers night before last tell how our men had come out of Fort Donelson and driven the Hessians back through their camps, and killed six thousand, and taken all the rest prisoners, and—and—"

"Very well, my dear, you needn't be excited at me. Have it your own way. Suppose we talk of something else."

"What is the matter with Mrs. Bowles, Dr. Warner?" asked his wife, with sudden suspicion.

"Well," replied her helpmate, slowly, "the faculty have different names for it. There are febrile symptoms, too much excitement in the brain. Nervous, hysteria."

"Stuff; but what has made her worse? I know it can not be she has heard any bad news about that everlasting Rutledge Bowles of hers, for you would have told me so when you first came. What has she heard? Something bad, I know."

"Well, yes. But you know, my dear, Mrs. Bowles permits her mind to run too much, really too much, on the events of the day—"

"Dr. Warner," says his wife, in alarming tones though lower than before, "will you tell me the news that came last night?"

"If you wish it. Remember it may be false; you will be sure it is. In any case I didn't do any thing to bring it about."

"What is it?"

"Fort Donelson has fallen, my dear. General Johnson has retreated into Alabama. Nashville has capitulated. A good many more items to the same effect. At least so the paper says. I dare say part of the news may be exaggerated, premature at least."

"It's a lie—it's a base, base, base lie! I'll bet a thousand dollars the man that prints that paper is a Yankee. He ought to be hung!"

"I DO BELIEVE THAT YOU, DR. WARNER, ARE A—UNION MAN?"

Perhaps it was owing to her cheeks having become some shades sallower that Mrs. Warner's lips seemed so much redder, her eyes and hair so much blacker than before. "Oh, if I was only a man!" she added.

Meanwhile her husband only arched his brows deprecatingly, and proceeded to eat his breakfast with a coolness, appetite, even cheerfulness, which contrasted greatly with the vehement, almost hysterical, wife at the other end of the table.

But, oh the exquisite satisfaction of Dr. Warner in imparting the news, unspeakable satisfaction at the very core of his heart, though all the rest of his anatomy might disavow it!

How you up there at the North rang your bells and blazed in all manner of illumination, and invoked the entire hive to help utter your gratification, Heaven and History well know. Your joy? It was as nothing compared with the electric ecstasy thereat which flashed unexpressed through all loyal hearts at the South. Heaven only knew it then; History shall know it forever.

"And if it is true, though I don't believe a word of it, there's some base treachery in it, or the officers were all drunk, or they were all a pack of cowards! To give up to Yankees! I do wish the Yankees had managed to kill them. I hope Davis will have them tried and hung," says Mrs. Warner.

"Why, my dear, it would take a perfect factory to keep you in rope," dares her husband, playfully but injudiciously.

"And you are not sorry a single bit!" responds his wife, turning the lightning of her rage zigzag in every direction that offers. "I do believe you are glad. I tell you, Dr. Warner, if I actually thought so, was satisfied of it, I would not care that, if we have been married so long. I'd—ha! no wonder you wouldn't get up that night the bells rung so. I had to hunch and hunch you ever so often before you woke even. And when you did wake, you said it must be fire, not even expecting a victory. Ought not to be too certain, you said, at the very time every bell in town was ringing as hard as could be. Dr. Warner, you are the worry of my life! And there you sit this moment just as cool—"

"But you know, Helen, I heard the news several hours ago. Besides, I've just drunk two cups of your excellent coffee. Then, my mind has been taken up with Mrs. Bowles's case. And, really, my dear," said the Doctor, eager to divert the conversation, "I'm getting uneasy about Mrs. Bowles. Such a sensitive, refined little body she is! perfect lady, too, in every respect; but she has given herself up to so much excitement for so long. Rutledge Bowles, too; the news night before last almost deranged her with joy. Then comes that news last night. The reaction was almost too much for her. I tell you what, my dear," continued the Doctor, with indolent hypocrisy, "I'm glad I have a wife who is stronger than her nerves. Glad, my dear, that you have such strong sense of your own to keep you steady these stormy times."

"No, Dr. Warner, you can't blind me. With all her aristocratic airs I know there are some things, at least, in which I can only pity. One can't help liking Alice. You never hear Rutlege Bowles from her lips—never opens her mouth about him, hardly. But, if you mean to say she loves the South more than I do—"

"But what is the use of worrying yourself? The armies are in the field, doing, I dare say, all they can. And you are doing all you can. You are out every day collecting for the soldiers, and you sing for them at all the concerts, act for them in all the tableaux, sew for them, knit, quilt. What more can you do? If one-half of the ladies of Somerville only did one-half of what you do—"

"Ah, Dr. Warner, I see what you are after!" said his wife, somewhat mollified; "but you are only from Tennessee, Eastern Tennessee at that, and you know where I'm from. What I want is for you to be more interested, excited, more like a warm-hearted Southern man. But there you go day after day with your old saddle-bags over your arm, just as you used to do, feeling people's pulses, dosing children, pulling teeth—you don't talk enough. But this news—oh, it can't, can't—"

"In your acquaintance among the ladies those that talk most, fuss most, do most of the work do they, eh? Why you told me yourself, Helen—"

"Pshaw! Dr. Warner, you know perfectly well what I mean. You are not sure enough the South is going to succeed. And you visit among those Union people just as much—more, I believe—than you do among good Secessionists. Nobody can get any thing out of you. Look at Dr. Ginnis."

"Which do you think the best doctor of the two? No, my dear, I'm a physician in large practice, I believe; all my time is taken up with my patients. Dr. Ginnis is more politician than medical man—talks about the war at the top of his big voice at the bedside of the sick, and, no matter how sick they are, for the hour at a time. If he likes, and they like, let him. I prefer to do my way, physic them, and come home to my family. You know what a quiet sort of man I am. Besides, you have patriotism enough for us both, Helen. Take your way, my dear—let me take mine."

"Yes, Dr. Warner. Oh yes; I dare say. Very fine. But what worries my life out is nobody can tell. When you are with Secessionists you are as mum as a mouse, or open your lips only to dispute something. When you are with those Union people, oh I know you! Why don't you denounce them, tell me that? Every body in Somerville is talking about you. Mr. Neely told me only last Monday, when he was here to see about Bub drawing those pictures on his blackboard, as if you can expect a child to respect a Yankee teacher!—told me, humph, much faith I have in him, loud as he talks—told me Lamum told him that Dr. Peel said he really believed you were nothing more'n less than a *Abolitionist*, if the truth was known!" But to describe Mrs. Warner's emphasis on the word is beyond the power of type.

"And this great Dr. Peel knows, of course, more about me—he has been here less than a year, I believe—than you do, or than any body who has known me here for ten years," says Dr. Warner, pushing away his plate from before him.

"I told Mr. Neely to tell Lamum to tell Dr. Peel from me that it was a lie, and he knew it," said Mrs. Warner, promptly enough. "If he hints such a thing to me, the big, bedizzened old puppy, I'll slap those ears of his! But don't you go and say any thing to him," adds Mrs. Warner, who had got her husband into hot water more than once in their married life, as he rises from the table.

"Not the least fear of me. I would be a fool to mind any thing any one says of me in these days," replies her helpmate.

"But this dreadful, dreadful news! Are you sure you are not mistaken? It can't, can't be true! I'll put on my sun-bonnet and run over to Mrs. Ret Roberts, she'll know all about it. Though, poor thing! how such a man as Colonel Ret Roberts ever came to marry her, soft, say nothing sort of a thing— Oh, one thing, Dr. Warner, engage me ten pounds of coffee at Mr. Ellis's. If any body has any conscience left he's— But, Dr. Warner"—and his wife seizes upon him as he passes her—"do you really think, really now, there's any doubt about the South succeeding?"

Nature gives every living thing some mode of defense, or at least escape. People that have feeble hands generally are compensated with admirable legs. Master Fox does not pretend to the roar nor to the teeth and claws of the lion; but then Sir Reynard is not deficient in cunning. This Dr. Warner can no more stand before the eyes and the tongue of his wife than he can before Atropos. Thin-haired, florid, unaggressive, fat, too, he does only what nature has left him to do—droops his head and takes it. It is a great deal he has to take, when she is fairly at it. Spare in frame as she is, but oh, the interplatting of her eyes and lips are about as awful a scourge as need be!

Sarah, and the rest in the kitchen, take their share of Mrs. Warner black and silent as night—such the shield nature supplies them. Bub and 'Ria, the two children, dodge and escape out of range, with steadily growing contempt for her in her bursts of fondness and preserves as in her anger and scolding. At last, the Doctor gets the largest share of Mrs. Warner and her black eyes; he escapes by never looking up while she is carrying on. The words he simply hears. Long habit helps him there. As the storm lulls he flatters—consciously, awkwardly, transparently flatters. But, then, flattery is sweet; and here was Mrs. Warner's only source thereof.

So that when his wife pressed upon him the question last recorded, one being asked at that period over every table at the South, what does the Doctor?

"Hush, Helen; Sarah out there might hear. I'll whisper, that is, I'll let you know exactly what I really think and feel," and approaching his lips cautiously to her ear, this deceitful practitioner pressed a rapid kiss upon the convenient cheek, disengaged his arm, and was gone.

It was a little strange, such disastrous news too, but it was the first time Dr. Warner had kissed his wife in two years!

THE AUTHOR ATTEMPTING TO DESCRIBE SOMERVILLE.

## CHAPTER II.

It strikes me, dear reader, that every writer ought to have, from the outset of his book, a perfectly clear understanding with his reader. You have often noticed that no public speaker succeeds in what he has to say unless there be such an understanding between himself and his audience. And, among speakers, he is an orator of the highest order who, from the opening of his lips to the moment he ceases to speak, is on terms of the closest and clearest mutual understanding with those to whom he addresses himself.

Now, there is one thing in which I will venture to crave such an understanding with you, dear reader. I can not describe. You will catch my meaning when I tell you that I have sat here some ten minutes nibbling at the end of my penholder, desirous of describing to you the good town of Somerville in which our story is laid, and find it impossible to do so. It may be some step toward this to say that Somerville is situated in one of the Southern States. Which of these States it may be in, try as I may to conceal it, the reader will be certain to find out long before he reaches the last page—it will slip out, I am satisfied. Each State has its own distinct individuality, a kind of personal identity which impresses itself upon each one of its children. Now, I have reason to believe that I could, after half an hour's conversation with a stranger, tell him to be a preacher, if he was one, and even the very denomination of which he is a preacher; and so if he be lawyer, doctor, planter, schoolteacher, or what not. So of State identity. Throw me one hour with a man, and I can give a shrewd guess whether he is a Southerner or not; and if I miss it in naming the very State at the South of which he is a native it will be the first time. And yet I must add one thing more, that the whole truth may be told. Very often have I met a man having all what are generally known as the peculiarities of the New Englander—reserve, caution, sharpness in trade, closeness in purse—and yet, who had never been outside of his native South in his life. And often, too, have I been pleasantly associated with one having all the opposite peculiarities of the Southerner—frank, cordial, generous, radiant with every noble impulse—what we somewhat boastfully claim to be the characteristics of a thorough-blooded Southerner, yet, at last, born and "raised" among the snows and nutmegs, not at all tropical, of New England.

The truth is, we of these American States are at last one people. Our origin and history~so far, railways, intermarriage, and other powerful processes of approximation and assimilation now working, all events and forces past and present are leavening us into one, and that altogether irrespective whether we like it or not. Those of us who look upon this continent from the point nearest to that from which the Almighty regards it, well know that all things, even the most unlike, are leavening our millions by a process, which is none other than the purpose of God, into a unity infinitely sublimer than any thing and every thing we have hitherto expressed by the word Union! You know this already? Well, but let me say it.

However, it is of Somerville we are now attempting to speak. And how shall it be described? To say it contains some twelve hundred people leaves but a vague idea upon the mind. Could I describe a river as meandering beside it, or forests as engirdling it, or mountains as towering above it, that would be some help. The only objection to this is, that it would not be the truth—a level, post oak, sandy plain is its location; no mountains, no river, and but a scrubby forest.

It may assist us to say that Somerville is mainly built along one principal street, with tributary streets, like rills to a river, emptying into it on either side. The court-house, too, should be specified—a square brick building in the centre of the town. But why should one feel the strong aversion I feel for that gloomy building with its brick-paved floor below, its well-worn and exceedingly dirty stairway, its breezy court-room above, its yellow walls spangled a yard up from the floor with tobacco juice, its bewhittled benches and hide-bottomed chairs, its doors and posts be-plastered with curt Sheriff's notices half print half writing, and with notices of cattle lost, written in all possible varieties of spelling and grammar?

The architecture of the four churches yields me nothing whatever to describe in regard to them. Places of worship they were—nothing else and nothing more—having in many respects a painful resemblance to the dreary court-house. And yet good, sound, practical sermons were often delivered in one and all. Sincere worship, too, as ever was offered in stately cathedral and towering minster, have those uninviting houses witnessed. Or, if there ever was lack of fervor in the morning and night services at which the white population attended, it was more than made up by the warmth of the worship on Sunday afternoons, when the black people took their turn in the churches. And you may talk as much as you please of the advantages of race and education in all respects, I defy any resident of Somerville to deny the assertion, that the practical Christianity of the colored professors of religion was on a level at least with that of the white communicants of the various churches in the place. Let us not mind so excessively much about our color and condition in this present world in other regards; if religion but land us safely in heaven there will be infinite, divinest influences operating on us there, with an eternity for them to operate in.

Nor will we say any thing of the post-office, two doors off from the principal hotel; if it will help us on to say that Smithers is post-master in the one, and Staples, Joe, host in the other, let that also be added; nor of the dry-goods stores, with the red blankets hanging at their doors; nor of the provision stores, sticky with sugar and molasses, and greasy with great piles of bacon.

I was aware of it before attempting the task; it is impossible to describe Somerville. In a journey across the State you pass through a dozen towns just like Somerville; you bear away nothing at all by which you can remember it from the other eleven; just the same sort of post-office at which the stage stopped with you to give out and to take in the mails, just the same groups idling in front of the groceries, just the same sort of tavern at which you snatch your hasty meal; like beads on the thread of your travel, the towns seem duplicates of each other. But there is to Somerville a focus, a point having the same relation to Somerville, and to the county of which Somerville is the county seat, even to the State in which Somerville is located, that the brain has to the body. I refer to the office of the Somerville *Star.*

Imagine a two story frame-house, not very far from the post-office. True, the huge sign-board on which is written Somerville *Star* is blown down, but then the largest half of what remains has been stood up against the side of the house on an end, and can easily be deciphered by those who already know what is inscribed thereon. All the printing is done up stairs. The editor's room you enter from the street, on the first floor. Nor need you knock; the door is never locked, and all you have to do is to push it open, if it should be shut, and walk in. You have only to introduce yourself, and you will be waved by the editor to a seat and to the last paper. If you are any body of importance, from any where outside of the county, a Judge say, or a candidate of the same views as Mr. Lamum, or a Colonel in some regiment present or prospective, you have only to make yourself agreeable, and in the next number of the Somerville *Star* you will read how "greatly gratified we were by a visit from our excellent friend," Colonel this or General that. "We are extremely gratified to learn from him," or, "We are much pained to be informed by him," and then you will read the information you may have incidentally communicated to the editor; but it will seem to you when in print vastly more important and decided in its nature than you had ever dreamed it to be at the time you mentioned it.

At the very moment Dr. Warner and his wife are conversing upon the news of the night before at their breakfast-table, Lamum and Dr. Peel are full of it in the editorial sanctum. This is not strange, however, as there is not an individual in Somerville—in the whole land, in fact, who is not at the same time conversing upon the same theme.

"I say, Lamum, between us, you know, what do you think of this news?" It is Dr. Peel who asks the question. He has read the bit of brown paper upon which it is printed some six times over, and holds it to read several times over yet before he is done.

"I think, Sir, that one half is false and the other half is exaggeration," replies Mr. Lamum, promptly. He has printed a paper too long not to know all about such things. We call him Mr. Lamum. The fact is, he is called Colonel Lamum and General Lamum and Major Lamum indifferently. Mr. Lamum by very few. Indulge me in the weakness of dropping all his titles and calling him simply Lamum. People never called him any thing else except in speaking to him.

An undersized man is Lamum. He may be thirty, and he may be fifty years old—you can form no conclusion on the matter merely by looking at him. Excessively lean; very much stooped in the shoulders; face very pale, and never changing color under any possible circumstance; nose long and sharp; thin black hair; of a swift gait in walking; prompt and sharp speech; very shabby in clothing—that is the man.

Although continually associated with people that do, Lamum never smokes, never drinks, never plays a game—at least of cards. You never catch him in a billiard-room or doggery, unless it is in search of some politician to be found nowhere else. Lamum rarely enters a church—never, in fact, save for some political reason, such as to hear a political prayer or sermon. Yet Lamum swears only when very greatly provoked. No one has ever breathed a syllable against him as a husband. In regard to his various pecuniary transactions his enemies violently assail him; but then his friends as vehemently defend him. As these transactions are enwound in lawsuits without number, it is impossible to decide upon them in advance of the jury.

One word expresses Lamum from his earliest manhood upward, heart and soul, body, mind, and spirit, conversation and conduct—in every respect from head to foot. He is a politician. Above politics, beneath politics—if it had any beneath—besides politics he has not a thought or emotion. All his reading is political papers; he holds no conversation, when he can help it, except upon political topics. He knows no ties to any living creature except political ties. As to his wife he sees her only across the table at meals, or, perchance, asleep in bed when he comes in late at night. His printer's devils have a joke that all his courting consisted of political conversation with his beloved—though why she married him Venus would have to ask of all the gods of Olympus to ascertain; perhaps Plutus could inform her. Certain it is, all of his street fights have been with political foes. There is nobody in the world—perhaps his wife excepted: he has no children, he has no time for such nonsense—loves this pale, cold, eager man.

There are many who fear him throughout his State; but oh, how unanimously throughout the State, which he rules with his pen, is he hated! Robespierre—yes, there must be a resemblance between the very appearances of the two men. Like Robespierre he loves politics not for the office or profit it brings him so much as for the dry sake of politics itself. Something like the intense fondness—not so much of a gambler for his cards as of a chess-player for his mystic game. He has a cold yet infinite zest in the intrigue, the twisting of facts, the magnifying of useful nothings, the diminishing of disagreeable somethings—the downright lying, the flattering, the bullying, the rewarding, the punishing—the wielding of Power, that is it! Robespierre had his guillotine, had he? Every Saturday's *Star* falls like an axe across some man's name if not his neck! Talk about the unscrupulous devotion of a Jesuit to his order!

Let it suffice to be said, Lamum was, in the most exclusive and intense sense possible to the word, a Politician, not in the sense of a stump-speaker. Lamum had a thin, feeble voice—he could not make speeches, never tried. But his pen! Ah, how powerfully he spoke through that! And how he ruled with it hundreds in every county in the State who did mount the stump.

"Look here, General," says his companion yet again, "you are going to print this ridiculous dispatch, are you? I say, you will fix it up in your paper? You know, between us, it won't do exactly."

"Hold on a moment," says Lamum, who has been writing rapidly ever since he entered the office. Dr. Peel resumes his brown dispatch. A large, dark man is Dr. Peel. What you might call a bulbous forehead, with very black hair and whiskers, singularly black. Dr. Peel possesses deep black eyes as singularly restless and eager in their motions. The Doctor has been in Somerville but a few months; shortly before the blockade was established over the Southern ports he arrived. Dr. Peel has long given up his practice, he says—has means enough to live.

And the Doctor *has* means, plenty it would seem—gold. No man can be more prompt in paying his board bill; nor does he make a single debt at a store, though he is continually in them, one and all, and purchases freely. The Doctor is partial to buggy-riding, and makes it a point to take some one of his acquaintances with him whenever he drives out. Though he has been in Somerville for so short a time he knows every body. Especially is he hand and glove with Dr. Ginnis, Mr. Neely, Colonel Roberts, old Mr. Juggins, the Rev. Mr. Barker, Lamum, and the rest of the genuine, from-the-start, out-and-out, no-mistake Secessionists. Of those who are suspected of being Union people he has the most unmitigated horror.

"Thank you, Sir; I wish to have nothing to say to such traitors"—he remarks—"I'd just as lief hang them as eat my dinner." He has frequently observed, "I'd put an ounce of lead through them, or six inches of cold steel into their white livers and black hearts as quick as take a drink, Sir, and a —— sight quicker!" and here his hands would clench, his eyes roll, and he would curse the individuals in question with a species of frenzy that left any other man far behind.

Not a war-meeting of any sort but he was the first to be present and the last to leave, the loudest to applaud and the largest to contribute. On one occasion, at least, he publicly offers from his own pocket twenty dollars in gold, in addition to the fifty-dollar bounty, to every man that will enlist in the new company being raised. From the earliest hour of the day till the latest moment at which he can find any one to converse with him, he has but one topic—Secession and the War. He can not cease from the theme even at table. It is confessed that he is stronger and louder and more violent in the matter than any other man in or around Somerville. There is a ferocity of manner, a recklessness of assertion, an insanity of feeling about him, which rather cools than otherwise the most violent of his associates.

Considering all the circumstances of his advent in Somerville; that he is so "flush of money—not paper-money, but gold, Sir, round twenty-dollar pieces—I'll be hanged, Sir, if I don't believe—why, the man has no occupation here at all but talk Secession and the War—I'll be ——, Sir, if I don't firmly believe that Dr. Peel is a—" And here the voice of the speaker is sunk into a whisper, and is received with a start and an oath by the hearer: such had often been the remark made in Somerville.

"There is my trunk, gentlemen," Dr. Peel remarked when a committee visited his room at Staples's Hotel to investigate matters. "Don't forget the lid part of it, please. My extra coats, waistcoats, and breeches are hanging on the hooks behind my door. I will take off the clothes I now have on also. Don't forget those extra boots under the bed—might have papers in the linings or between the soles. There you see my revolvers too; pair of bowie-knives also —examine the scabbards, gentlemen. My Enfield rifle stands in the corner. The mattress, too, and the books on the table. Make a thorough search, please."

No man could be more unembarrassed than Dr. Peel by the visit and the suspicion which led to it. One would have supposed that he would have been astonished at it, resented it, killed some one. Not a bit of it. Dr. Peel was not ruffled a feather by any thing of the sort.

There had been some singular discrepancies in the Doctor's statements in regard to the place of his birth, in regard to his having correspondence with his "old and intimate friend Beauregard," which he "had got confoundedly mislaid" when desired to produce; but no evidence could be found against the Doctor of a positive nature, and so he pursued his course louder than ever.

It was a little singular, however, the conduct of Dr. Peel, after having politely escorted to the door of his chamber the committee above referred to—Bob Withers, Simmons, and windy

Dr. Ginnis the committee were. Seating himself, having called out after them as they departed down the steps the last friendly, even cordial good-morning, with his hands in his lap, forefinger and thumb arched to meet forefinger and thumb, he first thought it over, then began to smile, at last rolled himself upon his bed, fairly convulsed with laughter, genuine, unfeigned laughter, sparkling from every white tooth, streaming in tears from his eyes, possessing him and shaking his burly frame from head to foot.

"Going to the war? I am going," the Doctor had often remarked, in answer to questions to that effect. "Do you think I'd stay away when there are Yankees to be killed? No, Sir. I am going; and if I was to see my own brother or father among them I'd send a bullet from my rifle here through their hearts first ones. Do you think money could pay me to stay behind?" And the Doctor would proceed to curse out the rest of the feelings of his soul on the subject in a way which left nothing to be desired.

And yet Dr. Peel's burly form was still to be seen in every store, at every street corner, before every bar. It was singular. "In constant correspondence with the military authorities, Sir. They are anxious to place me where I can do most for the glorious cause." Yet months rolled by; the Doctor left Somerville often enough, but he always came back again for a fresh start. It was singular.

But Lamum has finished writing. "See if this will do," he says to Dr. Peel; and he proceeds to read:

#### "THE NEWS OF TUESDAY NIGHT.

"Thank Heaven! we know our readers well enough to know the manner in which they received the news of Tuesday night, of which much, and a vast deal too much, has been said. In the first place, we take for certain that a large part, if not every syllable, of the news is utterly false. Months ago the North was taught, and the entire world was taught, for time and for all eternity, a fact which we of the South have always known as well as we know our alphabet—that Northern soldiers fly like sheep at the very appearance of our brave boys.

"Is it reasonable to suppose that this has been other than the case at Fort Donelson? Did not the last dispatch distinctly declare the utter rout of the Federal forces assaulting that fort? But yesterday we were rejoicing in what we expected as a matter of course—shall we pay the least attention to-day to the preposterous lies which have come to our ears? We feel confident our intelligent readers will treat such trash with the contempt it deserves.

"Even supposing the Federals have met with some slight success in Tennessee, it is but for a moment. At the news all the South will pour forth its legions by millions, and in less than one month from this day not only will the Federal armies be driven back, but our invincible hosts will be thundering at the gates of Cincinnati and Chicago! Looking at the news as we will, in any case we find in it ground only of rejoicing. Doubtless before this our Government has been recognized by every nation in Europe, hailing with enthusiastic welcome its advent among the noblest nations of the earth. The North, already execrated by the whole civilized world, can not endure two months longer its enormous expenses. For what we know, our independence has been acknowledged by the North even while we write these lines. This we will say—ever since the editor of this sheet could pen a line has he striven night and day to bring about Disunion; from his very cradle was it the warmest aspiration of his soul; its consummation is the proudest rejoicing of his life. Of the establishment of this nation, and that it will, from its very establishment, rank second to none else on the globe, we are as certain as of our very existence!"

"Good as wheat!" exclaimed Dr. Peel, as the editor laid down his blotted sheet on the table.

"Oh, that is only one article!" replied the editor. "I will have a dozen like it, longer or shorter, in the next number."

"It's good, very good," said his companion; "yet it seems to me you do not pepper it strong enough. Why don't you print as I talk, as you talk? Pitch in, you know; lay it on scalding hot. You don't let on your steam, somehow."

"If I did I would simply burst the boiler. No, Sir," said this Machiavelli; "that is the blunder other editors and all stump speakers are eternally falling into. They go it with too much rush—overdo the thing. It is in politics as it is in a battle, the head-over-heels people always get the whipping. It is the cool, deliberate ones that gain the victory. I show myself positive and absolutely certain; but no fuss, no fury. Strike the wedge too hard and it bounces out, you know."

At this moment a gentleman, evidently a country planter, entered the room. The editor hailed him as Colonel Juggins.

"This is Dr. Peel, Colonel," he added, with a wave of the inky hand toward his companion.

"Oh, I know the Doctor. Many a good, warm talk we've had over the Yankees," said the Colonel. "But look here, General," he continued, "what about this news? I tell you things is looking squally: this child came mighty nigh taking a scare."

"You've read the dispatch, Colonel?" asked the editor, indifferently.

"Yes, I hev read that doggoned dispatch," said his visitor, anxiously, "and I'm mighty anxious to get your next paper to see how you will fix it up. Fact is, I couldn't wait; I thought I must see you right away. I want to know what you think of things now!"

"And is it possible, Colonel Juggins, that a man of your sense can ask such a question, and you knowing the Yankees as well as you do?" began the editor.

"Don't know nothin' about them; never was there in my life; never want to be," interrupted his visitor. "Fact is, you and Mr. Neely is about all the Northern-born people I ever was to say intimate with, and I don't suppose such as you are fair specimens of Northern folks. Yes, I've known a lot of overseers in my time hailing from the North. Gimini! warn't they hard on the hands! But go on, General, go on; I'm anxious to hear what sort of a way you look on this here news. It's hard to swallow, I tell you!"

"Well," continued the editor, "if you don't know our dastardly enemies, you won't pretend to say you do not know our own brave boys?"

"I know, as well as you, General, they'll fight to the last drop. My Tom is among them. I suppose I ought to know. Fight!" and Colonel Juggins had not breath left to say more.

"Well, then," said the editor, "you know my opinion of the news."

"Yes; but look here. Evacuated Bowling Green, didn't they? Besides, what can the bravest fellows do, supposin' they meet over-whelmin' numbers, or their guns won't carry as far as the others, or they've got cowards at their head, or there's traitors about, or their fodder gives out, or—"

"If you will listen a moment I will let you know what I think," interrupted the editor; and he proceeded to read aloud the leader he had just written, besides one or two more to the same effect, to all which his visitor listened with the deepest and most painful attention.

"If you want any thing further to set your mind completely at rest, Colonel," continued the editor, "there is a whole pile of the latest papers lying about the floor there. Read them, Colonel, see what they say, all of them! You'll find there's not a paper there isn't just as confident as I am, and every Southern man ought to be."

"Well," said Colonel Juggins, with a glance of dismay at the quantity of newspapers on the floor, but with a sigh of relief, "I dare say it's all right. You see all the papers, General. Besides, you've lived at the North and ought to know the sort of people they raise there. What fellows they are to make things, calicoes and such like! And to invent machines, too. Reapers and sewing machines, and fifty thousand such contraptions. I'm glad you think they can't fight. Now we are in it you see we're bound to put the thing through. My place keeps me so hard at it, breakin' up and plantin', and cleanin' out the weeds and pickin', and ginnin', and pressin' all the year round, I don't hev any time to examin' into things at all deep like. One thing brightened me up a little," continued the old planter, as he settled himself to read, "Pete Shehan fell in with me as I rode into town this mornin'. It happened so, you see. Pete said he didn't believe one word of this doggoned news. If the truth was known, says Pete, Beauregard is this minute in Baltimore."

"Who is Pete Shehan?" asked General Lamum.

"Well, Pete isn't any body in particular, a sort of well-digger like," answered Colonel Juggins. "Irish, he is. He's been at me to hev him dig a well or two the hands need awful bad down at the quarters. I must hev them wells, but then

Pete he gets drunk all the time, and, what's more, he never gets sober. But Pete's all right on the goose—strong for Secession I tell you. Another thing Pete told me: he knew the British had recognized us; he ought to know, he said, since he came from one of the British islands himself. Pete's only Pete, but he cheered me up a heap. However, don't let me interrupt you, General," added Colonel Juggins, for the editor had taken his pen and was busily engaged writing.

"Make yourself at home, Colonel, you'll find plenty to encourage you in the papers," said the editor, never taking pen from paper while he spoke.

Colonel Juggins ventures on the first of the pile of papers.

"Don't forget to give it to those Union chaps this week," remarked Dr. Peel at this juncture. "I tell you what, gentlemen," he said, "when I got that news last night—I was sitting up till it came in—if I had met one of those Union men with any thing like a glad look on his face I'd killed him dead on the spot. If I had met one of them, I believe I'd have shot him down any how, I was so savage."

But in leaving out the oaths and curses with which Dr. Peel garnished his remarks, very cold and meagre and unlike the Doctor's diction is this record thereof.

"Look here, Dr. Peel," said Colonel Juggins, paper in hand, "I don't know about that. Every body knows I'm no Union man, but I can't chime in with you there. Them fellows is dreadful mistaken, but they've lived here longer, some of them, than any of us. All they hev in the world is in and around Somerville. They always was opposed to this here move, said it would ruin the country, and all that. They ought to go into the thing now we are in it, I know; it's a shame they don't. But we mustn't shoot them though. Almost every man of them is Southern born and raised; every soul of them owns his own hands—"

"Don't care," interrupted Dr. Peel, with a volley of oaths. "There's that Guy Brooks to begin with—"

"Why, Dr. Peel, Guy owns fifty hands!" put in Colonel Juggins.

"Don't care; he is from *Kentucky*, and Kentucky is as rotten as East Tennessee. Then there is that Parson Arthur—"

"Why, what has he been doin'?" asked the old planter, with amazement.

"Nothing, Sir, nothing at all, and that is the very reason he ought to be looked after. Compare him with Parson Barker! You find Barker on the streets all the week, using all his influence one way. Go to his church on Sunday, his sermon from one end to the other is the best sort of stump speech I ever want to hear. Did you ever hear one of his prayers?"

Colonel Juggins nodded in reply. "Oughter, one of his members," he added.

"I'LL READ YOU ONE ITEM FOR MY NEXT PAPER YOU MAY LIKE."

"There's a prayer for you; prays for the Confederacy, prays for Davis, prays for our army, prays for victory—and it's worth going ten miles to hear that man pray for the defeat and the utter destruction of the Federals!" and the Doctor sealed his cordial approbation of the Reverend Mr. Barker's prayers with the most emphatic oaths in his possession.

"Parson Arthur, I suppose you know," said the planter, "was born and raised at the South. Barker has *his* way of doin' up things, Parson Arthur is different. When we had that hurly-burly about Know Nothin'ism, Arthur he kept clear of it, though they lied about him then a heap; staid inside of his pulpit like. Brother Barker, you'll remember—no, you won't remember, you were not here, Doctor, the General will, though—Brother Barker he pitched in, went all over the country organizin' the Know Nothin' lodges. He preached Know Nothin'ism, prayed Know Nothin'ism! Oh, Brother Barker he is a full team, specially on a camp ground where things is full blast. Parson Arthur, he is different. Old Master didn't make him that sort; he's quiet, sober-like. However, mornin', gentlemen; must be goin'; ain't much of a hand read-in' papers, specially where there's so many. Glad to learn from you, General, things ain't as bad

as I feared. But they *did* look a little squally like. You see, I'm from old Tennessee myself, and all that about Nashville took me back. Maury County I was from. Good-mornin'."

"Hold on, Doctor, one moment," said the editor, as that individual was about to follow the planter. "I'll read you one item for my next paper you may like. Listen:"

"IMPORTANT NEWS!

"We stop our press to announce news which we well know will thrill every patriot bosom with joy. We have just had a visit from a highly reliable gentleman on his way through our place. He called to inform us that he had been credibly informed on his way to Somerville that the news of Tuesday night, which created such an unnecessary sensation in our midst, is, as we supposed it at the time to be, utterly false! The gentleman from whom he derived his information was reliably informed also, before seeing him, that Beauregard is in full possession of Baltimore. It is believed that the Federals fled at his approach in utter confusion, and that immense stores to the value probably of millions have fallen into his hands. If this be so, our next news will be of Beauregard in possession of Washington! He may be there even as we write!

"The same gentleman also informed our friend that there is no longer any doubt of the fact that the Confederacy has been acknowledged certainly by England, and, probably, by all the other powers of Europe. The gentleman who imparted this news is himself from England direct, and one who has had access to the highest circles. Being a foreigner, his cordial sympathy in our great revolution, impartial as it must be, is but an indication of the universal interest on our behalf now felt over the whole civilized world. We give this news as we heard it, but we think our readers may rely confidently upon its truth!"

"Why, General, how did you get it? when did it come? why didn't you tell me of it before?" asked Dr. Peel before his companion was well through, and, mingled with his oaths, there was a singular nervousness of manner which strongly resembled anxiety.

"You heard it yourself from Juggins," answered the editor coolly, even indifferently.

"What! his talk about Pete what's-his-name? Come, General, you don't mean to say—"

"Hush your racket, Peel," said the editor rather testily, while his friend indulged himself in convulsions of laughter mingled with hearty swearing.

"Lamum, you are a genius!" exclaimed he at length, wiping his eyes, and emphasizing his opinion with a string of oaths.

"But how if Juggins—?" he began to ask.

"Do you suppose the old codger will ever recognize it as being *his* information?" replied the editor, coolly.

"Recognize it, certainly not!" replied the Doctor, hastily. "Oh, but you manufacturers of public opinion are geniuses! I never was exactly so close among the machinery before. And then this item of yours will be copied in all the rest of the papers, with their favorable comments upon it! I see! But I say, Lamum, ain't you afraid occasionally?"

"Are you fool enough not to know that whatever appears in a paper to-day is knocked completely out of the minds of the people by what will come out in it to-morrow? It's with all sort of shavings we keep the pot boiling. Search those papers," continued the editor, pointing at the heaps of them which covered table, floor, and chairs of his very dirty and disorderly office, "and you will find they are made up of just such items. They originate now here, now there, and all the rest copy them, comment on them, swell them. The people read at little else all the time. Must do it, Sir; we've got into this war, and we have to fight our way out of it! They beat hollow drums and blow brazen trumpets to urge them on when in battle—we editors behind here among the people are doing, in our way, exactly the same thing. We are in for it! Any thing is better than the old Union. That we determined should go to smash—we don't care what comes so *that* is down. 'Regardless of all possible consequences,' was what Calhoun said; that is the flag we sail under—our motto in place of old *E Pluribus Unum!* I believe in what Pryor, and John Tyler's son there in Virginia, and all the rest of them say—any thing on earth so that the accursed old Union goes to hell!"

COLONEL JUGGINS GOING HOME.

## CHAPTER III.

COLONEL JUGGINS emerged from the office of the Somerville *Star* like an honest blue-bottle fly, only he carried away a good deal of the cobweb about him out of the den of a spider. And very much better the Colonel felt in leaving it than when he entered its door.

When he heard of the investment of Fort Donelson by the Federal forces, never had the Colonel been more certain of the rising of the sun to-morrow than he was of the repulse and destruction of the Yankees. When the news arrived that the fort had actually capitulated, that the Confederate forces had failed to make a stand even at Nashville, it fell upon his ears, and upon those of very many like him, more like the tidings of some great phenomenon, some unprecedented interruption of the laws of nature itself, than merely as the news of battle and defeat.

The instant and most painful impression was —Good Heavens! if we have been defeated—we of the South—defeated once, what may not happen hereafter? The truth is, the events of the war so far had settled the common mind in Somerville, and throughout the South, in the fixed conviction of that which had always been a decided opinion, that Northern troops could not stand before Southern. True, Bowling Green had been evacuated, but that was easily explained; it was a splendid stratagem to draw the Federal troops further South, and so make a total finish of them!

Future historians will write Manassas as the Waterloo of the Confederacy. The cup of Southern victory there drunk was followed by a degree of intoxication to the South, of a greater than which history has no instance. As has been said before, the universal opinion at the South of Southern invincibility had hardly need of any thing to establish it, and Manassas petrified that opinion into granite certainty.

Nor did the events following Manassas fail to increase this certainty, had such increase been possible. So thoroughly settled was the Southern mind upon the whole subject that the vague news of Northern preparation going on excited little or no interest. The same sentiment possessed alike the people, the press, and the officials—at least, from no quarter was heard a syllable but to the same note. Any one who had hinted otherwise would have been marked as but a poor creature, unsettled in his wits by an absurd attachment to the Union, which ought to be regarded as traitorous, if it were not so heartily despised as contemptible.

Even the most firm among the Union men were beginning to settle themselves down to what seemed the will of Heaven—casting about to make the best of an inevitable matter. Nor is all this to be wondered at, when it is remembered how successfully all intelligence from the North was excluded from the South. By a most mistaken policy, the Southern press copied from the Northern and European papers, as a general rule, only that which was favorable to the South. It was more than human to withstand an influence so unmingled and universal.

True, as to the inherent and unchangeable right and wrong of the matter, the minds of Union men were unchanged; but they had begun to bow to the thing as to a Providence too mysterious to be understood—a thing in which nothing remained but submission to the will of God—fate, destiny, whatever it was to be called. People in the Border States may have been less astonished, but to the people of the States farther South, thunder from a cloudless sky is less startling than were the tidings that Federal gun-boats had actually run up the Tennessee to Florence, that Fort Henry was taken, that Fort Donelson had fallen, that Nashville had capitulated! The dominant feeling was—bewilderment.

"My dear Helen," Dr. Warner remarked to his wife, in a calm which had followed one of his domestic tempests, "you may depend on it, and your own clear, strong sense will say yes to me in it, truth is much the best plan. Frankly and truthfully, from the first, with my patients is my plan. They have confidence in me then; they are sure to follow my prescriptions faithfully. There is a mutual understanding between us; no miserable dodging and deceiving on either side; and, whatever the result is,

we at least know that all has been done from the start that could be done. The South has been grossly deceived by its doctors, I mean its leaders, from the first."

"Yes, you always hated Secession," broke in the partner of his bosom, the canal-gates opening.

"I was not speaking, just then, of Secession, but of the course pursued since then; but it is all of a piece. Either our political doctors were themselves all deceived, or they deliberately and systematically deluded the unfortunate people who had been cast into their hands," observed the mild physician.

"Went it blind, ma," said Bub, who was making a kite on the floor beside his parents, and who could not possibly have been the child of quick-witted Mrs. Warner and not have been himself smart.

"Hold your tongue, Bub!" broke in his mother. "Nice thing, Dr. Warner," she continued, "you are not satisfied not to be a whole-souled Southern man yourself; you are poisoning even the mind of your own child. I have no patience with you, Dr. Warner—cool, slow, patient submissionist you are! The very idea of giving up to those vile Yankees! Before I'd do it I'd die a thousand times over! You laugh at old Colonel Juggins, I know; but if he is a coarse, ignorant, old man I only wish to goodness you were as hearty in the war as he is! He was always wondering what Johnson was doing, staying there at Bowling Green, when he ought to have been across the river into Ohio. And Davis, and the rest of them, lying there not more than twenty miles from Washington, month after month, instead of marching right on, taking Washington, catching and hanging old Lincoln. Set of cowards! You men are all alike. Oh, if I was only a man!"

"What would you do if you were a man?" asked her impassive husband.

"Do! I'd raise fifty thousand brave men, lead them right on into the North, burn every house, batter down every town, kill every man I could! I tell you," said thin Mrs. Warner, her black eyes sparkling, "I'd kill and burn and cut their throats till they'd be glad enough to make peace with us. That's what Mrs. Bowles and Dr. Ginnis say. Instead of that, they are evacuating Bowling Green—running away, I call it—and Davis there in twenty miles of Washington and not going right on! Next thing," continued Mrs. Warner, with bitter sarcasm. "we'll read some morning the precious news that they have evacuated Columbus—even Manassas!"

"My dear," said Dr. Warner, helping himself to another slice of ham—for they were at dinner on the same day as that in which we first introduced them to the reader—"my dear, I do firmly believe that if you were a man you would succeed vastly better than nine-tenths of our men. But we have to take them as we find them. However, if you were a man I would have missed the most active and excellent wife in the world, and Somerville the best house-keeper going!"

And it was only the fact ; Mrs. Warner *was* the neatest housekeeper in Somerville ; as to the other the Doctor lied, and he knew it.

But it was of Colonel Juggins we intended to speak in entering upon this chapter. Slowly rode the Colonel home meditating upon the news. Lamum and Lamum's pile of newspa-pers had relieved his mind somewhat, but not entirely. There is a certain mysterious assur-ance which a fact always carries with it wher-ever it flies : you may deny it loudly, you may hate it heartily; but when a fact comes to the ear, the mind receives it as such by some mystic affinity as a *fact*—recognizes it by spontaneous appetite as the palate recognizes its natural food. As well as he knew his name did Lamum know that the disastrous news from Fort Donelson was true. Dr. Peel knew it. Even Colonel Jug-gins knew it—acknowledge it? no—yet none the less every body knew it to be true. It was as if the sun had varied from his path. Gra-cious Heavens, what might not be the next news!

Somehow, before he alighted from his horse at home—some five miles from Somerville—all Lamum's consolation had been dissipated from his mind, and the ugly news remained in all its hideous reality. The Colonel belonged to one of the three classes into which all slave-owners at the South may be divided. As a representa-tive man of this class let us say a word or two in regard to the Colonel.

Tom Juggins was the son of a rich Tennessee planter. There had been six or eight children in all, but what with being thrown from unbroken colts, and cholera morbus from eating green wa-ter-melons, and chills and fevers, one by one all the children had died except Tom. As to him, he doubtless owed his special strength of consti-tution to the fact that he had been suckled from his very birth by a negro "mammy." In that mammy's cabin passed the days of his infancy, his mother being a confirmed invalid, and his father having an unfortunate habit of spending in town and in intoxication pretty much all the time he could spare from field and cotton-house. On the earth floor of his mammy's house Tom learned to walk, and around the chicken-coops in front of it were spent his first hours of play.

In her way never child had a more loving mo-ther than Tom had in his mammy, preferring him, as she decidedly did, to all of her own dark brood. And a very paradise of childhood Tom had of it ; permitted to get as dirty as he pleased, very little washing, and no switching whatever. Nor was his childhood less auspicious as it ad-vanced into older years. With a troop of little blacks at his heels he haunted the calf lot and stable-yard, worrying the calves, riding the horses to water "bare-back," hunting and eating all the eggs. With his allies to back him did he stone the cats and the birds, clip the tails and ears of the puppies, kill the snakes, paddle in the spring, and climb the trees. Among his sable associates, too, did he learn and practice many a vice peculiar to their semi-savage nature and easily ingrafted into his.

In due time Tom was sent to school ; yet it was very little Tom learned. What with playing truant, and "barring out" the schoolmaster, and holidays occasionally, and idleness all the time, it was very little Tom learned beyond reading, writing, and the beginning of ciphering.

The rest of the story is soon told. After a youth of breaking horses, and swimming and hunting, and accompanying the cotton-wagons occasionally to the nearest city, and frolicking a little at weddings and corn-shuckings, Tom fell in love with and married a neighbor's daughter, and settled down. The death of his parents not very long after devolved the "Place," with all its negroes, on his hands, and Tom went to work ginning cotton and selling it as his fathers did before him. The old log-houses in which his fa-ther lived did well enough for him. True, he did once take a notion to build, had vast quan-tities of stone and sand and lumber hauled for the purpose ; but something or other turned up to postpone the matter, and there the heaps of materials continued to lie, an admirable lurking-place for snakes, laying place for hens, and play-ing-ground for the swarms of little negroes, till winds and rain and towering weeds had made a medieval ruin of the whole.

Year after year in a row of wretched cabins did Tom, now Colonel Juggins, continue to live, as contented in his house as any hand in his lit-tle inferior but hard by. He had become accus-tomed to bobbing his head in passing through the low doorways, to walking over the rolling puncheon planks which composed the floors. As to the roof, a clap-board or two could be nailed on in half a minute to keep out the worst of the rain, and a rock or so, with a handful of mud, could close up the worst of the cracks between the logs of the wall. Abundantly able to build a stately mansion, the Colonel saw little in his limited travels to awaken desire for any thing beyond what he already was so accustomed to. Besides, the Colonel was fat.

And so rolled the years by with Colonel Jug-gins. Hardly would he do as a specimen of the terrible slaveholder of excited imaginations. Such there are, but not of that class was this Col-onel. His dwelling was first cousin to the worst which any slave on the place occupied. His clothing was rather inferior than otherwise to the Sunday suits of his men. As to his daily food, it was about the same in house and in hut. Very often, in fact, was Mrs. Juggins glad enough, when company unexpectedly came, to borrow of some of their "people" the honey, poultry, eggs, or butter with which to eke out the dinner.

True, the Colonel voted and his hands were denied that inestimable happiness; but, then, the Colonel knew very little more at last about the principles voted for or against than they would have done. The Colonel, having all the responsibility and bother of the "Place," was, upon the whole, much the least happy man on it, and, as to his religious principles, if he was a church-member, so was almost every one of his grown hands, and they had the opportunity of receiving just as much and as good religious instruction from Sabbath to Sabbath as he.

There are two other classes of slave-owners, each as distinct from the other as his is from both. The Yankee owner of slaves, Mr. Neely for instance, and the aristocratic slaveholder, Colonel Ret Roberts as a specimen. Of them we will speak hereafter. I am altogether unwilling to say that the Colonel's is the largest class, the base of the pyramid, because I am not entirely certain that it is so.

"What I've got to say is this: why can't they just stay at home where they are, mind their own matters, and let us alone." That was Mrs. Juggins's opinion in regard to the war. She always mentioned it at table when company was present and the war the topic. With her it was a plain, common-sense solution of the whole matter, embracing the whole thing entirely and conclusively. "We are not going where they live, and bothering them! Why can't they let us alone!"

But since the Yankees would come South "with their guns and things," Mrs. Juggins yielded to the necessity of sending Tom, their only son, to help drive them back. In her idea it was an operation precisely like having the chickens driven out of the garden—troublesome, but not very dangerous. Often had Mrs. Juggins heard the plan suggested of building a wall around the South, over which no Yankee was ever to intrude. It was intended as metaphor, but Mrs. Juggins adopted it as highly feasible. The fact is, Mrs. Juggins was the duplicate of the Colonel. Had you been introduced to the Colonel, and an hour after met his wife in a store, say for the first time, you would have said on the spot: "There is Mrs. Juggins, and I know it!" Both bore in weight about the same relation to two hundred pounds, both had the same large, red, good-humored country face. It was little education Mrs. Juggins had when she married, and she certainly had seen time for nothing except the management of the negroes and of her fast coming, fast going too, as for that, children since that event. Except an al-

manac, a Bible, and a hymn-book or two, there was no reading in their house save the papers.

Of those that he took the Colonel decidedly preferred his religious paper, which, while it gave him all the news of his church, gave him also Secession in its moral and religious aspect. But, ye Heavens! why is it that the mere say so of a mortal has so much more weight and force when printed than it has when only spoken? No mistake about that paper!

Never in his life could the Colonel read a paper, or any thing else, except aloud and very slowly. In consequence of this his wife managed to get her news without much trouble on her part. Every syllable was believed by the Colonel as he read it, and by his wife with a double faith, because of the fact that it came to her from the lips and backed by the comments and assurances of her husband. If angels are permitted to hover over mortals, one would think the very tongues of such visitants would have struggled to speak out and apprise this poor Colonel Juggins and his wife of the enormous falsehoods which they fed upon thus from day to day with such a pitiful, implicit belief. But no; the Colonel and his wife then in their cabins were but representatives of millions at the South—millions willing to know and to do the right, yet so systematically, so awfully, so utterly blinded! To keep them apprised of the arts by which they were deluded would have withheld the heavenly guardians from all the enjoyments of bliss in unintermitting activity. Ah, how even angel bosoms must have heaved to smite with flaming swords the guilty authors of the gigantic delusion! How patient is God! And if the inhabitants of heaven know what goes on upon earth, largely must they be partakers of this attribute of the divine nature—else would heaven cease to them to be heaven, at least so long as earth continues to sin and to suffer beneath it.

It was an immense relief to Colonel Juggins, as he entered the door of his house, to find Brother Barker there. Pete Shehan had assisted him in regard to Fort Donelson for a time as he rode into town, Lamum had cheered him a little for the moment, but Brother Barker was worth more than all besides. Pete, Lamum, and the rest were all very well, but what Brother Barker said fell on the ears of the Colonel with all the weight of religious truth. From his earliest recollection the Colonel had been accustomed to receive as certainly true what his preacher said whether in the pulpit or out of it. Besides, Brother Barker proved all he advanced from Scripture itself. To doubt Brother Barker's conclusions was irreligious, and the Colonel hadn't been a "member" for thirty years now—class leader, steward, and all—to do that!

"And what do you think of this last Fort Donelson news?" asked the Colonel, immediately after saluting his guest, and making himself comfortable by seating himself in a hide-bottomed chair and tilting himself back in it against the wall.

"As I see you do, Brother Juggins—painful, painful intelligence," replied the preacher.

"You believe in it, then?" asked the Colonel, slowly and with a sinking heart.

"Believe in it? Certainly I do. There isn't the least doubt, as I can see, but the Federals are in possession of Donelson and Nashville, Tuscumbia and Huntsville, too, for what we know!"

"Well, you take it easier like than I can," said the planter, with a gloomy brow.

"Why not, Brother Juggins? It is of the Lord, isn't it? Besides, what do I care, and what ought you to care about Donelson, Nashville, and the like, when I know and when you know what the end of it all is certain to be? Why, Brother Juggins, whatever I expected of a worldling I didn't expect it of you. A man out in the world, now, I wouldn't be surprised at, but you!" And the preacher was as cheerful as his host was gloomy.

"I was hopin' strong it wasn't true," said the planter, after some time. "To me it sounds mighty bad, no use tryin' to hide it."

"And that after all you know on the subject, after all the talk we've had! Well, Brother Juggins, you must pardon me saying it, but I am surprised and grieved," said the preacher.

"Surprised at what?" asked the planter.

"Bad news is bad news, I suppose."

"Strange; human nature; well: oh yes, of course; ought to expect it at last," mused the preacher, with his head down on his bosom as if in soliloquy. "So many thousands of years ago it was those Jews talked the same way! At it the instant they heard Pharoah's chariots rattling behind them. Very first sound of the wheels they forgot Moses, forgot God, forgot every thing except that Pharoah was after them. Umph! Well. Yes."

"I hadn't thought of it exactly that way," said the planter, accepting the reproof humbly, and seeing consolation in it.

"Did I ever say we would escape some fighting, some being defeated before we got through?" asked the preacher—"tell me now, Brother Juggins."

"You did at the firset, as I mind," said the planter, with a thoughtful brow. "Christian Israel you know we were. Baldwin, he made that plain in his book. Abraham driv out from his father's house, our forefathers driv of God over the ocean, God's special people in both cases. Thirteen tribes settled in Canaan, thirteen colonies settled in America. Some of them tribes split off from the rest, some of our States split off from the rest, too. And, you mind, when Secession first started, come to think of it, you proved from the Bible there would be no

fight, not a bit. God wouldn't let that fool son of Solomon fight the tribes that split off even when he wanted to. There was goin' to be no fight, no fight at all! God himself would interpose to hinder, you said. And it did look mighty plain."

"But, Brother Juggins—" began the preacher.

"In one moment, Brother Barker. I've been studyin' over it, and I want to speak about that Christian Israel idea while I remember. I've been wantin' to ask you; it don't seem to gee like. In the Bible the tribes that split off were all except two; in our case it's the fewer number has split off from the larger number. Then, and this hurts me worst, the tribes that split off were the ones that sinned against God in the thing, that became worse and worse, that went to—what did ever become of them?—while the tribes that they split off from remained the favored people of God, had Jerusalem, and the Temple, and all. I tell you, Brother Barker, it was all very pretty when you first look at it, but the more you study into it—there was that about there being no fightin' permitted of God between the tribes when the break-up took place. I declare, for one man, I don't understand it!" concluded the old planter, somewhat testily.

"Brother Juggins," said the preacher, gravely, "do I understand you to say that you have studied Baldwin's book from end to end, deeply, thoroughly?"

"No, Sir," said the planter. "It's near three inches thick, that book. I only skimmed over it—a little here and a little there."

"I really do not think, Brother Juggins," said the preacher, in a tone of expostulation, "that you ought to decide so upon what you say yourself you never studied to the bottom."

"Well, perhaps so," said the planter, as he remembered how ponderous was the volume in question, and how very little he had mastered its contents. "But there was not one syllable about Secession in the whole book, I know that, any how. It was Monarchy and Democracy that was to fight the battle of Armageddon in the Mississippi Valley. Not one hint about Secession!"

And Colonel Juggins was not the only one who had puzzled over the book in question—"ARMAGEDDON, OR THE UNITED STATES IN PROPHECY." You saw the thick and well-thumbed volume on every shelf during the two or three years before Secession.

"Brother Baldwin was mistaken about that," consented the preacher. "But he has found out his mistake, and, they say, is lecturing like wild-fire every where setting people right. I believe as certain as I do my own existence those prophecies in the Bible about the South and our Confederacy. I'll talk with you any day about them as long as you like. No man, at least no

Christian man, can study those prophecies and say they don't have reference to the Confederacy. But we won't talk about that now. Brother Juggins, will you favor me with a Bible?"

The Bible was found, dusted, and brought. Mrs. Juggins drew still nearer with her knitting.

"Brother Juggins," said the preacher, after he had found the place in the large, well-thumbed Bible, and putting on his pulpit manner as an Episcopal clergyman would put on his gown, "you often say you are a plain man. Well, you can understand a plain passage in the Bible—"

"That passage in Timothy?" inquired the Colonel.

"I know we've been over it often before," said the preacher, "but we can hardly have too much of the Bible, I suppose. This book was given to guide us. Brother Juggins? Sister Juggins?" Very solemnly. The persons in question nodded a hearty assent. "Now listen," continued the preacher, and he read, in a slow, solemn manner: "It's First Timothy, sixth chapter. 'Let as many servants as are under the yoke count their own masters worthy of all honor, that the name of God and his doctrine be not blasphemed.' Next verse isn't so much to the pint. Next is: 'If any man teach otherwise, and consent not to wholesome words, even the words of our Lord Jesus Christ, and to the doctrine which is according to godliness.' That is, any thing against slavery he's just been speaking about. 'He,' that is, every Abolitionist, 'is proud, knowing nothing, but doting about questions and strifes of words, whereof cometh envy, strife, railings, evil surmisings, perverse disputings of men of corrupt minds, and destitute of the truth, supposing that gain is godliness.'

"Now let us hold on one moment," said the preacher, closing the book, with his finger in the place. "I just ask you, Brother Juggins, Sister Juggins, isn't all that a description of the Northern people—the Abolitionists?"

"I suppose it is," said the planter for self and wife. .

"What I say," added Mrs. Juggins, "is just this. Why can't them people stay at their own home, mind their own business, let us alone? We ain't goin' up where they live to trouble *them*."

"Exactly, Sister Juggins. But here's what I want to get at," continued the preacher. "This is the Word of God we're reading. It says all that of the Northern people plain and clean. Next it tells us exactly our duty toward them—it's as plain as any part of the Bible. Listen:" and the preacher opened the Bible again, and, running his finger under the passage, read, very slowly and with prodigious emphasis, the rest of the verse, "'From—such—*withdraw*—thyself!'"

"Yes, just so; that was your sermon about Secession. I can't see how any thing *can* be clearer from Scripture than that," said the planter.

"Wait a moment, Brother Juggins; I'm not through yet. I want to ask you one plain question. Do you suppose God ever commands a man or a people to do any thing and then punishes them, or permits any body else to punish them, for doing it?"

"No, Sir!" said the planter.

"Well, we are beginning to see our way out, then. As you well know, Brother Juggins, the South was only obeying this direct command of God in withdrawing itself from the North and setting up for itself. A man is stone-blind who don't see that our Secession was the command of God. And here you are talking to me about Fort Donelson and Nashville," continued the preacher, becoming greatly excited, "frightened by the pursuing Egyptians, exactly like those Jews were, as if God did not *command* us to leave, as if God was not going with us in leaving! He lets Fort Donelson and Nashville be taken just to prove us and to try us, as he said to the Jews, and I'd like to know how we are standing the trial. He gave us that great victory at Manassas just to show us, in a way we couldn't help seeing if we was to try to, that God was with us. But what's the result? People forget God, say we did it all ourselves; we're waxing fat and kicking, and now He is letting us be whipped a little just to show who it is that raiseth up one and casteth down another."

"I liked mightily what you said in your last sermon, Brother Barker," remarked the planter, after a pause of rumination; "all that about the hearts of the kings bein' in the hand of the Lord to turn about as he pleased. Only I wish England and France would make haste and show some of it. Them Powers have been just goin' to acknowledge the Confederacy every paper I've read since we set it up; somehow they hain't done it yet—"

"Brother Juggins," interrupted the preacher, in a sad tone, "it was hard to wean you from your old notions about that old Union in the first place; it was like drawing your eye-teeth, you know; and now that you are on the right track it is awful work to keep you to it. It's true, we have been acknowledged by England and the rest before now, if we only knew it, or soon will be; but, don't you see, it's wrong in us to look to them so much. Trusting in Assyria and going down into Egypt will be just our sin, as it was the sin of God's other peculiar people. I tell you now, we're going to get it worse and worse from the North till we learn to trust only in the Lord. I believe you know I've had some experiences in religion—real, warm experiences; you want to know what is my strongest experi-

"WHAT I SAY," ADDED Mrs. JUGGINS, "IS JUST THIS."

ence now—the religious feeling which happifies me most?"

The planter and his wife looked up expectingly.

"It is that we here at the South are God's chosen people. Promises of Scripture have come out to me plain before now; but I just tell you this, nothing in the lids of this book has ever stood out from the page so plain to me as that. The North has gone off into Free-Loving, Garrisonism, Mormonism, Spiritualism, and that worst and blackest of all kinds of infidelity—

Abolitionism. There was some religion there once ; but that makes it worse — it's apostasy the North has fallen into, deep-reaching, widespreading, universal apostasy—and God has just given them over to it. But he has rescued the South—he has called us out. If there's one single *ism* here at the South *I* never saw it—not even Universalism. Talk to me! Can't you *see* that you may as well give up all the Bible if you give up what it says on our side? God on our side? The God *I* worship is! He to help those people who have apostatized from him! I'm as certain this day he's on our side as I am there *is* any God. As a just Lord he *can't* help those people—*can't* do it! Look at the Jews! Don't you *see* how he punished their enemies with sword, fire, pestilence, famine, and the like. If those poor, miserable, blinded Yankees only knew it—the ruin that is coming upon them from his hand! I never felt to pray for a revival in my life as I've felt to pray for their defeat and destruction. It's the Lord in me! Ever since they broke up our Church there in New York. in the General Conference of forty-four, the Church South has been praying and praying for this Confederacy. Glory to his name, he has heard our prayer! For one, I'll trust him for the rest!"

But it would be unreasonable to suppose we can record all that Brother Barker said. A small, pale man was Brother Barker, with thin, lank, black hair combed back off of his low and narrow forehead. Were you to see him in a crowd his small and stooped form promised little of the tremendous powers of speech possessed by him. There was a peculiar thickness and heaviness about his eyelids which gave an additional aspect of dullness to the man. Yet, let Brother Barker get fairly into the stand, and fully under way in a sermon, brighter and brighter grew his eyes, faster and faster flew his arms, and words rushed to his lips faster than he could deliver them. Like most of his denomination, the disruption of his Church in 1844 had begun in his bosom an alienation of feeling from the North which had steadily increased ever since disruption had followed in the other denominations ; but Brother Barker's Church was decidedly in the lead, as it was the first in the agitation.

Perhaps not a member or minister of the Church itself dreamed how deeply and thoroughly it was leavened in the matter. The act of Secession revealed an earnestness and intensity of alienation in the denomination to the North which surprised the Southern politicians as much as it gratified them. Bishops, presiding elders, preachers, papers, it was a powerful organization ready to the work--in their eyes a religious

work. As with every religious body the feeling was deeper and stronger than any merely political body of men ever know. Even the most heated politicians saw themselves utterly distanced by the almost frenzied zeal of such men as Brother Barker. It was not only heart, it was soul these threw into it. And no one can estimate the immense power exerted by such men in all the denominations at the South.

Accustomed to receive as religious truth every thing coming from such a source ; impressed, and which is far from being the popular feeling in regard to the politicians, with the disinterested, heart-felt sincerity of their spiritual guides ; aware of the moral purity, too, of these, no wonder the masses of the South were so moved by the unceasing efforts of their ministers. No one at all familiar with the South but knows that the Southern clergy accomplished more for Secession than all other instrumentalities combined. By far the ablest arguments and the most eloquent appeals for Secession were from ministers ; and what the mass of inferior ministers lacked in ability and eloquence in the pulpit and by the press they more than made up by their universal, incessant, and eager influence during the week, and the power of, at least, their public prayers on the Sabbath.

Assuming as impregnable that theological foundation for slavery which the last thirty or forty years has seen evolved from Scripture, those among the Secessionists who were believers in the Bible planted themselves thereupon as upon rock—making thereupon and therefrom their confident appeal to God for success. And since the universe afforded no 'other conceivable ground to stand upon in the matter, the pious were not the only ones to avow this as their position. Multitudes who never opened the Bible had awful reverence for this one divine institution if for no other decreed therein. Avowed infidels, too, accepted eagerly so much of Sacred Writ as proved slavery right, even though they scouted all the remainder as fable. And it is a fact worth recording, that, as a universal thing, the right and the wrong of the whole movement settled down, amidst a thousand side considerations, unanimously into this. The abiding of the appeal made to God in battle upon this point, in case it was decided against the institution, was a contingency which never entered the mind—no anticipation of or provision for that. History furnishes no instance of men more absolutely confident of the aid of Heaven. The nearest parallel to their confidence in history is seen in the case of the Zealots in Jerusalem at its bloody fall. Ah, direst of all infatuation to count with such confidence that Almighty God is upon our side when He is—not!

MRS. SOREL.

## CHAPTER IV.

BROTHER BARKER was in the full tide of the most confident and convincing assertions upon the state of the country when he experienced a sudden and singular interruption. This was none other than the entrance of a somewhat tall and slim but very neat lady, who was hailed by Mrs. Juggins with a cordial,

"Why, if here ain't Mrs. Sorel now! Walk in, Mrs. Sorel; glad to see you; don't take that chair, this here is an easier one; take off your bonnet; come to spend the day, I do hope; how are all at home?"

There was nothing specially wonderful in the lady, at least to look at. You could see that she must have been beautiful in her youth; the clear gray eye, regular features, and still graceful form, showed that plainly enough. Yet, being only a lady, clothed in some gray stuff, with a calico sun-bonnet, it was hard to account for the interruption caused by her simple entrance. The preacher stopped in his conversation, singularly abashed and confused. Even the old planter received her more like an overgrown boy caught by the owner thereof in the midst of a watermelon patch than the master of a household. And Mrs. Juggins, too, seemed endeavoring to hide something beneath the bustle of her welcome.

A close observer might have detected a peculiarly arch smile which passed over the face of the visitor at the sudden silence and evident embarrassment which attended her arrival, but it was gone in an instant as she saluted the company with quiet ease and took a seat beside Mrs. Juggins. It was evidently with an effort that conversation was resumed; and the burden thereof was thrown upon the visitor, who had herself to mention the facts in regard to the weather, which, in the section of which we are speaking, and probably all over the world besides, form the invariable introduction to conversation.

It is strange; yet if ever countenances expressed the sense of being caught at something wrong, the countenances of the persons thus interrupted expressed that guilty emotion. Certain it is, there was in the bosoms of the persons interrupted a sharp, sudden sense of guilt which surprised even themselves, but which their outward bearing was too true to their inward self not to manifest. Of all of them the preacher had the deepest, strongest sense of this; and a sense of it which, a moment after, he resented more than the others, being more violent and positive in his after-conversation from this very cause. Meanwhile, if any one could have known it from her composed and natural manner or not, Mrs. Sorel was saying to herself, as she took out her sewing—"Dear me, I wish I had known; but, as it is, I can not help it!"

With the rest, she felt that it was in vain to sit there five minutes and not get into the one, grand, only, all-absorbing, everlasting topic. That it should not, at least, be her fault, Mrs. Sorel immediately engaged Mrs. Juggins, who was her near neighbor, in conversation about the making of butter and the raising of chickens and turkeys. The scarcity of these was evidently leading into the topic of the war, so that it was necessary to avoid that theme also. The gentlemen had from her entrance ceased conversation; the preacher apparently engaged in reading the *Advocate*—the religious paper of the Church to which Colonel Juggins and himself belonged—and the Colonel engaged in smoking his cob pipe and solemnly thinking over Fort Donelson and Nashville.

Now there was no better soul in the world than Mrs. Juggins, but conversation formed no part of her excellences, so that it devolved upon Mrs. Sorel either to say something or to sit in silence. To avoid this and, at the same time, keep the thread of conversation in her own hands, Mrs. Sorel began in a lowered tone to tell her neighbor of her various devices in the economy of her household; how much a little alum had improved the candles she was making at home; how easy she found it at last to plat straw into hats for her household; how she had succeeded in making starch—a large sample of which she had brought over for Mrs. Juggins—from wheat bran.

"Yes; and just as good as any I ever bought of the store—Yankee made," remarked Mrs.

Juggins, as she examined the article carefully. "That is what I say," continued the old lady; "we can do without them, we don't want them here; why can't they just stay at home and—"

"But I must tell you how I managed about making shoes," interrupted her visitor; and she proceeded to tell how many soles of old shoes she had made the children collect from about the place; how she had soaked them well in water, and so made them again into shoes. Mrs. Sorel also informed her neighbor how keenly she had suffered under the dearth of bluing, then desolating all the wash-tubs of the country, and how she had found out that common blue ink, largely diluted, answered just as well.

"Yes, and ink went right up from two bits to fifty cents a bottle, soon's you found it out," moaned Mrs. Juggins.

Much more did Mrs. Sorel have to tell her neighbor, talking rapidly and in her most cheerful manner. Not, if she could help it, should the conversation glide off into the war.

"By-the-by, when did you hear from Frank last?" asked the Colonel, suddenly, in the midst of a description his wife was giving Mrs. Sorel of a loom she was having made.

Colonel Juggins had no such intentions, but his sudden question ruined every thing. He was an ignorant man, somewhat dull too, yet he had his intuitions the moment after that it would have been as well not to have asked the question. But it was too late. Even Mrs. Juggins saw that they were, as she afterward expressed it, "in for it now."

"Not for several weeks, Colonel," replied Mrs. Sorel.

"Your son is in Virginia, I believe, ma'am?" said the preacher, in his usual tone at the beginning of a sermon. Brother Barker always began his sermon in a low and scarcely audible voice: he got loud enough, however, long before he got through.

"With our Tom," said the Colonel, promptly. "And now, Brother Barker, suppose we take a look at that three-year-old I told you about; you circuit riders know a good animal when you see it if any body does: takes a Methodist preacher to judge horse-flesh!"

"In a moment, Brother Juggins," said the preacher, who was not to be interrupted in that way either. "I congratulate you, ma'am," continued he, "that you have a son to fight the battles of his country; it must be a great satisfaction to you."

Now, "Brother Barker was built for fight," had been a highly complimentary remark often made in regard to him by his friends. No knight ever went into tourney with greater zest than did this man into any theological controversy, whenever and wherever the lists were opened. But controversy upon the well-worn themes of Church Government, Election, Baptism, and the

like, had ceased entirely, had utterly passed from the minds of men. The one great controversy of the day, raging not only upon battle-field but in every village, in every knot of talkers, in every separate heart and mind, this controversy had swallowed up every other. To it men gave all the zeal they had hitherto squandered in dozens of different directions: certainly with Brother Barker this was the case.

"You are perfectly aware, Mr. Barker, that Frank's course does *not* give me satisfaction," said Mrs. Sorel, calmly.

"Ah, is it so?" said the preacher, raising his brows in wonder. Like every man who stakes every thing on a cause, falsehood favorable to that cause was a totally different thing from the old, abstract, abominable falsehood.

"You must pardon me, Mr. Barker," said Mrs. Sorel; "but I have observed from the outset that equivocation, departure from strict truth, has been a leading feature of Secession. You know perfectly well what my sentiments are to-day and always have been. Frank would not have gone to the war if he could have staid at home. He no more wanted to go himself than I wanted to send him. He was taught to love his country from his cradle, and from his earliest recollection he was trained to regard Secession as the greatest of crimes."

"You must permit me, ma'am," began the preacher.

"Only let me finish, if you please," said Mrs. Sorel, in a manner as cool as it was decided. "At the opening of the war Frank never dreamed of enlisting, at least not under *that* flag, but his case became more unpleasant every day. Hardly a day but he would say when he came home, 'I hate the thing as much as you do, mother, but what can I do?' Not a day, not an hour of the day, but his old companions were after him to enlist. So many of them were gone that he began to feel as if left alone in the world. The hints, too, about his being tied to his mother's apron strings, about his being afraid to go, and a hundred things of the kind, wore upon him till he could stand it no longer. One bitter, bitter day he enlisted! He did as tens of thousands of others have done—swept away against every prompting of reason, religion, and conscience—swept away in the wild tide that sweeps the land—and woe to the wicked men that set that tide going! I tell you, Mr. Barker, if to no others, to thousands of desolated mothers they will have to answer for it at the bar of God!"

If Mrs. Sorel had only spoken this in an excited manner and with raised voice it would have been a much easier thing for Mr. Barker to reply; but there was a calmness, a conviction, a sense of being unquestionably right, in her manner which embarrassed the preacher. Or, rather, there was a sense—struggle against it as he might—of being wrong in the matter in the bosom of this latter individual which he could not overcome. Loudly as he talked, abundant as were his arguments from Scripture, fierce as were his denunciations of the Yankees—all the time there was under it all that sense of being in the wrong which the preacher could not get rid of to save his life. However it may be with other men, the really pious man has a sense of right and wrong in his bosom which nothing *can* quench—it is the unquenchable spark within him of an eternal life.

"I would think, Mrs. Sorel—you are a professor, I believe?" asked the preacher.

"Mr. Barker," said Mrs. Sorel, with a steady and surprised look at him, "why do you ask such a question? You know that I am."

"Then I would ask, ma'am, why you do not have faith in God to leave your son in his hands? You should not grieve over your son, as I am told you do. Thousands of us—Sister Juggins here, for instance—have sons in the war—"

"And that is just the difference in my case," said Mrs. Sorel, breaking quietly in upon the preacher. "I do not grieve over Frank because he is away from me, or because he may be lying at this moment in some crowded hospital without a mother's hand to tend him. No. Nor if Frank was dying there of some disease or some dreadful wound, would *that* be what would break my heart. For all that I could and would trust him in the hands of the Lord—it is the *cause* he is engaged in that cuts me to the soul."

"Really, Mrs. Sorel," said the preacher, greatly excited, "your views are very singular, and they may be such as may injure you."

"Such have always been my views, Sir," said the lady, quietly and gravely, "and always will be. If I speak at all on the subject I have none others to express. And what I now think and feel was, a year ago, the sentiment of every individual in our then happy land, with the exception of a few desperate politicians who were even then plotting our ruin. Then they were regarded as bad men; to-day they are the rulers of a deluded people."

If Mrs. Sorel had only got angry as she spoke! But she was so entirely calm, spoke with such force of moral conviction, in such a tone as if of burglars or murderers whose guilt no one could deny, that, in spite of himself, the preacher was confused. A mere politician would not have been; but Mr. Barker, on the other hand, had a conscience.

"Were you not born at the North?" he asked, at length.

"Mr. Barker," said the lady, after a grave pause, "why do you ask such a question? You know perfectly well that I am a South Carolinian. Mrs. Juggins has told you that repeatedly—so have I."

"You are a strange sort of South Carolinian," said the preacher, with a sarcastic smile.

"Perhaps so," said the lady, quietly. "My father was a plain, sensible planter, living in South Carolina, as his people and his wife's people had lived from the settlement of the country. In the days of Nullification he was a Union man—not without some influence—the unpretending influence of plain, sober, Christian sense—in his neighborhood. He was murdered by a Nullifier, a leading politician then, and I never can forget the lesson I learned then—the calm, solid conviction of the one set of principles, and the heat and violence, the dueling, bullying, cursing, threatening spirit of the other. When I look over the country now I see the same difference between the two parties—only the noblest and best among us have, in many cases, been poisoned and borne away with the wicked spirit which was at one time confined to the bosoms of the desperate few."

"And is it possible, ma'am, that you, a Southern woman, can have any regard for Yankees?" said the preacher, with a strong emphasis, as of nausea, upon the first syllable of the word.

"Not for want of learning what a dreadful people they are," said Mrs. Sorel, with a smile. "Only last week Mrs. Juggins was telling me that marriage has been altogether abolished among them."

"Law me, yes!" broke in Mrs. Juggins; "so I'm told. Up there the women all wear pants like men, make speeches, vote, and, I *do* suppose, carry their revolvers, curse and swear, drink and gamble, just like the men! When any man and woman happen to meet any where and take a likin' to each other they just consider themselves married—free love, they call it!"

"And you remember, Mrs. Juggins," said Mrs. Sorel, "what you told me about Lincoln's having contracted with people to go through the South burning up people's houses by night, so much a house."

"And Mrs. Juggins could have told you, too," said the preacher, "that the North has apostatized into a universal infidelity."

"Mr. Barker," asked Mrs. Sorel, pausing from her work and looking steadily at the preacher, "do you believe yourself that the Christians of the North have thus apostatized?"

"I asked Lamum the last time I saw him," said the preacher; "he is a Northern man, too; he ought to know, and he said he didn't know that any one doubted it. Though," put in the preacher, with candor, "there may be—I say *may* be—some Lots in the midst of Sodom: for what I know there may be even seven thousand there that have not bowed the knee to Baal."

"Don't mention that man Lamum, Brother Barker, if you please," broke in Sister Juggins. "Preferred cold light bread, he said, that night he staid with us—a Yankee, a regular Yankee. He has a cold, creepin', calculatin' kind of a way. Bein' born and raised North, for my part

I don't see how he can help feelin' with his own people; it's *nature* he should. For all he says, take my word, he don't want the South to whip. He ought to be made to leave—put the other side of that wall!"

"Sister Juggins," said the preacher, "you forget. Charity believeth all things, hopeth all things. But never mind about that. Please hand me that Bible again. Mrs. Sorel is an intelligent lady, a believer in plain Scripture. I have been blessed to convincing a good many before now who were perfectly infatuated—you must pardon me, ma'am—about the old Union. If you will only listen a little! I would not mind it so much, but that you should be from South Carolina, and not— But here is the place."

And thereupon Brother Barker launched out upon the theme which had never been out of his mind, and scarce for an hour at a time, except when he was sleeping, off his tongue, for the last year. He adduced all the passages in the Bible which are considered as sanctioning the institution of slavery, and which were as familiar to his finger and tongue now as the proof-texts in regard to election and baptism had once been in less interesting controversies of old. Having established slavery as a biblical ordinance, he then assumed the infidelity of the North because hostile to that divine ordinance.

This position he confirmed by numerous references to the avowedly infidel writers and infidel practices of the North. Garrison, Theodore Parker, Gerrit Smith, Berlin Heights, Oberlin, John Brown, Lucy Stone, Antoinette Brown, Mormonism, Spiritualism, Millerism, Lovejoy, Lincoln, Lincoln, Lincoln! flew from his lips with a fluency and a force amazing to hear. These were the things which, like the well-worn pebbles in the calabash, the war rattle of a savage warrior, Brother Barker made deafening noise with. It was astonishing what a mass of ammunition he had accumulated upon the subject. But Mrs. Sorel ceased to wonder when he began to refer to the *Advocate*, lying on the table beside him. It was a very large sheet, and week after week it had come to Brother Barker, as to almost every family connected with the same denomination in the State, brimful of nothing else.

As the preacher proceeded he waxed warmer and warmer, louder and louder. But when he came to the unnatural, unchristian, despotic, malignant, fiendish, diabolical, hellish conduct of the North in actually waging war upon the South, recounting deed after deed of atrocity which he had gathered from the teeming papers, he seemed to have forgotten Mrs. Sorel—who sat by quietly sewing—altogether; seemed, in fact, even to have forgotten himself, for his language was rather that of an intoxicated bully than of a minister of the Prince of Peace. His sallow cheek became livid with passion, his whole frame trembled with the violence of his wrath. To Mrs. Sorel it was a painful spectacle, like the raging of a thunder-gust unpleasantly near—physically unpleasant, in fact. Even the Colonel and his wife hung their heads, deeply conscious how little in accordance with the gospel he preached was the temper and language of their pastor.

It took Brother Barker little time to get his feelings fairly wrought up when he began, but then it took him a still longer time to get them down again. Only when he was exhausted did he draw to a close.

"And now, ma'am, knowing all this, is it possible you can desire to be associated longer with such a people? Union! Union!" It is impossible to describe the loathing with which the speaker pronounced the hateful word.

"Mr. Barker," said Mrs. Sorel, very quietly, "I was told something the other day in regard to yourself. We hear so much that is false these days that I took for granted it was not so."

"What was it, ma'am?" asked the preacher, hoarse from his exertion, but pale and eager.

"I was told that Dr. Peel made a speech in Somerville, in which he said that if he supposed the Yankees engaged in this war went to heaven, for his part he would prefer going to hell. And it was said that you clapped your hands, with others, in applause. Will you permit me to ask you if that is so?"

"It is impossible for me, ma'am," replied the preacher, "to remember distinctly all I either say or do. If I did applaud such a sentiment, it was because I well know it is impossible for any one engaged in this murderous war upon the rights of the South to get to heaven!"

"I am free to say," observed Mrs. Sorel, after quite a pause, "that I am convinced of some things by what you have said."

"Ah! ma'am, I believed you were open to conviction—and what are those?"

"I think it is extremely probable," said Mrs. Sorel, gravely, "that those German soldiers in Missouri *did* break into the dairies and drink all the milk; because our soldiers have done the same to my dairy." And Mrs. Sorel looks up with a smile.

"I had hoped, ma'am—" began the preacher.

"Pardon me, Sir," continued Mrs. Sorel. "Your remarks have thoroughly convinced me of something more to the purpose than that I have noticed, and you are yourself as well aware of the fact as I am—that when one is entirely satisfied of the truth and of the moral and religious right of a matter, in regard to that matter they are calm. It is to them a something as clear and settled as is the existence of God, and I can not imagine a person getting into a passion in asserting the existence of the Almighty, or any other thing in regard to which his mind is entirely made up. Now, if Secession be a thing so certainly right—a cause approved from Scripture, and for which the Almighty is so certainly pledged—why such feverish excitement on the subject? why such incessant argument and assertion and violence? If the North is pursuing a course so horribly wicked why abuse them so? Why not leave them, with little emotion save of pity, to the certain vengeance of God? And yet that paper you hold in your hand is full, from week to week, of such terms as rascally, scoundrelly North! villainons, execrable Government! and the like. Before this thing began the editor of that paper, and all of you ministers—yes, and all Christians—would have shrunk with horror from using, in regard to any thing, language which is now the everyday speech of even ministers in the pulpit, to say nothing of Christians in private life. Can it be a holy cause which inspires such language? And we, poor Union people, why are you so exercised in regard to us? We are quiet and silent; one would suppose you would have a pity, a contempt even, for people so deluded! Why are you so uneasy about us? You see no passion in us, only cool conviction. Can we help convictions which are as clear to us as any conviction can be? We don't interfere with your views; why can you not leave us in peace to our delusion?"

"Mrs. Sorel," said the minister, more excited by the calmness of the lady than he would have been by her violence, "I tell you, as a friend, the Union people about Somerville had better look out. The feelings of the country are getting hotter and hotter every day. As sure as you live, every Union man, woman, and child will have to leave the country or be hung! We are not going to be trifled with, ma'am," and there was a dangerous fire in his eyes as he spoke. "It's with your church, like people like priest," he added, with bitterness.

"And what has Mr. Arthur done?" asked the lady, with a smile.

"He voted against Secession, ma'am, and," continued the preacher, "so far from being ashamed of it, he has been known to say that he will always rejoice that he did not stay away from the polls, as many of his sentiments did, but went and cast his vote, at least, against the measure."

"I always wished I could have seen him that mornin'," said Colonel Juggins. "I like Mr. Arthur, like his preaching—just a word or two from me would have fixed it;" and the Colonel resumed his pipe, greatly regretting he had left the magical words unspoken.

A close observer might have detected a slight motion at the corners of Mrs. Sorel's mouth, but she said nothing. The training in the art of holding the tongue, which Union people at the South underwent during the revolution, was amazing. Alas! the long and severe training, too, in all manner of equivocation, deception, and dissimulation which many of them submit-

ted to was one of the demoralizing influences of that most demoralizing of periods.

"Never you mind," interposed Mrs. Juggins, with a wise look from over the sock she was darning—"I know one will fix him, sure!"

"And who is that?" asked the Colonel. "Neely isn't the man to work on a man like Mr. Arthur. As to that Guy Brooks, he's worse Union than the parson himself. As to that red-headed Ferguson, somebody ought to get hold of that fellow! Only the last week or two I hailed him as he was riding by to ask the news. Would you believe it? he stopped his horse, threw one leg over the pommel of his saddle, and told me a long story of how Washington had been taken by Beauregard, and how Lincoln had been hung on a pole—flag-pole it was —on the dome of the Capitol, the Washington people hurrahing underneath like smoke, and all his dying confessions, and such like. He told it all as solemn—you know how dry he is—never stirred a muscle! And I was fool enough to believe it. Next time he saw me there in Somerville he came up to me, regretted —dry as you please—what he had told me was false! 'We hear so many things every day just as probable,' he said."

"Mrs. Sorel knows who I mean," said Mrs. Juggins, demurely. "Law me! it's no secret— Miss Ally Bowles. If she isn't sound nobody is, and if she don't make him toe the mark I'm mistaken."

"There is a true Southern woman for you!" broke in the preacher, by way of a severe hit at his late antagonist. "You remember, Colonel, and you, Sister Juggins, that day she presented the flag to the boys—I offered the prayer, you will remember. How straight she stood—as an Indian! Her hair down her shoulders, her cheeks as red as fire, her eyes sparkling. With her flag in her hand, and all, she reminded me of a picture of the Goddess of Liberty I saw somewhere once! Genuine Southern woman!"

"But they say Mr. Neely—" began Mrs. Sorel.

"A Yankee!" interrupted Mrs. Juggins. "Giaour!" may come very strong from the lips of an exasperated Mussulman, but it could not express more unutterable disgust than "Yankee!" did from the lips which then spoke it. "To lie like a Yankee" expressed a proficiency in the art which Satan himself might envy. "To run like a Yankee" left the old similes of deer and greyhound far behind. "A Yankee!" hurled by one boy on the play-ground at another was considered the quintessence of all insult and cursing. "Abolitionist" used to be considered strong language, but "Yankee" was stronger still —it meant the abolitionist armed and equipped and in full operation.

"Yet no one is a more ardent Secessionist," said Mrs. Sorel, in her gentle manner.

COLONEL JUGGINS READING THE "SOMERVILLE STAR" TO HIS WIFE.

"Fine looking fellow, too!" put in the Colonel.

"I don't care," persisted Mrs. Juggins. "I don't think Miss Ally could stand a Yankee. I don't care how much they make-believe Secession.

I hate them only that much more. Let them go back where they came from! What I say is, let them let us alone; we don't want to go among them that I know of. However, Ally'd rather marry even a Yankee than a Union man any

C

day. And if she did, there's Mrs. Bowles—it would kill her stone-dead !"

"Why, you are as piert as a tree-frog, old woman !" said her husband. "It's more than I feel after that Donelson news."

In a few moments Mr. Barker had left, carefully and cordially shaking hands with Colonel Juggins and his wife, and scarcely honoring Mrs. Sorel with a distant bow as he passed out. The subject of the war being exhausted with his departure, Mrs. Juggins and her husband were to Mrs. Sorel for the rest of her visit the same plain, cordial friends as before Secession was dreamed of by them.

But it was in vain, a day or two after, that the Colonel read aloud to his wife every word of the Somerville *Star*. That Fort Donelson had fallen, and that Nashville was threatened, was too evident. It is true the Colonel read several times over, with deep satisfaction, the important information derived from the gentleman direct from England ; yet even this news, new as it was and delightful as it was to the Colonel, produced but a momentary relief.

It was a satisfaction, however, to learn, as he did from the Somerville *Star*, that the recent disasters were all owing to the most unexpected and abject cowardice of the military leaders—an event which could by no possibility ever take place again. Besides, the *Star* had ascertained that the Tennessee and Cumberland rivers were both falling so rapidly that the capture of the Federal gun-boats and transports was a certainty. The *Star* even gave an estimate of the amount of provisions and military stores which would thus fall into the hands of the Confederacy—"brought to us by the fiendish enemy just when and where we needed them most."

Never had the Somerville *Star* shone more clearly than in the passing darkness of the hour. "Mark our words," said the *Star*, "if any of our readers fall in with any one who entertains a doubt, or the shadow of a doubt, of our success in this glorious struggle for all man holds dear, that doubter is a *traitor ;* yes, a TRAITOR to his country, and *should be dealt with as such !*"

---

## CHAPTER V.

ONCE in his life the Rev. Edward Arthur had a misfortune befall him which was really one among the most fortunate circumstances he ever experienced. If it will make this seeming paradox any plainer, let us say instead, the gentleman in question stumbled over an obstacle at the outset of his ministerial path, but so stumbled as from that moment to walk that path, when it had become a thousand times more difficult and dangerous, with a step firm and sure where multitudes fell never again to rise.

This most fortunate misfortune, this most beneficial blunder, happened on this wise :

Some four or five years before Secession was ever regarded as a possibility outside the State lines of South Carolina, a great political movement took place throughout the United States— a movement as sudden, as unexpected, and, it may be added, as much underground, too, as an earthquake. At first there floated a vague rumor, eddying about the street corners of Somerville, of something new and remarkable in the political world. To the people of Somerville it was, however, a something so little understood, and so very far away, that no one felt or expressed much interest in the matter.

The matter, however, which at first was only hinted at in the papers with a scornful item here and there, began to be more fully and frequently alluded to. Each successive paper contained news of sudden and amazing victories obtained by the new party in city elections here and there. The excitement rose rapidly. Overwhelming majorities for the new organization swept away whole States at once. The Whig and Democratic leaders ceased from their mutual strife in amazement ; not more astounded were the white-haired old generals of Europe when the youthful Napoleon rushed with victorious hosts over their obsolete tactics and old-fashioned battalions. The one thought with these leaders was how to take possession of the new party, so as therewith to defeat each his ancient enemy. But while Whig and Democrat thus schemed and planned the new movement swept them, for the time, both aside from its onward course.

Somerville was very far from being at the first of things ; but even Somerville became finally and deeply interested in this new thing under the sun. In vain, at the outset of the matter, did it look to the Somerville *Star* for light and guidance. For a time Lamum held both his tongue and his pen. Lamum was taken completely unaware, and was waiting to see. Weeks rolled by, friends and enemies alike waiting for the Delphic syllable from the lips of the renowned editor—friends waiting, afraid to step save after him who had so often led them on to victory, doubly afraid to place themselves in possible antagonism to that trenchant pen ; enemies waiting for fear of committing themselves to an organization until Lamum was pledged against it ; then, and not till then, could they be certain the organization was a thing right and good.

At last Lamum spoke. A thunder-peal was not more distinct, a lightning flash not more direct and destructive. The new movement was wrong, unprincipled, detestable in every point. Those who had gone into it were deluded fools or designing knaves. From that moment Lamum turned his artillery steadily and terribly upon the new party. It was enough. In a few days his followers had all abandoned and denounced it, his enemies had to a man united themselves to, and henceforth defended, it.

Lamum never hinted an explanation of his course in those days, but it was readily understood afterward. From his earliest political life the dissolution of the Union had been to him what it is said the conquest of Constantinople is to the Russian Government—the grand object and end of existence. If Lamum paused when the new party first rose into notice, it was only to ascertain whether that party could in any way hasten the destruction of the Union; could by any possibility he so wrought by main force as to be a new and effective engine to that glorious end. Had Lamum only been satisfied on this point he would have gone into it with all his—we will not say soul, the word does not apply to the gentleman—let us say intellect.

It was soon sufficiently clear to him that the new party was not available to this end; nay, it might even switch off the public mind upon a new track! Lamum was down upon it. Shrewd politician, men said afterward. Lamum had opposed and denounced Know Nothingism in the very moment it seemed certainly victorious over all opposition. Its sudden and universal unpopularity left Lamum amazingly in the ascendant. His influence was increased beyond computation. Yet all the shrewdness of the man, all the force, influence, success of Lamum rose solely from his having given himself up wholly to one idea. "The destruction of this accursed Union"—that was the thought, the passion, the end and aim of his life. He had cherished it years before he had dared whisper it even to his most intimate friend. He had attended years ago the Nashville Convention to plan toward this end, when almost universal contempt attended the step. Patiently, hopefully, unwearyingly had he toiled in this one direction. What amazing force it gives a man, the abandoning one's self to one purpose in life!

Had Europe known, had this continent known, how completely the destruction of the Union had been for long years the one fixed purpose in life of a few able men at the South, pledged heart and mind to this thing, Europe and this continent would have been less amazed at the attempt when it was made.

"Be at my office—can you?—this afternoon at four," said Guy Brooks one morning to Mr. Arthur at the rise of the great Know Nothing movement of which we have spoken. As he said this the lawyer — for Guy Brooks was a lawyer — had an aspect of meaning and mystery; and the expression thereof did not suit him either. A face franker and more open you might have searched even his native Kentucky for in vain.

"I can be at your office then," replied his pastor; "but what for?" Not that Mr. Arthur

needed to be informed; his friend's mysterious manner had already informed him.

"You come down and see," replied the lawyer. The young minister looked for a moment inquiringly, even doubtfully, at his friend, who had turned away to search for really nothing whatever among the pigeon-holes of his desk. After a minute's silence Mr. Arthur shut and locked the door and laid his hat upon the table.

"I suppose I know what you are speaking of," he said, "and I want a word or two of conversation with you just now and upon that subject." The lawyer took his seat, though it was evident he had much rather have waived the whole matter.

"Mr. Brooks," said the young minister, "you already know how I am situated—young, inexperienced, aiming to effect good here in Somerville, if it please God. I am resolved to be nothing else in this world and in this town than a preacher of the Gospel. Do you think it will be right in me to go into this new movement? Tell me frankly as a friend, as an officer of our church."

"Yes, I do," replied the lawyer. It was not so much in a positive as in a dogged manner that he said this. What singular creations we all are! Sitting there by that table those two men knew perfectly well, each and both of them, that they ought to have nothing whatever to do with the new party. Guy Brooks, burly, openhearted, open-handed, frank-spoken man that he was to the centre of his heart, knew with absolute certainty that he ought to go into no organization whatever with whose whole plan and purpose he was not thoroughly acquainted.

His pastor, too, knew, just as well, that, as a minister of the Gospel, he most assuredly had no business in any such affair whatever. If you had asked him, "Would an Apostle have enrolled himself a member of any such party—of any party at all?" the "No, Sir!" would have sprung spontaneously to his lips. "Would Whitfield, Wesley, Heber, Henry Martyn, any true minister of the Gospel, go into such a thing?" "No, Sir! no!" would have been the instant reply. From the first something within him had kept up a perpetual No! at the very possibility of his becoming an initiate in the mysterious Order. And yet both he and his friend persisted, none the less, in doing what all the time they knew well they ought to have carefully avoided. Such is this perverse nature of ours. The voice within, certainly in the case of a Christian, may be as still and small as that which spake to Elijah at Engedi, but it is perfectly distinct, and is the voice of God. From the greatest to the smallest thing in life, no man errs but does err, not that this voice has not spoken, but that, having spoken within him, he will not heed it.

The mischief is, that the young minister put

the keeping of himself in the matter out of his own hands into that of his friend. Almost feminine in his trust where he loved, it was his nature, then, to take a positive pleasure in looking to and relying upon others—at least in the way of advice about things better known to them than to himself. It was an amiable weakness, and a positive weakness if it was amiable. On the whole, after a man has become a man, if he lives in friendship with God, then to that man God within him is guide enough. Infinitely better be advising with Him in his Word, His Providence, and in prayer, than be running hither and thither in search of advice and direction from this one and that, who is himself a safe counselor only as he himself is counseled in the matter of God. Better live in one's own fellowship with the Almighty! With Christ on his own bark let every man hold the helm of himself with his own hand! Entirely too much do we depend upon and are we governed by each other.

AT THE KNOW NOTHING CEREMONY.

And so, that afternoon, was our youthful divine introduced, with a sense of shame and wrong-doing, into a miserable back-room of an old office, and there initiated into the mystic hand. It so happened that by his side, during the process, stood Brother Barker. Profoundly impressed was pale, lean, lank-haired Brother Barker with the ceremony. His peculiar, heavy-lidded eyes drooped not enough over his pupils,

but you could see the awe, the wonder, the intensity of his faith in the whole matter.

"Brother Barker," said the young minister, half aloud to his companion, about the middle of the initiation.

"Well, Brother Arthur," replied he, but giving all his attention to the ceremony.

"One thing I feel satisfied of. This"—and Mr. Arthur finished the sentence aloud—"is no place for either you or me!" And there was not a man there but knew the same, at least of the two ministers. But Brother Barker went into it, nevertheless! From that day none more zealous than he in the cause. No man in all the region organized, and, in every way, advocated the new party so efficiently and unwearyingly. "Brother Barker throws his whole heart into whatever he goes into, you'd better believe," had always been the remark among his friends of him.

"We ought—at least, of one thing I am certain, I ought never to have come here," said Mr. Arthur to Guy Brooks, as they walked away.

"Oh, I don't know!" replied his friend. Only he did know.

"You will act as you please," continued Mr. Arthur; "but I am done with the thing from this moment."

And yet not six weeks had passed when Guy Brooks recognized, and with regret, his pastor seated among the members of the Order at a special meeting for the purpose of nominating, which was the same as actually electing—the majority of voters in the place being members of the Order—certain county officers. The fact is, the young minister had been informed that Guy Brooks was that night to be put forward for an important office. The vote would be a very close one, it was urged upon him. "Attend for this once, your vote may elect him. Surely you will do that much for your friend!" And so again did he pass out of his own hands into that of others! Yet Brooks was not elected at last. The only vote cast for him was that of the minister, some sudden arrangement having been entered into just as the Order met, by which another man was substituted.

This was the first, and it was the last identification of Mr. Arthur by himself as a politician. In the sudden and overwhelming unpopularity of the Order which speedily followed, it so happened that no one was more thoroughly abused as having been a member of it than was he. Very bitter it was to the sensitive young man, the essence of the bitterness being that his own conscience joined its voice to those of his foes. Many a night did he lie awake utterly miserable, "That I should have erred so, I who so keenly feel the peculiar sanctity of the calling to which I have given myself. The severest of my enemies reproach me not half so bitterly as I do myself. But why should I be so singled out for reproach when every minister of every denomination in this whole region was also a member—all of them—active members! I opposed it in my very initiation, attended but once, and that for the sake of friendship, and yet I am so held up! Why should it be so?"

Why it was all so ordered he understood perfectly well not until years afterward. When Secession became the rage he was the burned child that dreaded the fire. His experience during the furor of Know Nothingism had branded into him several wholesome truths. He learned that a great political movement might swiftly rise and as swiftly cease. He learned that such a movement might at one hour number its millions of adherents, and at another after-hour have left scarce one to do it reverence. He learned that vast multitudes might, during a period, be roused to enthusiasm upon a certain point, professing the most thorough conviction, the most ardent affection, the most adamantine resolve in regard to that point, and yet in a very short time afterward that enthusiasm have utterly cooled out, that conviction utterly gone, that affection changed into as strong aversion, that resolve reversed to work exactly the other way.

His experience from Know Nothingism left him, and thousands like him, thoroughly prepared to resist the far more eventful Secession storm when it, in its terrible turn, raged over the South—resist it, at least, from sweeping them an iota aside. To that first experience did this son of Levi, at least, owe it that, from the outset to the end of Secession, he clung but the more devotedly and exclusively to his one business in life as a Gospel minister. And the wondrous dealing of Providence thus with him to this end awoke within him the sincerest faith and love ever thereafter in that Providence.

It was very early one morning, soon after the election of Lincoln was looked upon as a settled thing, that Guy Brooks entered the study of his pastor. That study was a little room in the rear of the church, amazingly convenient to the lawyer on his way between his house and his office down town. The lawyer had a half-concealed expression of anxiety as he entered the room, took his seat, unfolded a huge poster, spread it out upon the table before his friend, and leaned back in his chair with a "There! what do you think of that?"

As the minister read the flaming capitals the lawyer studied his countenance. It was the countenance of a poet as well as a preacher—oval brown eyes, clustering brown hair, quiet lips, almost too full to be so firm; an expression of thought, suffering, patience, and that altogether indescribable separatedness of the man from other men which characterizes the countenance of him who habitually looks within himself and above himself.

There was a marked dissimilarity and as marked a similarity between these two friends. The lawyer was of an unusually large frame—the singular characteristic of Kentucky—stature fit for those who man that outpost and bulwark of freedom, while the minister was but of medium size. The lawyer was angular, and somewhat awkward and cumbrous, while his friend was the exact reverse. The brown face of the lawyer would have been homely were it not for the frank and good-humored expression which pervaded it, while peace and thought gave to the face of the minister that which elevated and refined a countenance already prepossessing.

Even had the two men not been thrown together as minister and officer of a young and struggling church, in a new community having but little sympathy with religion, they would have been drawn together by an instinctive affinity. Genuine piety and heart-felt sincerity in both, the dependence of the lawyer upon the minister as his spiritual guide, and of the minister upon the lawyer as his counselor in matters of the world—these ties bound the two closely together. The lawyer found singular freshness and gentleness and elevation of sentiment in his friend in comparison with the rough and practical world in which he was struggling; and the minister turned with pleasure from his books and his own abstractions to the healthful, matter-of-fact, free-spoken lawyer. Not in vain, either, had they, side by side, learned the same lesson during the raging of Know Nothingism, and of all that followed upon its heels.

"Yes, but what do you think of it?" asked the lawyer, as his companion read the poster through, then, without a word, folded it up and returned it to its owner.

"Nothing at all. But where did you get it?" was the reply.

"Tore it down from beside the door of the Post-office," said the Kentuckian, with emphasis.

"It was hardly worth your while," said his companion; "you surely attach no importance to any effort of the sort."

"You are mistaken, Sir; terribly mistaken. Listen how it sounds!" continued the lawyer, and he opened the poster as he stood, and read it in a powerful and earnest voice.

"FREEMEN OR SLAVES!

"The die is cast. The unprincipled Abolitionists of the North have accomplished their diabolical purpose. Beyond a doubt Abraham Lincoln has been elected President. Are you prepared to submit to the iron yoke of an Abolitionist? Your President AN ABOLITIONIST? Fellow-citizens, we must strike for our liberty NOW, or be forever SLAVES! All those in favor of calling an immediate Convention of the people of this great State will meet this afternoon at the Court-house at 3 o'clock. Come one, come all!

"'Strike for your altars and your fires,
Strike for the green graves of your sires!
God and your native land!'"

"Well, and what of all that?" asked the min-

"THERE! WHAT DO YOU THINK OF THAT?"

ister, perfectly cool beside the excitement of his companion.

"What of all that?" replied his companion. "Is it possible you do not know what is to follow? Do you not know that South Carolina has already seceded? That Mississippi has probably followed? That the storm is just rising which is to sweep over all the Southern States? What of that? It means that our State, too, is to be hurled into the movement."

"By whom?" The minister patient with his mistaken friend.

"By the leaders of this meeting this afternoon."

"And who are they? Look at it, man. Lamum, first and foremost; Colonel Roberts; Judge Jones, who owes his late election to Lamum; Colonel Juggins will ride in, too, from the country; Dr. Ginnis; Alf Pike; Dick Simmons; Bob Withers; and the like. There may be others, but only as spectators, like yourself, Mr. Ellis, and Ferguson."

"You seem to take it for granted that I am not going into the thing," said the lawyer, composing his face.

"May God forbid!" ejaculated the minister, fervently, and somewhat anxiously.

"He has forbidden, he does forbid! But you do not estimate the thing right. Perhaps only a dozen or two of the professional politicians will meet there really determined to act. Lamum will be called to the Chair. Brother Barker, by previous arrangement, will open the meeting with prayer."

"Never!" interrupted the minister, eagerly.

"It shows how little you know, shut up here among your books. Brother Barker will open with a long and fervent prayer. His whole denomination at the South will identify itself, has identified itself with the movement. The strongest kind of resolutions have been written out by Lamum weeks ago, and will be introduced and passed. Not a hundredth part of Somerville will sympathize in the thing—the community as a community will heartily disapprove of the thing—yet Lamum will publish a blazing account in his paper, and represent the proceedings as the unanimous and enthusiastic expression of the whole county. Meanwhile, by letters and visits to all parts of the State, made weeks ago, months ago, similar meetings will be got up by similar politicians over the whole State; an enthusiasm will be kindled, will rage with fury over the State. Then a Convention will be held, Secession will be consummated, and then — God only knows what!"

"But the Governor—" began the minister.

"By—by nothing at all!" burst out the lawyer, deeply excited. "What a splendid opportunity for immortal fame that man has! Oh, if I could but be in his place to-day!"

"And what would you do? could you do?"

"Do? I would run up the flag of my country, rally around it by proclamation every true man in the State, and defy the devil of Disunion and all his infernal works! I tell you, Sir, three-fourths of the voters of the State would stand by me to the death. Lamum and his clique over the entire South—the *politicians*—are utterly distinct from the people in this whole matter. The politicians have a long-cherished hatred against the North burning in their bo-

soms; they want plunder and power. The people are busy with their crops and their families; they want only their rights and peace. Yet in one month—in two weeks from this hour, the people will have passed helpless into the hands of the politicians. And while this golden, glorious moment is passing away never to return, there they sit at the capital of the State, the Governor and the heads of departments, bewailing and deprecating and dreading the awful ruin they have at least sense enough to know is coming upon the State. Unwilling to shed blood! Imbeciles! Infatuated old women! As if the cause of Right and Liberty and Law, and all we hold dear as American freemen, is not the one cause to strike for, if need be to die for. Shed blood! As if *that* should paralyze us in this last moment. Only run up the flag of our country, rally around it the true men of the State, arrest every traitor; only a firm front and a bold hand for this next golden month, and the State is saved forever, just as old Kentucky will be!" And the lawyer walked the floor in excess of impatience.

"But the Governor?" insisted the minister.

"Understands the whole evil as well as any man; would do what is right; but—but—"

"Is too old," supplied the minister, in sorrowful tones.

The lawyer's head sunk gloomily upon his breast.

"You draw a terrible picture," said the young minister, after a long silence; "yet I do not feel at all dismayed. I have no certain faith in any human arm or brain. But I do feel a full and quiet faith in God. You believe in him as well as I. You know perfectly well that he orders all hearts, all minds, all events in infinite wisdom and love. This is a great Christian nation, has been founded as such. Ever since its peculiarly religious foundation was laid in prayers and tears by the holiest men then alive on earth, it has been a nation trained to piety. Think of the numerous and powerful denominations; think of the great benevolent associations for the advancement of Christianity at home and abroad, and of their millions of income. Why, Sir, this is a Christian land! I can not for a moment believe it is to be given up to disruption and ruin. I would as soon expect the sun to—to—"

"Go out?" asked the lawyer. "Well, and 'the sun shall be turned into sackcloth'—I don't remember the rest of the passage—'the moon into blood.'"

"Oh, that refers to the latter days," said his companion, with a smile of superior theological information.

"I myself can not think, can not bring myself to believe in the raging of a civil war in this nation—*this* nation. It seems preposterous," said the lawyer, as if reasoning with himself.

The minister laughed outright. "I did not dream you were ever troubled with such morbid notions, Mr. Brooks. Really Lamum frightens you altogether too much. Do you think that such men as Lamum, and the class whom he represents, are to be compared with the vast body of sober, sensible, Christian men who make up this great country? Or, if that is not strong enough," said the minister, with a pitying smile, "do you imagine that a million of Lamums are too powerful for the Almighty? For my part, the more I think of it the more composed I feel. War? Nonsense!"

"God often uses bad men to accomplish his greatest purposes," said the lawyer. "As to our Christianity, we may turn out to be not so Christian a people as we have fancied ourselves to be. And who knows," he added, looking at his friend in a way which both puzzled and awoke vague pain in his bosom, "but that the Almighty has a special controversy with us as a people—a *special* controversy? If He has, you depend on it no amount of Christianity, nor of national fasting and prayer on our part, will arrest His hand until that one matter be settled. We will see very soon. No matter about that just yet. The power of the bad men, the palsy of the good men just now! I declare it does look like the hand of the Almighty, though. However! It is the ruin of my native South, and by the rash hands of the South itself, that I fear. However, I am glad to find we think and feel alike in this matter. I was sure we would. Time for me to go to my office. Good-morning." And the visitor was gone only to look back again the next moment.

"I am afraid I know somebody with whom you will *not* be able to agree in regard to Secession," he said, significantly.

"And who may that be?" asked the minister, feeling his face suddenly burn as he spoke.

"Not the least use to inform you," said the lawyer with a smile, and closing the door after him.

ARTHUR'S WEAKNESS.

## CHAPTER VI.

It may tend to lower the Rev. Edward Arthur in the eyes of the readers of these pages; but none the less must it be stated that, although a minister, he was none the less also a man. Not an ethereal being, not an ideal of all excellence, but, from head to foot, a human being like the rest of us. Perhaps the intensest human part about him was his heart. His capacity for loving, his proclivity for loving, his unweariedness in loving from his earliest recollection upward was wonderful.

Of course it is painful to make the statement, yet it must be said that, from the day when just three years old, he was detected in the act of kissing behind a parlor rocking-chair a young lady-visitor of some six months or so less experience of life, onward he had never ceased to love. His own relatives, of course; but, in addition to these, all the little flaxen-haired companions of his childhood—there always being for the day some special queen of his heart in virtue of hair specially flaxen, eyes particularly black or blue, cheeks uncommonly rosy, and fair, and dimpled, dress remarkably beautiful, or, what was even more to the purpose, the being specially associated with him for the time of the little Cleopatra of the hour. Up to the very day of leaving for college he had not learned to master such nonsense.

With the development of lungs and brains and all the rest the heart had persisted in growing also. Not that, when he rolled away, just sixteen years old, in the stage from his father's door, he had as yet met exactly with his ideal. None the less did he bear away with him the image in his heart, the lock of her hair being in his Bible in his trunk, of the last, in the quick succession of the queens of his childhood; not so much because he loved *her*, as from the pleasure it was to him, the absolute necessity it was to him to love somebody.

His four years' course in college was a sudden and total interregnum in all this. Minerva set aside Venus with perfect success during those four college years. Heart had to content itself with merely keeping up the circulation while the brain was being developed. Vastly better would it have been could the two have shared the man more equally between them—not so cold and hard would those four years have been. Languages, philosophy, mathematics; mathematics, philosophy, languages all the session through, the impulse thereof bore him, like a locomotive over a break in the track, over the gap of each vacation with a jar scarce perceptible. That day Edward Arthur graduated he could have laid his hand upon the folds of the silk gown which covered his bosom and have truthfully declared his heart to have been, during the previous four years, wholly free from thought of woman. And as he descended the steps of the platform after Commencement, he could have safely declared that, leaving more sacred things aside dearer to him than the entire sex, from Eve down, was the honor he had obtained from Alma Mater, most revered and beloved of all her sex.

Altogether too short was the period which followed to think upon any thing but the immediate Past and the immediate Future. Bright and early that September morning following his graduation did he present himself in the chapel of the Theological Seminary to be matriculated; no man more free from every thing else in the world to devote himself to his studies for the ministry. And into it he plunged: Church History; Theology polemic, didactic, patristic, exegetic; the preparation and delivery of sermons; Hebrew; Chaldaic; Syriac; German. Grudgingly was the morning and evening walk granted to the muscles; only because it was a necessary nuisance was the stomach supplied with the regulation food at the regulation hours in the regulation refectory—it was the brain must be exercised, the brain must be fed. No wonder if, like the right arm of the blacksmith, it was developed beyond the rest of the body, out of proportion to the rest of the body. True, the heart was allowed free play in regard to things spiritual and divine, even stimulated and evermore prompted to this.

And, perhaps, it was well that such things should thus by years preoccupy the heart; obtain from long habit, the deep-seated, uniform custom of the heart, before its doors were opened to all the world. Yet, if its affection for all else could only be kept duly subordinate, the very exercising the heart in the love of all human things would fit it for the more vigorous loving of things superior to these; even as the eye and the hand, quick to see and prompt to gather every little flower flourishing by the way-side, is but trained thereby for the prizing and the gathering the more eagerly of all diamonds and precious stones, too, which may sparkle along the road-side of life. Is it altogether fanciful to remember here that, though the heart beat in the breast with but one throb, it yet has within itself two separate and distinct sets of organs,

an auricle and ventricle on the left side thereof, and an auricle and ventricle on the right side thereof? Thou shalt love God, and thou shalt love men, is the divine command. Only as we love either perfectly do we love both perfectly. Only as we love both as we should, do we, as we should, love either; only when both sides of the heart are whole, and keep the mystic time to each other, does the entire heart throb aright! "He that loveth not his brother whom he hath seen? And this commandment have we from him, That he who loveth God love his brother also."

One thing is perfectly certain, if ever there was a man prepared to love, prepared to love any thing and every thing which could be loved, that man was the Rev. Edward Arthur when he found himself, college and seminary passed through, pastor of the church in Somerville. Neglected, forgotten, the heart of the man was to assert itself—was to make up for the long-endured tyranny of the brain.

Let me pause a moment here. I have something to say which may greatly weaken the reader's estimation of the Rev. Edward Arthur. Shall I say it exactly as it was? Or shall I not rather carefully conceal the fact, so that the young minister may be that much the greater and stronger individual in the eyes of those who read these pages? Hesitate as I may to say it, ashamed as I may be to announce the fact, deeply conscious, as of course I am, of the damage it will do our hero from this instant to the end of his history, I must none the less say, because I can not possibly avoid it and be at all coherent in my narrative, that the Rev. Edward Arthur during the very first day of his arrival in Somerville fell in love! Pardon him, dear reader, he could not possibly help it; at least he did not help it. Pardon him, indulgent reader, for it was a love which, however hastily kindled, never ceased to burn thereafter with but stronger and brighter and purer flame.

The way of it was this: When Guy Brooks, Esq., years before Secession, had written to the young theologian to come to Somerville and organize a church in that new but promising town, and had received a promise of doing so in reply, he forthwith began, in a terrible hurry, to look around among the families of Somerville for some suitable home for the new minister. It ought to be among the members of the contemplated church, to begin with. Next, in which of these families should it be?

He himself was then a widower and boarded at the time at the hotel, and the hotel was no place for a preacher; half an hour in the bar-room or any where else about the house was sufficient to dishearten one of his calling through all the avenues of smelling, tasting, seeing, and hearing. Mr. Ferguson, the Scotchman, offered to share his bachelor home with the new-comer, especially as he was to be also a member of the church to be organized. Guy Brooks thanked him but declined. A most substantially and inflexibly good man was Ferguson, like all Scotchmen who are not utter reprobates; but, like every other Scotchman, reprobate or not, Ferguson was set in his way, notionate to the last degree. And cross, too; no tropical thunder-gust more suddenly, unexpectedly, and violently so. Upon Mr. Ferguson Guy Brooks counted confidently as upon a very oaken beam in the proposed church organization, but, as a host of the pastor thereof? No. The lawyer did not entertain the idea one instant. Suppose the guest should derange, should injure, should lose a Number from Mr. Ferguson's collection? The very possibility of such a catastrophe, with all its disruptive effects upon the proposed church, was sufficient to settle the matter. No one can dislike to pause more than the writer. The collection of Mr. Ferguson has been unintentionally alluded to. But now that it has been mentioned, it must be explained before we can proceed.

In Mr. Ferguson's bosom existed the instinct of collection. It *is* an instinct. Look at the magpie. We all know what a passion it has for stealing and secreting bits of raw cotton, shreds of rags, fragments of pottery, articles of jewelry, and the like. There is a story afloat in works on Natural History of another bird—a species of hawk—which has its nest in the centre of a thorny tree, and which impales upon these thorns all manner of grasshoppers, locusts, insects of all sorts, as well as the smaller birds. Toward the decline of its days this winged virtuoso has collected a perfect museum of natural curiosities, and lives and dies in its overshadowed nest, in the centre thereof, in scientific and serene content. However true this may be, we are certain of the instinct in the case of the magpie. And it is the same instinct which is seen in the collector of autographs, peculiar snuff-boxes, fantastic pipes, singular walking-sticks, rare editions of old books, and the like. Very strong was the instinct in the case of Mr. Ferguson. A Scotchman should have been more sensible; but in an old bachelor the object of his collection was preposterous—he had collected into a body every treatise on the subject of Infant Baptism he had ever heard or read of. It may have begun his making the collection, quietly and innocently enough, but it had grown into a passion—a mania.

The walls of a certain room in his house were devoted exclusively to these treatises. Books in folio, quarto, octavo, duodecimo, were there; thick books and thin books, and in every possible style of binding. Pamphlets, too, of all shapes, sizes, and ages upon the subject. Files of all such newspapers also as contained articles upon the subject, and the whole collection patched, pasted, annotated, in every stage of wear and discoloration. Then there were bound volumes of letters he had evoked from reverend and irreverent sources, in all degrees of angry *pro* and recriminating *con*. A bulky scrap-book or two contained every flying anecdote, paragraph, item, cut right and left, from every paper which he had ever come upon bearing upon the one theme. One stood amazed to behold how much had been said upon the subject in the world, and turned away aghast at the remembrance that, even yet, the question remained as unsettled as ever. The plain fact is, Mr. Ferguson took hardly the slightest interest in the subject discussed itself—it was in his collection upon the subject that his interest lay.

"No, and it would sicken him, too, for life of the whole subject!" laughed Guy Brooks to himself, as, after declining Mr. Ferguson's offer of a room in his house for the expected minister, he walked back to his office.

"He shall know of my collection none the less. And surely no room in Somerville could be so appropriate for a minister as just that room," said Mr. Ferguson, as he parted from the lawyer. In something of a huff, too; only he knew that no amount of huff on his part could provoke any thing but amusement and good-nature on the part of the frank and open-hearted lawyer.

There was Dr. Warner, also. He, too, was to be a member of the church. There was not a pleasanter house in Somerville than his, nor a better spread table.

"He can have my office in the front-yard," said Dr. Warner, after having previously received his wife's views upon the subject.

A nice office it was, too, as Guy Brooks knew, for it was therein, in retreat from his wife, that the Doctor entertained his gentlemen friends. On the shelves therein were the Doctor's rows of bottles and papers of herbs. Therein also was his mahogany case of surgical instruments. The wooden apparatus, too, was in the corner, with its complicated straps, in which Bub and 'Ria had more than once imprisoned Amos when suffering, in imagination, with the fracture of every bone in his body in consequence of a fall from the top of the stable. In the book-case were the Doctor's medical books, especially his large and intensely-colored Surgical Atlas, of the inside of which he was so careful Bub should know nothing, and yet whose every plate had been often and most thoroughly studied by Bub in the absences of his father, assisted by Amos, with 'Ria carefully locked out. Therein, also, was the good Doctor's collection, in glass jars and alcohol, of such tumors, bits of lungs and brains, amputated fingers and toes, embryos, and the like delicacies, as had come in his way in the course of his profession. And there, also, was a full-length skeleton in its corner.

"The first thing he will see in the morning, the last his eyes will close upon at night—have an impressive influence upon his meditations," said the Doctor, in commending the room for the expected arrival.

But no. There is a certain smell about that room, considered the lawyer with himself. Besides—and the idea struck the lawyer with considerable force—deprive the Doctor of that retreat from his wife? It would be a base imposition on his easy good-nature. And then, her tongue! Phew!—no!

There was Colonel Roberts also. Fine, commodious house; Mrs. Roberts an excellent woman, and member of the church. And who knows but he might be able to influence even Roberts? But the lawyer, charitable and hopeful as he was, shook his head even as he said it. The squat figure of the Colonel stood before his imagination on the instant — that black hair, those splendid black eyes, that full face, so much like that of a bull-dog, and yet so handsome! "What an unmitigated bully and blackguard that man is!" said the lawyer to himself, as the image rose before his mind—forgetting all about the minister. "Gambler, hard drinker, duelist, obscene to the last degree; unmatched and unmatchable in profanity; loose to dishonesty in the payment of his debts and in all his business transactions; avowedly a scoffer at the truth of religion and the virtue of woman. With all this, when he cares to be so, what dignity, what grace, what eloquence, what polished wit, what exquisite courtesy! That it should be possible to combine into one such a devil and such an angel!" murmured the lawyer to himself.

Colonel Ret Roberts! Nothing could be more familiar to the public ear and to the public tongue than that. He had been a bold young lawyer; then an indefatigable stump-speaker throughout the State—copious in anecdote, reckless in statement, vehement in invective; next an Elector of a successful candidate for the Presidency; then, for six months, Chargé at one of the minor European courts; after that Governor of the State. When Guy Brooks was debating whether or no to make him the host of the expected minister, he was drinking, gambling, playing at once the Edmund Burke and the bully in the United States Senate at Washington. All the State knew pretty well the kind of man Colonel Ret Roberts was; most certainly he disguised nothing of himself from any one. Yet all over the State religious, grave, and sober men applauded the Colonel's speeches; contributed gladly pigs, turkeys, and beeves toward barbecues in his honor; introduced him, with pride at the opportunity of doing so, to their wives and daughters, and voted him into whatever office he demanded rather than asked at their hands.

"As you say, my house is too far out of Somerville for the purpose; or, there being only Robby and myself here, I would be pleased to have Mr. Arthur with me," Mrs. Sorel observed, when Guy Brooks, throwing his energies into the matter, had ridden out to consult her upon the subject. There is Mrs. Bowles, thought Mrs. Sorel to herself, and she knitted and thought over the matter, as was her placid wont on every subject, before she spoke out. It was not altogether so clear.

"I have thought of the hotel, of Ferguson, of Dr. Warner, even of Colonel Ret Roberts, besides every other place possible," said Guy Brooks, after a somewhat despondent silence. "It ought to be in the family of a member of the church if possible."

"How old did you say he was? or did you say any thing at all on the subject?" asked Mrs. Sorel, at length.

"I do not know, somewhere under thirty, I suppose. You remember I never saw him," said the lawyer. "Ferguson, Warner, Ellis, and myself wrote to the head of the Theological Seminary to recommend some one to us for the purpose of organizing a church here. In reply Mr. Arthur was warmly urged upon us; we corresponded with him, he says he will come; that is all we know of him."

"Have you thought of Mrs. Bowles?" inquired Mrs. Sorel, at length.

"The very person!" exclaimed the lawyer, rising to his feet. "Strange I never once thought of her. That is, if she will consent. You know what a delicate, retiring lady she is. Besides, it would be an assistance to her, his boarding with her. Yes," added the lawyer, with enthusiasm, "and there is the office Rutledge Bowles occupied before he went to college in the corner of the yard. The very thing! She is a member of the proposed church, too. I do not think she would consent to the arrangement except on that ground. I will see her right away." And the lawyer took his hat to leave.

"There might be one objection," said Mrs. Sorel, accompanying her visitor to the door.

"What, what can it be?" inquired he, turning suddenly. Mrs. Sorel smiled demurely and continued knitting.

"Oh, nonsense!" said the lawyer, looking at her first, inquiringly, and then with a smile breaking over his wholesome face: "Beg your pardon, I didn't mean to use such language, Mrs. Sorel. But you never fear. We men, especially in such a new place as Somerville, with every thing before us to do, have no time to think about such things. You ladies flatter yourselves; really, I beg pardon again," said the frank lawyer, laughing at himself.

"Do we, Mr. Brooks? Well, perhaps we do," said quiet Mrs. Sorel, not at all cast down —quite confident rather.

"You would not really advise against Mrs.

Bowles on that account?" asked the lawyer, seriously, pausing hat in hand upon the front step.

"By no means, or I should not have mentioned it. Yes, see her, and see what you can do. Don't let me detain you. Good-evening!" But the wise, placid smile was still on her face as she said it.

"Stuff, nonsense! It is to be hoped he will find too much to do to think of such things! Oh these women, they think men never think of any thing else; sensible lady like Mrs. Sorel, too! Get up, Charley!" and with an unnecessary cut of his whip the Kentuckian cantered back into Somerville.

Mrs. Bowles came into the arrangement the moment the lawyer mentioned it, which he did with characteristic promptitude that same evening.

But it was after having most clearly and distinctly ascertained from the lawyer that the expected minister was not from the North, but from Virginia, born, raised, educated there. Good! If any spot on the globe could be said to stand next to South Carolina, in Mrs. Bowles's estimation, it was Virginia. "Though I have a great admiration for Kentucky also," Mrs. Bowles said, with the charming condescension of the daughter of a hundred Earls to a newly-knighted Baronet.

"If he will consent to live plainly there will be no inconvenience to us at all," she said to him immediately thereafter. "I have been so long without seeing even a minister of my own church that it will be a treat to me to have him. There is Rutledge Bowles's office. We can put .a bed in there for him, you know. It will do for his study, too. If I do not like the arrangement afterward, you know, we can make a change. But I am sure we will like it—yes, I am quite sure of it!" and excellent Mrs. Bowles was almost enthusiastic upon the subject, greatly to the delight of her visitor.

The truth is, Mrs. Bowles was enthusiastic in every thing. If she liked any thing or person she liked enthusiastically—could not see, would not hear or believe any thing to the contrary. And, it must be added, if she disliked she disliked as sincerely and vehemently as her piety would permit. It so happened that Mrs. Sorel and herself were from the same neighborhood in South Carolina, had been school-girls together. Yet it was singular that the same soil could produce two persons so unlike. Mrs. Sorel tall, dignified, grave, self-possessed; Mrs. Bowles rather *petite* and *spirituel* in face and figure, unconstrained, full of lively fancies, impulsive, quickspoken. Both were thoroughly ladies in the highest sense of the term—strongly attached to each other from memories of their childhood, still more from contrast of character; for while Mrs. Sorel could not but love the ardent and warm-spoken widow, so sincere and free in every

thought and feeling, Mrs. Bowles could not but feel a warm affection for one in whose judgment, strong sense, sober speech she had long learned to have the deepest confidence. She had long been in the habit of consulting Mrs. Sorel in every thing of importance—much more so since the death of her husband, the Major.

I wish our story could pause long enough to permit us to say a little, or rather a good deal about Major J. C. Bowles. You can gather all you may wish to know of his character and history by turning to any book of national portraits. You will find him there among the politicians of South Carolina of some forty years ago. A stately gentleman he appears to have been from the somewhat stiff portrait in question, the halflength painting, from which it was taken, hanging in silent grandeur in the parlor at Somerville. Often did the young minister sit in that parlor of summer afternoons and study, not only the biography of the man himself, but a vast deal of national history, too, in that imposing portraiture.

Evidently a commanding man the Major was, with his high rolled collar, huge cravat beneath his chin, and the locks brushed away from the broad forehead, only a blue ribbon across the bosom lacking to make it pass as the likeness of a royal duke. The painting in question represented him thus: the gold-headed cane presented him by his constituents after his great speech in Congress resting between his knees, the sword wherewith his father had fought in the Revolution hanging on the wall behind him, St. Michael's Church visible through the window, to show the portrait was taken in Charleston. But you can see it all for yourself, dear reader, by turning to the volume in question, and his life besides on the next page.

Let us halt here long enough, however, to say at least this: Colonel Ret Roberts and Major J. C. Bowles were as exactly alike, and as utterly, eternally, and irreconcilably unlike, as any two men can possibly be. Both were apparently gentlemen of the highest type of breeding and courtesy, yet Colonel Ret Roberts was only superficially so; it was as natural to him as a suit of the superfinest broadcloth is to a prince, and as much a thing apart from and external to his real self as such a suit. Major J. C. Bowles was a genuine gentleman to the centre of his soul. Colonel Ret Roberts was a talented, highly talented man. Major J. C. Bowles was not, even a little dull. With Colonel Ret Roberts, the Major believed to the hour of his death that South Carolina was the first State on the continent—in the world, in fact; unlike the Colonel, however, the Major never in his life cursed and commended to eternal perdition, as the Colonel did every day of his life, whoever and whatsoever was in conflict with him on this point. That Calhoun was the superior of Webster Major Bowles never entertained the slightest doubt; yet Webster was a rational, respectable, perhaps conscientious individual. This the Major sincerely believed, while the Colonel did not—or, at least, swore he did not. That the "peculiar institution" was morally, socially, religiously, politically, eternally right, the essential foundation of all correct government, a thing to exist for ever and ever by ordinance like that which rolls the stars, both heartily believed; yet Major Bowles fed, clothed, cared for his negroes like the Christian gentleman he was; seeing himself to it, with a deep sense of responsibility, that they were not overworked nor their religious instruction neglected. Colonel Ret Roberts, on the other hand, believed and acted in every sense in the belief that his negroes were only speaking animals, to be worked to the utmost by the strictest overseers. However, as Colonel Ret Roberts had but scant reference himself to his own higher nature as an immortal being made in the image of his Maker, you could not reasonably suppose he should imagine any such thing for an instant in reference to his slaves. When in good-humor he would treat them to tobacco, whisky, and all manner of frolics and idleness; but with the same feeling toward them in good-humor as in bad, that they were but animals, worth no more thought than the horses in his stable, petted as such, beaten as such.

Major Bowles had no specially rigid notions on the subject of religion, yet he was not an avowed and insolent scoffer at it like Colonel Ret Roberts; even attended church, at least occasionally, a thing that Lamum never could induce the Colonel to do even when the most important political object was at stake. Nor did Major Bowles admire any Puritanism in regard to morals: yet he never would have soiled his fingers with the greasy cards, the dirty dice-box, the dripping gin-tumbler with which Colonel Ret Roberts was familiar, to say nothing of the profanity, obscenity, and practical debauchery which peopled the Colonel's plantation with his mulatto offspring, as much to the Colonel, and no more, than the puppies littered in his kennels. And the Major had as supreme an adoration for honor as the Colonel; but it was a principle which would have made him blush to leave a debt unpaid, or to do even a deed of doubtful honesty, wherein the Colonel differed from him amazingly in practice. As behooved gentlemen of honor, both had "been out" with an antagonist. The Major had gone out only when grossly insulted, and then had coldly received his enemy's fire with erect bearing, afterward firing into the air. The Colonel, on the other hand, had ever been the one provoking the quarrel, and then eager on the field to kill; in which, to the number of some five or six foes, he had been remarkably successful.

But why speak of Major J. C. Bowles? Did he not waste his estate with too prodigal an hospitality, too utter a devotion to politics, and so subside, in his later years, first into what remained of his large property, a small home in Charleston, and a practice at the bar, for which he had become too old or too unused by political life to succeed, and then into his grave there in St. Michael's church-yard? Had he but had Colonel Ret Roberts's—what shall we call it?—some highly-polished synonym for rascality, he would not have lost acre or negro. However, so it was.

When somewhat advanced in life the Major married his wife, of as distinguished and of as decayed a family as his own. A son and a daughter were the children of his old age—Rutledge and Alice. These were both but children when, after the death of her husband, Mrs. Bowles moved out westward and settled in Somerville. The Major owned lands there; Mrs. Bowles could not endure to take a lower rank in Charleston than her husband had once occupied. Mrs. Sorel had preceded her, and had written, urging to the step. So it was, that, at the date of our story, Mrs. Bowles was living in her neat little cottage-home on the edge of Somerville. She had left South Carolina, it is true, but the soil was all of the State she had left behind her.

The young minister learned all this, bit by bit, after his arrival. Welcomed at the hotel door, as he stepped from the stage, by Guy Brooks, he and the lawyer were at home with each other from that moment; for where people are sincere they understand each other from the first sight of each other's face, from the first grasp of each other's hand. The energetic lawyer had his new possession into his chamber in a moment; and had him brushed, dined, and introduced to Ferguson, Warner, Ellis, and half a dozen more, within the hour of his arrival.

"You must feel yourself at home with us," he said to him, in his frank, hearty way. "We are all fragments of the church that is to be. Dr. Warner here is ready to doctor you the moment you say the word. Mr. Ellis has a store down town, a good place to drop into to get acquainted with people. Ferguson here—well, Mr. Ferguson can post you on the subject of Infant Baptism, if you need it at all. I am the only one not of much use. However!"

"Somewhat too young for my fancy; it isn't a fair-cheeked, brown-haired girl we wanted for such a place as this rough and unchristianized Somerville," growled Mr. Ferguson to himself, as he went back to his room.

The afternoon of his arrival—"Why not?" the lawyer said to himself—Mr. Arthur was carried over to Mrs. Bowles to be introduced, the lawyer explaining matters to him as they walked over.

"What a neat, home-like place!" the new-

"AND ARTHUR WAS IN LOVE."

comer said to himself, as they entered the front gate and advanced along the graveled walk between the altheas and rose-bushes to the door. Like all houses at the South not built by people direct from the North, a goodly portico was in front of the residence, admitting to a hall into which rooms communicated on either side. It was a May morning when the new-comer stood there, inhaling the fragrance of jasmine and mimosa, glancing around at the many evidences of a refined taste on every side, while they waited for the door to be opened. With Mrs. Bowles, a few moments after, so warm-hearted and cordial in her sables and gray hair, the young minister felt himself at once at home and at ease—there is so much, so exceedingly much, in refinement when warmed by a glowing heart!

"I have but a small family, Mr. Arthur," she said, at last. "Rutledge Bowles, my only son, is at college in Columbia." Mrs. Bowles did not say, "Columbia, South Carolina," because to her there was but that one Columbia in the world. "My daughter Alice—" she began ; but at that instant the front gate was heard to slam, hasty steps succeeded along the gravel, and a young girl threw open the parlor door, with sunbonnet in one hand, school-books in the other, her hair about her glowing face.

And the Rev. Edward Arthur was in love!

SEEKING DIVINE GUIDANCE.

## CHAPTER VII.

LET us linger a few moments longer before we plunge again into the stormy epoch of Secession with which these pages began. We will loiter but a moment. Heaven knows Secession will come soon enough.

Blessed forever be the quickening of the sap in the veins, the putting forth of leaves and tender blossoms hued like the rainbow, the eager joy of beginning the earliest rudiments of future fruit—the spring-time of youth! Never physician entered upon the case of his first patient, never lawyer undertook the business of his first client, never painter began his first painting, nor sculptor his first statue, nor poet his first poem, with more eagerness than did the young minister engage in his new charge. Only his was a diviner joy than theirs, as his work was a diviner work. He had dreamed of it all while yet a boy, for, from his earliest remembrance, the ministry had been the purpose of his life. A hundred times had he planned exactly what he would do, and what he would most carefully not do, after having charge, while yet in college. As to his three years in the Theological Seminary, not a day but he had determined upon some new evil to be avoided in his future ministry, upon some new virtue to be practiced. During all the long years going before, he had never known one of his own proposed profession, thrown with him in biography or in person, but he had said to himself, "By the help of God, when I enter the ministry, I will never, never be this and that as I see it in this individual. God helping me, even this heroism, this habit, this success which adorns this man shall be equaled, if it please God, surpassed, when I am fairly upon the stage."

That memorable morning after his arrival in Somerville, when he awoke in Rutledge Bowles's office, there in Mrs. Bowles's front yard, it was a feeling half of pleasure and half of terror with which he realized that his life's business, for which he had been so long training, praying, dreaming, was at last fairly entered upon. Ah, how fervently did he pray for aid as he knelt beside his neat bed! What expressions of his own inability to do aught unaided on his lips, and what perfect confidence of being able to accomplish every thing throbbing the same instant in his heart! No patriarch more dignified than he in conducting family worship that morning in Mrs. Bowles's parlor beneath the steady stare of the old Major from his gilded frame, Mrs. Bowles in her low sewing-chair, her daughter Alice upon an ottoman at her feet, and the two family servants seated solemnly near the door. Had he persisted, as he began, in reading the chapter expressly and definitely to Mrs. Bowles and her daughter, his manner would have continued artificial ; but, from long habit, after the first six or eight verses, he became deeply and devotionally interested in the words, and read them accordingly. And so of his prayer : nothing could be more natural because nothing could be more sincere. Were it only for the effect of it on one's consequent bearing toward his fellows, it is an admirable thing to possess a deep and habitual reference to, and heart-felt belief in, One supremely above the whole of us.

"The head of the table, did you say ?" asked

ARTHUR'S FIRST MEAL AT MRS. BOWLES'S.

Mr. Arthur a few minutes after, as they were seating themselves at the breakfast-table.

"If you please, Mr. Arthur, the *foot* of the table," said Mrs. Bowles, with a slight South Carolinianism of stress upon the word.

It was a dreadful moment for the bashful theologian, fresh from the barbarism of three years' eating with slouched and slipshod companions in the seminary refectory. His cheeks burned, and Alice's eyes danced with fun. But all the Latin, Greek, and Hebrew in the world can not destroy the true gentleman in a man where it exists by nature.

"You must pardon me, Mrs. Bowles," he said, with a frank smile, after pronouncing the blessing, and with perfect ease of manner; "but I have been living for the last several years like a sort of Robinson Crusoe upon a species of desert island."

"Yes?" asked Mrs. Bowles, to whom his manner was as an Open Sesame, while Alice's mirth became diminished as she found it shared with their guest himself. And so, during the pauses of the breakfast, their new acquaintance gave them in a humorous manner some description of his scholastic life. It was doubly interesting to the mother from the fact that her son was at college in Columbia.

"Really, Mr. Arthur," she said, at last, "it is almost like having Rutledge Bowles on a visit home from Columbia. He always occupied since the death of his father the seat you are now in. You remind me of him, I assure you." Higher compliment than that no new acquaintance could receive from her lips. "You were not educated at Columbia, Mr. Arthur?"

"At Hampden Sydney, Madam," replied her guest.

"In Virginia, I think it is?" asked she. Not quite as low down as Yale or Princeton; however, he was not to blame, she felt sure. Mr. Arthur replies in the affirmative. "You are a native of Virginia, I think?"

"Yes, Madam."

"You did right, quite right to enter an institution in your own State," said Mrs. Bowles, glad to find a defense for him. "I dare say they are not so extravagantly expensive where you were educated. I am almost shocked at Rutledge Bowles's expenditure. I suppose, however, his situation in such a place as Columbia requires greater expense than in other places."

And terribly expensive the fond mother did find her son's education there; but she stinted herself proudly for it; she mentioned it with unconscious pride in her tones; it was part and parcel of being at Columbia.

"Though, while we are upon the subject, there is one thing in regard to Columbia I have never yet fully understood," said Mrs. Bowles, after a while. "Rutledge Bowles has explained it to me over and over again in his letters—the perpetual revolutions in the College, I mean. From what Rutledge Bowles writes it has been impossible for the students to pursue, consistently with their own honor, any other course. It seems strange that the many Faculties of the College can not come to understand, any of them, what the youth of South Carolina are, and what they will not submit to. Strange! It is a great interruption to the studies, I fear. I

know very little of the institutions out of the State; but I fear it is something peculiar to Columbia," said Mrs. Bowles, though her fear sounded far more like pride.

Yes, in the history, eventful enough, of the College of South Carolina, at Columbia, you have, in epitome, the character and history of the State itself. Self-will, contempt for rightful authority, reckless disregard of every thing except the selfish abstraction of the hour! Gallant, generous, high-toned youth, they yield their own notions to that of their Faculty? No, Sir! Rather than that, let the institution be wrecked to its foundation! Rather than that, let their own education, and consequent success in life, perish! See the same youth when grown a few inches higher in stature and immeasurably more generous, gallant, high-toned, and all the rest; they submit their own ideas to the superior authority of the General Government? they yield a hair's-breadth from their own heated view of their own rights and wrongs—imprescriptible rights, infinite wrongs? By all that elevates the man above the brute and the negro, never, Mr. Speaker, never! Rather, Sir, let the General Government be wrecked till not a spar floats to tell where once it sailed! Rather perish the hope of the human race! Above all, rather, Mr. Speaker, we of South Carolina lose every negro from our fields, every cent from our coffers, every city from our soil, every son on the field of battle from our hearth-stones! Perish the universe and we, Sir, we with it, rather than it move save as we intend it shall move! From his birth to his death never in the ages such a conspiracy as against your South Carolinian. Nurse, parent, schoolmaster, College Faculty, General Government, opinion of Christendom, course of God's eternal providence—one early-begun, universal, incessant combination against him. But not more magnificent the coalition than the defiance thereof on his part!

Poor Mrs. Bowles! From its foundation was practical Secession the incidental but leading part of the Columbia Curriculum, and well was the lesson learned. The yellow-fever is, they say, a standing affair in Cuba; and there lives scarce a man beside the Pedees, the Congaree, the Edisto, and the Cooper and Ashley but inhaled Secession as his vital atmosphere. It was too strong even for the Gospel. Heaven defend us, even in the conventions of religious bodies. It was: Mr. Chairman, Mr. Moderator, it is painful to us, Sir, it is very painful, but on this point we can not yield. No one can regret it more than ourselves, but, if brethren will press this point, there is, Sir, but one course left us— *In secula seculorumque, aut South Carolina aut nullus.*

Sturdy, wrong-headed little State! Look at it on the map there, altogether unlike North Carolina even on the one side, and Georgia on the

D

other; tough, three-sided fragment of medieval granite, refusing to be dissolved or to lose an angle even in the rolling of the great waters of progress; requiring something besides the silent, serene processes of nature by which the craggy mountains are being melted slowly down and the rough globe rounded into shape; requiring the extra force and fury as of waters too long and too obstinately dammed back from their natural and inevitable course. Every soul of us, however, admires the South Carolinian at last. Only let him be master, and a truer gentleman never breathed. The Hardkoppig Peit in him is hidden under the Bayard, the Cœur de Leon. He is only a hundred years or so out of place, that is all. There is nothing to laugh at in Don Quixote except his living a century or two too late. Even then it is with pain that we smile at the ancient armor, language defiant of the universe, and, most sorrowful of all, poor old Rosinante which bears him up!

But Mrs. Bowles has made us forget ourselves. Breakfast over, the Rev. Edward Arthur sallied out into Somerville and his new life. Before night he had been introduced to more persons than during his entire academical course. "If I can only remember all their names!" he thought. And all along, as he went here and there over Somerville, he had it vaguely afloat in his mind, "Oh, if I can but exert a new influence, an influence for good, a divine influence on these!"

So pleased was his manner, so unassuming, too, that the impression he made upon all was decidedly in his favor. It was not particularly much that the people of Somerville cared for preachers; there was any quantity of them to be seen every day about the streets, and to be heard every Sunday; yet all had a vague respect for the special denomination to which the new-comer belonged. Besides, education and piety had given a certain elevation to the countenance and bearing of the new preacher. As to that, every thing new has its gloss, we know. Very faithful were the lawyer, Mr. Ellis, Dr. Warner, and his other immediate friends from that time, not only in making him known to the people, but in making them known to him; and all such knowledge kept up a running commentary thereon in the mind of the novice.

"What an agreeable gentleman this Mr.— Mr.—" began he, on parting from the last introduction one day.

"Simmons — not Mr. — Captain Simmons. Don't forget the Captain part of his name when you speak to him next," said the lawyer, who had introduced him.

"What an agreeable gentleman the Captain is!" continued the young minister. "You heard what he said about having led the choir before moving to Somerville. And his expressions of regard for our new organization."

"And the tears in his eyes as he told you about his good old father, and about his mother's death-bed and dying charge. Umph, yes; drinks," replied the lawyer. Drinks? And the young divine had on the instant planned a series of sermons on intemperance.

"Mr. Peters, this is our new preacher, Mr. Arthur; Mr. Arthur, this is Mr. Peters, a member and pillar of one of the Somerville churches," interrupted the lawyer, introducing him to a tall, spare, white-haired old gentleman.

"Don't call me Mr. Peters—Brother Peters; and you must call me so always, Brother Arthur," said the old gentleman, warmly grasping and holding in his own the hand extended to him. "I heard you had come; am glad to see you—glad to see you. And you are but a young hand at the great work—a young hand, a young hand, Brother Arthur. You'll find it a hard field, hard field. But you know where your help is. Bless your soul, I was not five when I joined, not five! I've been about a good deal since then; seen wonderful things. We must get better acquainted, Brother Arthur, better acquainted."

"Mr.—Brother Peters seems to be a warm Christian," said Mr. Arthur, after a long and cordial conversation with his new acquaintance, during the latter part of which his companion had endeavored several times, but in vain, to carry him away.

"I declare," said the lawyer in reply, pushing his hat back off his forehead, his fingers lingering indecisively a moment behind his right ear in consideration, "I do not know whether to leave you to find your new acquaintance out or not. Besides, I don't want to cast a damper on you. But the fact is, this Brother Peters—"

"Does not drink, I hope?" asked his companion, hastily.

"Oh no," replied the lawyer, quick to deny such a charge. "Sober as you or I, hard working, honest, kind-hearted, punctual at church as can be; nothing in the world against him but his awful lies. Lying Sam Peters is his name every where. He knows it as well as any one. His friends have talked to him about it, his church has worked with him for years, every new preacher they get makes a special effort with him; it does no good. He has lied so long it has become his nature to lie whatever he may happen to be speaking about, and always. Like an old swearer and his oaths, lying Sam Peters tells falsehoods from morning till night without knowing it."

Alas! that sudden sinking of the heart in the bosom of the young minister. It is a painful thing that sinking of the heart in the bosom of the young and sanguine. After a while the heart learns to beat more evenly through every thing. "Ah, yes, Ananias and Sapphira, the sin and the penalty of falsehood; I must preach on that subject," murmured Mr. Arthur to himself, some relief in that.

In the course of the day the two friends came upon Brother Barker, to whom the new-comer was made known. As soon as it could be conveniently done—a little sooner, in fact—Brother Barker felt compelled to tell his new brother in the ministry that there were certain doctrines held by that new brother's denomination which he really could not agree with him in at all; which, in fact, he regarded as against Scripture and common sense, and which really—really he regarded as—but he would not wound the young brother's feelings by saying all he deeply, very deeply felt on the subject!

" A series of discourses establishing our peculiar doctrines, and as soon as possible. Dear me, how much, how very much there is for me to do!" thought Mr. Arthur, as he parted from his new friend.

As to Brother Barker, the arrival of the new minister precipitated him for weeks after with a vehemence new even to him against the obnoxious doctrines in question. The spare frame of the zealous Brother fairly dilated with their enormity, as, in private conversation and from the pulpit, he fought against the detestable doctrines, with long, muscular arms, gleaming eyes, and feet in incessant motion while he talked, like an athlete in the arena.

Before the week was over the young divine had seen the pressing necessity of preparing, and delivering as soon as possible, sermons innumerable. He had incidentally been thrown with Bob Withers, who had told him on the second or third interview that he would have been a Christian long ago, instead of " the regular whisky-drinking, card-playing, cursing and swearing scamp, by George, which I now am, Mr. Arthur!" if it hadn't been for the gross inconsistencies he had observed, by George, in every single professor, by George, it had ever been his misfortune to meet with; not one single exception to the rule, Sir, not one! Strange to say, there is something attractive to Mr. Arthur in the round, sensible, good-humored face of Mr. Withers, his frank eyes and sincere manner. Although there is a glow as of ripe grapes in Bob's face, it is a vast deal sunnier and more pleasing than, in Mr. Arthur's opinion, Brother Barker's dry and lean, though rigidly correct, face. And that he must preach a sermon warning Christians on this point was only too evident to the youthful theologian.

Mr. Ellis, too—the mild, amiable, humble Mr. Ellis—whom Mr. Arthur had been drawn to from his first acquaintance with him, unintentionally even he had aided in dampening somewhat the ardor of his new pastor. In answer to inquiries over his counter at the store on the part of that pastor, he gave it as his opinion that the main obstacle in Somerville to the spread

of religion consisted in an intense worldliness. He readily agreed with his pastor that here was the grand evil to be aimed at. After Mr. Arthur had added parental neglect, Sabbath desecration, profanity, infidelity, and a score more of evils, to be immediately combated, to his list, he was fain to pause from the enumeration.

However, if he lay down a little wearied at night with accomplishing, in imagination, in Somerville vastly more than has ever yet been accomplished by all his profession put together for men since Christ left the world, nevertheless a sound night's rest sent him forth next morning to his studies and into Somerville as hopeful as ever.

And so the new church was duly organized. It was a small organization, very small indeed; yet, on second thought, even this was a new pleasure to the ardent pastor to know into what a noble size the church was to grow from that little seed. And those who were its members clustered around him so heartily, too. Energetic Guy Brooks, steady Mr. Ferguson, smiling Dr. Warner, devoted Mr. Ellis. Mrs. Sorel, too, punctual as the clock did she alight every Sabbath morning at eight o'clock with Robby, her bright little boy—Frank is old enough to have a class, and is there before her on his pony—at the door of the little school-house, which was answering as a church for the present, in time for the Sabbath-school just established. Mrs. Colonel Ret Roberts, too, never failed of being there with her children. A thoroughly-informed man of the world could have read the Colonel's domestic character in the pale cheek and bowed head and sorrowful eyes of his wife. To Mr. Arthur she was but an estimable, silent, refined lady, sorrowful by reason of ill-health. Ah, how devoted she was to her children, specially to her boy with his father's superb eyes and bold brow! And devoted a wife but naturally is when her love for her husband is spurned, nothing left for her to love but her children; doubly devoted to them she well may be, when all her care is required to undo all the evil influence upon them of their father.

Mrs. Bowles, too, how enthusiastic she was in regard to the new enterprise! Mr. Arthur never came home at night from his visiting but she had something new and hopeful to tell in connection with the church: some new family who had said they would send their children next Sunday to Sunday-school; some new young man whom she had ascertained to have had parents in connection with their denomination, and who ought to be looked after; some bran-new young lady who had agreed to teach in the school. Almost every night it was late after supper before her guest, as enthusiastic as she, could tear himself away from the sitting-room to go to his little office in the yard. At last Mrs. Bowles would run in upon him of mornings there in the midst of his studies, with an apology for interrupting him, only she thought he would like to hear this, that, and the other encouraging something about "our church." How much the novelty of the thing; how much a lively competition with the other denominations in the place, roused by Mr. Arthur's advent into fresh life and zeal, had to do with all this on the part of all of them, no man shall ask and no man shall answer on these premises. 'Tis in heaven only our motives will be perfectly pure. But unmingled? No, not even there.

And Alice, too. Mr. Arthur saw from the portrait of the old Major where she got her erect bearing and clear, haughty glance. Haughty is by no means the word, but aristocratic would be preposterous in this free land. Modest confidence, self-reliance, independence, queenliness, fearlessness—well, the language lacks the exact word, and we must do without. The reverend guest had taken up an idea that this black-haired, quick-eyed, open-browed school-girl must resemble Joan of Arc, say, before she had come out into the world, yet not unaware of herself even then. There was somewhat of the angularity of the school-girl—likes and dislikes sharply expressed, undisguised amusement at every thing odd in any person whatever, and a certain something in her manner that caused the guest to feel quite sure that she—if she did not dislike him, at least did not give him a thought. All this, and more, in her kept these two quite apart from each other.

The idea never definitely entered the head of their guest; yet, if his heart could have been taken apart and accurately weighed piecemeal, it would have been found that this school-girl all these days was to him decidedly more than all the world besides. You may say it was because he had to love some one of her sex by the necessity of his nature, and she happened to be the nearest and most convenient one to him for the purpose. It may be so. None the less was the unconscious Alice Bowles that person in all the world for whom he most cared. Perhaps if he had had a sister, or a brother, a mother, or even a father, to love, it would have been different; but he was without these, and all these Alice was to him, and he knowing almost nothing of her as yet. Yes, it was foolishness itself.

It took him a long time to keep from looking too much at her as she sat on her low seat at night studying her lessons for the next day, while her mother conversed with their guest. Her face had not settled down as a whole into its final beauty, but her lips had—so full, so red, so eloquent in their very silence. Once, months after his arrival, she had suddenly raised her eyes with an exclamation against her lesson, and had caught his eyes fastened upon her face. But Mr. Arthur was too fast even for her.

"Had I met your daughter, Mrs. Bowles, in London or New York, I could have told where she was born," he said, continuing to indulge the look under cover of the observation.

"Yes?" said her mother, with pleased eyes.

"I never flatter, Mrs. Bowles; but there is a certain something in you South Carolinians which marks you unmistakably," he continued. "But pardon me, I interrupted a remark you were making."

"Not at all," said the mother, abandoning the old theme for the new. "Only what you say we have ever regarded as a matter of course. And it is the same of you Virginians," said Mrs. Bowles, in tone cheerfully conceding the second rank in the world to Virginia.

"Why, as to that, Ma, you can say the same of any one from New England," said the school-girl, putting back her hair from her brow, and letting the book close upon her lap.

"Certainly, my dear," said her mother, with a meaning smile; "and we can always tell where an Irishman is from, or an Esquimaux. But Mr. Arthur left something more favorable to be inferred from his remark, I presume."

"Oh, how I do hate the Yankees!" concurred the daughter. "There is that Miss Moulton at school, her lips pursed up, her elbows drawn down, prim, precise old maid; forever talking about her dooty toward us and to our pa-rents, with her system of education, rewards of merit, marks of approbation—"

"My dear, hush! You should be ashamed of yourself!" said the mother, interrupting her daughter's mimicry of her teacher's words and manner. "You must remember Miss Moulton is employed as your teacher. She is a very respectable person, I know. And you forget that she is not to blame for her place of birth. They may say what they please of the Yankees," continued the mother, turning with charming candor to her guest, "but for my part I think they are extremely useful people in their way. I can not say I have been used to like them very much, but I will say that. We had at one time an extremely deserving young man in our family in South Carolina from the North as tutor for Rutledge Bowles. I am afraid Rutledge Bowles did not make his situation as comfortable as it should be, but I am sure the young man really wished to be of service. He remained but a short time. Rutledge Bowles disliked him; treated him, in fact, so—so scornfully that we were compelled to dismiss him."

Again we touch the chord whereby we at least intended this chapter should be keyed, and repeat, Blessed be the spring-time of youth! How swiftly the days melted into weeks, and the weeks into months, with the young pastor. His sermons were most carefully prepared—too directly aimed at the point in view to be very rhetorical, but pleasing from their evident sincerity and pith. To pay more attention to the fullness and flow of words was a lesson he was afterward to learn. It was, you know, as he grew old that Edmund Burke grew so sublimely rhetorical. But no one could be more ignorant of exactly the kind of sermon he was to preach on any occasion than was the preacher himself. At one time he would prepare with great eagerness some special discourse, to find, in actually preaching it, that it was nothing special at all—the reverse rather. Again, he would go into the pulpit with some preparation of which he was heartily ashamed, to find, from his own feeling and the evident interest of the congregation, that it was far better than he had ever done before. One Sabbath when he would count confidently on having quite a crowded congregation, he would be chilled to the soul to find but a small one. Another Sabbath, counting gloomily upon but a sparse attendance, he would be encouraged by a house full. Now he would be led to count assuredly upon certain persons becoming members of the church, to be disappointed instead; and to receive, unexpectedly, persons into membership of whom he had never hoped such a thing. To-day would he be encouraged by the unaccountable presence of certain individuals at church; and on the next occasion annoyed by the unaccountable absence of others.

This week he would attend some funeral, and wonder at the apathy to the important spiritual concerns thus brought to mind on the part of those present; wondering most of all at his own inability, standing beside the open coffin, with the cold face beneath his hand, to set forth, as he would, those spiritual truths. The next week would be illuminated with some unexpected or long-expected wedding, with all the incidents therewith connected.

And there, also, was the pastoral visitation; the conversing with persons from whom all the machinery of Archimedes could not have drawn out more than Yes and No during the interview. However, there was placid, sensible Mrs. Sorel; practical Guy Brooks; delightful Mr. Ellis, with whom he could converse. Crusty as Mr. Ferguson was, too, the young minister soon learned to keep plenty of sea-room in conversation between himself and the Scotchman's hidden reefs; learned even to keep aloof, with a mariner's instinct of a storm, from the Scotchman altogether when that Scotchman was all reef and breakers. And so passed the days along.

Perhaps there was not one thing in his charge in the least degree as he had dreamed it would be—pleasures and pains all different; yet it was a great work and a good work, and a work in which he laid himself out with joy. The very buying of the ground for the new church, the planning of the building, the raising the money, was an epic of interest for months. And the actual erection of the edifice, from foundation to weath-er-vane, it was a daily joy and rejoicing. We say nothing of his intercourse with the workmen during this period; with almost every nail and shingle and plank the young pastor had intimate acquaintance from their arrival on the ground until finally adjusted to their place.

The months of picnicking—if we may so speak —in the covered in but unfinished church, with loose scantlings on tressels for seats, and a pine table a foot across for pulpit, was accompanied with a purer pleasure than the worship in many a stately edifice all granite and walnut, fresco and velvet. The obtaining of the church bell, from the instant of the conception of the idea in the head of Mrs. Bowles, until its first peal rang upon the ears so attentive to hear it that Sabbath morning, was one long and pleasurable excitement. And the painting, pewing, furnishing the church throughout, in which the ladies threw themselves with their inseparable and inalienable love for adornment in all its ramifications—was that a matter without deep interest to the pastor, as well as to many others? There was the organizing a choir; the most unexpected discovery of Mr. Ferguson's splendid bass, a mere growl hitherto under his grizzly beard, developing now into music—a hard and stiff old Memnon smitten by the sun; culminating in the suggesting, subscribing for, obtaining, and actually using an instrument. It is impossible to pass lightly over that. And the Ladies' Fairs also, from time to time, for this object and for that; the Sabbath-school celebrations of ribboned and rosy and hungry children; the grand efforts at tract distribution for the entire town; the purchase and arrival of a grand Congregational Library; the building of a study for the pastor; the presenting him of sudden sets of linen and altogether unexpected writing-desks.

Oh, blessed period of life, when a man is fairly at his life's work, with Youth and Health and Hope his close companions! Blessed period when, like a swimmer fresh to his task, there is a joy in every fibre at the very encountering and mounting and leaving behind the opposing billows as they come! Time of exultation, when every defect discovered in one's self is a joy, in the hope of henceforth destroying the same; when every enemy unintentionally made learns the novice how henceforth to act so as to secure instead a thousand friends; when every opposing circumstance is but a something, the path over which leads one that much higher above what he was before! But, O youth thrice blessed, when the Telemachus accompanied by Mentor is realized, more than realized, in him who, engaged in the service of an incarnate God instead, walks ever with that God during all the day, kneeling morn and night in communion, fellowship, friendship closer and sweeter than the world knows beside with that friend and brother! There is too entire an identity between the life of him who is doing the will of God on earth and him who is doing the will of God in heaven, for the happiness and energy of the one in heaven not to be very much the energy and happiness of the other on earth.

In nothing was it more evident how fully engaged the young pastor was with his work, and how entirely it filled and satisfied his heart and his hands, than his entire forgetfulness as to the making of money; that is, as to the accumulating any property at all. It never occurred to him to place at interest what remained over of his salary at the end of the year; it went every cent to gifts for the children of the Sabbath-school, and donations to benevolent objects. When he first arrived in Somerville had he only bought a few town lots at the nominal price then asked, in a few years he would have had even wealth. It never occurred to him for an instant; even the purchasing of a lot for his own home in the future was done only at the suggestion of friends. People who owned a few head of cattle when he arrived in Somerville had whole herds thereof by natural increase in a few years. Why could he not have done the same? There was Mr. Neely, the schoolmaster—with his first earnings from his school he had bought a likely negro woman, and now he had quite a family of young negroes, upon even the youngest of which he could have realized five hundred dollars any day. "And why," Mrs. Warner frequently asked, "could not Mr. Arthur have done the same thing?" Yes, it is with pain that we frankly state this new weakness in one whom we would fain have the reader love. Devotion to his calling? Certainly. But such thoughtlessness, such utter lack of reference to his future wife and children! We would paint him in brighter colors if we dared; better tell the truth of him though. Truth is, "The children of this world *are* wiser in their generation than the children of light!"

One thing is certain—he grew steadily in the confidence and esteem even of those who acknowledged his deplorable lack of worldly wisdom. Yet "men will praise thee when thou doest well to thyself;" perhaps they would have thought that much the more of him if he had been accumulating property all the while; but let us recount nothing but the truth about him though the heavens fall.

Yes, so far in his ministry the young pastor toiled with enthusiasm and joy. From the first he can be said to have had but one definite trouble; and that trouble had quick, sharp, black eyes, which saw every thing going on in Somerville and a great deal more; and that trouble had a tongue, and such a tongue! Perpetually was Mrs. Warner seeing something dreadful here, and strongly suspecting something worse there, and painfully but positively assured of disaster in the future, and pouring all herself abroad upon such matters every where. Any chemist who had enumerated the ingredients composing the atmosphere of Somerville, and, in mentioning oxygen, nitrogen, vapor, and carbonic acid, had failed to mention Mrs. Warner as a chief constituent element of that atmosphere, would have been woefully mistaken. That one lady managed to keep the place surcharged with anecdotes, rumors, suspicions, surmises, prophecies—all personal, and all of a painful nature to a degree surpassing human power of production. To do Mrs. Warner justice, her own servants, children, husband—household, in fact, was the theme upon which she dilated most freely and fully. Neat and energetic housekeeper as Mrs. Warner was, it was certainly not at home only that she washed her "dirty linen." Some of it showing, in her hands, so very dirty, too.

As the years rolled by the canal gates had been too often opened to close now at all. But her children did not particularly mind, her servants had grown used to it, her husband was too old a sailor upon the tossing deck and amidst the whistling gales of his home not to have come to regard it all as the ordinance of nature. Every day he grew fatter and balder and more stooped about the head, more slovenly about the person, quite a weather-beaten mariner, but wonderfully forbearing and mild. But then her table, and her exquisitely neat and clock-work household! If one were but stone-blind and perfectly deaf, or a philosopher—Socrates say—he could live even under Mrs. Warner's roof.

And all these months Mr. Arthur continues with Mrs. Bowles. The idea never occurred to her in that form; but her guest was to her all that Rutledge Bowles would have been had he instead tenanted the little office in the front yard all this time—rather more perhaps.

"And Mr. Arthur is such a vast assistance to Alice in her studies," said Mrs. Bowles to Mrs. Sorel one day; "and they have read a great deal of history together, too. Mr. Arthur takes a pleasure natural to a scholar in such things. Really I believe Alice is improved beyond her years—more thoughtful, too. I hope to return to Charleston as soon as Rutledge Bowles is settled in the practice of the law there. It is too soon to speak of such things yet, I am aware; but if Alice is finally married into one of the old families there I will be satisfied."

And placid Mrs. Sorel only smiled in her quiet way, and said nothing upon the subject whatever.

THE NIGHTLY CONFLAGRATION.

## CHAPTER VIII.

THE current of events presses more and more powerfully upon us as we near the roaring, foaming vortex of Secession. Let us resist it for a moment longer; for even in the waters, comparatively calm and smooth, just outside that vortex, there is a quickening and a current toward that fatal circle, and toward that circle's fatal centre, and all its disastrous result among the black rocks and the surging waters.

Months, and even years, had passed over the young minister at his work there in Somerville. His charge has increased wonderfully from the little seed of its organization. It is no longer an experiment, but a regularly established church and congregation, having a strong family likeness to churches of the same denomination the land over. The old Major gazing down upon his family had heard Know Nothingism wondered over as the last new thing under the sun. He had heard his daughter Alice say one night to the young minister, lifting her eyes from her slate after having satisfactorily reached the Q.E.D. of her proposition—she was getting fast toward the end of her schooling now—"Mr. Arthur, what is Know Nothingism?"

"I know nothing about it, Miss Alice."

"Oh pshaw!" Miss Alice has said; and is engaged in making a rapid but not flattering sketch upon her slate of her music-master as he appears at the piano.

"What an expression, Alice!" says Mrs. Bowles, looking up from her sewing. Her eyes are not as strong as they might be, as they were years ago when the Major overhead first surrendered to them; but Rutledge Bowles must have his shirts. Rutledge Bowles has left college now—not graduated exactly, but left it. More than once had he consented to waive the past and return to Columbia from Charleston, in the earnest hope that the College Faculty had come to their senses. The last time, however, it was too much, really too much—their course—for him to endure. In company with the other students he again withdrew as to *Mons Sacer;* but this time he could descend no more—could not even entertain such a proposition.

In fact there is, just now, no college at Columbia to descend to. For the time, Student-Secession has killed it. Rutledge Bowles is now in the law office, at Charleston, of one of his father's old friends. That is, he is occasionally in it. What with cigars and wine-parties, games at billiards and the like, he really has but little leisure for the office. Besides, politics must be attended to. Being in Charleston, the *Mercury* and the *Courier* must be read, at least glanced over, after breakfast, and an hour or two spent in discussing with the nearest friend the last points of the case. As Rutledge Bowles retires rather late of a night, and rises rather late of a morning, when he has done with the papers and the conversation thereupon after breakfast, it is altogether useless to go to the office that day at least.

Not that he has no purpose in life. Rutledge Bowles has plenty of talent, undisciplined as it is, and superabundance of fire to warm it. He has a purpose before him in life—a purpose to which he would gladly give all his energies. If he could only get to stand upon the floor in Congress, make one good, full speech containing all he would like to say against the North; see the Abolition Members writhe in their seats beneath it, and then have it printed and circulated over South Carolina and the rest of the South, a copy carefully mailed to his mother, he could be content to die, naturally or in any duel which might turn up. Rutledge Bowles has his ideal of human glory, too. Let him have justice done him. Congressman Brooks is the idol of the hour in his latitude—but not with him.

"No, gentlemen," he has said in his knot of friends, "you must permit me to differ from you. I perfectly agree in all you say or can say about that most contemptible fellow, Sumner. But Brooks was wrong to cane him. With all respect for Brooks, the club is not the weapon of a gentleman. Under no circumstances is cudgeling a gentlemanly deed. My idea is simply this: Calhoun would not have done it! If the fellow was a gentleman, call him out. If he is not a gentleman, be unaware of his existence."

But his friends can not agree with him for an

instant. He does not know it; but it is the old Major, his grand old father, speaks out in him. And it is amazing in Rutledge Bowles. Not only the young approve the cudgeling; even white-headed men, members of the church, officers of churches, even venerable pastors, think, "under all the circumstances," that Brooks was right. They regret he was compelled to do such a thing in just such a place; but, as it was, he was right, Christ and all his apostles to the contrary notwithstanding. No; Calhoun is Rutledge Bowles's ideal of earthly glory. Not exactly Calhoun the hard student in his youth; nor Calhoun the cold dialectician; nor Calhoun the spotless husband and father; nor Calhoun the irreproachable gentleman only—but Calhoun the scourge of the North. More than once has Rutledge Bowles, strolling along the street there in Charleston, thrown down his freshly-lighted cigar at the door of the public edifice wherein it is enshrined, and gone in yet once more to have another good look at Powers's statue of the old Roman. And Calhoun is an awful presence, standing there in a marble coldness which harmonizes with his character. Only lava cold from Vesuvius could have been better and more significant material. There he stands, his outstretched arm shattered to the shoulder by raging waters and foundering ship. Did Rutledge Bowles read no omen in this of another tempest, another foundering bark, shattering in the future more than that?

"I am astonished at you, Alice," said Mrs. Bowles. "Mr. Arthur tells you he knows nothing of the matter about which you ask him, and you say, Oh pshaw!"

"Yes; but, ma, the girls all say that is just what all their brothers and fathers say when they ask them—and they members of the Order all the time. That is the way it came by its queer name," said Alice, giving unnecessary length on her slate to the fingers of her music-master's widely-extended arms.

"You are right, Miss Alice," the minister replies. "But I am in earnest. And, what is more, I never intend to know any thing more of this new party than I do now."

He was in earnest when he said it; yet we saw how he afterward fell from this his high estate. And it is almost a positive satisfaction to know that he did err herein. The weaknesses of these ministers are so often internal and undiscovered by the world around, that this error of the Rev. Edward Arthur will help the reader to believe the assurances of the writer of these pages that he was by no means an angel. On the contrary, a man, and a very imperfect one at that.

Yes; Know Nothingism had come and had gone, accomplishing its specific something for God in the land, certainly in this individual. It had been entombed beneath editorials, pamphlets, speeches, as beneath autumnal leaves which had once been so fresh and flourishing. People had subsided somewhat into merely youths and maidens, husbands and mothers, when suddenly they are brought back to their condition of citizens with a shock. Lo another excitement begins, literally, to redden the horizon!

It had amazed Mr. Neely very much—Mr. Neely was from New Hampshire, and taught school in Somerville—when he first arrived in the South, not to find the negroes working in irons all day and carefully locked up all night. Why they were not in a condition of incessant and universal insurrection had been a puzzle to him, and multitudes with him there, when he left the North. Mr. Neely had often read items in the papers before he left the North, and he met with them in the papers of the South after settling in Somerville, to the effect that the blacks in such a county and in such a State had been discovered to be in a conspiracy to rise on a certain fixed day, murder all the whites, plunder and burn all the houses, and—who knows or had any idea of what they *would* do next? It was a thing in which Mr. Neely took the liveliest, deepest, most nervous interest; yet, for the life of him, he could never get the exact facts of any such case. Every few months he would read of some such conspiracy being discovered, now in this county, now in that, in the State in which he had settled. Oftener still he would hear accounts, to the same effect, of which the papers made no mention. It was always the same story—a conspiracy existing, embracing it was not known how many negroes; a discovery thereof just before the day it was to break out; certain white men mysteriously involved therein; a dozen or two of the negroes hung in company with one or more white men.

Always exaggerated, the facts were in some cases substantially so. Yet Mr. Neely could not understand the matter for his soul. Who were the white men? What was their motive in exciting the negroes to insurrection? Was it hope of plunder? Was it revenge of private grudge against certain owners? Or was it nothing other than desperate fanaticism? There must be some powerful motive to induce any one to undertake such terrible risk. What was the motive? The detected conspiracy was always followed by confession on the part of some one or more of the parties involved. What was the confession? Among so many discovered conspiracies, taking place during so many years, why was no more understanding arrived at of the germ, and process, and end aimed at? The fact and philosophy of the thing—that is what the inquiring mind of Mr. Neely wished to get at. But Mr. Neely never found any body who could cast the least light upon the subject.

Nor would he if he had sought for information throughout the entire South. When such things take place people in the immediate neighborhood thereof are terribly excited; rigid investigations are made; negroes and others are hung; but at last the whole matter remains as much as ever a puzzle and a mystery. A regular organization of white men to excite the negroes to insurrection, with agents abroad? or each case a private, isolated, spontaneous matter? The people of the South know no more on the subject than did Mr. Neely, or than the North from which Mr. Neely came.

So that when, one mid-summer morning, Mrs. Bowles asked her guest, at breakfast, "Mr. Arthur, what *do* you think of these dreadful burnings we hear so much about?" Mr. Arthur could only reply, "The accounts are greatly exaggerated, madam, I feel confident; beyond that I really do not know what to say or to think."

"We were speaking of the subject last night at Mr. Ellis's house," said Mrs. Bowles. "Mrs. Ellis told me about it before Mr. Ellis came in from his store, and he confirmed all she had said. Stables, mills, private houses have been burned in great numbers; all in different neighborhoods, but all about the same time. In every neighborhood, too, negroes have been arrested and hung. Mr. Ferguson happened to be in to supper. I believe it is the only place in Somerville at which he visits; and he says it is amazing sensible people should be such fools. He does not deny the many simultaneous fires, but accounts for them by the great heat of the summer, which has turned every thing to tinder. Under such circumstances, when the least spark will produce a conflagration, his only wonder is that there are not more fires. We all know Mr. Ferguson, however," Mrs. Bowles adds, with a smile.

"But how does he account for the torpedoes and matches which are said to have been discovered among the negroes—the arms and powder also?"

"Oh! you know Mr. Ferguson. All stuff and nonsense, he says."

"If you will permit me, here is General Lamum's view of the matter," said Mr. Arthur, unfolding a damp paper—the Somerville *Star.*

"We all know Lamum is a bad, unprincipled man; but, Yankee as he is, nobody doubts him to be a genuine Southern man, as far, at least, as he *can* be, poor man!" said Mrs. Bowles. "Please read what he says."

"'We have long looked for it,' read Mr. Arthur—'have even wondered why the work was not begun before. It is fairly inaugurated, however, at last! True to their infernal principles, faithful, as madmen ever are, to their diabolical threats, the Abolitionists have entered upon their work of fire, and blood, and plunder at last! From innumerable parts of the South and of our own State we hear of awful conflagrations and of, detected conspiracies among the blacks.

That the whole North is entered upon a crusade against slavery we have no more doubt than we have of the shining of the sun. Advices from Texas are to the effect that over the whole of that State conspiracy reigns triumphant. From sources which place the information beyond all doubt we know that there exists a powerful organization, secret, and amply supplied with men and money, sworn to the work. This secret Order has its peddlers, map and book agents, furniture-varnishers, school-teachers, preachers, and the like, traveling over the entire South. To-day are these infernal emissaries among us, in intimate intercourse with the negroes, poisoning their minds, supplying them with torpedoes, strychnine, and arms, preparing them for what is to come. The signal has already been given. Any night we may wake to fire and carnage unprecedented in the annals of the world. Our homes, our wives—'" But here Mr. Arthur stopped. There was much more to the same effect.

"You need not fear my nerves, Mr. Arthur," said Mrs. Bowles, with a smile. "I have heard and read things to the same effect in South Carolina ever since I can remember. I am used to it."

"It reminds me," said Alice, after a pause, "of what you read to us, Mr. Arthur, in Carlyle's 'French Revolution' the other night. You remember the negro alluded to therein standing before the magistrate in St. Domingo, with black seed in his palm covered with a few white seed. He shook his hand: the white seed had disappeared, only the black seed seemed left! And after that came the awful convulsions there!"

Mr. Arthur ate his breakfast in silence, the negro servant, a smart mulatto boy, waiting assiduously on the table, and hearing all that was said. That was never thought of by any one there. Talk about excluding Abolition emissaries from the South! No public speaker for years past has ever mounted the stump in any part of the South but he has had negroes by scores among his audience: negroes with white children in their arms; negroes attending to the horses; negroes bringing water; negroes loitering around from curiosity. And when, for years past, has any stump speaker failed in his speech to dwell upon Abolition, conveying to his negro hearers, and through them to every black in the South, all the information any human being could convey to them on the subject? It had struck the young minister as a little odd, hearing, on a grand barbecue occasion, Colonel Ret Roberts deprecating from the stump this very thing, when, all the time he was speaking, half a dozen of the brightest mulattoes in the county stood in eager attention within almost arm's-length of him. Save beings to do the work, needing in consequence just so much food, clothing, and the like, the house-flies were little less heeded, save in parentheses of excitement about insurrection.

"For my part," said Alice, motioning Charles, the waiter, to hand her the sirup—she was school-girl enough yet for that—"I wish you had never read me that horrid book, Mr. Arthur. All that description of the peasantry of France in the first part, and how they rose afterward!"

"It was no selection of mine, Miss Alice—" began the guest.

"Oh! I know that, Mr. Arthur; but I do wish, with all my heart, all the negroes were in the Red Sea!" And none but a school-girl could have made such an irrelevant remark, with such singular emphasis too.

"One thing I hardly need say," observed the minister, as they lingered still around the table, "I am not a blood-thirsty character, I believe, and I abhor Lynch-law; but if there be agents among us inciting our servants to insurrection, they are guilty of the most terrible of crimes against us, and against the negroes themselves. They can not be watched against too carefully, nor dealt with, when detected, too severely."

"Yes; but what I hate," broke in the impulsive Alice, "is, that we should be in a condition requiring us to be afraid of any body, requiring us to be keeping up a watch all the time. I am a genuine Southern girl," continued she, erect as an Indian, with glowing cheek and sparkling eye, "and I can't bear to think the South should have to be always in a panic about Yankees, and emissaries, and conspiracies. They want us even to be looking around to see if any of the negroes are near before we speak; watching lest they be peeping through keyholes and listening behind doors; whispering and talking low, and using all sorts of devices to hide our meaning. It's a cowardly condition to be in!"

"You foolish girl!" said her mother, smiling at her energy of manner. "Don't parents have things they never speak of freely until their children are sent out of the room? Do we say all we think before our acquaintances even, and friends? What a child you are!"

But, like a willful child, the young beauty only arched her brows and shook her head.

"I only know pa always taught me, and you have always taught me, and all I have read has taught me to admire England; and I'm sure there's nothing of the sort—the continual trembling and apprehending I mean—there; is there, Mr. Arthur?"

"There is in Austria and in Italy," replied that gentleman. "I have read about the Chartists of England, and the Irish, the French, too, over the Channel; but to what degree they are feared I really can not say. But I must go to my books."

As the weeks rolled by matters became more and more alarming. Every number of the Somerville Star was taken up with accounts of new burnings, new conspiracies, additional hangings. Several fires had taken place in the vicinity of Somerville. One day Somerville was thrown into the intensest excitement—a carpenter's shop was suddenly discovered to be in flames. Not a man of the many speedily on the ground but had his revolver girt beneath his coat. It was discovered, however, to be the work of poor Jack Sampson's children, the unfortunate carpenter himself. Like other unfortunates in this world, Jack had altogether too many children, and every one of all he had was perpetually in mischief and in trouble of some sort or other—a broken leg, or a chopped foot, or a blued eye, or a bad burn, or a "Deary me! somethin' goin' wrong all the time with them children; it breaks my back to nurse 'em, and breaks my heart to raise 'em!" was poor, slouchy, sallow, worked-to-death Mrs. Sampson's continual expression of the matter.

"Just as I knew!" said Mr. Ferguson. "And if every one of these fires could but be thoroughly investigated it would be found to be the same case in all. Incendiaries? Stuff and nonsense! Look at Sampson's shop; those piles of shavings baking under this hot, dry summer for months; the wonder is they have not caught fire long ago. All those fires in stables, too; any man in his senses must see that the heaps of straw and litter about such places are tinder during such a season as this."

Another fire in Somerville! A dwelling-house this time, and by a negro boy of some ten years old. He was seen to fire the building in broad day! In fact, he never denied the thing. The town authorities had prohibited the usual services for the blacks on Sunday afternoon at the churches; and the boy avowed that he did the deed partly because they had stopped his going to church, but chiefly on account of the over-weight of the white babe he was required to nurse.

"I heern tell of de black folks burnin' houses all de time, dat's what made me fust tink of it," was his candid explanation to Mayor and Council. "Nobody put me up to it," he persisted. "Mass George he say sha'n't go to church, an' dat baby weigh five hundred pound!"

Now what to do with this negro boy? that was the question. For four weeks Scip lay in the jail; that was all. Longer than that his owner could not do without him. Hired to somebody else, bearing a lighter infant, he sinned no more. But for months he considered himself rather a hero than otherwise. More than once, as he drifted about Somerville on warm Sunday afternoons with his charge, in answer to the question, "Whose baby is that boy?" "Mass Bolling, what lives down by de steam-mill, an' I is de boy what burned down de house by de gully," was his prompt reply.

Another fire! This time it originated in a grocery. By this time Mr. Withers had fallen from being only a drinker of whisky to the lower degradation of being a seller thereof; and " All I know about it is this, gentlemen. Late one night I fell asleep against the counter, by George! There were a good many newspapers, I know, lying on it. Was a candle any where near? Of course there was! Do you think I was sitting, by George! in the dark? I don't pretend to say how my place caught afire," continued Mr. Withers; " but one thing I do know, Jem Budd's gun-shop is next door—was, by George!—to my place, and we can easily guess why any incendiary would want that burned down. The other thing I know is, that I am regularly cleaned out this time—nary red! Not able to get even my daily liquor except on tick!"

Another fire! A cotton-gin this time, a few miles out of Somerville. The excitement was becoming fearful. Could Lamum's explanation be the true one? Was the country really filled with incendiaries? It certainly looked like it. Mr. Arthur found no satisfaction in Mr. Ferguson's theory. Dry and hot as the summer was, there were altogether too many fires. To do Mr. Ferguson justice, with every new conflagration he became more positive upon the subject, fractious even. It had become one of his storm reefs, which his pastor had learned to avoid.

Another increase of excitement! Mr. Isaac Smith, the painter, had been out of his shop all day painting at Colonel Ret Roberts's new office. He did not return to it until bedtime—Mr. Smith was a bachelor, and slept in his shop. After entering it, and while groping about in the dark for his candle and matches, he was astonished to observe flashes of light under his feet. On lighting his candle he found scattered over the floor white grains little larger than the head of a pin, which burst into flame on being trodden upon or rubbed in the hand. Not that Mr. Arthur himself got to see any of these torpedoes, but the story was told him by a dozen lips.

By this time the panic was fairly under way. Even Mrs. Warner disappeared, so to speak, in the universal excitement. Lying Sam Peters, lingering about street-corners, found himself singularly tame and uninteresting where every body was talking. Every fresh number of the Somerville *Star* was filled with the topic, to the exclusion of every thing else; conspiracies detected, men hung, the whole North engaged systematically in the work of Southern destruction. The paper was frenzied in its descriptions, assertions, invectives; and it was but one of hundreds of sheets employed, few with equal, none with greater ability, to the same end.

"What *do* you think about it?" asked Mr. Arthur of his friend Guy Brooks. It is impossible for any human being to live for any length of time amidst universal and intense excitement and not be affected thereby. Physically, mind, as well as mentally, the human magnetism, electricity, sympathy, whatever you may choose to call it, which binds men together, insures that.

"I have my own deliberate opinion on the subject," replied the lawyer. "But we won't bring it up just now. Let us keep cool, and wait a little. The temperament of Somerville just now is too much that of Sam Peters; the whole place talks too much like Mrs. Warner to believe all we hear. No man likes Dr. Warner more than I do," said the lawyer, apologetically; "but Mrs. Warner is really, really—ah, well, we all know Mrs. Warner!"

"But, Mr. Brooks," persisted Mr. Arthur, "I would like to know what you do think upon the subject. It certainly is a mysterious matter, one affecting us very—"

"It certainly is," interrupted his friend, gravely. "But we won't venture an opinion just now. My case is not quite made up, as we knaves at the bar say. Wait. I certainly have my fearful opinion on the subject. But it is really too bad to utter. I may be mistaken. God grant I am! If I'm wrong I'm glad of it. If I'm right time will show." And that was all the generally frank lawyer could be induced to say.

It was the next Sunday night after this conversation that Mrs. Bowles was aroused by a tapping on her chamber window.

"Don't be alarmed, Madam; it is me—Mr. Arthur," said that gentleman, in answer to her hurried exclamation. "Please get up and dress yourself—Miss Alice, too—and don't be alarmed; I trust there is no occasion to be. I will be out upon the front porch."

There Mrs. Bowles and Alice found him when they had hurried on their dresses. But no need to ask him why they had been aroused. Even before they left their bedroom the ruddy glare upon the walls told them of another fire. As they stood upon the front porch the whole conflagration was distinctly visible, turning night into day, and throwing the shadows of fence and trees darkly upon the ground. Full in view from the eminence on which it stood, the Somerville Factory was one vast blaze from the ground, and with flames which towered high above the lofty roof. A six-story edifice, recently completed, thoroughly furnished, and owned by a Northern Company, the establishment, a good deal sneered at as "that Yankee concern," was none the less the boast and pride of the place.

For a time not a word was spoken as they stood gazing upon the sublime spectacle, listening to the hiss and roar of the steam from the heated boilers. It was remembered by all of them afterward that no shouting was heard, no one was seen hurrying past their house to the scene. In fact, though all in Somerville knew of the fire, few besides those immediately connected with the mill were there.

"You need not remain with us," said Mrs.

THE WARNING.

Bowles, at last. "Perhaps you would like to assist at the fire. The Major always hurried to them when we lived in Charleston; he liked the excitement. If Rutledge Bowles was here he would not even have stopped to awaken us."

"I have no desire to go, I thank you," said Mr. Arthur, quietly; and Alice noticed now that her brother's double-barrel shot-gun, rusty from long disuse, was leaned in a corner of the porch behind him. Beneath his hastily-buttoned coat, too, she saw the butt of a revolver gleaming in the light of the conflagration. And not a man or boy in Somerville that night but remained at home armed to the teeth. It is strange the new and singular emotion which stirred in the bosom of this young and impulsive girl as she stood beside Edward Arthur that night, aware, she hardly knew how, of his palo face and set lips and fixed resolve. Not that he said any thing. Mrs. Bowles engrossed the conversation with reminiscences of South Carolina, and the magnificent scale on which that State indulged itself in its conflagrations.

Like all the other school girls, Alice had made abundant fun of the young preacher among her companions, the truth being that reverence was a trait as yet undeveloped in her character. Her novel emotions are easily accounted for. You have often observed that when you are suddenly awakened at midnight from a sound sleep by music there is a freshness of feeling about you which makes the music far sweeter to you than the very same strains heard on any other occasion : and it was out of a very sound sleep that Alice had just awakened. It might be incidentally remarked that these young people had been closely associated now for some time, not only as dwellers under the same roof. It is amazing how much of history and poetry they had read together; how much, in consequence of that, they had conversed, thought, and felt together—all in a natural, imperceptible way—from week to week. We will say nothing about any impression which may possibly have been made upon her by Mr. Arthur's purity of character and refined breeding, and, above all, his enthusiasm in his profession. You may not have thought of it before, but an honest enthusiasm in any good cause is one of the most beautifying things in this world : it imparts a light to the lip and to the eye, an uplift to the whole person ! A quiet, unfathomable enthusiasm is the light and bliss, the element of heaven.

Not a more unpopular man existed than was Mr. Ferguson the next day, when, true to his native heather, he was as Scotch in his belief of the accidental nature of the fire as ever. There is nothing people in a panic hate more than the man who coldly refuses to go with them therein; there is an affected superiority to every body else, a self-assertion in such a course which is positively insolent.

"Every sensible person in Somerville has expected the burning of that factory from the outset of the summer," said Mr. Ferguson. "It was one pile of tinder from top to bottom : cotton, wool lying all about, and a raging furnace in the centre of it. Incendiary? Stuff and nonsense !"

Not an adherent did Mr. Ferguson have to his theory. He only held to it with the zeal of thousands concentrated in himself. Besides, he had entered upon a new collection. It had occurred to him during the last few days to collect and preserve all things in his reach which had so far been published upon the subject of the burnings and conspiracies. "A rare treat it will be to read them after the delusion is over," he said to himself; and he entered with an enthusiasm upon the subject which he had not experienced even in making up his treasure of documents relating to Infant Baptism.

But the excitement in Somerville, as well as throughout the whole region, who can describe ! Nothing else was thought or talked of. Arms of all sorts were cleaned, loaded, and laid in readiness. Hardly a lady in Somerville but took lessons, with a hundred "Oh my's !" and "Oh, I am so afraid !" in the art of using the rifle and the revolver. You could not walk past a dooryard without hearing the crack ! crack ! of pistol practice on the part of the inmates of the house.

As to the blacks, the Sunday afternoon service had been long stopped. Now patrols scoured the streets from dark till broad day, firing promptly upon all negroes attempting to run when ordered to stop. By an arrangement of Mayor and Council the room and trunk of every negro in Somerville was searched at the same hour by a large committee.

"And nothing found—not a thing !" said redheaded Mr. Ferguson, in triumph.

But at least some few arms, boxes of caps, even powder, was found, was the general rumor. In one case, at least, several glass bottles of powder were certainly found in a negro's cabin. Very promptly was he had up before the Mayor, but as he seemed more amazed at the discovery than any one else, he was as promptly released. "I need not say, gentlemen," remarked pursy Dr. Ginnis, the owner of said boy, during his examination, "that if Jim had any hand in putting that powder there, you may string him up, and welcome. But my boy Jim ! I'd take my oath he knows no more about it than I do. Why, gentlemen, Jim was raised with me ! Nursed by the same mammy ; wrestled together a thousand times. He thinks more of me than if I was his own brother." And while Dr. Ginnis waxed short of breath, and redder in the face, and puffier even than before upon the subject, Jim stood beside him open-mouthed, thoroughly bewildered, undeniably innocent. It was singular the lack of definite, decisive, undoubted proof upon any one point in the whole mysterious matter.

"I am more and more convinced," Guy Brooks had said more than once, or even twice, to his friend, Mr. Arthur. "But I may be mistaken. Wait. Let time show." But of what he was convinced he altogether refused to state.

"It really seems to me as if this excitement were deranging the whole of us," said Mr. Arthur one evening to Mrs. Bowles, about a week after the destruction of the factory, as they sat out upon the porch in front of the house enjoying the moonlight. For several nights now he had slept upon a pallet in the hall of the house, dressed, two loaded revolvers within easy reach of his hand. Mrs. Bowles said nothing to him about it, but she saw to it that every table-knife in the place was under lock and key before she lay down at night, counted and safe; the silver-mounted carving-knife, wherewith the Major had carved at his hospitable table many a joint and turkey, rested safe under her pillow. And her guest never spoke to her on the subject; yet, before lying down, he never failed to take the axe from the woodpile and secrete it, restoring it to its place before dawn next day. And he could not but confess to an almost sheepish, if not mean, feeling as he did it—a sense of being ashamed of himself, he knew not why.

And now, as they sit upon the porch, they hear a rapid foot along the street. Every ear had grown painfully attentive, every eye keenly alert lately. The person stops at the front gate, shields himself in the moonlight behind one of the gate-posts, and begs Mr. Arthur to step there a moment. Mr. Arthur does so, and finds an Alderman of Somerville there. The Alderman is fat as becomes an alderman, although turtle soup smokes not within half a thousand miles of Somerville, and is panting from his rapid walk.

"We have learned, Mr. Arthur," he says, as well as he can—"learned but an hour or so ago that the negroes have arranged to rise, and that to-night is the time appointed for it."

"But, Dr. Ginnis, is there any foundation," begins Mr. Arthur.

"Can't tell; fear so; in fact, we feel almost certain upon the subject. But I have no time to stop," said Dr. Ginnis, in the same low, hurried tones. "We are alarming every family in Somerville, and glad we knew of it in time to do so." And the Alderman has hastened on to apprise other families of the impending insurrection, with that keen gratification in having news of moment to impart which the heart *will* feel, though the news be the death of one's own father.

That night Somerville sat up.

With the single exception of Mr. Ferguson. Leaving every window of his house open and every door unlocked, the Scotchman made a point of going to bed earlier than usual, and of sleeping particularly sound, in open defiance of the panic of the hour.

If Dr. Warner could only have been induced to do so, he could have deponed under oath that, from supper time till breakfast next morning, Mrs. Warner never ceased speaking; the impression produced on the Doctor's mind thereby being that, in some inexplicable but undoubted way, he, Dr. Warner, was to blame for the whole

thing. It was also currently reported afterward that Mr. Neely, the schoolmaster, had abandoned his own bachelor home, after locking in his negro woman with her children, and nailing down all the windows, and had taken refuge, armed to the teeth, and making ten thousand inquiries as to the contemplated rising, when it was to begin, and how it was to be met, in the centre of a crowd of watchers at the hotel. "White in the gills, by George; actually frightened out of his wits!" was Bob Withers's statement on the subject afterward. However, it was morally impossible for Bob Withers to speak of a Northern born man save in scorn and contempt.

As the young minister returned to the house from receiving Dr. Ginnis's information, perplexed for a moment what course to pursue, he finally concluded that here, as in every thing else, the frankest course is the best.

"I do not think there is any ground for apprehension," he said to his companions; "but then I can not be positively certain, not knowing upon what the Mayor and Corporation rest their belief."

"But have they adopted no plan in case there is a rising? Suppose the negroes do attempt it, what are the men going to do? Will the negroes move in one body, or will they rise separately, the blacks on each place attacking their own people? When are they to begin? What are you going to do, Mr. Arthur? Oh, if Rutledge Bowles was only at home!" And Mrs. Bowles showered question upon question on the head of her guest. Not at all hysterical either. The least frightened persons that night in Somerville were the females. Bless their inexplicable natures, they shriek at a spider, but look a lion undaunted in the face!

It was little their defender had to say; but after the servant boy Charles and his wife were gone to their room to bed, he quietly locked them in to begin with. Next he laid the double-barreled shot-gun within easy reach in the hall, and plenty of ammunition on the chair beside it. As to his revolvers, they were girded on as a matter of course and of custom. But while he made every possible preparation for any event, he treated the whole as a needless alarm—a good joke, in fact, to be laughed over hereafter.

It was strange, but Mrs. Bowles seemed rather to enjoy the excitement than otherwise, recounting innumerable like alarms passed through in South Carolina, especially one, in which the Major patrolled the streets by night for two weeks at a time. So excited was she that she refused to go to bed at all; and it was after midnight before she at last fell asleep, with South Carolina on her lips, in her easy-chair, seated with them on the front porch. Softly adjusting a pillow beneath her mother's head and a shawl around her shoulders, Alice again seated her-

A NIGHT ON THE PORCH.

self on the step of the porch, leaning herself against the column.

Mrs. Bowles's house—Rutledge Bowles's property she preferred calling it—stood by itself on the outskirts of Somerville, no other house within several hundred yards. The moon had now gone down; only the clear bright stars illumined the serene summer night. Seated in a chair above her on the porch, somewhat in the shadow of the vines which overhung it, her companion abandoned himself in silence to her loveliness as she sat, her face and eyes turned up toward the shining stars. Ah, that feeling of love, first love, love unuttered as yet even to the object thereof, why should I describe what we all know so well? It is the purest, sweetest emotion felt beneath those stars. He felt unwilling to break the silence by a word, while he blessed the fat Alderman for his news, forgetting for the time the nature of the news altogether.

It seemed suddenly to occur to his companion that the situation was becoming an embarrassing one, and she uttered what came first to her lips: "There was something I overheard Charles tell Sally, his wife, the other day, Mr. Arthur," she said, without taking her eyes from the stars. "I do not know what they had been speaking of, but I only heard Charles say: 'Never mind, never mind, we'll be free soon, any how;' and Sally answered, 'You'd better try an' see if you can't tell me some *news!*' Such a singular emphasis on the word news.*'*

"You have not mentioned it to your mother?" began the minister.

"No; but she knows how it is with the rest of the negroes. There is not a day but some negro says something of the same kind, especially when they are whipped, or are threatened with a whipping. And Charles and Sally were born, too, and have lived all their lives in the family, and if ever servants were indulged they have been."

"The truth is," said her companion, after a pause, "they hear so much from the public speakers and from the conversation at table—I mean all the negroes do—I do not wonder they get such ideas in their minds. Besides, there are several of the mulatto boys in town who can read, who do read all the papers, I am told, and they communicate all they know to the rest. You know the reason why their Sabbath service was stopped: one of their preachers—I know not how true it is—is said to have been so swept away in the fervor of his prayer as to have prayed most fervently for Freedom. And where they got their notion of their being like the Jews in bondage in Egypt, one day to be delivered by God, it is impossible to say, but they certainly *have* such an idea."

"Do you think they would be better off if they were free?" asked his companion.

"No, I do not. I confess the whole thing is a puzzle to me. Their parental relation and"— her companion was about adding marriage relation, but checked himself in time—"is not as the Gospel requires it to be among Christians. Many of our Southern ministers are writing, even preaching, upon the subject. Besides, we do know that in many respects the institution is a positive evil to—well, to us—at least I fear so. But what to do with them is the question. If we were to send them to Africa—and how *could*

we ship off the three millions of them?—they would relapse under its climate into barbarism. They do not do well in any sense when free, either here or at the North. I confess it is all a puzzle to me." Mr. Arthur spoke earnestly.

"And how is the puzzle to be solved?" said Alice, her eyes fixed upon the fleecy clouds rolling rapidly by over the deep blue.

"The Providence of God will solve it, and in His own time and in His own way. I am content to wait," said her companion, quietly.

"It is strange, Miss Moulton making us read Guizot's History of Civilization," said Alice, after a while, in a dreamy manner. "I do not know what makes me think of it to-night. It was very dry at first, but I became deeply interested in it at last. I have never thought of history in that way before—a plan, a purpose of God in the whole, from first to last—you know we were speaking about it."

"Guizot is a Protestant, you know—has read his Bible, Miss Alice, though, like a Frenchman and a philosopher, he almost ignores the existence of such a book. Yet he has stolen his whole idea from it. From creation history is the slow overturning of all wrong things toward the development of the race and the establishment of God's dominion again upon earth. It seems a very, very slow process through so many ages. At times the tendency seems to be in the other direction altogether."

"I have been reading Dickens ever since I can remember," said Alice, after a long silence; "and there is one theme running through all his pages, and I do believe it is his dwelling so eloquently on that theme which makes his books so popular. I hardly know how to describe what that theme is—a steady denunciation of all that wrongs human beings, even the lowliest; a continual dwelling upon the excellence of loving-kindness toward the meanest and humblest."

"Peace on earth, and good-will toward men! Yes, and this Song of the Angels at the birth of Christ is becoming every day more and more the substance and staple of all popular literature. Perhaps," added the theologian, "Glory to God in the highest may come to be blended in the strain also as the world nears its consummation."

In what a singular, thoughtful mood they both are! The still night, the romance of the hour, the desire to entertain each other.

"Do you remember Tennyson's lines—'Ring out, wild bells?'" asked Alice.

"And its close—'Ring in the Christ that is to be?' Perfectly well."

"And that

'One far-off divine event,
To which the whole creation moves.'

So unlike Byron, Scott, and all the old authors. There is Locksley Hall, all full of the same theme," continued Alice, her head still leaning against the column behind her. "You remember,

> 'Slowly come a hungry people, as a lion creeping nigher,
> Glares at one that nods and winks behind a slowly-dying fire.'

Who do you suppose he means by that, Mr. Arthur?"

"All enslaved people; those in Hungary, Italy, every where," said her companion.

"He means them too when he speaks, in one shape or other, so often, of 'a slowly-dying cause,' I suppose?" said Alice.

"The fact is," said the minister, after a pause, "all Scripture is the Prophecy of, and all History is the Record of, the slow, steady destruction over the whole world of Feudalism—yes, *Feudalism* is the best word."

There follows hereupon a long silence. Both were thinking exactly the same thing. Like all persons at the South these two had, from their childhood, singular ideas at times to flash upon their minds—ideas easily staved off, but often returning—uneasy ideas, disagreeable ideas; ideas one prefers to leave in their present nebulous condition. Both have a sense almost of guilt in entertaining such ideas an instant. Both would deny ever thinking such a thing, if plainly charged with such a crime. As to uttering such thoughts, both are thoroughly afraid to do it.

"How, then, about our 'Institution?' It is an ugly word, isn't it—Slavery? I wonder if it must go down too?" ventures Alice, at last, being the braver of the two. "Strange," she adds, "how full of fancies one feels such a night as this!"

"Only one hundred years ago, or so," says her companion, our 'peculiar' institution, as we well call it, existed over the whole world: nothing peculiar about it then. Just look at it to-night. Outside of the South, of all the civilized world only Brazil and Spain retain it. Brazil! Spain! And here, on this continent, it was once unrestricted of its whole area; now it is crowded down—a thing abhorred and hunted down by the world—into the South."

"You forget Russia," said Alice.

"I beg your pardon; the Czar has already decreed its extinction. Serfdom ceases in Russia March 17, 1861," replies her companion, eagerly.

"And here we are to-night watching against an insurrection of slaves among us. That there should be slaves among us—*slaves!*—it strikes me sometimes so oddly! And the movement which has overthrown slavery every where else, under *us* too this very night. Pshaw! what nonsense! and for a South Carolinian too! What I hate about it is that those Yankees at the North think they are so wise," said Alice, gayly. "But do you think it *is* to cease among us, Mr. Arthur?"

"I certainly do. I am as certain of it as I am of the existence of God," he replies.

E

"Yes, but how?"

"I have a sort of theory of my own, Miss Alice. I believe slavery is now driven to bay here at the South. I believe, too, that it will fight desperately, perhaps with struggles which will deluge the land with blood and shake the world—long after you and I are dead, though. Of the result I am as certain as I am that every wrong thing must go down before God. No use attempting to make a China or a Japan of the South. Open the gates *must* fly, down the walls *must* go; the Gospel *will* have free and perfect access to every human being that breathes. Just see those stars, great worlds they are, all moving so unswervingly, so musically upon their paths beneath the hand of the Almighty; how do they assure us past doubt of the presence and power and love of God! Such a still night as this, the jarring voices of men hushed, God's great universe moving so serenely under his loving care, one feels content to leave this little star we live in, too, in the same hand that cares for all the rest of the worlds. I don't intend to preach a sermon, Miss Alice," added the minister, in earnest tones, lowered, too; "but you believe it all as well as I. Just think of it. It was on this world alone of them all that God dwelt in person, living here, dying here for its inhabitants; putting on then, and wearing forever henceforth, the nature of its race, God and yet a man forever! With such assurance of His special interest in us, I am perfectly content to leave this world and all its events in His hands. And to think that He is no respecter of persons; that he died for, and wears the nature of, and cares equally for, the least human being that lives! You remember the trial we are to undergo at his bar: as ye did it, or as ye did not do it unto the *least* of these little ones, ye did it or ye did not do it unto *me!* When you think of that sublime Will moving us silently on in the accomplishment of his gracious purposes toward every being on earth made in His image, how idle and senseless and despicable do all our strugglings against it seem! To acknowledge and bow to that Supreme Will is the act of every sane intelligence. To acquiesce in, to exult in that glorious Will as in that of one's own personal friend and father and saviour, seems to me the very essence of piety."

It was not much all this; it was the low tone in which it was said, it was the mood in which it was heard. It was soul in communication with soul.

Both knew how near henceforth they stood to each other. And well did Alice know why Edward Arthur did not long ago, and did not to-night, say things of a nature more interesting to them even than all this. Being proud herself, she understood his pride, admired it, was vexed at it in the same instant.

"And you do not have much faith," said

Alice, after a long silence, "in the success of any movement in defense of slavery, or in the permanence of any government based on slavery?"

"Not the least in the world," said her companion, quietly. "Nor will such a mad experiment ever be tried."

There was a long pause in the conversation. How utterly had they both forgotten fat Alderman Dr. Ginnis and his insurrection! Both felt like any thing else rather than like those sitting on the crater of a volcano that night.

"Yonder is a fire at last," said Alice, really gratified thereby, pointing to the reddening horizon.

"Yes, Miss Alice, but one kindled by no human hand—it is the dawn," said her companion, and with any thing but the emotion of them that watch for the morning.

"Dear me, I never dreamed it was so late—I mean so early!" exclaimed Alice, but a blush followed the words.

"Any insurrection yet?" inquired her mother at this juncture, wakening and rubbing her eyes.

"Not a bit, ma; and, oh! I am so disappointed," laughed Alice; "and after sitting up for it all night, too—it is too bad!"

"We used to have some ground for such things when we had our alarms in South Carolina," said Mrs. Bowles, patient and forbearing for failure in the present instance. "We must write to Rutledge Bowles about it, Alice; it will amuse him."

In fact, there was a general sense of disappointment that morning throughout Somerville, a sense of having been cheated and defrauded, as people yawned and stretched themselves. Alderman Dr. Ginnis sank fifty per cent. in the opinion of every body. However, like all other light yet bulky bodies, his depression on the surface of things was but for the moment; his imperishable property of bobbing up again when wind and wave might serve.

"Of course, do you suppose they would rise after they found we had put every body on their guard?" chorused Mayor and Councilmen.

As to Mr. Ferguson, coming down that morning from his peculiarly sound and refreshing sleep, more inflexibly Scotch than ever, he was insolent even in his triumph, hard to be endured by people surly after a sleepless night. However, people were used to Ferguson.

"And who sat up with you, Alice?" said the school-girls to her next day.

"My mother, of course. And, dear me, how stupid it was! No rising at last, either. I was so disappointed!" said Alice.

---

## CHAPTER IX.

AND so we return at the point from which these pages set forth—the fall of Fort Donelson, and all the boundless astonishment which follow-

THE FALL OF FORT DONELSON.

ed it. We unmoored our bark and set sail under the strong wind beginning to blow at that date; and though we have been compelled to reef sail, and lie by for the last few chapters in order to get our ship's company thoroughly acquainted with each other, we will from this moment spread all sail, drive before the ever-increasing blast, and gain such haven in the end as it may please Heaven to grant.

"Exactly as I have all along said it would be, only far worse," Guy Brooks, Esq., is remarking to his pastor in the study of the latter at the very hour Brother Barker is reasoning over the same topic—the fall of Fort Donelson—with placid Mrs. Sorel under Colonel Juggins's hospitable though somewhat leaky roof. In fact, every person in the South—doubtless in the North also—over ten years of age is eagerly engaged at this instant upon this same theme. There in Somerville, the excitement being so intense, it is but natural a warm-hearted, large-limbed Kentuckian like Guy Brooks should feel deeply also. And strongly disposed to converse, too. Not in public, however. The time had been when no man spoke his mind more warmly and freely before Bob Withers, Sam Peters, Brother Barker, Colonel Ret Roberts, Colonel Juggins—ay, even before the dread Lamum himself, apt to put it all in savage print ten minutes after; before all Somerville, for that matter, than the lawyer. On the streets, in his own office with his heels upon his table, in good Mr. Ellis's store, and every where else, the Kentuckian was wont to give his opinion upon whatever the topic might be.

Not so in these days. The lawyer has altered into a grave and silent man, with only occasional eruptions, showing that the fires within are only intenser for being smothered. What he would have said every where before, he now utters only when with such intimate friends as Mr. Ferguson and his pastor.

In every city, village, and neighborhood throughout the South it is touching to see how the Union men cling to each other. The ship having passed completely into the hands of mutineers, these poor disarmed passengers in the cabin below, the hatches battened down upon them, cluster instinctively together for comfort, speculating with each other under their breath upon the storm raging around and the breakers ahead. One of the cruelest effects of Secession was the breaking up on every square mile throughout the South of many a friendship between even the oldest and most intimate friends. Worse still, families were broken up, son turned against father, brother against brother, wife against husband. In this latter and worst case, in nine instances out of ten it was the wife who was the Secessionist, while to many a husband nothing was left but either to engage in bitter and unceasing strife at home, or to play as well as he could the patient part of poor Dr. Warner. Yet it would be telling only half the truth here if we did not add that, where friends and relatives did hold to their country alike, the ties between them were immeasurably strengthened thereby; friend loving friend, father loving son, brother esteeming brother, wife valuing husband just so much the more as they thought alike, felt alike here, where thought and feeling had their intertwined roots about the soul's very centre. Ay, and persons never before acquainted, at enmity even, came now together into cordial friendship upon this one and sufficient ground.

"I frankly confess," said Edward Arthur, drawn toward his burly friend as he had never been before, "every thing is altogether unlike what I anticipated."

"Of course," replied the lawyer. "You ministers are only too ignorant of human nature, especially its darker side—which is all over," added the lawyer. "You preach total depravity from the pulpit as an abstract doctrine, yet ignore it in all your dealings with men or expectations from them. Do you remember that day I brought the first placard here for you to read? I prophesied then how it would be. As I knew at the time, the whole programme had already been arranged by Lamum and Colonel Ret Roberts, the Colonel at the very time solemnly sworn as a member of the United States Senate to uphold its Constitution—only one instance of a thousand similar perjuries. And yet we were all so horrified at Louis Napoleon! As

we all know, there is a Colonel Ret Roberts and a Lamum, in some stage of development, in every town throughout the land. The meeting called and held by them in our Court-house here, not a corporal's guard of the people there; the furious resolutions adopted calling a State Convention; the blazing account thereof in the paper, was but a specimen of like meetings engineered by like men over the State. And this was the spontaneous, indignant, unanimous uprising of the people! You know it all. Before the masses can realize it, lo! a Convention is in actual session—a Convention voted for, and delegates thereto elected, by only a miserable minority of the people.

"And who composed that minority?" said the Kentuckian, becoming more and more excited. "First, the politicians themselves—men whose trade and living is politics—men who saw their power and plunder passing forever from their grasp unless they made just that last desperate move. And even they accomplished their end only by superhuman exertion through the press and from the stump. Next come the set in every neighborhood, following their party leaders from the very force of habit. Last, the people, fancying Secession the only remedy against the North. Remedy? Good Heavens!"

"You forget, Mr. Brooks," said Mr. Arthur, "there were really sensible and excellent men—"

"Who voted for the Convention, and for delegates to that Convention?" interrupted the lawyer. "Yes; Colonel Juggins, for instance, and all his class; and why? Because Lamum assured them Secession was only a step to Reconstruction—merely a peaceful Secession! He and his no more voted for the dissolution of the Union, and for war if necessary, than did you or I, or Ferguson, Warner, Ellis, and the rest of us who refused to vote about a Convention at all."

"I half thought at the time a terrible mistake was being then made," said his companion. "If Union men throughout the State had all suddenly come into the idea of a Convention when it was first proposed by the Secessionists, had voted for it, had voted true men into it, then—"

"We would have seized their one piece of artillery, turned it upon the Disunionists, and with it blown them to the—the moon!" said the lawyer. "Ah, it is easy to talk! Or, if the Governor had but planted himself upon the Constitution from the first. But what is the use of talking about that now?"

"You know Secession was submitted to the vote of the people afterward," suggested the minister.

"And with great difficulty was that precious Convention induced to do it," said his friend. "And when it was done! By that time hadn't the politicians fanned the fire into a conflagration? You remember how it was commonly declared then that the man who refused to vote Secession was a base submissionist. As to him who voted against it, that man was an Abolitionist, and the sooner hung the better. Freemen! And yet tens of thousands of the best men in the State, scattered apart as they were among the excited, infatuated—"

"Don't let us say fools," interrupted the minister. "We can not keep our tongues too carefully from the violent language of the day."

"Did not dare to vote," continued Mr. Brooks. "You and I, Ellis, Warner, Ferguson, and the like, did vote against Secession; but I know, and you know, many a man who dared not go to the polls; was sick himself, or had a sick child or wife, or had pressing business somewhere, some cowardly excuse of the sort. Even of those who did go to the polls, how many were prevented by the crowd about the boxes, and couldn't wait, or who disliked going into such excitement, and all that, didn't vote at last. I tell you, Sir," said the excited Kentuckian, "the Signers of the Declaration of Independence left an illustrious name; but I will hand down the fact that I voted against Secession to my posterity as the noblest act of my life; my declaration of independence of falsehood and folly, made when at their highest flow."

"But a majority of the votes cast were for Secession," said the minister, after a pause.

"A majority of the votes *cast* you may well say," replied Guy Brooks. "But you know as well as I whether it was a majority of the voters in the State."

"And then came the raising of troops against the South," said Mr. Arthur, reflectively.

"Yes; and no man in the South had, in the flush of the moment, more disposition than I to meet force with force," began the lawyer. "At first it was a feeling sudden and universal. I think you were not altogether as clerical in your language, Mr. Arthur, my friend, as you might have been," he continued, with a smile. But there he stopped.

Ah, that terrible test of conviction and principle! Guy Brooks sat in silence, tugging gloomily at the hair behind his right ear with restless fingers, his broad, brown face no longer open, but full of such anxious thought as men know only when bosom and brain are at cross purpose, when feeling and principle are at strife for ascendency.

He said nothing, but he thought, thought! And multitudes at the South were at the same instant thinking, thinking, thinking—not saying a syllable of their thoughts even to brother or wife.

If his disjointed thoughts could have been written down they would have run somewhat in this manner: "We of the South—Southerner! Democratic right of self-government. But that democratic old Andrew Jackson and his native

South Carolina in 1832? Humph! The old General would not have actually fought Carolina? Perhaps. South fighting for its very existence as a nation? Yes; and the United States Government fighting, since need is, for its prior existence. Secession in this case? Then Secession legitimatized at the North, East, West, in the South over and over again. Humph! Universal disintegration, dissolution, death! Wrong to fight against *that?*"

And on and on—millions at the South on the same track that instant with him—plodded Guy Brooks slowly, painfully through mire and fog. Alas, the systematic effort to drown one's own soul with the clamor of the times! Multitudes of the noblest men of the South were forced to conceal their trains of thought from others, from themselves. Alas, for the laborious process of self-silencing! Miserable dissembling to one's own self as well as to others.

With some it became settled into a hopeless habit, for which "the peculiar times are to blame, Heaven knows, not I; *I* can not help it!"

With many, very many, the soul came out of the mire at last, to see clearly, to stand firmly, to speak boldly. But that daylight has not arrived as yet to Guy Brooks, sitting there that hour in his pastor's study.

"I am as well satisfied as a man can be on any moral question that Secession is a great wrong, a crime against man, a sin against God." The minister, as he says it, walks to and fro across his study, his hands clasped behind him, his chin drooped upon his bosom. "But then the Battle of Manassas! At the time it seemed to me God's approbation of Secession. Not that I thought for an instant the Almighty approved of Secession," said the minister, hastily correcting himself; "that I never can bring myself to believe. I mean, it began to seem as if the Almighty intended permitting the deed, as he permitted the partition of Poland. So far as we could gather from our papers, the North had pretty much given the South up. But now this sudden, determined, apparently overwhelming advance upon the South—"

The speaker hardly uttered the rest of his sentence. You who know, could you have found just at that date a Southern-born man at the South who would then have intimated even to himself, much less to his dearest friend, a wish for the success of the Federal arms?

Guy Brooks and Mr. Arthur never were more busy than in keeping themselves from distinct thought upon the matter.

"And do you suppose," said the lawyer, at last, "that the politicians did not know all this time of the immense preparations being made by the Federals on shore and sea at the North? No, Sir. It was no ignorance on their part. From the first they have studiously kept the people at the South in profound ignorance.

THE PARSON AND THE LAWYER.

Look at Bowling Green! Who dreamed the Confederate Army there was so small?"

"It certainly was poor policy," said his companion.

"Knaves are *always* fools in the end," was the lawyer's remark. "It is all of a piece. You remember that summer of the burnings?"

The minister nodded his head to this altogether unnecessary question. If no one else remembered it, Edward Arthur certainly did, the memory of his heart assisting therein the memory of his head. That serene, starlight night upon the front porch sparkled in his memory amidst that dark time like a diamond set in jet.

"You may remember," continued his friend, "I had my idea then, as well as Ferguson his, as to those fires, poisonings, conspiracies, book agents, and all. I did not utter my suspicion then to a soul. I could not believe it possible. I do believe it now," he added, with a blow of his huge fist on the pastor's table, sending his heavy Concordance inches in the air.

"Well?" inquired the other. "I confess I am just as much puzzled this hour upon the subject as I ever was." And he paused in the midst of his walk before the lawyer with curiosity in every line of his face.

"Sir, I suspected it then; I know it now," said the lawyer. "The whole excitement in the South then was the result of a regular conspiracy."

"So Lamum said at the time," not so innocent, however, of his friend's meaning as the words would indicate.

"And the unprincipled—yes, it is better to use no epithets; it may become a habit these awful times, and become oaths—the unprincipled man," continued the lawyer, "was right. Only he was himself one of the conspirators. The whole plot was devised and worked by him and his masters. I tell you, Sir, not more than a dozen or two of the ablest and most desperate of the leaders may have been in the secret; but as I believe in the existence of Satan, so do I believe that the whole excitement that summer was plotted and carried on by them and by their agents to prepare the people at the South for Secession. It was not enough to split the Baltimore Convention, and so bring about the election of Lincoln—that was in the programme. But they knew that even if Lincoln was elected —a Black Republican I mean, whatever his name might be—the South was not ripe for Secession even for that; and that is the way they ripened the South, as by a hot-house process."

"And the John Brown Raid?" asked Mr. Arthur, with a smile. "No, Mr. Brooks, I can not agree with you there. I have long thought that political ability, and political success, too, whether on the part of Louis Napoleon, or of Jeff Davis and his set, consists not so much as people suppose in creating or even in anticipating events. No; it consists rather in instantly and adroitly seizing upon events, even altogether unforeseen events, as they arise, exaggerating them, turning them, working them toward their own end. The destruction of the Union being the end fixed upon, the politicians in Congress, from the stand, by the papers, and in every other way, have strained every nerve to make every event a help toward that."

"And all the time the people, intent only on their daily matter, dreamed of nothing about their country but that it was the greatest and most permanent government on earth!" said Guy Brooks.

And yet a great many people at the South hold with the lawyer upon that incendiary summer up to this hour. Not Mr. Ferguson, of course. As to every thing being worked by the Disunionists to their own deadly end, he believed that as firmly as any man. But for those burnings, the excessive dryness and heat of the season is the full and sufficient explanation.

"Look at the papers if you doubt there being a systematic conspiracy as I say," urged the lawyer. "Do you not see how invariably they are exaggerating into the utmost importance every thing favorable to their Confederacy—invariably, systematically distorting or suppressing every thing in the least degree unfavorable to it? The tremendous clatter they keep up on the bells at every rumor of victory, only a part of the same thing. They desire to establish a manufacturing interest at the South; they have begun it with a vengeance in the manufacturing of lies—out of all material, and out of no material at all."

As we have observed, it was just after the fall of Fort Donelson that the lawyer held this conversation with his pastor. Time was to teach him something of the capacity of human nature to produce, and to believe in, falsehoods beyond what he or any other man could at that day have deemed possible.

"'NASHVILLE OCCUPIED BY THE FEDERALS! NOT ONE SOUL THERE SO BASE AS TO WELCOME THEM. INHUMAN ATROCITIES ALREADY COMMITTED THERE! NORTH ALABAMA THREATENED! GRAND ADVANCE UPON VIRGINIA! FLEET TO DESCEND THE MISSISSIPPI! ATTEMPT SOON TO BE MADE ON NEW ORLEANS! OUR AROUSED PEOPLE READY TO HURL THEM BACK. THEIR VERY ADVANCE PERMITTED BY OUR GENERALS AS PART OF A BRILLIANT STRATEGY SOON TO BE SEEN IN ITS FRUITS!'" read Mr. Arthur from the headings of the last Somerville Star lying on the table. "It really does seem as if the North was about making a determined effort," he continued, after a pause.

"It does indeed; you may well say so," replied his friend, with tones in singular contrast with the gloomy shake of the head which accompanied them. And it was not only singular, but to the last degree exasperating to Lamum and his set, the way in which the Union people began to swarm out into the streets from their retreats, like bees on the first burst of summer; and the frequency and fullness and unction with which they spoke of "the late most disastrous news."

Good Secessionists shrank instinctively from all conversation with them: but there was a wonderful degree of sudden visiting among themselves on the part of the Union people. No two of them could meet on the street, or upon the roads around, but they must stop to shake their heads together in sad concert over the "terrible intelligence," and to agree that "matters must be much worse even than our papers represent them, if we only knew." Very sad their brows, very doleful their tones, very desponding their hearts, like to the grief of the next heir beside the dying couch of the present owner.

"I lay awake last night thinking, and I am ready to make you a prophecy this morning about this war," said Mr. Arthur, slowly tearing the disastrous news into strips.

"No, Sir, I had rather not," said the lawyer, promptly. "I had enough of prophecy last night to last me a long time. Brother Barker dropped into my room at the hotel last night, and kept me up till midnight. 'I am not speaking with an infidel, but with a believer in the Scripture; and I feel to believe I can convince you from the Bible the Confederacy is of God, and that God is going certainly to establish and bless it,' he said. With that he whips out of his pocket his little black Bible, and goes at me exactly as he used to do about points of doctrine, only with far more zeal."

"I do not remember any Scripture bearing upon Secession," began Mr. Arthur.

"You are behind the times, Sir. You have seen a book, written by a Dr. Baldwin, showing how the United States is clearly alluded to in Scripture. Since Secession Baldwin's idea has been seized upon and arranged to admit Secession and all its glorious results. Oh, I can not remember half the man's nonsense! I listened to it as part of the insanity of the times with some curiosity. Abler and better men than poor Brother Barker originated the idea; he has jumped upon it as his last hobby, and is riding it to death. Even Captain Simmons has caught the infection. Fullest of memories of Sabbath-school and Scripture when drunkest, the Captain's religious knowledge until so warmed being as invisible as the writing in lime juice, he now brings, when drunk, an amazing number of scriptures to illustrate the subject in hand."

"Can you not remember at least one of his texts?" said the minister, all the theologian beginning to stir within him. "I am curious to know what even insanity can find to favor the Confederacy in Scripture."

"Well," said the lawyer, his fingers busy behind his right ear, "there is the stone cut out of the mountain without hands which smote the image—in Daniel, I believe. The mountain is the United States Government; the stone is the Confederate Government, which is to grow into a great kingdom, and in some way or other fill the whole earth. Ah, yes, the stone being the Scripture emblem of the Confederacy, you have only to turn to the places in which it occurs in Scripture to find plenty of reference to that Government! Whoever fell upon the stone was to be broken; upon whomsoever it was to fall it would grind him to powder—I do not remember where it occurs in the Bible—emblematic of the victorious strength of the Confederate Government. 'The North and Europe sneer at us on account of slavery. Very well,' says Brother Barker, 'the Bible expressly says of the Confederacy, it shall be a stone of stumbling and a rock of offense.' All the rest of the world is infidel, is his notion, because it rejects the Bible doctrine of slavery as a divine right. In other words, the Confederacy is the last, lingering abode on earth of pure religion. 'Perfectly clear that,' says Brother Barker; 'does not Scripture say on this rock or stone I will build my church, and the gates of hell shall not prevail against it? which settles the result of this war upon us by the North,' he said. Yes, he thinks when once you have what he calls a key, like the symbolical meaning of the word stone, you can unlock all prophecy. There is the word seven also; he makes it refer in Scripture to the seven States which first seceded; and he runs that word down through the Bible. Seven women shall lay hold on one man; that means those seven States laid hold upon, to feed and protect them, a Confederate Government over them all, and so on. Then there is a prophecy about the Mount of Olives; mountain in Scripture, he says, means the old United States Government splitting asunder by a line running east and west, referring to Secession. 'Thou breakest the ships of Tarshish with an east wind;' Europe lying to the east of us, this is a prophecy of the raising of the blockade by the European states. There was a vast deal more to the same effect, but I have forgotten it. But to do every body justice," continued the lawyer, "though people rather like to hear Brother Barker's expositions of prophecy, feel strengthened by them, I have not heard of any one as yet decidedly embracing them. 'They may be correct; we hope they are correct,' is what his hearers say, but that is all."

"To me such a thing is one of the darkest features of the times," said the minister, very sadly. "If ever there was a time when religion and the ministers of religion should hold themselves aloof from the infatuation of the hour it is now; for if there is no restraining influence exerted on the rising tide of worldliness and wickedness by these, what is left under heaven to restrain? I know of no other influence used of God for this purpose."

"I fear matters are going to be far worse than you or I have ever imagined. And this brings me to the matter I called this morning especially to see you upon," continued Gay Brooks, rubbing his upper lip with his rueful finger.

Ah, that sinking of the heart, which tells more surely in the bosom of impending evil than does the mercury in the barometer of approaching storm! Not yet had Edward Arthur got used to it; though he was to be made a stronger man, and by this very process.

"What do you mean?" he asked.

"I fear we are going to have trouble in our church—great trouble," said his friend.

"I think not," said the minister, earnestly, but with more hope in his tones than in his heart. "You remember I announced from the pulpit, at the outset of Secession, that I intended to confine myself exclusively to the peculiar duties of my calling, and to keep politics utterly out of my sermons and my prayers."

"It doesn't matter," replied his friend. "Do you suppose there is a person in Somerville but knows your views in regard to Secession?"

"I can not help that," replied the minister. "I have the deepest and clearest convictions on the subject--how could I but have? I have all my life been accustomed to express myself frankly to my friends in conversation on every topic which came up. Upon this topic, one so continually up, one in which I can not but feel the deepest interest, I have done the same. What else could I do? You would not have me dissemble my honest convictions, I know. I have sometimes wished I had been able from the very first never to have uttered a syllable on the subject one way or another to a human being."

"You would have possessed supernatural strength to have done so. And even if you had," continued his friend, "your very silence would have had the worst possible construction placed upon it. How could you be silent, people would have said, amidst the universal enthusiasm, unless because you could not, would not join in it?"

"But what have I done to imperil the church?" asked the young pastor.

"You do not pray for the Confederacy."

"Why, Mr. Brooks, you know how often we have discussed that question. 'The powers that be are ordained of God,' and to the present powers that be I have submitted as to the providence, for the time, of God. The Bible commands us to pray for these powers. So I do every Sabbath from the pulpit in the exact language of the Scripture."

"You have never prayed for the success of the Confederate Government," said the lawyer.

"No, Sir," said Mr. Arthur, "I never have in private nor in public. What is more, I never will. Mr. Brooks," continued the minister, deeply agitated, "I believe in my soul, as before God, that this whole movement is a wrong, a crime, a sin. Men better than I may not believe so, but I do believe so. For my life, after all the thought, reading, and prayer I have given for years to the subject, I can not but believe so, always have believed so, always will. Can I, then, pray for the success of a wrong, a crime,

a sin? I believe this whole movement is ruinous in every sense of the word to the whole land. I believe its success would be specially disastrous to my native South. Can I stand up, then, and ask the Almighty to bless, to prosper, to grant success to the movement? No, Sir, I would die first! Scripture distinctly commanded what Timothy and every other minister then was to do, Nero being then on the throne, a usurper, and the vilest of tyrants. The command is left for the guidance of every Christian now. I obey that command literally and fully in my prayer every Sabbath in the pulpit—more than that I can not do."

"I perfectly agree with you; I heartily and entirely approve your course," said his friend. "The plain truth is, I would not, a good many of us would not, enter the church if you pursued any other course. Yet it will not satisfy the Secessionists in our church. They have been growling at it for some time. As the excitement deepens, and it is deepening every hour, they will not stand it. They—"

"You know I have often offered them my resignation. It is ready at any instant," interrupted the young minister.

"Yes, and your resignation is the closing of the church," said his friend, gloomily.

"I had thought my course met the approval of at least the overwhelming majority of the church," said the minister.

"So it does," said the lawyer; "but times are rapidly coming when even those entirely with you in sentiment will not dare to say so. You see I know men better than you. And I may mistake, but I dread even more than that. You who by habit give yourself to religion, and keep aloof from the excitement of the streets, can not imagine how this excitement is beginning to eat into the very piety even of those who entirely agree with you in political sentiment. Unless I mistake, you will find even they will cease taking any interest in religion; will cease from attending public worship even, such is the paralysis creeping over even the best Christians."

The heart of the pastor had been already too full of forebodings not to acknowledge the truth of all this.

"But what do you advise?" he asked at length, so sick, so deadly sick at heart.

"Simply that you pursue the even tenor of your way," said his friend. "I have told you all this in order to keep you thoroughly aware of the exact state of matters. You should feel no mortification at it as at a matter personal to yourself. You need not I should tell you the sentiment of the church toward you. But we are passing through a terrible revolution—a revolution social and religious as well as civil. Your trial will be that of, I suppose, every pastor in the land. If you were a Secessionist that would not mend matters, for then the Union people would be against you. Let us bear up as we best may ; no man in the land but is smitten in some shape by the accursed step we have taken off the precipice," said the lawyer, disregarding in his excitement all the rules of rhetoric. " I am sorry you are so cast down ; you are as pale as a sheet."

And long and sad was the conversation which followed between the friends, drawn now nearer together than ever before.

"There is one thing I hardly need say," added the lawyer, as he rose at last to leave. "We are entering on times of great scarcity and pressure. At least do not let *that* trouble you. To my last cent you may depend on me. There is Ferguson, too—but I am ashamed even to suppose you do not know all this without being told. Good-by !"

With the door locked, the curtains down, all the raging madness shut out, Edward Arthur sank upon his knees before One nearer to him and more to him than all the universe beside. Amidst the wreck of all else, this seemed all that was left him. It was not only his church, his old friends, Alice too—Alice? But he never dreamed of regretting his opinions. They had been as much a matter of course to him as his breathing. Long he kneeled there in earnest, fervent prayer. He had had troubles before, but here was the wreck to him of all things at once. Alas, he was only entering upon the trial! It was to him but as Gethsemane ; the awful remainder of Agony was yet before him.

"I fear you are unwell, Mr. Arthur," said Mrs. Bowles to him that night at supper. "We wondered you did not come to dinner." But Mrs. Bowles was not in her manner and tones the Mrs. Bowles of other days. And Alice, too!

"But I can not help it!" groaned Edward Arthur.

## CHAPTER X.

It is late one afternoon, a few weeks after this, that Edward Arthur, seated in his little room there in Mrs. Bowles's front yard, hears the front gate open and shut, and sees through his window Mr. Neely walking toward the house. In that one glance he sees that Mr. Neely is carefully dressed in his very best ; sees all that Mr. Neely has come for ; knows almost every syllable of all that Mr. Neely is going to say ; sees and knows all this with a sudden glow which tingles him from head to heel—a glow followed by as sudden a chill. We must endeavor to excuse the young minister, the fact being that he has lain wide awake all the previous night on account of the bells.

On account of the bells! At nine o'clock exactly the night before, Bill Perkins, the stage-driver, had driven up to the door of the hotel.

MR. NEELY.

Long before he could rein in his horses a dozen voices from the crowd, which now awaits his every arrival in the ample porch of the hotel, hails him—"Any news, Bill ? What's the news?"

Bill Perkins is aware of his importance, and is silent and even dignified accordingly. No man there so calm as he, though his team is all in a foam, and he an hour earlier than usual on account of the news which burns in his bosom. Their classic reading being extremely limited, the series of stage-drivers of which Bill Perkins is one are not aware of the fact that they strongly resemble the runners in that one of the old Olympic Games in which each one bears at full speed, and transmits in full blaze to the one next beyond him, a lighted torch. During the last hundred hours or so, each driver on the line, catching the news, with the reins and whip, from the one before, has borne it on like a torch indeed, setting aflame with the great and glorious tidings all the country as he drives along. Perhaps it is on account of its being transmitted so far, and from hand to hand so often, that the torch blazes larger and brighter for every mile it is borne over, as with the very rapidity of its transmission.

"The news! What is the news?" says Bill Perkins, at last, very slowly, and with considerable irritation in his manner. "Ask me if there's any news! I guess there *is* news !" And Bill Perkins is thereupon silent, enjoying the dependence of the assembled crowd, and all Somerville behind it, upon his single tongue. Here is the possession of power, and, like all of us, he greatly enjoys it. The moment his news is spoken he vanishes from public attention, and he knows it.

"I tell you what it is, you Jake," he says to the negro hostler, amidst the breathless attention of the crowd, "you'd better have them horses a little cleaner when I come to leave to-morrow than they were last time; better had, or I'll Jake you till your very wool 'll come out o' curl! No, they ain't any passengers. What are you unbuckling them straps for? Think I kerry trunks about behind jest fur the fun o' the thing? Gentlemen, do shet up till I kin—News? I rather guess there is news! Great battle at Corinth! Glorious victory! Yankees whipped all to smash! Beauregard's taken prisoners all he hasn't killed, an' that's fifty thousand! Battalions, gun-boats, brigades, all keptured! Sydney Johnson killed, only that's known to be a lie. But get out o' the way, gentlemen, I must drive to the Post-office. Can't you wait till the mail is open and get your papers?"

And having keenly enjoyed his momentary importance, Bill Perkins subsides, as he drives off, into private life till the next time.

But the news! It is to the crowd like fire to powder. Such a brightening of faces, such a shaking of hands, such a chorus of yells! People hurry off to their homes to tell it to their waiting families. Men who live in the country can not wait till the mail is opened, but mount their horses, tied hard by, and gallop off at the risk of their necks through the darkness to tell the news at home, then to gallop back again for their papers. Lamum only stops to say, "The bells, boys, the bells! Every bell in Somerville!" and is in the Post-office and his hand in the mail-bag almost before the Postmaster can unlock and draw out the chain through the iron loops thereof.

It is a little strange about Dr. Peel. Up to the arrival of the stage he had been one of the foremost, and certainly the loudest, of the crowd at the hotel awaiting the stage. No man so confident as he that, "Mark my word, gentlemen, there'll be great news to-night;" consigning his soul most emphatically to perdition if his prophecy is not correct. But Dr. Peel has made many a similar prophecy similarly emphasized before; in fact, he never ceases from prophecies to the same effect all day long and all over Somerville, so that people have come to attach not so much meaning to his words as they used to do. It is strange, then, that he is not among the foremost in pressing around Bill Perkins when Bill first drives up. Nobody notices him when Bill has first announced the great news. They would have been surprised at the singular pallor of his face as he stands a little back in the shadow cast by the large lamp hanging in front of the hotel from one of the pillars of the porch.

Nobody notices him in the wild excitement of the hour; but he is silent, has ceased even from cursing, is suddenly shrunken from his burly prominence, ague-struck, dumb. It is not for long, however. Ten minutes later, and Dr. Peel's lumbering form and heavy black brow and exultant profanity is foremost as usual. He can hardly make his voice heard, for three citizens are ringing at the tavern bell, while Joe Staples, the hotel keeper's little boy, is beating the gong, relieved in turns by such of his companions, specially favored thereby, as are not engaged in firing their revolvers and ringing the church bells.

"Gentlemen," he roars, with stentorian oaths, slapping down a twenty-dollar gold piece on the hotel counter as he does so, "there's twenty dollars toward powder to celebrate this glorious news; and there's another ten toward liquor for all who will help me drink success to Beauregard and perdition to the Yankees!"

But there must have been a good deal more than twenty dollars' worth of powder fired off that night from the two cannon, the four anvils, and the innumerable rifles and revolvers in Somerville. As to ten, it was rather many hundreds that went that night across the counters of every grocery in Somerville for liquor; the bells scattering the news meanwhile over all the country for miles around.

All night Lamum is busy in his office reading the papers, writing editorials, answering questions to the crowd pouring through it like a thoroughfare, all flushed and noisy but he. With stooped shoulders, face beaked like a kite, and thin, sharp voice, he is the acknowledged intellect and oracle of the hour, ruling by his very paleness, confidence, and coolness. There is a tone of asperity even in the manner in which he alludes, from time to time, to the excitement of the hour. "Acting as if you did not know who would whip!" he says. No outward sign thereof; but, ah, how keenly he enjoys the hour! Sweeter taste of bliss this man will never know so long as his soul endures.

All night long people came galloping in on horseback from the country. The dispatches are read over and over again at every bar in town; beside the hotel lamp in front of the hotel; by fathers at home in shirt and drawers to the mothers in night-gowns, and the children starting up from cradle and trundle-bed, wondering and crying. All night neighbors are hurrying into each other's houses to talk it all over; and so, from where the news smote, like a stone in the centre of a lake, there at the hotel door, the waves roll and spread until they die off into all the country around miles away. There has been a slight misunderstanding between Captain Simmons and Bob Withers at a grocery, however. "What I say is, by George, I want to see all this news confirmed first! Suppose it shouldn't be *true*, by George!" is what Bob Withers has remarked over and over again as he holds on to an awning post in front of a blazing bonfire.

"Look here, Bob Withers: I tell you, Sir, you mustn't say that; you oughtn't to say that," Captain Simmons has remarked, as drunk as Withers, but only the stiffer in attitude, and the more quarrelsome on that account.

"Confirmed, gentlemen, that's what I say; confirmed is what I want this news to be first. Yes, by George, *confirmed!*" hiccups Bob Withers, regardless of the Captain.

"Any man, such a glorious night as this, who can refuse to believe news, *such* news, is a traitor!" says Captain Simmons, still more sternly. Unlike poor Bob Withers, the Captain prides himself upon being a gentleman in the genteel sense of the word. Were not his parents highly respectable people, members of the church, specially careful in his training? Hence it is the Captain never dresses except in black, even in summer. As to Bob Withers, the drunker he gets the lower he descends. The drunker Captain Simmons is, only that much higher he ascends. When sober, which is becoming a very rare thing with the Captain, he is but a common sort of person; but as he waxes intoxicated his reminiscences of parents, and church, and Bible-class, and college, and the term he served in the Legislature, and all his past respectability in general, become more and more vivid. It is when at his deepest possible stage of drunkenness that the Captain is in bearing and language the very Chesterfield of Somerville. He now stands regarding Bob Withers with lofty indignation.

"Confirmed, gentlemen!" exclaims Bob, still more loudly, more dogged in his insane notion, blinking gravely with owlish eyes upon the crowd, "that's what *I* want, by George!"

"This most disreputable individual is a traitor, gentlemen," says Captain Simmons, slowly and solemnly; "a Yankee at heart, an Abolitionist in disguise. By sainted parents I was carefully instructed never to fight, never even to associate with drunken squabblers. This case must be made an exception. He is inebriated, I know, but even his pitiable condition shall be no protection." And the Captain, lifting his cane and advancing upon him, is prevented only by the crowd from inflicting merited chastisement.

But Colonel Ret Roberts is at this juncture dragged out of Lamum's office, after having been called for in vain for the last three hours. Dr. Peel has opened a basket of Champagne, and Colonel Ret Roberts is very drunk by this time, though Dr. Peel and Lamum are not. But zealous friends stand close around the hogshead upon which the Senator totters to catch him when he falls.

Oh, divine gift of eloquence!—given not to one man in multitudes, and not by one man in thousands to whom it is given used but for the basest of purposes. People have heard Colonel Ret Roberts before; no wonder, as the news spreads that he is speaking, all groups break up from hotel, grocery, bonfire, street corner, and hurry toward the spot. In a little while hundreds of excited faces show around him through the half light, half shadow of torch and bonfire as he speaks. The frantic applause as he steadies himself to begin drowns even the sounds of scattering shots and the pealings of the church bells, intoxicated with their own clamor.

The bells! As the suggestion had broken from Lamum's lips boys and men had raced off toward every church in Somerville. True, the doors of each church were locked. But what difference did that make? The news, the glorious news! Sashes were smashed in, doors burst open, the very churches made to take—alas! and not in that way alone during these days—the noisiest, rowdiest part in the jubilee. And it is of no use stopping up the access to the bell-ropes afterward. During all these days they hang within open and easy reach to the hand of whosoever chooses to pull.

But the voice of Colonel Ret Roberts rises clear and strong and fascinating above every other sound. Falsehood, fact, fierce invective, anecdote, prophecy, appeal—how smoothly they flow from his lips! No belted earl in Europe has so supreme a contempt for the people as has this South Carolina cavalier; hardly concealed even. He speaks now, as always, not so much to the mob around him, nor for their hearing, as just because he thereby gratifies himself. He speaks as naturally and as necessarily as a river pours its water, or as a mocking-bird sings.

And how they applaud! Men stand there yelling with laughter at his jokes whose daily business is utterly ruined by what Colonel Ret Roberts and his set have brought to pass. Colonel Juggins has ridden in by this time, summoned through the night and the mud by the bells and the cannon. How cordially he agrees in the speaker's bitter descriptions of the Abolitionists, not even dissenting at the exciting instant to the horrible oaths with which it is peppered! Colonel Juggins with his plantation swarming with negroes, and so ignorant of the fact that it is just that speaker there before him who, aided by his like, have secured the speedy emancipation of every negro he owns! Abolitionist! For practical abolitionism Wilberforce, Clarkson, Burdett, Beecher, Garrison, Brown, and all the rest, with all their meetings, petitions to Parliament and Congress, speeches, books, papers, pikes, and torches, are, in comparison with Colonel Ret Roberts and his class, but as the jury to the executioner. And not a man in that excited crowd dreams of it!

There is Sampson, the carpenter, listening with

COLONEL RET ROBERTS MAKES A SPEECH.

both ears, never wincing even when the Colonel culminates his denunciation of the Federal army as being composed of "base mechanics!" Staples, the hotel keeper, has left his hotel to take care of itself while he can hear Roberts. How he exults in the demoralization of the North, its speedy bankruptcy and ruin, as prophesied by the speaker; so ignorant that, of his three boys turned by the Colonel and his set from thriving citizens into soldiers, one lies at that

moment dead at Shiloh, another is to suffer am-
putation, and consequent death, to-morrow at
Corinth, while George, the last but one, is to
be returned at the end of the war a drunken loaf-
er until his death. Yes, there stands Staples,
his hat left behind in his hurry, his red and
enormous crop of hair on head and face full
one-fourth of the man it seems, for Staples is but
a small man, and was once a tailor; disheveled
and bristling and electric with the glorious news
in every fibre, with eyes sparkling through it
like those of a ferret, mouth agape, hands ec-
static, how he listens and laughs and applauds,
more of a lunatic than sane to-night!

In the name of God's eternal justice, if Benedict Arnold deserved death for attempting to betray and ruin his country, what do Colonel Ret
Roberts and his gang deserve—deserve at the
hands of the South, who have so terribly succeeded therein? Let them escape the gallows,
unhung as traitors, none the less will they swing
forever in the chains of history as the greatest
criminals that ever blundered through blood and
mire since the days of Cain—criminals whose
wickedness was exceeded only by their folly!

"Sheep, sheep, sheep," Mr. Ferguson has been
murmuring to himself all night; "and herded
here and herded there, as sheep always are, by
smart dogs," adds Mr. Ferguson to himself, from
recollections of his native hills and glens. As
to believing in the news of the night, not exactly. Mr. Ferguson disbelieved it in advance
when he first heard, that night, the rattle of the
approaching stage. He disbelieved it still more
strongly when he heard the uproar which followed its announcement. Truth is, by this time
Mr. Ferguson and Somerville occupy in regard
to each other opposite ends of an ever-moving
plank, like children playing see-saw. When
Somerville goes down in heart up goes the Scotchman, never so cheerful as when his friends and
fellow-citizens are gloomiest. To-night Somerville revels in the ascendant over Yankees and
universe, but very low in spirits is the Scotchman, indignant all the time at himself for being
so, the news being, whatever it is, so absurd!
Not that he went down from his room to ascertain its nature; being all a lie, why should he?
There was one satisfaction in it—he would
have another flaming sheet to add to his collection. Beginning with the summer of the burnings, he already had a large one. Not a placard
posted on the walls of Somerville from the first
in relation to the matter, not a notice of thanksgiving for victory, not a sermon upon the war
preached by minister or bishop, not a document
of the kind had so far come within his reach
but he had seized upon and placed it, in its due
order, upon file.

If any man tried desperately to sleep that night
Mr. Ferguson did; but Mr. Ferguson did not succeed, the bells were too strong even for him.

As to the Union people in general, you saw
few of them on the streets that night. Doctor
Warner went to the office for his paper—but
that is no rule. Mrs. Warner made him go.
She read the paper on his return, sitting up in
bed in her night-cap, the Doctor holding the
candle, and enduring in his own person, from
his wife, the whole Federal defeat of Shiloh over
again. There were others of the Union people
who glided swiftly and stealthily into the office,
obtained their papers, and studied them on their
return home—gathering far less cause for the
pealing bells and the reports of cannon and guns
than others found. It is astonishing, it is perfectly amazing, they should find so much to exult in! they said to themselves—and, in strict
confidence, to each other next day of the people
of Somerville; yet they themselves were far,
very far, from being as cheerful under all the
circumstances as, according to their own views
of the tidings, they should have been.

In Somerville, as in every town on earth,
there existed what may be called the wavering
one-third. That is, one-third of the population
was sincerely and decidedly in favor of Secession—firm believers in the Millennium it was
about producing; another third was still more
decidedly of the conviction that the South was
wrong, and had nothing but evil to expect in
consequence; the remaining third believed in
nothing so clearly, inflexibly, and consistently
as this—that the winning side was the right
side. When with Unionists the waverer was a
Unionist too, but, "Bless me, we must be guarded in our language during such times as these,
you know!" When with Secessionists the waverer was, "I confess, somewhat doubtful about
the step at first, but now that we are in it, of
course there is but one course left us; we are
all agreed in that, I suppose!" And now that
this last news has come, the waverer, when with
the Secessionists, shakes hands and smiles amidst
the universal smiling and hand-shaking, gladly
lost among the crowd. When thrown in private
with his Union friend the waverer has nothing
special to say—only arches his brows and gives
a mournful shrug of his shoulder at the delusion
of the rejoicing. The sympathy of the waverer
with such a man as Guy Brooks just now—Corinth pealing with all its cannon in his ears—is
very much that of the Frenchman who took off
his hat to the antique statue of Jupiter. "Who
knows," said the Gaul, "but he may get his
head above water once more!"

When the first stroke of the first bell smote
on the ear of Edward Arthur, studying in his
room, it struck like—it may be an awful thing
to say of a Southern born, Southern raised man,
but none the less must the truth be told—a cruel
blow.

"It is the last desperate effort of the Yankees
to subjugate the South," Mrs. Bowles had said,

before the news came, that night at supper. "They obtained a partial and greatly-exaggerated success at Fort Donelson, on account of their gun-boats. Our Generals were inexperienced, perhaps cowardly, then. The South was slumbering in full belief the war was over; but now the two armies are in front of each other near Corinth you will see a different result. Their gun-boats can not help them then. Our Generals are experienced and brave. The entire South has swarmed to their assistance. I believe in our army; I believe in our cause, as that of a people struggling to be free from cruel tyranny, I believe in a just God, above all, and I know already the victory is ours!" said Mrs. Bowles, with glowing cheek. "If it was not that Rutledge Bowles is at the head of his Company in Virginia, soon to be victorious there, I would only regret he is not at Corinth to share that great victory!"

And now hardly has the pastor seated himself after this in his room before the bells, and the shouts, and the roar of cannon announce that Mrs. Bowles is right. As he sits he can hear the instant and joyful bustle in the house. He hears Mrs. Bowles hurry the negro Charles down to the office for the papers. He hears Alice and her mother conversing eagerly together as they await his return. He hears Charles return; can hear Alice reading aloud the dispatches to her mother; hears Mrs. Bowles's loud "Oh, thank God! thank God!" mingled with even weeping. Had it been in regard to any thing else in the world he would have been with them, and one with them.

But as it is? A great gulf yawns between him and the rejoicing town; between him and the very family in which he lives, heretofore one in every thing; between him and Alice! There is a pause; and then the voice of Alice at the piano rings clear to the song of Dixie, and then of the Bonnie Blue Flag. There is another pause; then Alice plays more slowly, sings more sweetly: it is a Psalm this time—the Forty-sixth Psalm. Edward Arthur well knows why: it was the Psalm sung, he has often heard Mrs. Bowles tell, in the Major's father's family by the whole household, white and black, after the news of the surrender of Cornwallis. All this, and he sitting there in his room separated from all the world.

Shall he dash away from him every thing, go in the house, congratulate them on the glorious news, rejoice with her—with Alice—with the whole world rejoicing around? He sinks his head upon his hands resting on the table before him, and tries to go over the whole question of Secession from the first. Was Secession a right thing? During these last two years he has, in reading and in conversation, made himself perfectly familiar with every thing that can be said on both sides of the question. He had brought to the investigation no prejudices or partialities except in favor of the South, in which he has lived all his life, out of which he never expects or desires to be as long as he lives. Distrustful of himself, he has ever sought divine guidance herein. Leaning his brow upon his table he sinks upon his knees, and goes again over the whole subject in the language and feeling of prayer. How ardently he desires to believe Secession, under all the circumstances, to have been a right thing before man and before God!

But with all the loud opinion of Somerville ringing at the instant in his ears, for his life he can not effect the slightest, most momentary agreement in himself with that opinion. Secession was—is a wrong thing. But so many at the South disagree with him here? He can not help it; to him Secession was—is a great wrong. But so many pious Christians, learned and pious ministers have believed in it, have written and preached in its favor, have entered into it as the very cause of right and truth and God himself? They are more learned, more holy than he a thousandfold; none the less to him Secession was—is wrong, wrong! He may be deluded, may be insane, but to him that night, reason as he may, Secession is to him as clearly a crime as ever.

Only a little time ago, he remembers, the whole land, North, South, East, West, thought and felt as he thinks and feels to-night. All were unanimous then, at least, on that point— the believers in Secession being regarded, such a little while ago, and by the whole land, with contempt as deluded, with horror as wicked men. He can remember how that sentiment ran through the speeches of all public men, the leading articles of all editors, the sermons of all preachers, the platform addresses on all anniversaries, the very school readers and hymns for Sabbath-school celebrations, the entire country over. And to-night, like a man in full health suddenly drugged into a hideous dream, he finds himself, as it were, alone in this same sentiment, all the world changed as in an instant to believe with all their soul in exactly the reverse. But he has not changed with it; he almost wishes he could have done so; but he has not, and he can not help it. It was—it is a great crime!

Then all that good Mr. Ellis said to him only yesterday comes into his mind. There is no man in Somerville with whom he has held such sweet and intimate communion, for years now, as with Mr. Ellis, the member and pillar of his church. He has a friendship for Guy Brooks, but the lawyer has not the deep and devotional piety of Mr. Ellis. He has often conversed, and very agreeably, with Guy Brooks on church matters; but he has never conversed with him as he has with Mr. Ellis, deep into the night, there by his study fire, or here in his chamber, upon doctrines precious alike to them both, unveiling to him in Christian friendship, the closest and sweetest of all on earth, the deepest experiences of his soul. He has often knelt with Guy Brooks in prayer in private; but it was Mr. Ellis whose devotional spirit rose with his own in agonies of entreaty, in the very wrestlings of living faith for the common cause of their hearts. Was there a proof of affection and esteem for him which Mr. Ellis had not given? Blameless in life, prudent in speech, sincere in soul, liberal of his means to the last cent, above all devotedly pious, Mr. Ellis had been the man of all men he had ever known to whom he had clung closest.

"You know I was a Union man to the very last," his friend had said to him only yesterday. "We agreed perfectly in sentiment on that point. But the case is altogether changed now. We are both Southern men; have and desire to have no country but the South. Well, the South has established itself as a separate nation from the North. We both opposed the step, but it has been taken, and we are not responsible for it. In the providence of God the Confederacy being a nation, and we the citizens thereof, our duty is clear. You know the maxim: 'My Country, may she ever be right; but my Country, right or wrong!'"

And here Mr. Arthur had cried out against this maxim, but all the argument only left them where they were before.

"When the North actually declared war upon us"—Mr. Ellis continued, at last—"war upon us, think of that! Actual war, simply for desiring a peaceful separation from them, from that time my feelings have undergone a complete change. I am glad we did separate from a people capable of taking such a step—such a wicked, diabolical step! Henceforth I have no wish but for the success of our arms, and for the defeat, destruction if need be, of the Northern Government. You have not a warmer friend in the world than I am," adds good Mr. Ellis, taking his pastor by the hand, the tears standing in his eyes as he speaks; "from my soul I admire and love you—am your *sincere* friend. Don't persist in your course—don't, I entreat you, for the sake of our friendship, for the sake of Christ's cause—"

If Edward Arthur could only have got his friend then and there to have united with him in prayer, first for wisdom, and then have discussed together the one thing at the core and centre of it all—Slavery. But he dared not do it. An *Abolitionist!* Horror. Why Mr. Ellis would have—what would he *not* have said and done?

As if, deep down under all, Mr. Ellis, and every other Christian at the South was not thinking, in various stages of advance, exactly the same thoughts!

Yet it was strange, too. Long after war had been begun Mr. Ellis had little to say upon the subject. Week after week had the pastor, Guy Brooks, Mr. Ferguson, and Mr. Ellis, besides other church-members, met for prayer. On every one of these occasions Mr. Ellis had led in prayer, had prayed for peace, had prayed that God's will might be done, but had never once prayed distinctly for the Confederacy, nor for the success of its arms and the defeat of its foes. As the months rolled on, Mr. Arthur, standing still himself, could perceive a change in his friend. At first he would have scouted, and did scout, with horror the idea of his son Henry going to the war. "It was like causing Henry to pass through the fire to Moloch," were his own words often repeated to his pastor. But, at last, Henry did go. Henceforth Mr. Ellis was indeed changed. Now he began to pray earnestly for the Confederacy, to give freely up to and beyond his means to all the demands upon him toward it; to feast upon the papers, believing all they said of success to the Confederate arms; to seek and join eagerly in all meetings and street conversations; in a word, to outdo many even of the most violent "from-the-start Secessionists."

As the young minister knelt there in his room, with the bells pealing in his ears, he well knew that no man in Somerville was rejoicing more than Mr. Ellis in the news. "We must cease looking back, cease reasoning upon the matter," Mr. Ellis had told him yesterday, "and must give way now to our feelings, to our natural and hearty feelings, as citizens of a nation invaded by a brutal foe."

"But was not Secession a wrong thing?" Mr. Arthur had asked.

"Well, yes, in a certain sense it was," Mr. Ellis had replied.

"And is not this a war, on the part of the North, but an energetic attempt to put down a wrong thing? Is it not, this war, a desperate attempt on the part of the South to establish this wrong thing? Can you hope for the blessing of God, Mr. Ellis, on any effort to establish any wrong? Dare you deliberately pray to God to give success to the wrong?" said the minister.

"All this is mere morbid fancy, Mr. Arthur. Fight? yes, it is the duty of every man in the South to fight. I have sent Henry! I tell you, Sir," continued Mr. Ellis, a fire gleaming in his eye which no man had ever seen there a few months agone, "if there are any among us who are unwilling to go and fight for the Confederacy I would have them torn by force from their homes and made to go; if they are of *no* other use on the battle-field they will make breast-works there for those who *do* love their country."

Mr. Arthur had never been calmer in his life than when he replied, rising as he spoke: "Mr. Ellis, we once thought and felt exactly alike in this matter. You have left me. I stand this hour exactly where I have always stood—must always stand. Wrong is of the Devil. Right is of God. A Wrong is eternally a Wrong, and a Right is eternally a Right. He who fights for the Wrong and against the Right fights for the Devil and against his God. May my right arm wither from its socket before I strike a blow for the one and against the other!"

Only Secession the Wrong? No vague, unde-fined, instinctive apprehension of a deeper, more desperately wrong thing than that, *under* that, out of which, as from a giant and deadly root, Secession had naturally sprung?

Yes, Edward Arthur—the bells pealing in his ears—went over the whole subject which he had gone over and over and over again so often dur-ing the weary months past. Has not the South passed into the hands of the very worst and most desperate men in it? he asked himself. Many a Mr. Ellis drawn into it now; perhaps many a better man than I am deluded into it from the outset—but that its leaders are men who occu-pied, two years ago, a position in the esteem of the country the reverse of that to which they have now risen who can deny? And, suppose Secession successful, what is that but the certain crumbling apart, both at the North and at the South, of States held together by so fragile a tie? Will not Secession be ever before the mind as the easy remedy for any dissension among States? And what is my country, my *nation*, then? What permanency in such a Confederacy toward nations abroad? What permanency in such a loosely-bound nation for the building of railways—the founding of great institutions? What hope for the peaceful spread of civilization and the Gospel in a region perpet-ually in danger, at least, of crumbling to frag-ments? Shall I desire and pray that the South may succeed in this effort to make itself another South America of wrangling and warring prov-inces?

And suppose the Confederacy successful as against the North—does not the one existing cause—Slavery—still exist? With such a line of frontier, with such hostility to Slavery North, with such jealousies and rivalries, could a peace between two such nations last six months? That, *Slavery!* Old, and stale, and hackneyed reason-ings these, now; but to Edward Arthur that night they were living things with which he wrestled as for his life!

It is as one exhausted with long conflict that, on this afternoon after the night of bells, Ed-ward Arthur sees Mr. Neely enter the house of Mrs. Bowles, on a little visit to the mother, and especially to the daughter.

Just a word or two in regard to Mr. Neely while he waits on the front porch for Charles to answer his knock. A tall man is Mr. Neely, with fair hair and florid face. When he first came South Mr. Neely had always replied, "Kentucky," when asked where he was from. Because having made an extensive tour of that State before settling in Somerville, he *was* from Kentucky. But his fair and rosy face was against him; he had always to acknowledge, at last, that shameful and painful fact of having been origin-ally from New Hampshire; in fact, hard to say, "*born* there." If Mr. Neely's body was in per-petual motion—hands, eyes, feet, tongue—it was only because it was an instrument thoroughly adapted to his active and restless mind.

One definite purpose Mr. Neely had in life—to succeed. That is, to obtain as much position and property as he could, in which he is very far from being singular. Starting from New En-gland with just one hundred dollars in gold, a good suit of clothes, an old-fashioned watch, once belonging to his father and his father's father, a pleasant person, a ready wit, he had gone into the Book Agency Business because it was the first thing that turned up. But it had occurred to him as a thing still better to study Law, and now he is teaching in Somerville as a means of support—glorious Daniel Webster be-fore him in that—while he masters enough legal knowledge to obtain a license. Mr. Neely is not an unprincipled man; Mr. Neely would not do a dishonest deed for the world—an undoubted-ly, undeniably dishonest deed, you know—but Mr. Neely, all this apart, is resolved to suc-ceed.

Now it is not in New Hampshire that Mr. Neely is expecting to succeed, but in Somerville and the South. Therefore Mr. Neely must adapt himself to Somerville. Point out to him that "Hadn't oughter" grates upon the ears of Som-erville, and never again does that expression pass his lips. It is part of his creed that though there are such quadrupeds as cows, the universe owns nothing answering to the name of keows. Well does Mr. Neely know that the calling any one to an account for a thing is vastly better ex-pressed by the phrase "calling him to dew for it," but he would prefer death to such language. Mr. Neely often speaks of "throwing a rock," but of such a thing as a "stone" he has never read, except in the Bible. Cheerfully does Mr. Neely inter-change "evening" for "night," and as freely does he give up "chores" for "jobs;" and so of all forms of speech unadapted to his new meridian. There now lingers not even the knowledge of one in his mind. It is rather the custom of Somerville to substitute negro labor for one's own labor, and to no man there has it become so indispensable as to Mr. Neely. No man denies the piety of Mr. Neely; but it was after ascertaining which of the churches in Somerville had the largest at-tendance that he united himself to just that church —and of that church's choir Mr. Neely is a prom-inent member; but as to introducing, or even alluding to any of the tunes so familiar in New

Hampshire and in the old church there, and so unknown in Somerville—why, Mr. Neely has long since ceased even to whistle them to himself, on principle. "Identify myself with the South" is Mr. Neely's one, plain path; and the only question on any and every point with him, great and small, is simply, which is the Northern, which the Southern side of this matter? and magnetized by this, Mr. Neely repels the Northern and clings to the Southern Pole of the question by a second nature which has become an instinct.

In a word, Somerville contains many hundred Southern-born individuals, but Mr. Neely is the most intensely Southern person there. That is, in comparison with the born Southerners, we mean. There are a plenty of other men there —Lamum, Barker, and the rest—born at the North, as Southern as he. Let us pause to inscribe this fact on the page of the times for future analysis and inference by whosoever chooses to undertake the task. Among the people, in the army, in political office, in the pulpit, on the stump, as editors—in all things at the South, Northern-born men are the most intensely Southern Southerners there. Pugnacious and self-conceited old Dr. Johnson once dreamed that he had an argument with some one in which he was defeated. We all remember how he consoled himself on awaking in this defeated condition: "At least, Sir, it was I myself, at last, who furnished my imaginary opponent with all the arguments with which he defeated me!" The North may flatter itself or bewail itself on the fact as it please, but, in a goodly measure, the desperation of Southern resistance was owing to muskets and pens in Northern hands under the flag of the Confederacy, New England wit and New England resolve where raged the battle fiercest in council or in field.

"I was born in Columbia, South Carolina, Sir," Dr. Peel had one day replied to Mr. Neely. Dr. Peel was a dark, superb-looking man, almost ducal in dress and bearing, and the words were spoken with his black eye full upon Mr. Neely, and in tones, to Mr. Neely's ear, so distinct and regal! "I am a prince of the blood, Sir," would scarce have sounded nobler. Ah, how mean New Hampshire, and how plebeian Mr. Neely to himself in comparison!

By no one was Mrs. Bowles congratulated, that day after the bells, in her parlor, more cordially than by Mr. Neely. No one had a brighter smile or a more hearty grasp of the hand on the occasion. If there was any defect in Mr. Neely it was that he was too glad, too fervent. But this one thing, brought with him from his bracing mountains, Mr. Neely could not unlearn; this one Southern thing he had not yet learned—to be still. Not that Southerners are not demonstrative enough, but then they are quiet withal; and this Mr. Neely could not be.

F

"A most wonderful victory, Madam," said Mr. Neely, rubbing his hands; "the complete rout of the Yankees. You will observe in the dispatch, Beauregard remarked on the spot that it was a more complete thing than Manassas even. I rejoice sincerely in it."

And no doubt Mr. Neely did. He opened his school with prayer every morning, and never had he failed since Secession to insert a petition therein for the victory of the South, and for "the speedy and total defeat of our cruel and implacable foes." Of late he had got into the custom of making little addresses to his school, descriptive of the wickedness of the North and of the glorious and successful revolution in which the South was embarked. As to giving the boys a holiday after the good news of last night, he would certainly have done that if the boys had only come to school that morning, which, however, they did not do, having voted themselves a holiday already, and altogether irrespective of Mr. Neely—the fact being that Mr. Neely was the most thoroughly governed individual in the school. "Old Neely?" any boy would indignantly exclaim on being remonstrated with on some special act of insubordination to his teacher, "why, old Neely is a Yankee!"

Yes, it was hard, very hard! No man could have been an earlier Secessionist or a more consistent Secessionist than the schoolmaster. His whole language had from the outset been of unwavering and unmitigated hostility to the North. Other men would venture to make exceptions in favor of "some, at least, it is to be hoped—some, however few," at the North; Mr. Neely could not in conscience make any such exceptions. In teaching his boys History he constantly kept up the striking parallel in their minds between the Revolution of '76 and that in which the South was now engaged. He required compositions from every pupil old enough to write them upon the topic of the day, and applauded most highly those in which the Yankees were most terribly demolished. "Nero was the Tyrant of the Roman Empire, and Lincoln is the Tyrant of America," "Only Powder and Steel can cure the North of its Phrensy," "Jefferson Davis is the Washington of our New Nation," and the like, were the copies set by him for his pupils. More than once highly patriotic songs had appeared in the Somerville Star signed N., which Mr. Neely had never denied as being from his pen. In fine, if Mr. Neely left any thing undone in proof of his sincere devotion to the cause of Secession it is impossible to imagine what that thing was. When he arrived in Somerville he possessed a Daguerreotype of his father. A large one and a very good one it was, and an honest, fatherly, clear-countenanced old patriarch the elder Mr. Neely seemed to be therefrom. Shall it be recorded here that the son deliberately broke to atoms and stamped, in his own words, "to flinders" beneath his heel that likeness in the first fervors of the war? Shall it be added that of this he afterward boasted with all phrases suitable to such a deed? Artistically considered this ought not to be mentioned, on account of its improbability, yet was it simple fact.

And yet? True as it is of the teacher it is equally so of all other Northern-born Secessionists—they never were thoroughly trusted and believed in as being really "sound."

"It isn't nature," Mrs. Juggins was continually remarking to husband and visitors, "for any body to turn so agin their own people. You needn't tell me what good Secessionists that Lamum an' Neely an' the rest are, I don't believe a bit in them myself. And there's Brother Barker," adds Mrs. Juggins, after a long pause, approaching the subject with reluctance. "Oh, I know how well and how much he talks. But —somehow—yes. Ah, well, don't it 'pear to you Brother Barker is too feverish like, kind o' over-het?" and Mrs. Juggins looks you anxiously and inquiringly in the eyes as she knits.

And this was the universal feeling whether expressed or not. The more violently Southern Northern men were, only that much the more did people murmur, "Only put on; you'll see one day if it isn't!" It matters not how violent and consistent in his course Lamum, for instance, was; though mortal could say no more against the North and for the South than he; though he harped perpetually on the infamy and the merited halter of "the traitors among us," at last people were only suspicious—"Yankees all of them!"—to the greatest degree. Had any one of them been detected in the worst practices of the incendiary and Abolitionist, one universal chorus would have broken forth, "A Yankee! I always knew it!"

Mrs. Bowles was pleased to see Mr. Neely, however, and conversed eagerly with him on the glorious news—an unconscious condescension running through all her manner as of a South Carolina lady conversing with a New Englander —a condescension not more assumed on her part than taken for granted on his. To no female born and living at the North would or could Mr. Neely have been so obsequious, so deferential. It is an unpleasant thing to write, but it is a fact. But in all Mr. Neely's conversation, though he addressed himself mainly to Mrs. Bowles, it was with chief reference to Miss Alice that he spoke. The truth is, the man really admired and loved the beautiful and queenly girl as he never loved or admired a woman before. There was a majesty in her erect bearing, a dignity inherited from her stately old father the Major, in her reserve, a serene soul in her full and steady eye, which was more to him even than her glowing cheek and coral lip. It is a shame to hint such a thing in America, but it was the old story of

plebeian and aristocrat, squire of low degree aspiring to the hand of noble dame. Marrying a South Carolinian! It was next to being born there!

"And it must be a great gratification to you, Miss Alice," he said, at last, "that the flag you presented that day to the regiment was in the fight." And Mr. Neely went back in memory to the day of its presentation, Alice standing on the platform with the colors in her hand, saying her few thrilling words more with eye and cheek and attitude than with tongue, a goddess to him from that moment henceforth and forever. For the moment Alice had endeavored to believe herself then and there a sort of "heroine of '76" over again. But, under all this cry of "Our Country!" "Our Glorious Revolution!" "Our gallant Army!" "Our despicable foes!" there steadily ran this fact, we are fighting for our negroes. Ugly thought, we are fighting for our —slavery! No, not a thought, an unpleasant but undefined consciousness thereof.

"Yes," said Alice; "but I am more anxious to know the fate of the men that received it, just now, than any thing else." Whereupon Mr. Neely skillfully turned the conversation upon their bravery, mingled with reasonings to show why he did not think, at least sincerely hoped, they had not suffered much in the contest. "And you have not heard, you tell me, from your son, Captain Rutledge Bowles?" he said at last, turning to Mrs. Bowles.

"Only that he is at the head of his company in Virginia," said Mrs. Bowles.

"I suppose we shall be compelled to inflict another Manassas upon them there. Perhaps one more defeat of the kind may satisfy them," said Mr. Neely.

"Rutledge Bowles was then in Charleston," said Mrs. Bowles, "in obedience to orders. He assures me in his last letter that he will be in the next battle, orders or no orders, wherever he thinks it likely to take place. I regret that he and many of the youth of South Carolina can not feel as satisfied with Mr. Davis and his arrangements as could be wished. It is a little hard that South Carolina should be second to Mississippi, taking the lead in the revolution the way my native State did. It is only for the present, however."

Thereupon Mr. Neely entered upon a glowing eulogy of South Carolina, adroitly worded, too, in the midst of which the bell rang for supper.

"Really, I had completely forgotten myself," he said, as he arose. "Only when one gets to speaking of South Carolina—"

"Stay to supper with us, Mr. Neely," said Mrs. Bowles, with a warmer manner than when he first came, and with perhaps somewhat more of hesitation and of apology for possible intrusion than was necessary, Mr. Neely at last consented.

"You will excuse me, Mr. Arthur," said Mrs.

Bowles, when the family were seated at table, "but you are really looking as if you had just risen from a severe illness." It was a fact; the pale, care-worn face of Edward Arthur contrasted strongly at the moment with the rosy and happy countenance of Mr. Neely by his side.

"Yes, Madam, I had no sleep last night," was the reply of that gentleman as he endeavored to assume a more cheerful manner.

"Why, as to that, none of us slept last night," said the schoolmaster. "Glorious news! Was it not, Mr. Arthur?"

Oh, the temptation, the pressing, the almost hourly temptation to lying those days! What is the use of talking about dissembling, evading, getting out of telling the truth, and all that? Satan is Satan, God is God, a lie is a lie! And the lying, downright lying, on the part of the Union people at the South—multitudes of them at least—was one of the most terrible demoralizations of the times. If ever necessity, the fear of consequences, the unparalleled nature of the case, justified people in this, of course they were completely justified. But can any thing make a wrong to be a right? Does God ever so place man that he *must* sin? Alice was cutting cake at the moment, but how keenly she was on the alert for Mr. Arthur's reply, though she raised not her eyes.

"Has any confirmation of it as yet arrived, Mr. Neely?" was Mr. Arthur's calm reply.

"Confirmation? It needs no confirmation!" exclaimed astonished Mr. Neely. "The victory is one we already knew would take place whenever the armies joined. The only question was one of place and day."

"You must pardon me if I seem to cast a gloom on the matter, but I frankly confess that my dominant feeling since the news came is one of sorrow," said the minister.

"Sorrow, Mr. Arthur!" exclaimed Mrs. Bowles and Mr. Neely in the same breath.

"At the awful destruction of human life," said the minister, and Alice breathed again. "You know my profession has habituated me to look on things in that light. Pardon me; but to think of a civil war in our country, not in France or Italy, but actually in America! A battle on our soil, with all its hideous carnage! I say nothing about souls hurried by thousands, unprepared many of them, into eternity. Again, pardon me, but you must blame my profession."

And thus Mr. Arthur told part of the truth; but did he tell really the truth in telling only a part?

But not for nothing had Mr. Neely been born in New England. "Why, Mr. Barker is of your profession, and I saw him last night listening to Colonel Ret Roberts, and I really believe he was the happiest man there!"

Mr. Neely was right. Brother Barker *was* there, and was as happy, to say the least, as any man on the ground. So happy, that in drinking down the Colonel's speech he had no time on the instant even to object mentally to its innumerable oaths, and to its blood-thirsty atrocities. Yes, no man laughed louder, or applauded every sentiment with both of his long hands more eagerly than he. What though Secession had arrested at once the operation and income of every Bible Society, Tract Institution, Missionary Cause — domestic and foreign — as well as every other Benevolent Association in the land; what though it was pouring over the land, through the prostrated embankments of Law, Order, Religion, and Society such a torrent of Profanity, Sabbath Desecration, Intemperance, and all kindred vices as the most gloomy-minded had never dared even to fear: what though ministers were starving at their ministry, or driven from it into other pursuits, churches were being split into fragments and dissolved, all religious worship being comparatively abandoned save to hear political sermons and proclamation prayers; members of churches and even ministers backsliding and apostatizing by multitudes; what though the minds of worldly men were being hardened a thousandfold more in irreligion; even the coming generation blasted in advance by the arrested instruction, and the inevitable corruption, mind and heart, by the times, of the very children. What though the cause dearest, avowedly, to Mr. Barker of all on earth —that of the Gospel—was perishing beneath the deadly influences of war in the land—civil war —yet was Brother Barker the loudest, and happiest, and heartiest among all beneath Colonel Ret Roberts's eloquence that night.

Ah, if Brother Barker had been the only minister of the sort! It was indeed the hour of the Saviour's crucifixion afresh. Never speak of the soldiers gambling at his feet, spotted with his falling blood, nor of the taunting multitude, nor of the darkening sky above and the earth quivering beneath, next to the hiding of the Father's face, the darkest, bitterest thing was that, even of Christ's disciples how nearly may we come to reading: "They all forsook him, and fled." We speak not of you who clung all the closer to your Master, with separatedness from the reigning spirit of the world, with strong crying to God during all that hour of darkness. You who, heartily with the North then, or as heartily with the South then, kept most heartily of all to Christ—one with each other at least in that— alas that, North and South, your number seemed so small in those days of Satan's hour, and the Power of Darkness!

"For my part I do not wonder Mr. Barker should rejoice," said Mr. Neely, after having waited in vain for the minister's reply. "With him, I believe the entire North to have become thoroughly infidel. This is a religious war—a war for Scripture doctrine in regard to Slavery against Abolitionism and all the other infidel isms of the North. Mr. Barker rejoices in the defeat of the North as in the defeat of irreligion itself—so do I."

"Mr. Neely," said Alice at this juncture, "how then about England and old Scotland—all Protestant Europe?"

"I do not exactly understand your question, Miss Alice," said Mr. Neely, intensely on the alert.

"I mean, only for argument sake, you know," said Alice, "does Protestant Europe stand on this question with the North or with the South?"

"Really, I am not sure," began Mr. Neely. But he saw that Alice knew, and knew that he knew, the facts of the case. "With the North, I believe," he added, under the stress of her clear and steady eye.

"And are they all infidel?" began Alice.

"I tell you what I frankly think; I mean I will frankly say what I really and truly believe, and that is, that almost the whole Christian Church is becoming infidel, Jacobinical. By Jacobinical notions I mean the old French notions of freedom and equality."

"I think I know what Jacobin means," said Alice, her eyes still bent with inquiry upon him.

"In this strife, Miss Alice, between Jacobinism, then, and Conservatism, between infidelity and the Gospel, in fact, I do believe that there is only one spot on the globe in which the pure and genuine Gospel lingers, and that is in the South. I wish to flatter no one," added Mr. Neely, "but of all the South I do believe that piety, the purest and most strictly in accordance with the Bible—Old Testament as well as New—is to be found in South Carolina. I myself was born at the North," continued Mr. Neely, with engaging frankness; "but, if one may say such a thing, I would give millions to have been born, of all the world, in South Carolina."

Yes, Mr. Neely actually said just that!

Mrs. Bowles cordially approved the sentiment, and assured Mr. Neely how highly she felt flattered. Alice never raised her eyes from her plate.

"Therefore," said Mr. Neely, after some further conversation, "if I, a Northern man, rejoice so in the success of Southern arms, I am sure you must, Mr. Arthur."

"It is impossible for me not to rejoice in whatever may be for the interest and real welfare and prosperity of the South, Mr. Neely," replied the other. "I have every inducement, and it would be unnatural and simply impossible that I should feel otherwise."

And yet, somehow, his reply did not satisfy Mrs. Bowles.

"I am perfectly ignorant of military matters," said Alice at last, "but I do not understand what is meant when the dispatch says that Beauregard fell back from Shiloh some twenty miles to Cor-

inth. I am confident of the gallantry of our soldiers; but why fall back?"

Thereupon Mr. Neely hastened to explain matters, showing that it was a kind of military strategy almost invariably adopted by victorious armies. Alice listened, but replied not.

"Oh, you mustn't mind Alice, Mr. Neely," said Mrs. Bowles, at length. "She is a willful girl, and she has an independent habit of her own. She is always endeavoring to form her own conclusions on every subject. When she once gets a notion in her head it is impossible to reason with her. She reminds me more and more of her father, Major Bowles. But, Alice, do let us have some music. We are not tired of Dixie yet—what a low name for the South!—or the Bonnie Blue Flag—any thing."

"What do you say to Yankee Doodle, or Hail Columbia, or the Star-spangled Banner, Mr. Neely?" said Alice, looking back upon that gentleman, with her hands upon the keys of the instrument.

VICTORY AND TIME.

## CHAPTER XI.

As the days and weeks creep by, it is very slowly but very certainly ascertained in Somerville that the great and glorious victory near Corinth was not, at last, quite so complete and final a rout of the Yankees as was at first believed. Somehow they have not fled utterly away—the miserable remnant left of them—but are still lingering, in a singular manner, near or upon the very battle-field. And it is so strange of Beauregard, that he has not long ago descended upon them again from Corinth like a thunder-bolt. Why does he not make a finish of it? What is he staying there at Corinth for? people are beginning impatiently to ask.

Like many another military idol of the time, before him and after him, Beauregard is slowly waning in public estimation. Good Mr. Ellis thanks God for it. "The career of any one General, like Napoleon, in our cause," he avows, "would be fatal to our liberties. We wish victory to be won for us in such a way that to no one man, but to the whole people, and to God above all, the glory may redound." Certain it is, though there were ever so many just on the point of becoming the Marions, the Washingtons, the Napoleons of the war, in some way or other each just missed it as by a hair's-breadth, but missed it altogether.

But the Yankees are even approaching Corinth. Lamum fills the Somerville *Star* with ample reasons why. Beauregard is hatching some great event within his intrenchments at Corinth, and people say they hope so, and that he will be quick about it; but there are sinking hearts in every bosom in Somerville. However, there is Island No. 10. It has been made a perfect Gibraltar. It is fully demonstrated that the passage of that Island in the Mississippi River by the Federal fleet is an absolute impossibility. Every Number of the Somerville *Star* exults in "Island Ten," and in the laughable notion of the Yankees that it can be passed. And so for weeks; slow as the first approach of an epidemic the rumor gets afloat that Island Ten has been evacuated.

It was not Lamum's fault! To do him strict justice, never from the first had any item, or any particle of an item, appeared in his columns save of good news for the Confederacy. Many a prophecy did he make of great and glorious events; many a statement did he continually repeat, on the best authority, of something or other highly favorable to the Confederacy. Steadily as the days rolled by were his prophecies unfulfilled and his statements disproved, yet you would never gather a syllable to that effect from his paper. And no reader thereof filed away each Number of the *Star* for future reference as carefully, or with such deep satisfaction, as did Mr. Ferguson.

Lamum had remarked: "If our gallant heroes *should* evacuate Columbus, it will be only to make a more impregnable stand at Island Ten." Long after Island Ten was evacuated Lamum casually remarks in his columns: "If our able and experienced Generals *should* evacuate Island Ten it is only to make a stand at Fort Pillow, but a short distance below;" and thereupon follows

several columns of such minute description of Fort Pillow—its natural advantages and its armament—that even a child could understand that of its capture no one need entertain the least fear. "Deluded by their frenzied leaders they dream even"—Lamum was frequently observing in his paper—"of capturing New Orleans!" If Colonel Juggins read Lamum's full and enthusiastic description of Fort Jackson and Fort St. Philip, and the other Gibraltars by which New Orleans was secured from the possibility of being taken, once, he read it a dozen times. The boom costing millions of dollars stretching across the river below the forts seems to him a waste of money. And then, the gigantic steamships building at New Orleans to dash to atoms the Federal vessels, to the Colonel they had assumed a grandeur of size and armament under the hand of energetic Lamum from which even a Brunel would have shrunk aghast.

"From what I learn of that splendid ship of war," good Mr. Ellis had said to his pastor, "even if the Federals should pass the forts below, of which I have no fear, that vessel alone, moored as it is in front of the city, could drive them back."

"But the papers speak of it as not yet completed," ventured Mr. Arthur.

"One side is, one side is," urged Mr. Ellis, warmly, "the side toward the river: the guns on that side are enough, amply enough."

And to this his friend had no reply.

Stealthily and awfully as the deadly blast of which the Spaniards say, "It kills a man but does not put out a taper," comes the news that New Orleans, too, is captured! A painful thing it is to state, but imperceptibly to themselves men begin to distrust Lamum and all his herd! Undefined, unacknowledged even to themselves, men begin to reason that, if the editors had so often deluded them upon such points as Bowling Green, Columbus, Fort Donelson, Island Ten, Fort Pillow, Roanoke, Pulaski, New Orleans, Corinth, might they not have been unsafe guides on all other points also relating to Secession and its consequences? Slowly, slowly.

"I think I am beginning clearly to see the hand of Providence in lengthening out this matter," Guy Brooks remarked one night to his pastor as they sat together in the study of the latter. "You know my brother, Paul Brooks; he has been down lately from his solitude among the Pines. He was always fond of solitude and reflection—old bachelor that he is. He has been giving me the benefit of his months of thought up there. We are, he thinks, passing through a revolution indeed, not only a political, but a social, moral, religious revolution. Were it only a political revolution, the establishment of the Confederacy, or the putting down of Secession say, it might have been a thing begun and over in a few months. But it is to be, he thinks, a total revolution in our deepest and dearest convictions on many subjects of vastly greater importance than the mere question of Secession and Union. Such revolutions of thought, belief, opinion, feeling can not be effected all at once. To be sincere and permanent, people must have time to think; yes, time, plenty of it, to *think.*"

"For the divisions of Reuben there were great thoughts of heart," said the minister. "I have been much struck with that passage of Scripture myself of late. Yes, the political leaders have full space, for instance, in which to show themselves—"

"From the tips of their horns to the points of their cloven feet," interrupted the lawyer. "And the people are slowly but steadily finding them out: it is a lesson being very slowly learned, but once learned it will never be forgotten on this continent forever."

"Unless I greatly mistake the South is learning other lessons also," said the minister, after a thoughtful pause. "God is causing us to read over again, beneath the blazing torch of his providence, other matters in which I for one was as thoroughly settled and satisfied as any man could be. We will not speak upon that matter just now—let us wait and see."

"We will see one day," the lawyer remarked, "the wonderful dealing of the Almighty with us in permitting this war to linger so long. Suppose Manassas had resulted the other way, the Confederacy been crushed in the bud, it would have been a mere victory of force—nothing else. There would have been nothing of a radical cure of the evil, nothing safe and permanent afterward. I tell you, Sir," continued he, rising to his feet, and leaning his burly form against the mantle as if the idea was too large and free to be expressed save upon his feet, "especially we here, at the South, are slowly, steadily coming toward convictions, conclusions which shall be those of our *own* minds and hearts. The bayonets are holding the question open only till we have had time to think the whole matter to an end. As firmly as I believe in my own existence, I do believe that this whole continent is steadily coming to such a oneness of sentiment as will make us such a Union—such a nation as—"

"The old Union was but an emblem of a scaffolding toward," the minister added for him. "I tell you, Mr. Brooks, Southerners as we both are, we can not disguise from ourselves the fact that, on some points, we of the South lag in the march, are a century or so behind the sentiment, the conviction, the Christianity of the times. I have had an uneasy conviction of the kind for years, but quieted myself with the knowledge of its being the providence of God, his peculiar dispensation in our case. And it is only God's providence in present events which I am now waiting to understand. For one I have no no-

tion of fighting against God. Nor have I any intention of being upon the obsolete side, the waning side of a great question. If you glance your eye over the history of the world you will notice that there are certain periods of time when you can run, as it were, a pencil line between where one era ends and a new and better era begins. And there always is a party for the old era fighting blindly and desperately for it! God helping me, I belong not to the old, worn-out era which the world is sloughing off, but to that era which is better, which is sure to succeed, which is that much nearer the Christ that is to come. My happening to be born in the Sandwich Islands would have been poor excuse for me, therefore, to have fought against civilization and Christianity when they had actually landed from God on its shores!"

And it was well for Edward Arthur, and for the many like him scattered throughout the South, that he and they had a belief in those days clear enough, strong enough, inspiring enough, to bear them up through poverty, and the alienation of their dearest friends, and the hatred and insult of innumerable enemies, and death always threatened, in some cases actually inflicted; a belief, thank God, which grew clearer, stronger, more inspiring, as the darkness and the peril became more dense. Easy enough it was for you, Sir, living outside the South during those days, to possess convictions clear and right upon the great question. You heard nothing else all day among your friends. You read nothing else in your papers, pamphlets, books. You had the one conviction poured upon you from the platform with all force of argument and eloquence. You had it urged upon you in every engraving that met your eye, flashed upon you in every transparency, waved before you in every flag, thundered upon you in cannon exulting over victory, and in the infinite hurrahs of the people! Little merit in your going with the right—how easy it was to you!—when you were in the centre of a great torrent pouring irresistibly onward.

But look at this man, Edward Arthur, one case in multitudes at the South during those long and dark months. From the first hour of that suicidal Secession he received no line of correspondence from any one outside the South, nor any during the first two years of the war, at least, from a correspondent within the South, save in enthusiastic support of Secession. Such of his correspondents as shared his convictions were prudently silent, well aware that the seal of a letter was no bond whatever against the reading of the letter by dozens before it could reach the owner's eye; at the utmost an innuendo, a carefully-veiled sarcasm, a word here and a phrase there, capable of being understood only by the one to whom the letter was addressed. From that hour, during the same length of time, no Northern or European paper, pamphlet, or book met his eye—every printed line which did meet his gaze being in furious advocacy of Secession. Except as their arms proved it, scarce a hint glimmered through the darkness of opinion and sentiment outside the blockade. By himself, even his friends entertaining similar views, confining those views mainly to their own bosoms, often speaking and acting in direct opposition to their own real opinions; thinking, alone and unaided, by himself and for himself, he arrived at those opinions to which he held as to his life itself, as to more than his life, the grasp upon the opinion being for him to relax his hold even upon life.

And it was better as it was. Only, never wonder at the clearness and energy with which Southern men hold to views which they have thus attained. No man values his gains so much as the man who has earned them with sweat and toil: the belle of the ball-room holds not to her pearls with the convulsive grasp of the diver who has brought them up from the depths and darkness of roaring waters.

"Lamum says, in his last *Star*, that I am a traitor to my native soil," the lawyer said, after a long pause. "I really wonder if I am," he continued gravely, weighing the proposition in his mind with his finger behind his ear. "What is my pay for being a traitor? It isn't office. Months ago Colonel Ret Roberts told me that any thing I would have he would see that I *did* have if I said so. It is a singular fact, but not one, not a single one of the leaders in Secession in or around Somerville but are this hour in receipt of salary in some form. Roberts is a Confederate States Senator; Lamum has the printing of the Confederate laws; Tim Lamum, Lamum's nephew, is a Commissary; Colonel Juggins has a contract for corn; Dr. Peel is making thousands by his contract for beef; even Captain Simmons is clerk, when sober, of the Confederate Court; and Bob Withers is a Tax Collector; Joe Staples is Receiver of Confiscated Property—not a man of them but has a fat office, or, if in the army, but is a Colonel or a Quartermaster. Bribe? On account of my opinions my business is ruined and nothing else to look to; my best friends will hardly speak to me. I hold to my original opinions upon Secession against every thing on earth. As to abandoning them—the fact is," added the lawyer, "as Paul, that brother of mine, says, either I am entirely and hopelessly deranged or the Secessionists are."

It is weeks ago now since it had occurred to Mrs. Sorel, knitting, spinning, weaving, making starch, soap, candles, hats, caps, shoes, and every thing else at her place near Somerville, that it would be a great favor to her if Mr. Arthur could occupy the vacant front-room on the left-hand side of the hall in her house. She has

nobody, now Frank is gone, but herself and Robby. It was a delicate matter to bring about under all the circumstances. But women are the best *diplomats* in the world. Talleyrands are they by sex; and Mrs. Sorel had her purpose accomplished and Mr. Arthur safely at home in her front-room almost before he knew it was a thing in view. The truth is, he himself and Mrs. Bowles felt the propriety of the step as well as Mrs. Sorel, and only Mrs. Sorel could have managed it so quietly and pleasantly. Robby Sorel is a sober little fellow, fond of his home and his book and his quiet sports, the very image of his mother; it will be a pleasure to Mr. Arthur to direct his studies, another reason for the arrangement.

The propriety of the step! Only you who read these lines, after painful experiences of your own, can understand all the bitterness of meaning herein implied. Not a day but Edward Arthur was made to feel and see it. The strong Secessionists outside of his church had long since removed all doubt from his mind in regard to their opinion of his position. Colonel Ret Roberts had never entered his church in his life. That, however, of course. Gentlemen of his stamp never go to church. People not members of the church never had, as a general rule, much desire to attend church—now they have none at all. If some preacher who is also Colonel of a regiment is to preach, or if Brother Barker is to give clear Scripture proof of God's cordial approval of Secession, if there is to be some Sabbatical variation of the one strain of glory to the South in the highest, on earth war to the knife, and eternal ill-will to the Yankees, men go to church to be that much more encouraged in a cause in which they are beginning to feel more and more the need of encouragement. But not to hear the old Gospel? To be told over again the old, old story of their being sinners and of Christ being a Saviour? No, Sir! heaven pales its ineffectual glories and hell its fires in contrast with the lurid flames of the war.

Where professing Christians have become so apathetic in regard to religion Mr. Arthur expects nothing of the rest of Somerville. Yet it touched him keenly that Sabbath morning when Mrs. Roberts made such a point of meeting him, when he visited her class in turn, and shook him with such special cordiality by the hand. He well knew what her eyes worn with weeping meant, and now filling again with tears as she turned from him and stooped as if to tie again the scarf around the throat of her little boy, looking up with bold brow and splendid eyes so like his father's. When immediately after Sabbath-school she left with her children, not waiting until service, her pastor knew as well as if she had told him of the letters from her husband at Richmond requiring her never again to hear her pastor preach; knew as by intuition all the oaths and abuse against him with which Colonel Ret Roberts sustained his own spotless reputation of patriotism. He had forbidden her entering even the church. At first she resisted so far as the Sabbath-school was concerned; but it was too painful, better stay at home altogether. How painful to her pastor was that vacant seat henceforth only you who occupied a like situation, and there are many of you, in those days can tell!

And with Mrs. Roberts there fell away many even of his warmest friends in days of old. "Mr. Arthur was a good man; they had known him too many years to doubt that; but now that he was a Union man!" Of what use to call upon them in their homes? Only political discussion, warm, perhaps heated. And so, what was left him but to pursue the even tenor of his way?

"Resign? No, Sir. The great body of the church are content that you should continue preaching to them the Gospel as of old," said Guy Brooks, whenever he consulted him upon the subject. "You can in conscience do only what you are doing. Let us be as quiet as possible; let us wait and hope." And most punctually and faithfully did Mr. Brooks, and Mr. Ferguson, and the many like them, attend at service, listening as if with double attention, greeting him on every meeting with triple cordiality.

"You can hardly imagine how painful it is to me," said Mr. Arthur to his friend the lawyer, one gloomy evening as they sat together in the study of the former. "Men whose esteem I hoped I had secured forever pass me without speaking. Even many who do deign to greet me do it coldly and harshly. Even those who I know do fully agree with me in my opinions, and who would not enter the church if I pursued any other course, seem afraid to be seen speaking with me on the street."

"And have not a syllable to say in your defense when you are cursed, as you most continually and fervently are, over Somerville," added the lawyer, who, in his own despondency, would have been a friend in keeping with those around Job as he sat on his dunghill.

And it was well it was so. Too dependent on others for his happiness, Edward Arthur was fast learning to stand firm in the consciousness of his own integrity—to dispense with all friendship besides in appreciating and enjoying, as he never before conceived of doing, the presence of Him who sticketh closer than a brother. Pale and thin and worn, he was only at a lesson which was to last him his life—the lesson itself was not to last forever, but its *results.*

"I declare," said the minister, after a pause, "the opinion that I am a traitor to my soil seems to be so universal an opinion, and is so unceasingly expressed, that I have at times almost a sense of shame as for actual guilt. However,

that only keeps me at a perpetual reconsideration of my original views. And, alas for me!" he added, with a sigh, "those views are only deepening and strengthening every hour."

"If you were only fixed as a minister my brother Paul lately heard of it would suit exactly. Paul was telling me of it when he was down from the Pines. It is a minister as conscientiously opposed to Secession," continued Guy Brooks, "as I am or as you are—oh, decided, strong, cast iron on that point. But he is an Episcopal minister, you see. His bishop has written out the prayers for him, and strong they are for Secession as language can make them, for the blessing of God upon the Confederate arms, for the speedy and total defeat of the Federals, and all that. Twice every Sunday that Union minister stands solemnly up and offers those prayers. Worse than that, the bishop has lately appointed a special prayer-meeting, with prayers to match, to be held two or three times during the week, for the success of the Confederate armies."

"And, true to his canonical obligations, he prays them?" asked Mr. Arthur. "Singular position for a worshiper of God to fill—deliberately, continually, kneeling before the Almighty, one set of petitions on his lips, exactly the reverse set of supplication in his— Never mind!" said the minister, interrupting himself, "it is none of my business."

"But it keeps all so straight and pleasant," reasoned the lawyer. "Every now and then the bishop fills his pulpit in his regular visitation; and he always preaches a sermon full and most decided for the Confederacy—Brother Barker over again, only in lawn and with manuscript. But no wonder; the Bishop's negroes have been running away dreadfully of late. His expenses for dogs alone in trailing—"

"My dear Mr. Brooks," interrupted the minister, "do let us speak of something else. A milder, more pious, more sincere man than this bishop before these troubles neither you nor I ever knew. The times have changed him, as they have changed so many of us. There was a time when there lived not a minister at the South who dreamed of alluding in the pulpit to political matters. And now! Would Paul, would Peter, would Heber, Simeon of Oxford, Wesley, Whitfield, Nettleton, Daniel Baker do it were they now alive? Would the Saviour do it did he to-day—if such a thing can be imagined—walk the soil of North or South? To me the *side* the minister happens to be on is a mere nothing in comparison; it is his abandoning the Gospel that is his deadly sin, whether he preach Secession or preach the Federal Union. I feel to-day as if I had somehow become suddenly obsolete—as if the whole world had passed by and left me in the rear—as if I was far behind the times."

"And you are," said the Kentuckian, "behind the times? Yes, Sir, eighteen hundred years! But Paul says it is the richest thing in the world—that Union minister standing up in the pulpit, as he has to do once every two or three months, reading long pastoral letters from the bishop to his diocese, political vindications of the South, you know, the poor fellow reading it with the necessary emphasis and inflection—queer position for a free man to occupy!"

Mrs. Warner did not think so, however, when Mr. Arthur called there next. Of all his pastoral duties none more unpleasant than a visit to Mrs. Warner—until, at least, the minister took a lesson from Dr. Warner, and sat and merely listened. Of late any one could tell, just by seeing Dr. Warner on the streets, that the gusts at home these days were more violent than ever. The Doctor's neckerchief was always to one side now, the long ends hanging out, and dreadfully frayed. There was a crushed appearance about his linen; a strip or so of the lining of his coat hanging loose to the breeze from wrists and skirts; more buttons off than of yore from waistcoat and pantaloons; a wild and disordered state of his hair, too, a good deal of it gone altogether, which caused him strongly to resemble a mariner just out of a terrible tempest. And, storm-tossed and weather-beaten as the Doctor was, he was only the fatter for it all. In fact, beaten upon as the Doctor was by the eternal gusts, he had got into the habit of retiring completely within himself these days, and his body had expanded itself to make room for him.

"What I regret, what Dr. Warner regrets, if he would only say so—only he is one of those men who never will speak out as he ought—is, that you do not pray for the Confederacy as you should, Mr. Arthur," said Mrs. Warner to that gentleman, sitting in her parlor this last time. "If you do not feel prepared to preach sermons for the Confederacy and in denouncement of the Yankees, like Brother Barker and ever so many ministers more, well, you needn't do it—that is, if you can feel it in your conscience not to do so; though I am sure our revolutionary forefathers took their swords and muskets even into the pulpits with them. But why don't you pray for the Confederacy—pray for it warm and strong? There's Brother Barker—and he a Northern man too!—he prays every Sunday, I'm told by Mrs. Staples, that the Almighty will defeat, destroy, annihilate the Federals; that He will entrap them in snares, deceive them in policy, decimate them with measles, small-pox, and yellow-fever; not leave enough of them alive next battle for the survivors to bury the rest! Pray? yes, and for their eternal damnation too. They are fiends, they are devils, they are worse than the worst savages; they richly deserve the agonies of the pit! Why, look at it, Dr. War—I mean Mr. Arthur! They are invading our soil, they are burning our cities and homes, they are slaughtering our men, women, and children; they want to set our negroes free; they are hiring them all the time to rise and cut our throats, and wash their black feet in our blood! Suppose those Yankees succeed; they make us their slaves, to hew wood for them—yes, drawers of wood and hewers of water to them long-legged, tallow-faced, peddling, cheating Yankees! I'd die first—die a thousand and a thousand times over! I've learned how to shoot with a revolver, and I'd kill them as soon's I would a snake. A snake?—yes, a genuine, Southern-born rattlesnake is more respectable than a Yankee! I've had our carving steel sharpened to a point for a dagger: if they come here I'll stab the first Yankee that enters that door! Come here? I tell you, Doctor—Mr. Arthur—I'll burn down my house with my own hands before they should have it. I'd make Doctor Warner shoot down every Hand he's got—and they all came to him through me—before he should let the Yankees get them. That's what Brother Barker says, Dr. Peel too, Lamum, and all. Did you read Colonel Ret Roberts's last speech? Only his wife is such a poor, downcast, silent sort of a woman! But you must pray for the Confederacy stronger, Mr. Arthur. Every body in Somerville is saying you are an Abolitionist. And just suppose they was to hang you some day; you may not know it, but people have threatened long ago to hang you. Ain't you afraid? You know they have hung ever so many." And oh, how much, much more!

And Mr. Arthur sat, holding, instinctively, hard to the arms of the large parlor rocking-chair in which he sat—sat while the upraised gates of the canal locks poured their tide upon him—sat waiting till the gush would flow itself out.

And so Mrs. Warner went on, taking snuff with her stick energetically all the time.

But the snuff which she so copiously dipped is not Mrs. Warner's only cause. Last night another of those wretched letters, written to some one in Somerville—nobody knows whom—from somebody near Corinth, has announced that Beauregard has actually evacuated Corinth, and is retreating South in confusion! But a day or so before there had been a well-authenticated report in Somerville that Beauregard had ordered his army to prepare for an immediate move upon the enemy. Lamum had filled the last *Star* with it; the thrilling address of Beauregard to his soldiers before the great victory that was to be; the enthusiasm of his army; the utter demoralization of the Federals; the whole regiments that had already been shot in the Union intrenchments for mutiny; the almost unanimous unwillingness of the troops, Yankees though they were, to fire another shot upon the Confederates.

"Hopeful as we have always been in regard to matters at Corinth," said Lamum, "we are now positively confident of a great and glorious victory, full particulars of which we will give in our next. Slowly but steadily has Beauregard been maturing his brilliant plans. All information from Corinth agrees that the thunder-bolt so long in forging has doubtless been launched long ere this. We congratulate all true Southern men in advance upon the great victory. As to the wretched traitors among us, let them know their day of doom is at hand!"—and vastly more to the same effect.

But one of those miserable letters has arrived, saying that all Beauregard's preparations were not for the rout of the Yankees, and for an immediate march either on St. Louis or Chicago, as Lamum and all others had so confidently predicted, but for a hasty retreat—a retreat under the fire of the Yankees—and leaving behind innumerable deserters. And, somehow, in ten hours after the arrival in Somerville of the letter, every body knows its contents—believes them too, no matter what they may say ; past experiences have taught Somerville pretty thoroughly by this time that, amidst the perpetual rumors afloat, the rumors favorable to the Confederacy are almost invariably false, and the rumors of an unfavorable nature as invariably true—or, at least, too near true to be comfortable. Those wretched letters! Nothing could have been done that was not done. A full list had been furnished the postmaster in Somerville of those persons whose letters must be looked into before it could be decided whether their owners are to have them or not. Faithfully did Mr. Smithers, the postmaster, obey these instructions, but with a painful sense all the time of deserving the Penitentiary therefor. Yet almost every week somebody or other in Somerville was receiving and spreading abroad the astounding contents of some letter which should never have been written ; or, if written, should never have been read except by an official ; or, if read, should never have been whispered to a living soul—never. These foolish letters! Written from the various seats of the war by people who had reference in writing only to the facts, and not at all to the influence of those facts ; unknown, unofficial people—in short, unsalaried people, who, in tenderly sustaining the Confederacy against every shock, had no most unusual income to nurse and protract thereby. The contrast, the steadily running contrast, between the printed information from the seats of the war and the undercurrent of private information from the same sources was amazing. Between the cross-streams of public and of private intelligence the air was always filled with all sorts of rumors as with the flying froth of conflicting waters.

Here is a bright summer morning upon which Dr. Warner casually drops in upon Guy Brooks in his office. "I would not have my name mentioned in it, you understand," Dr. Warner says, in a low, mysterious tone to the lawyer, "but there is a rumor afloat this morning that Richmond has been taken. Of course I do not vouch for the truth of it. Sam Peters was telling me this morning—let it go for what it is worth—that he overheard Lamum and Captain Simmons speaking earnestly together about Central America, tracing the route to it on a map open on Lamum's table. Of course we attach no importance to what Sam Peters says, but it really looks as if the leading Secessionists were contemplating a speedy flight, taken in connection with the other report from another source, you observe!" and the mild Doctor wipes his perspiring forehead, from which the hair is being blown away so in his high winds at home ; quite bold the Doctor is becoming.

"I pay no attention to such things," says Guy Brooks, with brightening eyes, "but it may seem somewhat of a coincidence, the Secessionists—the leaders I mean—have had a remarkably depressed look about them of late. Pshaw! it's all nonsense ; but I suppose you have heard about some lady or other suddenly coming in upon Mrs. Colonel Ret Roberts and finding her bathed in tears with her children around her. She had just heard, the interpretation is, from Roberts at Richmond that the game was over, you see." But the lawyer is ashamed of himself as he says it.

"We are kept so completely in the dark—taking all these things together. Ah, well, we shall know sooner or later," says Dr. Warner, shaking his head as he considers it all over.

"And so Dr. Ginnis is running off with some of your patients?" inquires the lawyer at last.

"Such a loud Secessionist, you know. I can not help it. It is impossible for a man to think and feel except as he *does* think and feel; and I make such a poor hypocrite do the best at it I can," says poor Dr. Warner.

That very day the Scotchman was telling his pastor of this same rumor. "It is all over Somerville ; people really believe it," said Mr. Fergnson. And he was right. Only wish to believe any thing, it is the easiest thing to do so. "It *may* be true, you know," said the Scotchman, before he had done referring to it ; always scoffing at all news he did *not* wish to believe, too.

"Do you see this port-folio?" asked the Scotchman of a ponderous scrap-book lying open upon his table, with covers of blue pasteboard a yard square ; half a foot thick the volume is. And he turned lovingly over the irregular leaves—pamphlets, speeches, sermons, placards, hand-bills, written notices of all shapes and sizes, newspapers, too, from a yard across down, toward the later dates, to sheets of eight inches, and of all the colors of the rainbow, according as wrapping paper was being resorted to under stress of the

MR. FERGUSON AND HIS RECORD.

blockade. "Now, here is a complete set of the news and the rumors since the beginning of this awful delusion," continued Mr. Ferguson, turning over his collection with the pride of a virtuoso. "You see, I own lands in the State. My business used to be selling those lands. I have none to sell now, not a rood, for paper-money, you understand. So I have a good deal of leisure to spend on this collection. When a rumor is afloat unprinted, I write it out myself and paste it in ;" and he turned in succession to several pages of his own writing carefully interleaved with the rest of the ponderous volume: his best hand it was in, and with date in full to each rumor, and plenty of capitals and marks of exclamation.

"And each one of those items was in its turn as a dose of ipecac to those who did not want to believe it, and as—"

"A glass of usquebaugh to those who did," said Mr. Ferguson, completing the sentence for his pastor. "Now I have even classified these items for a regular index, here in this blank book, to the volume," continued the Scotchman, laying his hand upon it. "I have almost nothing else to do; and I have become interested in it as a systematic study of this war, and of human nature during it. Would you like to hear my classification ?"

The Scotchman had a grizzled beard covering all his mouth, and a dry, didactic way of speaking, with his chin fixed steadily between his shirt collar, and in crisp sentences. He walked with a stiff, short step, never turning his head right or left, favoring his most intimate friends with the slightest possible motion of his head, strictly up and down on its vertebræ, never a shade to one side or the other, when he met them. It had often occurred to Mr. Arthur that Mr. Ferguson, if himself classified, would have been labeled of the *Linnæus* species—a botanist caring for flowers only for analysis, without the slightest reference to their hue or fragrance.

"From the beginning of this delusion," continued he, with the dry precision of a lecturer, "all of the innumerable rumors I have classified as follows:

"*First*—The Confederacy is on the verge of recognition by Europe. I have put this first, as being the most frequently repeated and the most steadily believed.

"*Second*—The North is bankrupt, and can not carry on the war beyond the fifteenth of next month at the farthest. This was a more frequent rumor at first than it has been of late.

"*Third*—A great revolution favorable to the South is impending at the North.

"*Fourth*—France, England, and Spain have determined upon an instant armed intervention unless their terms are agreed upon by the end of this month ; and the papers all contain these terms, drawn fully out, article by article, in diplomatic style.

"*Fifth*—An impending 'mutiny of the entire Federal army against the accursed scheme into which they have been hounded.'

"*Sixth*—Great and glorious victories, with the slaughter of half of the Federal army and the capture of the other half, stores, arms, gun-boats beyond calculation. To the same head belongs the repeated capture of Washington city.

"*Last*—The arrival, 'at last,' of the Confederate fleet, iron-plated, fully armed, from Europe, and the impending destruction of the Federal navy. Such are the classes of rumors, one or more of which are continually afloat. It matters not how often a rumor has been abroad and disproved before ; like the balls of the juggler, one or more of them is continually in the air none the less.

"I mention no such small matter as the death —now by pneumonia, now by wounds, now by the hand of some brave Southerner penetrating into his camp for the purpose—of, in turn, every leading officer of the Federal army. Perpetually are they being killed and buried. If they are perpetually rising again from the dead it makes no difference. If they are proved to be alive to-day they are certain to die of disease or to be killed again in the papers to-morrow. There is not a single one of their deaths that I have not down here," said the Scotchman with pride.

"It is amazing how readily the report of yesterday is dropped," said Mr. Arthur. "It was eagerly heard and believed yesterday, yet its disproval to-day hardly excites a remark. It puzzles me."

"Not at all," said the countryman of Reid and Brown, in his sententious manner. "There is a reason for every operation of the human mind. Yesterday's news is forgotten because to-day's news is so much more glorious ; then, yesterday's rumor was false, it seems, but that of to-day is certainly true. Besides, the hearty *wish* it may be true is so unfailing. One thing that interests me in this continual stream of news is my studying therein the working of the leaders of this most disastrous delusion. Like the paid pyrotechnist of a Fourth of July night, they see to it, out of sight themselves, that some rocket is always in the air to keep the gaping populace amused. They have such a supply to select from," said Mr. Ferguson, laying his broad and hairy palm on his foolscap classification. "It is but to dash off the lie best suited to the hour in a few rapid lines, send it to the next paper, and in a few days it is read and believed over the whole South. If you had studied this collection as I have, Sir, you would find that just when all the appearances are at their darkest for Secession, then, and exactly then, the largest and most splendid lie is whizzing overhead. It comes down a stick, to be sure ; but it answers the purpose of the moment, and, on the next occasion, up goes another."

Mr. Arthur did not care to say so to his friend —he was too weary of strife for that ; but he knew it was all only a whimsey of notionate Mr. Ferguson. Like multitudes of other men, the Scotchman ascribed to the politicians far more than was at all due them ; for far more than they ever even dreamed of doing they had all the curse or all the credit, as the case was, thought the minister. They lashed the placid ocean into tempest, he said to himself, as he rode slowly home to Mrs. Sorel's. What long-continued and superhuman exertion it required! But now that they have fairly wrought it into commotion, the waters howl and heave and sparkle with all phosphorescent fires by the force of their own fury.

Arrived at home and gone to bed, Mars, not Morpheus, presided over his slumbers. Slumber? During the first hour or so after lying down he tossed as on the wild waves, wrecked, and the bottom of ocean miles beneath his struggling feet. The waters around him are thick with men and women clutching at and hurled off from each other, the drowning and the drowned. How red they are, too, the waters slimy and clinging, so that he can hardly even struggle in them. How many upturned faces rise and sink there! Can that bold brow with the large-set eyes be Colonel Ret Roberts? The thin face of the postage stamps jostled cheek by jowl with Bob Withers's ruby countenance and the pale cheek of Lamum? Horror! There floats by him a fair form, every lock of whose streaming hair is dearer to him than life, thrust aside by the sudden countenance of Colonel Juggins, giving place to that of Mrs. Juggins; and amidst all the gurgling, gasping terror the dreamer hears as from her lips, "What I say is, why can't they stay where they come from? We warn't interruptin' them that I know of," and the sleeper is awakened by his own laughter.

"Look here, my friend," he reasons with himself, "along this way madness lies." He is right there. Only give up to the thoughts pressing like the Eumenides after you just now, and you are in the highway to whitened hair and brow prematurely wrinkled, and insanity and suicide. Millions at the South are on that path now, suffering along all its degrees. Sleeplessness? For the first year of the war men could not sleep o' nights for the horror of the thing. However, as nature creates, they say, a sort of integument, a callous membrane about a bullet lodged in the body, so there grew a kind of covering, a callous accustomedness about the horror of the hour in the hearts of men, enabling them to endure it.

With solemn resolve to go to sleep, Mr. Arthur, after pacing the floor an hour or so in forming it, lay down again. He is just getting into a comfortable doze when the thought smites him up and out of bed again: "Suppose at the North Christian men and Christian ministers are as frantic, rabid, raving, unchristian, bloodthirsty for the Right as Brother Barker and his kind are here for the Wrong?" And he travels miles up and down his room upon that track of thought. About his three-hundredth turn at the wardrobe at the end opposite his bed the idea smites him full abreast, and halts him there for long minutes: and isn't this just the process, you poor creature, by which the whole land, North and South, is being prepared, through the deep humiliation of the church, for the greatest religious reaction the land and the world has ever known—to follow, can't you see it, on the heels of the war?

And the Rev. Edward Arthur goes again to bed upon this opiate, and sleeps sweetly until morning.

IN LOVE.

## CHAPTER XII.

WE really can not and will not permit our attention to be drawn off one moment longer from Dr. Peel; he looms altogether too conspicuously upon the Somerville horizon for that. It is impossible longer to ignore the deep and widespread impression he has made upon that intelligent community.

"Describe him to you?" says fair Anne Wright to an old schoolmate, with whom she is conversing, on a visit from an adjoining county. "I can not, Laura; you must see him for yourself, child."

"Oh, well, you can at least give me some hint," urges her curious friend—naturally curious from the perpetual reference she hears made to him beneath that roof. "Is he a big man?"

"At least not a little man," laughs Anne. "Yes, I do really believe he is the largest—I mean the grandest man I ever saw in all my life.

Such a noble chest! His forehead, too, high and prominent. And then his eyes—the finest you ever saw—eyebrows, and hair all as black? That isn't the name for it. But his eyes—the most splendid you ever saw—look as if they were actually alive!"

"Why, so they are if the man isn't dead," says her more prosaic friend.

"Oh, nonsense, Laura! I told you I could not begin to describe him," says Anne, who is a fragile and lovely blonde. "There is a sort of soft fire in them, except when he gets roused; then how they glow and flash and scorch! And then he has such a voice, child; I do know it is the sweetest and deepest. And pa tells me he makes speeches in Somerville the most powerful—makes the people laugh one moment, and cry like children the next. And when he denounces the Yankees or the Union people! Why pa says his voice, when he lifts it, can be heard for miles. Pa says he is equal to Colonel Ret Roberts, if not superior. And then he dresses so splendidly! The finest broadcloth, the whitest and finest linen, the richest vests. I do think his neck-ties—figured silk scarfs, you know—are the gayest and the brightest. One notices such things so much more these days when we are all wearing our old things on account of the blockade—this old calico, for instance. And his jewelry, too! Pa objects to that in Dr. Peel. And I didn't like it in gentlemen either till I saw Dr. Peel. He wears several rings on his fingers, large ones, one or two diamonds among them. Then his heavy gold watch—I have noticed it when he takes it out to see if he ought not to be going—it is so massive and rich, with such a heavy gold chain to it all across his bosom. But you ought only to see his breast-pins, Laura! A different one every time, at least, he has called out here—the richest! What is most uncommon about him is the quantity of perfumes he uses. Pa almost swears about it. I don't object to it. Why, Laura, in his appearance, bearing, and all, his olive complexion, too, he looks like a Spaniard—a Spanish prince, so large and sumptuous and magnificent in comparison with us plain people."

"Why, the man must be rich," says Laura.

"Everybody says so. He always has plenty of money, and he pays it out as freely as a king. The ladies there in Somerville have only to go to him to get any amount they want, provided only it is for the war in any way. Not our miserable, ragged, dirty paper-money; great round twenty-dollar gold pieces; and, you know, they are worth ever so much more than paper. And as to his politics, pa says he never saw—"

"Give for the war? He must be a good Southern man," says Laura, threading her needle afresh.

"I was just going to say, pa says he is most determined, active, liberal, confident; 'the most splendid specimen of a Southern gentleman I ever saw,' pa said, after Dr. Peel left here last Saturday. And that's just what we like him most for," continues Anne Wright, with enthusiasm. "You know what a hot Southern man pa is; but Dr. Peel is ahead of him, of anybody I know. I've always been a good Secessionist, which is more than you can say, Laura. Now don't be offended, dear, but it's actually awful to hear Dr. Peel talk about the Yankees—the most despicable people, he says, in every sense of the word; yes, and proves it in a thousand ways. And then to hear him speak about the South, its extent, resources, glorious victories, future prospects, how essential its success is to the whole world—I can't remember it all, but it is like reading an oration."

"Yes; but why isn't he off for the war?" asks Laura, whose people, by-the-by, have been dreadfully suspected of entertaining Union sentiments. Plague take them! as Mrs. Warner is steadily remarking, you find them here and there and everywhere.

"You silly child, he is in the war. Not a private soldier to dig in the trenches, or to be shot down like common people. If you were to see him once you would see how absurd that would be. No, Dr. Peel fills some high position or other. He is often away from Somerville attending to military business; in correspondence continually with President Davis, General Beauregard, and the rest. He brought a superb sword all the way out here to show me, one that Davis had presented him with, gold scabbard, silver hilt, with a great red gem of some sort in the end, silver chains to it, and all. Pa pressed him to tell us more particularly about his position—it was only last Saturday. You ought to have seen his manner as he said it—'It would give me much pleasure, Major Wright, to inform you. I flatter myself it would interest and astonish you if I was only at liberty to tell. A gentleman of your intelligence, however, will understand that there are elevated and difficult duties—duties which require oaths of secrecy.' And then he drew himself up with such dignity I couldn't help thinking what a splendid Confederate senator he would make. Don't whisper it, Laura; but he has already told us that he has some promise, when the war is over, of the mission—you know we will have embassadors like other nations—to Austria or Russia or Spain, he was not assured yet which. But, my dear," ran on Anne, generally the quietest of girls, enraptured with her theme, "you ought only to hear him tell about being taken for a Federal spy there in Somerville, oh, months ago. He told us about a self-appointed Committee visiting his rooms at Staples's Hotel to examine. The idea was so funny, and then the way he took off Bob Withers and that fussy old Dr. Ginnis, pa like to have died laughing. And such splendid teeth, speaking of laughing, you know, he has! He had met with ever so many singular adventures in his life, he told us, but that being taken for a Federal spy he did think was the richest of all. He sat down on the spot, he told us, and wrote to the President a full account of it, just to give Davis, he said, one good laugh if he never has another. How they tumbled over his things, peeped into his boots, and all—pompous Captain Simmons and the rest. But he was glad to see it, he said; it showed the people were active and wide awake for the Confederacy."

"Why, he must have been out here quite often?" said the friend, with a smiling malice in her eye.

"No, not very often; that is, not very, very often," replies Anne, very red and then quite pale. "But we won't talk about him any more; I'm tired of it. How do you fix these gathers, Laura? you are such a wise body, and I am such a poor little good-for-nothing."

"Oh, you artful little goose," broke in her friend, "if you ain't in love with the man my name isn't Laura Rice!"

"What nonsense, Laura!" says poor translucent Anne, blushing very red, and then turning so pale it was unpleasant to see. "I never thought of such a thing. Me? I would as soon think of the Emperor of Russia. If you only knew him, what a great, magnificent—"

"Nonsense yourself, Anne, don't I know," says her visitor, who, being quite plain, was that much the more strong-minded and sensible. "If you don't know you ought to know that just such fair-haired, blue-eyed, nice little bodies as Anne Wright are the very ones your big Spanish princes are most apt to fall in love with."

"You ought to be ashamed of yourself, Laura," said her friend, flushing with pleasure one moment, almost ready to cry the next. "You ever whisper such a thing, and see if I don't tell every body you are Union. Dr. Peel may have shown me a good deal of attention at balls in Somerville, concerts, tableaux. He may have been out to talk with pa about the war. I never once thought, I never dared to think of such a thing. If I was only a strong, beautiful girl, high-spirited, like Alice Bowles say—but poor little me? Why, he could put me in his vest pocket almost. Me, child! You think yourself mighty wise, but you never were more mistaken in all your life." And Anne vows she will never mention Dr. Peel's name to any body again as long as she lives, rattles off upon other topics for a while, and then becomes so silent as to be but poor company for her friend.

And Dr. Peel is a magnificent-looking man, no denying that fact. As Anne Wright said to her friend, he did look "the very hero of a novel, dear; Byron's Corsair, and all that. And sings? You only ought to hear him sing!"

He looks all this the more strikingly these last

few days from contrast with Lieutenant Ravenel. The Lieutenant is a late arrival in Somerville. He and Dr. Peel, to whom he has brought letters of introduction from South Carolina, are inseparable. Any one can see what particular pleasure the Doctor takes in introducing him to all his friends—that is to say, all the gentlemen, not Union men, to be met on the streets. "A genuine bit of Charleston aristocracy, Huguenot blood, distinguished for his gallantry in the war; on important business from the War Department, though what that business is I can not get out of him," says Dr. Peel aside to his friends in billiard saloon and street corner.

If you observe them in Mrs. Bowles's parlor on a visit they make that lady, Dr. Peel looms up peculiarly large in comparison with the small, almost girlish, size and form of the Lieutenant. The Doctor is quite swarthy, while the Lieutenant is exceedingly fair and rosy, no perceptible beard yet—too young for that. A handsome fellow, too, in his way, in his neatly-fitting gray suit, the sleeves richly embroidered; the military cap sitting jauntily on the side of his head is off now, of course, and you can not fail to admire his light and curly locks. "My dear mother fitted me out before I left Charleston with her own hands," he told Mrs. Bowles in return for some compliment upon his attire. Such frank, open, cordial manners! Fun, too, always lurking in the corners of his dark eye and chiseled mouth, breaking out continually in ready laughter, artless and unrestrained as a child, over dimpled chin and cheek. Every body likes the Lieutenant on the spot warmly; you can not help it.

"By George! and those slight-built, pretty-faced fellows, girlish as they look, are the very ones to fight, you'll bet; perfect devils incarnate when a battery has got to be stormed. That's what the English people found out about their London dandies there in that war with the Russians," says Bob Withers in reply to Dr. Ginnis's sneers at Lieutenant Ravenel.

For a wonder Dr. Peel sits comparatively silent in Mrs. Bowles's parlor this evening, and lets the Lieutenant do all the talking. And Mrs. Bowles is in a flutter of delight over a visit from one direct from Charleston, and has a thousand questions to ask about Charleston and South Carolina. Lieutenant Ravenel knows almost every body and every thing there. She has vague recollections of having often seen the Lieutenant himself when a little boy playing on the Battery there at Charleston. His family she knows, of course, ever since she knew any thing. And the Lieutenant has a world to say about Rutledge Bowles, with whom he has been intimately associated, and whom he likes almost as much as his mother.

"Only, you know, Madam, there is no merit in that. Every one admires and likes Rutledge

Bowles. How much he is growing to resemble his father in the portrait—of the Major, I presume it is, Madam?" says the Lieutenant, with a wave of the hand toward the old hero in his frame overhead.

"I am pleased to know it," says little Mrs. Bowles, all the mother kindling through her refined and thoroughly lady-like manner. "Did Rutledge Bowles send his photograph by you?" she adds, eagerly.

"He would have done so, Madam, for I heard him speak of desiring to send it only the week I left. The fact is, I was not intending then to leave Charleston, much less come so far south as this. Intending? Upon my word, Madam, I had no such intention. Just ten minutes before the Augusta train ran out of Charleston my Colonel caught me on the street with dispatches in his hand and a sealed note of instruction for myself. 'You will hardly have time to throw your linen in a valise and run,' he said. I did run, hard as I could tear, Madam; barely in time to catch the train as it ran out of the dépôt. You remember it is a good distance from the Post-office, where I was when the Colonel caught me. At the rate they hurry us a pair of fresh feet ought to be served out every few hours as a regular ration, Madam—a relay of wings, or something of the sort." The Lieutenant is so perfectly a gentleman, at the same time so overflowing with life and fun that he keeps Dr. Peel and Mrs. Bowles and Alice laughing, the first named especially, all the evening.

"I could wish Rutledge Bowles was a little more lenient toward the faults of his subor—I mean his superior officers, as they are called in military language," says Mrs. Bowles, not without pride. "He seems to be always in some difficulty with them. Yet Rutledge Bowles has, though young, a good deal of his father's, the Major's, accuracy and energy of character too. He lately sent me full drawings of all the defenses of Charleston, with an exact statement of the number and disposition at the time of our troops there."

"Was that not rather—excuse me—against rules?" began the Lieutenant, politely.

"So he said in his letter. 'But since you have written for them, mother,' he wrote, 'I will risk it.' It was a foolish curiosity I had, not to see the drawings and that, but to see how well he could do it. Friends here also would like to see what Rutledge Bowles could do. Still I did not wish him to come unnecessarily in conflict with his—superiors."

"Oh, we all know Rutledge Bowles," says Lieutenant Ravenel, gayly. "For my part I do assure you, Madam, I have talked with him upon that very point often. You see, Madam, we were students together at—tut, pshaw, was it at the Citadel or—"

"Columbia," suggests Mrs. Bowles.

"What am I thinking about? Columbia. I prepared for Columbia at the Citadel. Columbia, of course. I could take the liberty with him, you observe; it is not every one who can. If Rutledge Bowles has a fault it is pride. But I could do nothing with him. Ah, before it escapes my mind, those drawings you spoke of, would you be so kind? And all the papers, in fact, if it is not too much trouble?"

It is no trouble at all. Mrs. Bowles knows exactly where the package is. Lieutenant Ravenel glances rapidly over them, but is so pleased with them that he begs permission to take them with him, will return them in the morning—they are well worth an hour's study. Mrs. Bowles consents, of course. The dear lady glows up to the smooth parting of her silvered hair with pleasure. A visitor, and a Ravenel too, from Charleston!—it is as an angel stooping from Eden to banished and pining Eve. What with South Carolina, the war, and Rutledge Bowles, the evening passes rapidly by. The gentlemen consent to remain till tea, Alice entertaining them while her mother absents herself, making some special arrangements connected therewith.

Neither of the ladies have any admiration for Dr. Peel's sumptuous attire, jewelry, and essences. But on account of the Lieutenant, who remembers Alice, often met her with her nurse in King Street—her mother also, only it is so long ago, at Hibernian Hall he thinks it was—they can not refuse to pay the Doctor all due attention. Yet the Lieutenant is the soul of the evening, at tea-table, and after tea till near midnight. The war is, of course, second as a topic only to Rutledge Bowles, and Lieutenant Ravenel regards the attempt of the North to prevent our independence as the choicest of jokes. He describes their cowardice, how they scamper and squall for quarter in every battle till Alice can not help laughing heartily, while Mrs. Bowles's cheeks are wet with tears of mirth. "Not that I do not from my inmost heart pity them," says good Mrs. Bowles. "The madness, the frantic folly of their miserable leaders it is excites my anger. Poor creatures, the Federal privates—mechanics, I presume, most of them, ignorant persons. Yet they, too, have wives and children to sigh and weep for them."

The gay Lieutenant is grave in an instant. In low, soft tones he recounts sad, sad incidents which, he is not ashamed of it, have moved him to tears even in battle. "Poor, poor creatures! I agree in your Christian sentiment, Madam; yes, we can well afford to pity." But the Lieutenant is familiar with the plans of the Confederate generals, narrates skirmishes of which Mrs. Bowles and Alice have not as yet had opportunity to read. Nor, owing to their retired situation, have they had such full particulars of the noble fleet being built in Confederate ports and in Europe for the Confederacy. The

Lieutenant tells them, too, of certain negotiations then in progress with foreign powers; imparts the fullest information in reference to the great revolution, already arranged and soon to break out at the North for the overthrow "of Lincoln and—pardon me, ladies—his hellish crew." A vast deal more to the same effect, all in a manner so sparkling yet deferential as to bring back to Mrs. Bowles those happy, happy days in dear old Charleston.

"Really you should see the editor of our paper—a Northern man, I regret to say," begins Mrs. Bowles.

"Lieutenant Ravenel has already seen Lammm, Madam," interposes Dr. Peel. "We spent yesterday evening with him. The *Star* will contain in its next issue more really interesting information than any number since the war began."

And it did contain just that. Somerville read it with keen pleasure or the reverse, according to the political tendencies of the render. Mr. Ferguson regarded that number of the *Star* as one of the most valuable in his whole collection. The visit of Lieutenant Ravenel was an event in Somerville. Somerville, in fact, remembers it distinctly to this hour.

But it waxes late. The gentlemen really can not consent to trespass upon the ladies any longer. "Only one piece of music more before we leave," says the lively Lieutenant, who has been beside Alice at the piano turning over the leaves for her, even joining in with a well-trained voice, as she played and sang this and that for the last hour.

"Well, if I can," says Alice, with a smile, her fingers on the keys.

"Hail Columbia. Only for the fun of the thing, you know," says her visitor, laughing.

"You must excuse me." Alice has a taste for fun, but finds no amusement in doing just that, she does not ask herself why.

"Well, then, the Star-Spangled Banner."

"Excuse me, Lieutenant Ravenel," quite decidedly, too.

"Pardon me, only Yankee Doodle, just for the amusement of it," pleads the Confederate officer, with hands clasped in comic supplication. "You play so well."

"I can be guilty of no such—such mockery," says Alice, surprised at her own depth of feeling and energy of refusal. With heightened roses, too.

"I really am amazed at you, Alice," says her mother, as Alice rises from the instrument. "A willful daughter, much like Rutledge Bowles in character, Lieutenant Ravenel. But since you have given us so pleasant an evening, Sir. Of course I respect your aversion to the North, Alice, but then— If you will excuse my poor practice, Lieutenant Ravenel—"

And Mrs. Bowles, who is a fine player, sits down to the piano. She does not exactly see the joke, but it is the request of a guest, a favored guest. Yankee Doodle first. She had almost forgotten it. The servants in the kitchen positively refuse to believe their ears. The Star-Spangled Banner next. Charles and Sally, in the hall by this time, listening, paralyzed with vague ideas that the Yankees have arrived at last. The Lieutenant beside her strikes in with the words after the first line. Mrs. Bowles glances up nervously, to meet the laughing eyes of her guest. What a willful, handsome, foolish fellow!

"Now Hail Columbia, if you will pardon my folly," pleads the volatile officer. It is a severe strain upon her good-breeding, but she has no time to refuse. This time Dr. Peel is on her other side, his deep voice swelling that martial melody. It is better sung than played, but splendidly done as it is. Alice is turning over a book on the other side of the room, the tears, to her own astonishment, trickling fast and free down her cheeks. Her emotions? The variation of magnetism not more beyond her analysis or control.

"It will be such a joke to tell Rutledge when I see him," says the laughing soldier. Mrs. Bowles is three-fourths ruffled with him, but there is a fascination about the young Carolinian which she can not resist. With the last note of the magnificent anthem the gentlemen take their hats to leave, apologizing for their long stay. And Mrs. Bowles has to apologize also for Alice, who has left the room.

"I fear I have offended Miss Alice by my whimsey in regard to that old music," says the handsome Lieutenant, seriously, and with penitent face. I am heartily ashamed of myself. I fear levity is my besetting sin. Apologize for me, Madam; she must forgive me on the ground of our being both Carolinians. And may I beg," adds the Lieutenant, coming back into the parlor after taking his leave, "that you will not allude to my visit in writing to Rutledge? There are reasons—in fact, I am here on secret service." His peculiar position prevents the officer from saying more. No one has finer tact than Mrs. Bowles. She anticipates him, understands the whole, and hastens to express again her gratification at having met him. And so they part.

"I do solemnly declare, Fairfax, you are a trump! But look here, man, you carried it too far to-night, entirely too far." It is Dr. Peel who makes this remark over and over when they are safely in the streets, and once again with new emphasis when they are seated in the Doctor's room at Staples's Hotel.

His companion pays no attention to him until he has completed an accurate copy of the papers from Rutledge Bowles loaned him by Mrs. Bowles.

G

"HAIL COLUMBIA!"

"Beautifully done," says Dr. Peel, after examining the work. "What a draughtsman you are, Fairfax! And the list, too; useful documents."

"Worth coming all the way to this little Somerville to get. You see we can buy any number of papers of the sort on the spot. But those are made to sell, perhaps to deceive; this we know to be correct. My conscience hurts me awfully, however," adds the Lieutenant.

"What a perfect lady she is; and so unsuspecting! But that music was grand, wasn't it? That is the food I was raised on; very little else I have heard off and on these last two years; but I never enjoyed it in my life as I did to-night. By Jove! here in the heart of the rebellion, and the sincerest of rebels playing the accompaniment! Did you ever know such a joke?" And the young man stretched out his legs under the table, threw himself back in the chair, and laughed as only the young and happy can laugh.

However, for her life Mrs. Bowles could not see the point of the fun next morning. She felt condemned, guilty. And then passers-by having stopped, horror-stricken, to hear the music, poor Mrs. Bowles had to explain and explain the matter for weeks after. Most annoying. But when Mrs. Warner, on a special visit, with upraised eyebrows, "really could not believe it, Madam. Hail Columbia, Yankee Doodle, Red, White, and Blue, Star-Spangled Banner—all those miserable old songs, and over and over again, I'm told. Why, Mrs. Bowles, you must have heard how Alonzo Wright, only a month ago, when down the country for cotton, shot a man dead, dead on the spot, for only whistling Yankee Doodle thoughtless-like, for the man was a good Secessionist!"

"Mrs. Warner," interrupts Mrs. Bowles, very quietly, but with all South Carolina in her manner, "my daughter Alice and myself and our guests play and sing, and do now, and at all times, exactly as we see fit. You will pardon me, Madam; but how did you say your little Maria is? Well, I trust."

So that nothing is left Mrs. Warner but "Good-morning, Madam!" and to leave.

"But, Fairfax, I'm in earnest about it, in the interest of Government as much as in your own, do you not risk too much?" urges Dr. Peel there in his room upon his young friend.

It is amazing how changed is the Doctor's manner with the Lieutenant from what it is with Somerville; not an oath hardly, gentle as a lamb, not the least bit of a bully or a blackguard. Sumptuous Dr. Peel is a totally different Dr. Peel in every sense from what Somerville has known him. And he wears a business air, too, with the Lieutenant, his natural self evidently.

"Never mind about me, Peel, old fellow!" says his friend, gayly. "The only way to cross rotten ice is to skate your swiftest. You have your way out on this business; I must follow my way. I wonder if I have not had some experience by this time? My way of doing matters has carried me over many and many an ugly place—will carry me over many an uglier yet. The fact is, Peel, I wonder—by-the-by, what your name really is. Never mind about that. The fact is, I'm a man walking the edge of a precipice: over a scantling laid across an abyss: if I stop to look down I'm lost. But I'll be shot if it isn't fun alive, the whole thing. I always had a genius for fun—about the only truth I told Mrs. Bowles to-night. There, at the University of Virginia, we fellows used to think we knew what fun was. I rather flatter myself I was a kind of ringleader. Smoking the Fresh; deviling the Sophs; putting pigs up the belfry, tied to the rope, so as to ring at it all night, you observe; putting tubs of cold water over the tutors' doors, so as to benefit their debilitated systems with a bath as they came out; dyeing the professors' dogs and horses a lovely crimson—things of that sort. But this is a joke ahead of them, I rather think. As to the danger, that is the spice of the whole thing."

"And you never were in Charleston?"

"Not before the war; often since—on business, you observe, confidential and excessively private. Carolina, with a plague on the heroic little humbug, except that, I was never in it in my life. Thank you for your hints about Rutledge Bowles, only his mother gave me enough during the first five minutes. I was intimate with him, wasn't I? Splendid fellow, I have no doubt."

"His proud beauty of a sister was too much for you," began Dr. Peel.

"Glorious girl, isn't she?" broke in the Lieutenant, with enthusiasm. "And I'll tell you something, Sir, will astonish even you. That girl is Union, Sir—Union true blue—Stars and Stripes to the centre! You needn't whistle. I ought to know the signs by this time. While you were telling the mother that preposterous story about your acquaintance with Calhoun, I gave the fair damsel a full trial, just to be certain of it. I couldn't get her faintest assent to a syllable I said in glorification of the Confederacy, not even the assent of her eyes, steady arrière pensée there the whole time. It was to tease her as much as any thing I asked her to play those pieces. A Secessionist might do that, refuse as she did, probably would, but the manner of refusing! And with her brother and mother so dyed in the wool. Glorious girl! I could have hugged her on the spot for her principles. But, as to that, how any woman can stand Jeff Davis, Secession, war for slavery, and all, is more than I can understand—blind feeling."

"Exactly as a woman clings to a red-faced, foul-breathed, roaring, drunken husband, who curses and beats her and the children. It is my husband, you see. My country! The delusion lies just there," says Dr. Peel, with a sneer.

"Oh, as to that, it is amazing how many people I find all over the South who continue to know what their country is, cling to it, too, with all their souls. By Jove, Sir, I honor them," says the young officer—"honor them more than words can utter. They are the very best people, too, of the places where they live. I fall in love with them on sight, especially when they are females. I often meet with wrinkled, toothless old ladies. You see they know people can not well hang them, so they can speak out to their heart's content. And they do. I have heard them abuse Secession even to my satisfaction. I could have taken the dear old things in my arms. Whenever I chance with Union people off by themselves you can not tell what a severe temptation it is to tell them a little something. I can play upon them as a girl can on a piano; tell them tremendous tales of the success of the Confederacy just to see how melancholy they get, their faces growing as long as your arm in spite of themselves. And to see how they brighten up when I slip in a little good news the other way! They do not believe a word of it, of course; or shake their heads in such a melancholy way, their eyes sparkling. How they will rejoice when the old flag flies over them again, and all the air blows Hail Columbia! True as steel they are; but if one could only tell them how certain the thing is! However, all this isn't business, and I'm off in the morning. People might get *too* fond of me, you know. Lieutenant Ravenel, Confederate States service—good!"

"Well, I am ready," said Dr. Peel, producing a package of papers from his bosom. "Not much more in addition to what we have attended to already. But, first, there's a receipt for that last thousand you brought; much obliged to Uncle Sam and secret service. Now then. Here's—let me see—ah, yes, a statement of the rebel forces and so forth in my district, present and prospective sustenance, and so on. Tell them they may rely on it; I got the statement from head-quarters myself. You do things your way, Lieutenant Ravenel of South Carolina, but if you fancy there is a genuine Southerner of higher standing than Dr. Peel in all this district you are mistaken. By-the-by, here's a private letter. Do me the favor to leave it at its address in New York. It is exchange on London for five thousand pounds to my credit, you know; they'll understand it. A good joke, since you like jokes so well, in connection. That represents a cargo of cotton safe over the water in payment by the Confederacy for I have forgotten how many pounds of powder—"

"Permit me, Dr. Peel," interrupts his guest, with a total change of manner. "Do I understand—"

"I am astonished at you, Fairfax. Don't you *see* that the article was manufactured for this express purpose? We found it would throw up the ball in the metre about, say, three degrees. The standard in our service is rather over that, I think. You ought to have seen the proud satisfaction with which it was received. I volunteered to see to the stowing of it away. Necessary to take special precautions lest it should explode. Explode! And there it is at the Arsenal this instant, all ready in case of need."

"But," began the delighted Lieutenant, "how in the mischief—?"

"Oh, I had specimens plenty for trial, Dupont's best. The Governor shook me by the hand warmly. 'Splendid article,' he said. 'You see I'm an old soldier, and ought to know,' says he. 'We are under obligations to you, Doctor.' I rather think wooden nutmegs will cease to be quoted hereafter. The articles in the way of caps, arms, powder, clothing, every thing that Yankees in Havana, France, England, Belgium, have passed off for genuine cotton upon these poor devils is shameful. Not Yankees only. It does seem that the entire world has conspired with the leaders here South against the South. I am glad of it to my soul," adds Dr. Peel, with a savage oath. "That is what I like most in the thing—the cool, deliberate, thorough suicide in it from the start. Burned towns, railways destroyed, wharves leveled, whole regions stripped bare, to say nothing of the killed and the orphans and widows. Curse on them!" continued Dr. Peel, with a torrent of curses, all his soul in his bad eyes—"no man can hate them worse than I do, and even I am almost satisfied. And then all that is yet to come! I am more than satisfied, almost beginning to pity—*perhaps*," he adds, with the expression of a devil.

"Hallo, I say, look here, man," says his companion, looking keenly at the speaker. "War is war, I know, and these people would force their heads in the cannon's mouth. But I don't believe in the way you look at it. Take care what you say. If we are whipping them a tough enough job they are giving us of it, all our numbers and navy to boot. Besides, I am a Southern man myself, every drop of my blood." And the gay young officer had changed into a sharp observer upon Dr. Peel. "Besides, you talk too loud. How do you know but there may be some one listening? If there are, up we go, you well know," added he, with a peculiar gesture of his right hand, and resuming his gay manner.

"Never fear, I know what I am about. I'm too anxious to live if it is only to see the delicious ending. I have taken every precaution. Besides, I don't believe any possible event could make the people here even doubt me. The credulity, the super-astounding gullibility of these people is one long treat to me. I do love to work them up, and have them yell and brag and soar to heaven in glorification of the South. Such double-distilled fools!" says Dr. Peel, melting into contempt, and so becoming cool again. "However, business. There, that paper explains itself—the exact date, as near as I can get it, of that raid to be made into Tennessee. I think I have been tolerably accurate heretofore. There is another paper—sealed, you see; private even from you, Fairfax. Ah, that is a little petition of some friends about that Sergeant Boldin. He deserted from Grant—you must have heard of it—after getting himself scarified on the back some way—something like it in one of the old sieges of Babylon, is there not? It was his information gave us that delicious blunder of the rebels below Corinth. The Sergeant died like a man. You'll find the address of his family there. Seward ought really to do something handsome. Ah, here is that list of the Union men in my district who may be relied upon at Washington. If you are caught, destroy that whatever you do; if it gets into rebel hands they'll smell out the cipher, and in that case good-by to the men. That would be a pity. There are two Judges, a Secretary of State, three Superintendents of conscripts, several officers in actual service. It amazes me, Fairfax, and every day—pshaw! no, it does not amaze me. But the *rottenness* of this whole thing! Talk of Southern chivalry! If you only knew as well as I do the frantic eagerness of these military men—not civilians mind you, but the officers, the very chivalry itself, to make money! All that is a thing, of course, with Yankees, but I did think there would be at least that difference. Why, Sir," adds Dr. Peel, with an oath, "there is not a dodge to which most of them do not resort to make a fortune out of this war."

"Laying up for exile and confiscation, man," says his companion. "And as their paper pay depreciates they will be more desperate in the work than before."

"And to do the South justice," continues Dr. Peel, with something like a sneer, "even you have little idea how very many Union men there are South, and a man of them even attempting to make a cent out of the war, dumb, dead weights upon the rebellion those of them that escape hanging." The Doctor says this while selecting another paper from his package. "There," he adds, laying it upon the table, "read that, Sir; something actually done for the cause; the amount of stores destroyed is rather under than over the mark."

"Flouring mills, card factory burned; ten powder wagons blown up, two more upset in crossing the river—hum—hum; train of mules run off from—hum—hum. Why, Doctor, you are the very—steamer *Eliza* burned; thousand stand of—six pieces small cannon, fifty thousand pounds powder—hum, hum; machinery of percussion cap—"

"That was really a shame," puts in the Doctor, with a display of his remarkably fine teeth. "If you only knew the months of modeling, casting, contriving before they could get the thing to work. Just as they got all ready—I was really sorry for them, such a bitter disappointment. Reminds me of a little thing I didn't think worth putting down. I was on a visit over

at the Penitentiary—a distinguished visitor, you observe. The Colonel insisted on showing me over the whole establishment. In one room they had an iron trough filled with the detonating mixture for caps. Very much interested I was, so much so as to visit the room again next day; had a handkerchief full of lime under my cloak, and—if those caps explode I'm mistaken."

"Destruction of the Arsenal at Jackson!" says the young officer, glancing over another paper placed in his hands. "You don't mean—"

"Certainly," says Dr. Peel, with an effort at seriousness. "The women and children I regret as much as any man. But war is war, and they *would* have it. You observe, there is no neighborhood in all the South in which one can not find plenty of hands. The blacks are too dull often, but the mulattoes are smart enough. Bless your soul, you don't suppose I do my work with my own hands? No, Sir, not if I can help it; besides, what is the use when I have so many ready for any hint from me. You could not do my work; it requires a peculiar gift. In one month I could lay almost every town in my district in ashes if I only gave the word. They are sometimes caught, often hung, yet they never divulge any thing—at least, never any thing to hurt. Miserable animals they are, of course," adds the speaker in peculiar tones. "Mere monkeys, apes, gorillas, but as mischievous as monkeys. They can not plan, have no idea of combination, yet they can do what is planned for them. They are called 'hands,' you know. And then they have such an innocent, ignorant, stupid look with it all."

"I am sick of the whole thing—sick, sick," says his companion, with ill-concealed loathing for his friend, and resting his face, covered with his hands, upon the edge of the table.

"How you reason!" said Dr. Peel, towering above the Lieutenant, bold and bad as Lucifer. "Forty odd blown up at Jackson. Why, Fairfax, those people had already—women and children, mind—had already made cartridges enough to have killed many thousand times that number of our men, and were hard at it still."

"How do we know, at last, but you are humbugging us?" says the Lieutenant, glad of some mode of showing his aversion, raising his head, and looking his companion defiantly in the face. "Who knows but you take the credit of mere accidents?"

"That is for your superiors to decide, Sir," replies Dr. Peel, even haughtily. "They have had no occasion to doubt me so far."

"Oh, well, it *is* none of my business," said his companion, hastily, drawing his cap down over his forehead. "Let us get through."

"Well," he adds, when Dr. Peel has handed in, without further conversation, his last report, "it is a disagreeable business. I'd rather take it out in open field. Yet few men in the field are as useful as I am—and as you are," he adds, with some hesitation. "Certainly none in such danger."

There is a long silence, during which Dr. Peel, business over, is refreshing himself with a cigar as he sits at ease in his superb dressing-gown, rocking himself in the best rocking-chair Joe Staples's Hotel affords. The Lieutenant, meanwhile, is securing the papers about his person.

"Being a Yankee," he begins, as if suddenly impelled into conversation by some new motive.

"I beg your pardon. Figuratively a Yankee, you mean. You are a Virginian, you know," interrupts Dr. Peel, holding his cigar in his jeweled hand, and emitting a long puff of smoke from his lips.

"There is nothing very wonderful in your knowing that," replies the other. "Others besides yourself know me inside our lines. No, what I was about saying is this : being a curious sort of man, I will be glad if you will tell me exactly what prompts you to your well known—I will add wonderful—zeal and energy. I don't think I am an idle man in the cause, but you leave me far in the rear."

"I have no objection to tell you," is the reply, "provided you will tell me why you are so active. I won't stop to be complimentary."

"Soon told," answers the young officer, who has entirely resumed his light and dashing manner. "I am a Southern Union man, ten times intenser Union than any of those Yankees North can be if they tried, because it is my native South which I'm helping to rid of the double curse of Secession and—I wouldn't have said it three years ago, I do say it now—slavery. I got my devotion to the Union from father and mother; had it deepened by the stand I took for it at the University ; since the war began it has become my very life. The assassination of some of my dearest friends by the rebels, the death of my old father, and the destruction of the old place at the same hands, have helped matters ; and I have an old mother—as splendid a specimen of a Virginia lady as ever lived—living at Fredericksburg, who lays her hand on my head and blesses me in my work whenever I see her. Martha Washington, Sir, over again," adds the officer, with enthusiasm. "Precious little I care for old Lincoln. In fact, I've had more cold water thrown on me at Washington than any where else. It is the rescue of the South from that wretched old Repudiator and his gang, and their abominable delusions and knaveries, that I fight for. You know all about the Crusaders and the war for the Holy Land."

"But why engage in this particular sort of service ?"

"It just happened so : At the opening of the war a particular piece of information had to be obtained from within the rebel lines for a very special reason. No one would go and get it ; so

I had to do it. It became a habit, you see ; the excitement of the thing, the success, a little praise from head-quarters, and all. And I always had a taste for masquerading—for the joke's sake. Why, Sir, I've passed any number of times for Davis's nephew ; once or twice as his son—dangerous work that, as I do not know whether the old scoundrel has any son ; but every man has nephews, you know. There is hardly a prominent officer in the rebel service whose near relative I have not been somewhere in my travels. I am a native of every State of the South, hailing, at some time or other, from almost every leading town in every State South. I have filled almost every minor office under the Confederate Government ; been in every battle, without exception. Masquerading! Why, Sir, I've passed half a dozen times as a lovely girl driven from my home in Maryland, Kentucky, Nashville. I have been the belle of balls in Richmond and Charleston! You would have died of laughing to see me managing my crinoline and tossing my curls ! By Jove, I can handle a fan and a parasol so well, at times I almost get to believe I am a woman, and not so ugly a one either ! I have had love made to me by any number of military men ; have been so enthusiastic for the cause ; have had so many charming little ways—'Now, do tell me, General !'— 'Please, Colonel, how many men have we got here ?' and so on—that I've got more information than I dared hope for. But I've no time to talk. Isn't that the morning breaking ?"

And the young officer rose from his chair, washed his face at Dr. Peel's wash-stand, combed his hair before the glass, and sauntered about the room as fresh as if he had just risen from a full night's sleep.

"Four o'clock," he added, at last, consulting his watch, "and the stage leaves at half past. Have up that breakfast, Doctor, you promised. I have already settled my bill—nothing to do but to eat and leave."

That Dr. Peel was a Power at the hotel was evidenced in the rapid manner in which a hot breakfast was served up in answer to his call to that effect down the stairs. The very countenance of the mulatto who waited on them with it would have indicated to a close observer that Dr. Peel wielded some unusual influence over him at least.

"You said you were in London, I think," said the Lieutenant, who, declining to sit down, stood beside the table eating. "I don't expect any sympathy from you, but did you notice the tomb of André in Westminster Abbey ?"

"There were really so many objects of interest—"

"Well, I did. My father took me over when I was a boy ; told me the whole story as we stood looking at it. I was fascinated. I suppose there may be some similarity in our dispositions

—not our fates, however, I hope. There was a sort of harum-scarumness; a dashing mixture of Achilles and—by-the-by, what a fellow Achilles was for a masquerade! I never thought of it before! Months, you remember, in disguise at the court of King Something-or-other! Isn't that the stage coming up the street? And I had almost forgot. What is your motive?" said the Lieutenant, making a rapid finish of his meal, snapping together the lids of his valise, putting on his cap. "I'm all ready to be off—what is it?"

"None of the motives you speak of," said Dr. Peel, grim and sullen, behind the coffee-pot. "I don't object to the pay; it is to me an easy life; some other reasons, perhaps. But the chief reason," he added, suddenly, "is hate."

"Hate?" Lieutenant Ravenel of South Carolina weighs the words as he draws on his beautifully-embroidered gloves, looking keenly in his companion's face. "Hate?"

Few men sharper than Dr. Peel. "I would not have printed all that wild young scamp told you," he had said to Lamum after the issue of the *Star* containing the Lieutenant's information. "Lamum was wrong to do it," he remarked to Somerville generally. "Chaps like Ravenel are fond of exaggerating, making a great blow. Take my word for it, you'll find half he has been telling us is all a lie." With a tremendous oath, "I don't know but what his very letters of introduction to me were all a forgery!" Yes, very smart, indeed, was impetuous and magniloquent Dr. Peel.

Not sharper than young Fairfax. As that gentleman stands drawing on his gloves and looking steadily at his friend seated before him, the stage horn blows a second time, and with it the negro hostler comes into the room for the Lieutenant's valise, and "Mass Bill Perkins say, come or be left."

"You told me to take care I didn't carry it too far. You had better take particular care yourself, Dr. Peel," such singular meaning in the speaker's tones. "Upon my soul, I can hardly blame you; the times whirl so fast I hardly know how to think or feel; but, fact is, I have found you out, Doctor."

One can make nothing of the Lieutenant's countenance, the expression is so strange.

"Why, what do you mean?" asks Dr. Peel, at last, but by no means the Dr. Peel he was up to that instant.

"Oh, pshaw! I know it. You are ——;" and he places his lips to the Doctor's ear to say it. Not over half a dozen letters to the word, yet grand Dr. Peel falls back from the whisper as if struck by a bludgeon, and his lively young friend is gone.

MRS. SOREL'S COMFORT.

## CHAPTER XIII.

MRS. DR. WARNER had remarked to her husband only yesterday: "Dr. Warner, *will* you tell me what we are coming to? Flour forty dollars a barrel, sugar four pounds for a dollar, salt twelve cents, coffee one dollar, molasses two dollars and a half, lard forty cents, chickens fifty cents, eggs one dollar, butter a dollar and a quarter—those fiendish Yankees! And not a calico in town under a dollar a yard, domestics a dollar and a quarter, shoes ten dollars, a paper of pins five dollars! If I only had all the Yankees right in front of a cannon—Lincoln and all—loaded to the muzzle, and could shoot that cannon off, I could die happy. And there's snuff, not a grain of it to be had!"

Mrs. Warner stopped; words failed to express her indignation. In fact the English language had long since been used up by Mrs. Warner. Its very strongest words had been hurled by her so long and so continually upon the heads of the invaders that they had become insipid and meaningless to her. It is weeks now since she has first remarked that, if she but could do so, she would with her own hands send the North into atoms so small that Omniscience itself should never find them, nor Omnipotence itself put them together if found.

From Colonel Ret Roberts's last speech that was; but even that had become language too feeble to express her loathing and abhorrence. Having said fifty times a day that the Yankees were worse than devils, and that even hell was a punishment too light for them—said this in all possible inflections of the idea; what else could *he* said? Even Mrs. Warner was conscious of a sense of exhaustion.

As to the Doctor, what had he to do but to be as little at home as possible, put in some word of flattery whenever his conscience and a lull in the storm permitted, and so endure? The Doctor agreed in all the fulminations of his wife upon those who had brought about the ruin of the country, with this slight difference only—that the Xantippe of his bosom located these authors in Washington, and he located them in a somewhat lower latitude. When the infinite diversity of sentiment between the Secessionists and the Union people at the South during the war is considered, the wonder is, not at the alienation that existed there on that account, but rather that no greater explosion followed. But then there was on the part of the Union people an amazing amount of—what is the softest possible word for dissembling?—and a still more astonishing degree of silence. And there was an ominous meaning in that very silence, taken in connection with the class character of the Union people, hitherto and in all other matters, for forecast and prudence, which disquieted their Secessionist acquaintances exceedingly.

There is Mrs. Sorel. The times bring many troubles to her besides the absence of her son at the war. She goes out very little these days. None of the Union people do so any more than they can help. But she meets, as all Union people do, with coldness, sometimes actual denunciation, in company when she does enter it. Often is she under the necessity of entering the small room adjoining her chamber, where is little furniture beyond a chair and a table with a Bible upon it; oftener than of old, and she remains there longer in these days. Yet she always comes out from it calmer and in happier mood, if possible, than even in her palmiest days of yore. Nothing can be more placid than the conversations she and Edward Arthur, her guest, hold across the neat little table at breakfast, dinner, and supper; for Mr. Arthur is rarely away from home in these days any more than Mrs. Sorel. Mrs. Sorel has even to remonstrate with her guest upon his confining himself too closely to his studies.

The truth is, in the absence of the papers, reviews, and new publications of all sorts in which he once delighted, Mr. Arthur has taken to the old English divines in his library, volumes yellow with years and near a yard long, for which he has hitherto found little time. Into these volumes, as into pools pure and deep, he plunges over head and ears, and so forgets the times and himself. Nor are these the only pools into which he plunges. Every morning, to keep as fresh and as strong as possible, he is up and away on his horse to a creek miles off in the dense forest, into which he goes headlong, to return by the time the sun is up, glowing with his bath and the exercise, hopeful of happy days beyond Secession, hungry for his breakfast and for his studies afterward. A little Virgil occasionally; periodic Greek Testament likewise; and Hebrew also, straying away in its elephant tracks far away from Secession, across Canaan, through the rocky gaps of Sinai and Horeb, and on toward Abraham and the Creation.

What with these, the Old Divines, and his exercise, he is preparing sermons having more of the pith and essence of the Gospel in them, leagues away while so engaged from Secession and civil war. It may be only his imagination, but he has an impression that he is just now in special training for a work after Secession is over—some great work in which he is to accomplish more than he has ever dreamed of so far. At any rate he will prepare himself as thoroughly as possible.

Here is a morning, some weeks after his last conversation with Mr. Ferguson, when the gallop and the bath before breakfast do not quite suffice. It is in vain after breakfast that, after getting through his lessons with Robby, he essays the folio of theology. It may be a deep pool at other times, but this morning it seems a frozen one. He can not penetrate beneath, but slips and falls continually on the page as on a surface of ice.

On account of the bells last night! Even from Mrs. Sorel's, three miles away, he could hear the great rejoicing in Somerville—all the bells, all the cannon, all the smaller arms. He woke at midnight with the first stroke of the Methodist bell, by far the largest in Somerville. "If Providence is willing, I am," he said to himself in the act of awaking; but there was no more sleep for him that night.

Somerville has been quite despondent of late, and the reaction of joy over victory is immense. Colonel Juggins has a negro boy over at Mrs. Sorel's with the paper long before breakfast. Mr. Arthur has read it to Mrs. Sorel at that meal. Cause for rejoicing, indeed! There have been a series of battles near Richmond lasting several days. M'Clellan has been captured, with his entire army! The gun-boats have managed to escape down James River, but that is all: 60 generals, 140 captains, 30,000 Federals killed, 80,000 captured; stores, batteries, colors without computation! The war is virtually over! Colonel Juggins comes along after breakfast.

"Of that vast army, ma'am," he says to Mrs. Sorel, "Bill Perkins was saying last night only 75 privates made their escape, and at last.accounts our army was in full pursuit of them!" And Colonel Juggins, brimmed with enthusiasm, insists on reading over aloud the whole paper from end to end to quiet Mrs. Sorel washing up the breakfast things.

No, Edward Arthur can not get into the merits of the folio this morning. He evades Colonel Juggins, goes to the stable, saddles and mounts his horse, and rides slowly away he does not care whither. It runs like a ditty in his mind over and over again—"If Providence is willing, I am!" Odd passages of Scripture come to the surface, in his memory, of themselves—"'His ways are not as our ways, neither are His thoughts as our thoughts. He doeth according to His will in the armies of heaven and among the inhabitants of the earth. None can stay His hand, or say what doest thou......' And yet if Secession *could* but have been put down! One country again; one flag again; universal amnesty; peace and prosperity again, firmer, greater than before!" His mind runs over it all as it is: "The success of the great Wrong! The triumph of wicked men! Anarchy victorious North and South! And is it possible, after all, that such men as Lamum, Roberts, Barker, and the long tail of Captain Simmons, Bob Withers, Tim Lamum, and the like are right? Right? Pleasing to God? And all who think unlike them are wrong? their opinions displeasing to Heaven, and now justly rebuked?" It was partly broken rest the night past, but Edward Arthur felt as he rode along as if the very foundations of reason and religion were out of course.

The seven days of Chickahominy were days of disaster to you loyal hearts at the North, were they? Believe it, your deepest feelings in regard thereto were but, in the phrase of old Cervantes, "as cheese-cakes and cream-tarts" to the agony of hope deferred, nigh destroyed, in the bosoms of hundreds of thousands of us at the South, loving our common country as much as you. As much as you? Far more. Though trembling lest you should lose it, you still possessed it. We at the South, actually stripped of all we loved, of flag and country, were yearning for their return. In the great wreck common to both, you were as those of the wrecked still holding on to the floating fragments, though they seemed slipping from your grasp; we were as those drowning without even that, praying and clutching—ah, how desperately!—amidst the roaring foam.

It is raining heavily, and the rider looks around to find that his horse has stopped of its own accord under the roof of an old gin. He has been there before in his excursions. The gin is an abandoned one in the centre of a tract of land, which the furrows, nearly leveled by the rains to a plain, and a fragment of an old rail here and there, show to have been once cultivated. There is the screw, too, hard by, its long levers, with their little cap of a roof, idle evidently this many a day. The pit beneath is caved in. There are scraps of rope, shreds of bagging, great piles of cotton seed blue and steaming in the rain around. Yes, many a bale of cotton has been planted and gathered and ginned and pressed and wagoned away from this deserted spot. Edward Arthur is in full sympathy with the scene this morning; how much better to be there just now than in the hotel in Somerville, or even at Mrs. Sorel's. As he alights from and ties his horse to one of the huge posts which support the upper room of the gin-house, the under story being open all around, he is glad he has not to converse with even Guy Brooks this morning. Mr. Ferguson, too—he knows that the Scotchman is that instant in his room there in Somerville contemplating the blazing dispatch which he has just filed in its place in his ponderous scrap-book. There is a gleam of satisfaction in the young minister's mind as he sees, in imagination, the peculiar expression which is that very instant tinging, so to speak, the very tips of the Scotchman's grizzly beard.

But he is to have company at last. There is a galloping of a horse across the old field. It is a lady; she rides her pony in under the protecting roof, and is off and shaking the drops from her riding-skirt before he can get to her assistance. She raises her head as he approaches. Of all persons on earth it is the person whom he would most desire to meet just there and then. Of all persons on earth it is just the person whom he would there and then most ardently desire not to meet.

It may be owing to the fact that we have double lobes to the brain and a double set of organs to the heart; but certain it is a man may have in brain and heart, and at the same moment too, a double set of thoughts and emotions —double and strong, and in exact conflict with each other. And it is with a man in such a case as it is with a steamer, say, when the engine on its one side is propelling, with the engine on its other side backing. Round and round, morally speaking, goes the individual, but not an inch does he advance either down stream or up current. At least Mr. Arthur certainly had, at this moment, just such speed.

But who can venture to assert what her opinion of the chance meeting in that lonely spot was? If you gather any thing from her blush on first perceiving her companion, what are you to gather from the pallor which, the moment after, left her face in such striking contrast with the black velvet cap upon her head, and the black plume which drooped, heavy with rain, down to her cheek? Prompt enough to speak, however:

"All my fault, Mr. Arthur!" she said, gayly. "I have been spending a few days with Anne Wright, an old school-fellow. I determined to ride home this morning, come what might.

Anne told me it would rain, but I thought pony would get me home first. Mr. Wright is in Somerville; the hands were off in the fields with the horses, so I had to come alone. I deserve it for starting. But I *will* have my way, mamma says. How came you here?"

Mr. Arthur has but a disjointed reply to make. Disjointed, because he has no reason for having ridden there at all. And because she is so beautiful—ah! how beautiful! He has not seen her, to converse with her, for many weeks now; and she has changed so! It is all in the sex. Boys do not change so. The youth of eighteen is very much the individual he was at sixteen, only taller—no coming out of any chrysalis with *him*.

But here is Alice Bowles. When Edward Arthur removed to Mrs. Sorel's Alice was but a girl—a lovely girl, but only a girl, although Mr. Neely *was* in the habit of visiting her so often. But to-day Alice Bowles alights from her pony in the old gin a woman. Her face is full, and her ruddy lip, and clear eye, and gentle yet firm expression, is that of a woman—no longer a girl. She always bore herself in that erect and imperial manner—a something about the white brow as if made for a crown—a bend about the neck as of Marie Antoinette among the *sans culottes*. Before, it was a manner that went and came with her varying moods; but to-day it is herself. It may be the plumed riding-cap she wears; it may be her long riding-dress, which brought up vague memories of grand ladies in their trains at court; it may be it was in the excitement of her rapid ride causing her face to glow so; it may be the contrast between the young beauty and the littered earth on which she stood and the dilapidation around her; or maybe it was her sudden advent through the dreary morning, and upon him in a mood as dreary; but, whatever was the reason, she came upon him there very little else to him than an angel from heaven. Had he not loved her at first sight, years ago, when she was only the bud of what had now opened into the perfect rose?

There was one advantage he had over her. He had not come upon her in her retreat there, in the out-of-the-way old gin, but she had come upon him; and, somehow, from the first he had yielded to her the burden of the conversation. His first look as he met her had said so much that he felt, and she felt, he had little more to add. Ah! how she talked, in order to keep from hearing or saying any thing!—cutting with her riding-whip at the shreds of cotton on the ground, shaking the drops of rain from her riding skirt, smoothing her already smooth hair on each side of her brow.

" And oh, Mr. Arthur, I nearly forgot. What *is* the news?" she suddenly asked, after all other topics were exhausted. " Anne and I could

hear the noise all the way to Mr. Wright's. What great and glorious Something has happened this time?" And she entered on the topic with a sense of indefinable pain, and yet of indefinable pleasure too.

Mr. Arthur related the contents of the dispatches. Quite accurately, too, which was a wonder in those days. As a general rule it was a thing impossible, quite impossible, to do then. A man might try to tell his eager neighbor the contents of the last dispatch the moment he laid it down, but he never *could* repeat it accurately. If he was a Union man his version was far more unfavorable to the Confederacy than at least the printed lines warranted. If he was a Secessionist the news he repeated from the paper was much more encouraging for the Confederacy than even the largest capitals of the sheet just in his hands would justify.

" I need not ask your opinion of the news," said his companion, more thoughtfully. " I presume you will say of it, as you did of the news from Shiloh—it is partly true and partly false. And you were right. But it is a pity one can not believe the whole of a matter from the first, and with all the heart. One could enjoy one's self so !"

" You have no apprehension about your brother—?"

" Oh no !" interrupted his companion. " Did not mamma show you—ah! I forgot at the moment that you do not live with us now. No ; mamma received a letter from him only ten days ago. He is in Charleston—under arrest, I am sorry to say. There was some Mississippian or Georgian put over him in rank. Very foolishly he neglected to obey some order, something of the kind, I do not exactly understand it. At any rate, Rutledge—Rutledge Bowles, as mamma always persists in calling him—is under arrest in Charleston. Since Rutledge can not bring himself to comply with the wishes of his superiors, it is a great pity they can not make it a rule to comply with his. At least mamma almost says so," added Alice, with a good deal of demure fun at the corners of her rosy mouth.

Her eyes being intent on the particular shred of cotton she was switching at with her riding-whip upon the ground, Mr. Arthur had an opportunity of looking at her. Poor young fellow! she was so beautiful ; so full of life and grace! And Secession has put them as far apart—not as the East is from the West; that similitude is obsolete in these days—but as far apart from each other as the North is from the South.

" You know I have never seen your brother," said her companion, seeing at the moment with great satisfaction that the rain was beginning to fall heavier than ever. " But is there not—?" and in his half hesitation Alice hastened to finish the question for him.

" A strong resemblance between Rutledge and

myself? In character, yes, I dare say there is. We are both of us altogether too impatient of control—too much in the habit of having our own way. It *is* a dreadful defect of character, Mr. Arthur," she said, looking up only for an instant at him, and then resuming her chastisement, though it was at least "an inch" of "a king," of the unfortunate piece of cotton; "but I do not see how either Rutledge or myself are to blame for it. We inherited it from our father, who was celebrated for his fixedness—if there is such a word—of opinion; and we have been trained to it from our cradles. If pa had only lived it would have been far better for us both; but you know how indulgent mamma is."

"I for one would not have you otherwise than as you are for the world," Mr. Arthur said, emphatically—only it was to himself, not a syllable of it reaching his lips. And yet she knew as well, in the silence which followed her remark, that he was saying just that as if he had said it aloud.

"Only to think," she hastily added, therefore, "of the thousands of brave men that must have been killed; that is, if there really was any fighting at all in Virginia."

"And of the many thousands that are yet to die in hospital and upon battle-field before this war is over," added her companion. "We read of Roncesvalles and Fontenoy, and the gallant knights dying at Chevy Chase, and all. Yet the simple truth is, old Froissart, whom you remember we read together last summer, tells of no brave gentlemen nobler or braver in every sense of the word than our Southern soldiers. Chivalry boasts of nothing which the South is not equaling every day, and every hour of the day."

"But we of the South deserve and wear the name of Chivalry, Mr. Arthur, only *too* well," said Alice, after a pause. "I wish I could not think of it as I do; but, somehow or other, we seem to be as antiquated as Chivalry is, too. As to the nobleness, generosity, courtesy, and valor of our armies, I suppose all the world is agreed; but, with all that, I can not help having a vague but painful sense that we are classed by Europe with Spain, behind the age. If one half of the feeling of the world in regard to us is admiration, the other half of that feeling is pity. I am afraid it is owing to some book or other which I should never have read; or it may be some natural perversity of my character, but it does seem to me as if our armies, gallant as they are, are warring against—what shall I call it?—against Destiny."

It may have been some improper reading, or it may have been the independence of her nature rebelling against whatever happened to be dominant; but it had pained her mother that Alice was not as thoroughly under the rule of the enthusiasm of the day as she desired her to be.

Perhaps Mr. Neely had visited her too much—had overdone in his conversation the topic of the hour. Devotedly, too, as she loved her mother, she had known Mrs. Sorel too long not to acknowledge to herself the calm superiority of her sense and judgment to the mere impulse of her mother, beautiful as that impulse was—not that Mrs. Sorel had conversed with her on the great question of the day. At least not for months now had she heard a word from her lips upon the merits of the quarrel. In truth, very rarely indeed in these days were the families thrown together. Mrs. Sorel had always spoken frankly on the subject when she spoke at all, and Mrs. Bowles was as decided in her feelings on the subject as Mrs. Sorel was in her convictions. Feeling *vs.* Conviction—that was the case at issue.

"If you will permit me, Miss Alice," said her companion, "I may be able to explain you to yourself. If you had read and thought as little upon the whole question now convulsing the country as the mass of those around you—I mean upon both sides of it—I dare say you would think and feel exactly as they do. Or if, notwithstanding all your thought and reading, your character admitted of your forgetting every thing of the kind, and giving yourself up blindly to the popular emotion, whatever it was, then, too, you would feel and think, as, for instance, your friend Miss Anne Wright does. I do not mean to flatter you, Miss Alice, but I can not say what I wish to say without seeming to do so," he added, knotting the lash of his riding-whip industriously as he spoke.

"I only wish I was as happy as Anne in her whole-heartedness upon the subject," said Alice. "How she does abuse the Yankees! I do believe she thinks if the Yankees succeed they will actually make her go to the wash-tub for them, enslave her, make a house-maid or a field hand of her. I'd like to see them come cavorting around *me*, her father says. Anne says she'll die first. I would certainly hate to eat any dish of her preparing, if I was Mrs. Lincoln, or whoever her future mistress is to be; it would be far from wholesome, I was telling her so last night," said Alice, with a laugh. "But, then, there is my dear, dear mother," she added, with sudden gravity.

"Will you forgive me, Miss Alice?" said her companion. "My admiration and affection for your mother are second only to your own, and I venture to say only this," he continued, gravely, although he saw the color rising in her cheek: "if you had been born at the date of your mother's birth you would have felt and thought just as she does to-day. It may be your misfortune, but you were born some thirty years after your mother. There has been a vast change in the very fashions worn since then. Look at your mother's miniature, taken when she was a bride.

There is—whether we like it or not—a still greater change in the opinions of men. A person of active intellect—one who reads, thinks, arrives at independent conclusions—can not be the same in opinion with one born a third of a century before, unless you lived like Robinson Crusoe on a desert island, or unless you lived exclusively in your own section, like the Chinese, or unless you went—"

"Fast asleep, like Rip Van Winkle," interrupted his companion. "Dear me, how it rains! How mamma will scold me for venturing out from Mr. Wright's! You must excuse me, Mr. Arthur; but the plain truth is, I hate to think in these days. I wish I could stop thinking, I'm sure. I would give all I possess for a good drink from the flagon that put Rip Van Winkle asleep!"

"To come out of your cave at last, as he did, and find all the world changed by other hands than your own. Well, perhaps so. And yet if there is indeed a great change for the better to be brought about by human brains and human hands, I confess I would prefer not to live altogether apart from it. I would like—at least in my happiest moments I feel so—to have a heart and a hand in the work. But it is a wearisome thing to think upon so steadily. I never felt it more so than to-day."

Although Alice did not look at her companion she none the less saw the care and pain, even anguish, upon his face. With a woman's quick insight, however, she saw that the anxiety and uncertainty almost which used to—or which she months ago fancied used to—mark the countenance of the young minister, was giving place to a twofold expression of confidence and peace; an expression growing from day to day through great suffering into an aspect of certainty and joy. Yet Mr. Neely was much the handsomest man of the two, so fat and rosy and full of cordial sympathy with the invaded South.

"If a person does not agree in sentiment with the people of the South what does he stay here for? Evidently he ought to be with that people in whose opinions he agrees. If I was with the North I would go there, and I would stay there." That was Mr. Neely's decided opinion in his last conversation with Alice—or rather in his last conversation with Mrs. Bowles when Alice was present. Mr. Neely did not mention Mr. Arthur's name in that connection: so that he could, of course, have no reference to him; certainly not.

"But suppose, Mr. Neely," Alice had innocently asked, looking up from her sewing—a soldier's shirt it was, one of a dozen made from the cover of her piano, cut up for that purpose as the only material to be had—"suppose you possessed property at the South, valuable property, all the property you owned in the world. I believe it is the certain loss of property in the South

for a person to leave as you advise; if you held the sentiments you mention, you would leave, as you say, at the sacrifice of all you possessed?"

"I certainly would, Miss Alice," he replied, enduring her clear look. Perhaps in such a case Mr. Neely would. But perhaps in such a case Mr. Neely would not, also.

"Then if you were now at the North, entertaining the sentiments you do, you would instantly leave the North for the South, giving up all you owned there to do so?" asked Alice. Her beautiful eyes were full upon him. What could he do?

"I would, Miss Alice, I certainly would!" Oh, Mr. Neely! Not to know that you knew, and that she knew, whether you spake true or not. But, then, the temptation was so great, to Mr. Neely the greatest temptation possible in the whole world.

"Suppose, Mr. Neely, though you disapproved of the step taken by the South, and agreed in the course pursued, in consequence of that step, by the North, yet you shrank from engaging in actual war upon your own people, or even from being surrounded by such as were, how then?" Alice had asked.

"These are no days for such nice distinctions, Miss Alice," the school teacher had promptly replied. "As one feels and thinks so should he act. A man must adopt one side or the other, and without a particle of reluctance or shame in doing so. And men will do so whose views are clear. He that is not against us is with us; he that is not with us is against us—plain as the multiplication table, Miss Alice."

Alice really did not know what to reply. But it seemed strange to hear this gentleman from New England speaking so freely of We and Us's in connection with Southern affairs. The possessive pronouns in all their inflections were used with painful frequency by the Yankee Secessionists. "Our brave boys!" "The way We are whipping them, too!" "The diabolical designs meditated against Us by the Federals!" and kindred phrases, were more frequent on the lips of men like Mr. Neely from the North than of those who had never been outside the South in their own selves, or in the persons of their ancestors, since Jamestown was settled.

It seemed somewhat of a coincidence, then, with Mr. Neely's previous remarks, that Mr. Arthur should say now, loving Alice as he did, and answering her very thoughts:

"I do not wish to speak of myself. Here in God's providence I am. Not a day, or a moment of the day, that I do not feel how painful a thing it is to differ from public sentiment, especially from the sentiments of those among whom we have lived all our lives, than whom there are none in all the world whom we esteem or love more. I have done my very best to become a Secessionist, but I can not. I have done my utmost to believe, at least to hope that, after all, the Confederate Government will be a success and a blessing to the South. For my life I can not think so. I can not get away to Europe, and if I could I would feel very much like Jonah on his way to Tarshish, storm or no storm. No, I am in charge here as a minister of the Gospel. So long as I am permitted to do so, I will continue the duties of my office, obeying faithfully the Scripture directions as to the Government over me. I was, I may almost say, in agonies of mind at first. I am getting used to it. I have within me such a settled sense that I could not have acted otherwise than I have done that I am coming to feel as quiet in mind as a man can be—a kind of solid quiet greater than I ever possessed before. And my experience, though I am not so situated as to have correspondence, or the least intercourse in any way, with one of them, is that of perhaps thousands of my brethren in the ministry at the South, and, in some respects, of hundreds of thousands of the very best men, all Southern men, and destined to do a great work in and for the South yet. But if I knew this hour, Miss Alice, that I was the only Southern man in the whole South entertaining the sentiments I do, I could entertain them not a jot the less for that. It may be my misfortune, it may be my crime, it certainly is my case. As to the future of myself and of my country I am learning to leave the whole in the Hands that *are* managing it, perfectly satisfied in advance as to the result. You must really excuse me, Miss Alice," he added, with a smile. "It is the first time I have spoken to you thus of myself. I assure you it shall be the last time. It has only happened so, you see. You must endure it as one of the accidents of this rainy day."

But Alice did not hear these last words. It was only a few days ago that she had been reading Milton, and why she knew not, but the lines were passing through her mind as he spoke:

"So spake the seraph Abdiel, faithful found
Among the faithless, faithful only he:
Among innumerable false, unmoved,
Unshaken, unseduc'd, unterrify'd
His loyalty he kept, his love, his zeal;
Nor number, nor example with him wrought
To swerve from truth, or change his constant mind
Though single."

Her head drooped until the plume of her riding-cap almost concealed her face. But, at last, Edward Arthur said nothing to her of himself which she did not know already, and know fully as well as he did himself. She stood still, occupied with the shred of cotton on the ground at her feet, But no longer cutting at it as before, moving it rather hither and thither with the lash of her riding-whip, lovingly, caressingly even, as if it were some living thing which she would not hurt for the world.

"No, but Miss Alice, what I want to know"

—Mrs. Warner had said to her in the court-house where the ladies met to work for the soldiers only the week before, and it was after a long stretch of remark by Mrs. Warner on the one topic—"what I want to know is just this: do you not believe that the Yankees, invading our country, burning our homes, killing our women and children, are worse than the very devils in hell?"

"How should I know, Mrs. Warner?" Alice had replied. "I have never been to the abode of the evil spirits you speak of. I never saw a devil in my life. If I was to come upon a person possessed with one I would keep as far off from—dear me, you must excuse me, I must go and get Mrs. Sorel yonder to give me some more thread."

"I tell you, Dr. Warner," Mrs. Warner remarked to her husband at supper that night, "there is something wrong about that Alice Bowles. Her mother, Mrs. Bowles, such a genuine Southern woman, too. You are their family physician, and sure enough I am your influence on her has not been favorable for the South. You are the plague and misery of my life with your milk-and-water way of thinking and talking, or rather not talking at all upon the subject. How a man of your years, one who reads the papers every day, can be as mild as you are! And, then, knowing *my* feelings on the subject, hearing every day and hour of your life all *I* say —I do believe it is just to cross me. Because I am so strong for the South you are exactly the opposite!" Which statement, by-the-by, was not far from the truth. But Dr. Warner only ate his supper with the shower-bath droop about the head, and nathless so endured.

"Alice's father was a stanch Secessionist years ago," mused Mrs. Warner, aloud, striking her tea-spoon against her empty cup. "That is his portrait hanging up in their parlor, grand enough to look at; only it's a pity he couldn't have left a few more negroes to his wife and children. There's Rutledge Bowles, Mrs. Bowles is so everlastingly talking about. A worthless, drinking, gambling fellow, there in Charleston, if half I've heard about him is true. He'd better be here at home making money for his mother. But he's a good Secessionist, was active in the taking of Fort Sumter there at Charleston. Did Alice ever visit the North?" asked Mrs. Warner, suddenly.

"I believe not," replied her husband.

"Because it always has the worst effect on Southern people. Spending the summer at the North! I reckon that old cry is over. I never was out of the South! And a far better Southern man *you* would be, Dr. Warner, if you had never spent that time in Philadelphia, attending medical lectures. If I only had my way," said Mrs. Warner, for the three thousandth time. "no Southern citizen should ever visit the North on any pretext. Nor Europe either, for that matter; they are just as rank Abolitionists there as

ARTHUR AND ALICE AT THE OLD GIN.

at the North. Won't recognize us on account of Slavery, Yancey said there in his speech in New Orleans! Yes, if I had my way I'd build a wall a hundred feet high all round the South, in real earnest; nobody should go out and no-body should come in. To think how they used to flood the country with their books and papers and peddlers and things! Hang them!"

"I am sure Alice has taken an active part," began the Doctor.

"Presenting that flag? Sewing, and singing at concerts for the soldiers, and all that?" interrupted his wife. "There's something wrong for all that. I began to think so that day she opposed having a lottery for the assistance of that regiment. It was against the rules of religion, she said, and there is a law of the State—wonder how she came to know that?—expressly prohibiting it. As if any body would dare enforce such a law these days. And as if Brother Barker himself did not go in for it, and have the meeting to arrange for it in the very church. But, opposed or not, we had it any how. No, I know exactly how it is," said Mrs. Warner, in a lower and more intense tone, peering at her husband under mysterious eyebrows, and shaking the tea-spoon at him like the thyrsus of a magician. "It is *Mr. Arthur!* Haven't I got eyes? Never tell me! And he living there for years, now; helping her in her studies, and all that stuff. He's gone to live at Mrs. Sorel's, I know. He doesn't visit at Mrs. Bowles hardly at all. I met their boy Charles on the street and asked him only the other day. I know they ain't engaged, for I asked Mr. Arthur himself when he was here last. But there's something wrong in Alice's mind about Secession, and it came there just in that way, you mark my words. And how people—you among them—*will* continue to go and hear him preach these days is more than I can understand. For my part I'd just as soon—"

But we have no disposition to share in Dr. Warner's martyrdom.

A very smart woman was Mrs. Warner. Long and unwearying investigations into the affairs of others had given her a remarkable power of insight. Who will deny all of her reasonings in this matter? The being a Union man involved, at that period of the war, in general estimation, the being either a fool or a knave. Now Alice could not believe that Mr. Arthur was either, so that her faith in the desperate depravity of Unionism may have thereby been shaken. And there was Mrs. Sorel too, such an old friend, one whom she had so long loved and esteemed, a South Carolinian too; her sentiments were all against Secession. It only happened so, you see. But was ever fly entangled in a web so terrible? It was Spenser's ever old and forever new Song of the Fair Una traveling through the wildernesses. Ah, how dark and brambly the way! Consider this Southern girl—for hers is but one case of how many thousands of her sex: born on the bosom of the old era, tended by it from birth with its ten thousand tenderest touches; all the deep aversion of early and life-long prejudice repelling her from the bringers-on of the new era; all the warmest sympathies natural to the bosom with soil invaded, kindred slain, valor struggling against overwhelming odds: add to this the ever-present force of an almost universal enthusiasm. And the new era dawning over her, with skies so dim and with hints so vague of its coming clearness. Happy are those whose lot is in the centre, say, of one era—Luther's parents, let us instance. Happier still those who live in the centre of the era which follows—those possessed of a perfected Protestantism, we will say. But the transition period between the two eras—how stormy and full of all perplexity! In every transition period the perplexity lies not without only—it is within one's own bosom that the shadow is darkest, its strife bitterest. Easy enough to do the right when a sincere soul but *knows* the right—the agony is to know with sufficient clearness what *is* the right.

If one dare plagiarize from Brother Barker his mode of finding the times in prophecy, we might be tempted as we read to let finger and eye linger upon this prophecy as bearing upon the days of Secession: "It shall come to pass in that day that the light shall not be clear nor dark; but it shall be one day which shall be known to the Lord, not day nor night: but it shall come to pass that at evening time it shall be light." Only look in Brother Barker's little black Bible. You will find the margin of the two verses immediately before this passage is all worn away. Brother Barker, standing in the pulpit a hundred times during Secession, has kept the fore-finger of his left hand pressed just there, holding on like an anchor to the passage, while all the rest of his body swung about wildly in a tempest of declamation, proving that therein Secession and its glories were set forth with a distinctness which left only the inference of judicial blindness upon those who could not see it. Let us do the brother justice; only recognize the fact that the passage in question does refer to Secession, and it is striking, very striking indeed. However, Brother Barker never put *our* interpretation upon—if you have curiosity to look them up—those sixth and seventh verses of the fourteenth Zechariah—the reverse, in fact.

The rain is falling less and less heavily upon the leaky roof of the old gin-house, if the parties within only knew it. Twenty times has the young minister said to himself, "No, Sir, no; this is neither the time nor the place." But there is something about the drooped head and the hue upon the cheek, even in the motion of the gloved hand holding the riding-whip, as it toys with the shred of cotton on the dust, that emboldens him. He has been speaking out his soul, his heart; and how soft and affecting are the tones of the voice when one does so!

"And, next to the approval of my own conscience, do I desire *your* approval," he is beginning to say, when Alice raises herself and looks across the old field plashy with water. She has heard nothing, but a woman's instinct of approaching danger is strong upon her. And at last she sees only a man on horseback hundreds of yards away riding slowly toward them. It is strange how swift the sex is in its reasonings and conclusions.

In the instant of seeing the approaching horseman she says, and she says it hurriedly:

"May I ask it as a special favor, Mr. Arthur, that you will mount your horse and leave me? You see the rain is over. Excuse me, but please do." How earnest she is!

Mr. Arthur hears, with sense of pleasure at the tones, but with surprise at the request.

"I know you will excuse me and comply with my request if you only knew why I ask it," she said, still more hurriedly, her eyes upon the horseman, her gloved hand resting upon his arm.

"Really, Miss Alice," her companion began.

"Oblige me this once, Mr. Arthur," she continued, in tones of entreaty and apprehension. "Yonder is Mr. Wright. You know his character and sentiments. I have a fear that he may be intoxicated—"

"You must excuse me, Miss Alice," interrupted Edward Arthur, gravely and coldly. "I understand your apprehension, but I can not do as you wish." And a flush almost of anger mounted to his temples.

It was too late. Alice busied herself with her pony, leading him in front of her companion, who assisted her to mount.

"Why, good-morning to you, Mr. Wright," said Alice to the horseman, who had now reached them, in tones of gayety singularly in contrast with those she had just used. "I will be glad of your escort back to your house. I *would* start this morning for home in spite of all Anne could do. But I have got wet; do let us make haste; the rain is over." And she lifted her reins, gathered in her hand as if to start, keeping herself, however, still between Mr. Arthur and the person she addressed.

With an "Excuse me, Miss Alice!" Edward Arthur struck her pony a slight blow with his riding-whip, and Mr. Wright, who had reined in his horse with drunken dignity, sat staring at him face to face.

Alonzo Wright. As refined and agreeable a gentleman as you could meet with any where when sober. When drunk, a devil incarnate. Long ago had he killed his first man. It was when he was intoxicated, and because he fancied at the time the individual in question, a merry youth of sixteen—Jim Hartley—was looking impertinently at him. Very rarely had he got drunk since then. But when he did become intoxicated the passion for killing some one again came upon him as a mania, as part and parcel of his drunkenness. It all took place before Mr. Wright removed to his present home; in fact

he had come hither on that account; but, unless rumor lied more even than it usually does, if Jim Hartley was the first he was by no means the last man Mr. Wright had killed. Every body knew Alonzo Wright; and when drunk Nero on his throne had not courtiers more abject. That is, such of them as did not fly the spot. Shunned as his house was by almost every one except an unselect few, it was on that very account that Alice had felt specially drawn to poor Anne Wright, her school-fellow, and hence her visit to her.

As Alice anticipated, Mr. Wright was drunk, very drunk. How could it have been otherwise in Somerville last night after the arrival of such news? There had been a military prohibition on the sale of liquor in the place for several weeks now; but the authorities themselves "raised," as they styled it, "the blockade on whisky" to celebrate the glorious victory over M'Clellan. Men who never drank before got drunk in Somerville last night. Men whose whisky had been cut off for the months past drank last night in Somerville with the frenzy of long abstinence. Even Lamum was shocked at the state of Somerville last night, Tim Lamum, his nephew, wallowing and vomiting on his office floor in the experiences of his first "regular spree." And Mr. Wright, having an entire grocery abandoned to him during all last night, had so far killed no one. He was riding home with an unsatisfied craving in his heart, his loaded revolver ready for any emergency that might arise. Vague wrath slumbered in his bosom against whatever negro might come out to hold his horse as he should dismount at his gate. Not a negro on the place, however, but will find pressing business on the remotest part of the plantation when it is known that "Mass Lonny is comin'."

Such is Alonzo Wright, a slight-built, sandy-haired, pale-faced man, who now sits on his horse gazing upon the young minister, of whose presence he was not aware until Alice and her pony had moved from between them.

It all takes place as in a second of time.

"And who are you?" Mr. Wright says, with a sudden half-closing of his eyes and an oath.

Edward Arthur knows perfectly well who and what Alonzo Wright is. More than once has he been received with the most gentlemanly courtesy by Mr. Wright in visiting there. But that was months ago. Besides, it was under Mr. Wright's own roof; and, drunk as he is, were it under that roof he was now meeting Mr. Arthur, he would have treated him as a gentleman and a guest. But they are not in Mr. Wright's house; Mr. Wright is drunk, and this Mr. Arthur is strongly suspected of being a Union man. Nothing more abhorred by Mr. Wright even when sober than that.

"My name is Edward Arthur," replies that gentleman; but his manner is stern from his knowledge of the questioner and of what may follow.

"A preacher and an Abolitionist," says Mr. Wright, with a volley of oaths.

Mr. Arthur has nothing to reply, but has turned to the post at which his horse is tied, and is slowly unfastening him to return home.

"And now you are going to run, are you? what you Yankees always do. Hold on!" exclaims Mr. Wright, in a tone such as only men like those of his class can use. "Get out of the way!" he adds, with a cut of his whip across the head of Alice's pony, which she is endeavoring to ride between them. He hears not a word Alice says—is not aware of her existence. His eyes, almost shut, are fastened upon his prey.

"Look here," he adds, slowly, drawing his revolver from his girdle as he speaks, "I've got one boy away in the army fighting the Yankees. Ten to one he was killed in that last fight at Richmond. If there is any thing in this world I would like to do this morning it is to kill an Abolitionist. Now, you say 'Hurrah for Jeff Davis!' or you are a dead man."

Knowing his man, hearing that indescribable tone of his voice, Edward Arthur had no doubt that he meant what he said.

"Do, Mr. Arthur, for my sake, my sake, my sake," Alice keeps on repeating, still endeavoring to force her pony between them. But pony fears Mr. Wright's whip and shies off.

Unarmed, no chance of springing upon him before he can shoot, there is no alternative.

"Fire when you please, I will die first!" he replies, as pale, as cold, as rigid as a statue.

There is the sharp crack of a revolver, with Alice's shriek on the air. It may have been that Mr. Wright has been drunk too long, or that there was an extra quantity of strychnine in the whisky of last night; for the genuine liquor is running very low in these days of the blockade—but the bullet sings by Mr. Arthur's left ear, and he stands erect and unhurt. And next, what? He thinks of springing upon the desperado, but he knows there are five more charges in his weapon! Mr. Wright curses his nerves and again presents his weapon.

"One more chance, Abolitionist," he says, "Hurrah for Jeff Davis and the Confederacy'—out with it!"

The young minister has no reply at all to make this time. Pale, cold, rigid he fastens his eye, glittering like ice, upon that of Mr. Wright. No attention at all does that individual pay to Alice, who has leaped from her pony and stands at his side pulling with both hands at his coat, weeping and entreating. He keeps his weapon leveled at the forehead of his intended victim, his finger on the trigger full a minute.

There is neither flinching of muscle nor quailing of eye there. The desperado slowly lowers his weapon. "Well!" he exclaims, with an oath, "you are as brave as a man can be. I'll do you that justice if you are an Abolitionist. I could not kill even old Lincoln himself if he was looking me as straight in the eyes. We'll cry quits if you say so;" and he rose in his stirrup to replace his weapon comfortably in its sheath at his waist.

"No, Sir," said Mr. Arthur, sternly, "I am not a specially brave man that I am aware of. But it happens to me just now that I am not particularly in love with this world, and I am, I trust, prepared for the other. Besides, I am not in your hands or in those of any other man; now, as always, I am in the hands only of God."

"It looked very much as if God had turned you over to me just now; one touch of my finger on that trigger and you would have been in the other world sure enough. However, we won't quarrel about it. Ah, this is you, Miss Alice," he continued, "is it? You must really pardon me any rudeness. But we do not capture a M'Clellan and his entire army every day"—the ruffian instantly lost now in the polished gentleman. "Shall we ride? Anne will be glad to see you."

"Thank you, Mr. Wright," said Alice, who was by this time seated again on her pony, "I believe I will ride on home; Mr. Arthur will be kind enough to escort me. Good-morning;" and the two rode slowly off, leaving Mr. Wright carefully buttoning up his waistcoat to protect his cherished weapon from the damp, hesitating but what he ought to use it yet. And long sits Mr. Wright upon his horse, looking after them as they ride away, doubtful in reference to the course he has pursued in failing to kill some one, especially the chance, in his very hands, too, of having neglected to kill a Union man! Dissatisfied Alonzo Wright is with the event and with himself. Stop! Ten to one some of the hands have been up to something on the place since he left yesterday. Want to be free, do they? Only one good chance at any one of them—and with appetite quickened by new hope of food, Mr. Wright spurs from under the old gin, and rides rapidly home through the drizzle.

Alice rode along the miry way in silence, weeping and mirth struggling with and neutralizing each other in her bosom. It is remarkable how little these two can find to say to each other under the circumstances all the way to Mrs. Bowles's front gate in Somerville. Mr. Arthur is almost haughty in his bearing, certainly very cold and quiet. And so, assisting her from her pony, they part, Mr. Arthur declining to enter the house on the plea of neglected studies.

Yet all the way to Mrs. Bowles, and when he parted with Alice at the gate, our clerical friend fancies that his companion sits on her pony with a form more erect, and the morning as of a new purpose breaking on her face. "Only fancy, I

H

"ONE MORE CHANCE, ABOLITIONIST."

dare say," he said to himself as he rode homeward, "only fancy!"

"Proud? For any one to speak of my being *proud!*" Alice says to herself, as she stands in her room, her hand wandering mechanically about the fastenings of her hat. Unconscious of herself utterly, because so conscious of another, and that other not Mr. Bezaleel Neely either, immaculate Secessionist though Mr. Neely is! Four years since the writer has seen a copy of Tennyson—not a copy at present in hundreds of miles, from memory let the lines be ventured :

" Love took up the harp of life, struck on all chords with might,
Struck the chord of self, which, trembling, passed in music out of sight."

## CHAPTER XIV.

"BUT I do sincerely hope, my friends, that we are ready by this time to turn away from these second and seventh chapters of Daniel. There are a host of other passages in Scripture I am anxious to show you. Astonishing, is it not, that men should have supposed so long that America was not referred to in the Bible? Why there is not a day passes but I, for one, find some fresh allusion in it, especially to our glorious Confederacy. Yes, let us leave this behind us as settled. By 'the Ancient of days' here in Daniel is clearly meant the old United States. By the 'one like unto the Son of man' is as undoubtedly meant the Confederate States. The 'mountain' refers, as we have seen, to the United States also. The stone 'cut out of the mountain without hands,' which is to dash all other nations to pieces, and become the great central Christian nation of the millennium, is, as we have clearly shown you, the Confederate States. Any flaw in our reasoning is simply impossible. The man that can not perceive this is hopelessly rotten. Heaven forbid, dear brethren, there should be a Union man among you !"

And here Brother Barker pauses, wipes his streaming face and then his moist hands with his very damp handkerchief, lays it beside his Bible to dry, takes another sip of water, and begins afresh. He is in the pulpit on his regular monthly appointment in the Pines, a country neighborhood some fifty miles from Somerville. A log church it is, densely crowded to-day. On his last regular Sabbath there Brother Barker had preached a thanksgiving discourse upon the defeat and capture of M'Clellan at Richmond, so powerful as to bring him into a state of hoarseness from which he is not recovered even yet. "I'd rather wear out than rust out," he has remarked ; and to-day he is delivering one in his series of sermons upon the Confederate States in Scripture.

The fact is, it is long now since Brother Barker has preached any thing else except the war. Nothing in the world more insipid, behind the times, obsolete for the present, than the Gospel. But has he not taken up prophecy instead ? And is not prophecy as much a part of Scripture as the old gospel ? And Brother Barker frankly disclaims all credit as the discoverer of his new interpretations of prophecy ; they are discoveries too splendid for that.

" I only use the investigations of other divines at the South," he said. " The documents themselves can not be circulated as widely as they ought owing to the dearth of paper. But so conclusive are these discourses, so exceedingly encouraging to every Christian patriot, that so far as my poor bleeding lungs will allow I am making them known by word of mouth to all under sound of my voice. I learn there are up here in the Pines some who hold to the old Union still ; few, very few I do hope. If the brutality of the North, if the justice of the Confederate cause have not convinced such of their error, Scripture surely must. Scripture, brethren, *Scripture !* And right here let us turn, if you please, to another passage.—But wait a moment. Look at me," says Brother Barker, folding his long arms upon his narrow chest, and standing back a little from the pulpit. " As you all may know, your unworthy speaker was born at the North. I have some half dozen brothers alive there this very Sunday, I suppose. Do you want to know the Scripture that cured *me* of my last love for the North? Turn then to Genesis forty-first, fifty-first. Wait a moment. What was the first great battle of our revolution ? Manassas ! Very good. Now read the passage: 'And Joseph called the name of the first-born Manasseh : For God, said he, hath made me forget all my toil, and all my father's house.' See?" And with the finger of his left hand on the passage, Brother Barker spent a vehement five minutes in showing how entirely the South had in and by that battle been made to forget its long slavery to the North, all affection even for that the home of its ancestors.

"Scripture prophesied enough for me here," he said, with both palms on his Bible. "My old father? Manassas! My brothers there? Manassas! The North, and all in it, now, henceforth, and for evermore? At the very least utter forgetfulness and eternal alienation. In other words, Manassas, Manassas! And yet there are people who doubt whether our war is referred to in this Holy Book!" added the preacher, with an air of patient resignation.

Another application of the handkerchief to face and neck and hands; another sip at the glass of water.

"Let us turn now to Isaiah sixty-sixth, seven and eight." And Brother Barker reads—"'Before she travailed, she brought forth; before her pain came, she was delivered of a man child. Who hath heard such a thing? who hath seen such things? Shall the earth be made to bring forth in one day? or shall a nation be born at once? for as soon as Zion travailed, she brought forth her children.' Now remember," continues Brother Barker, leaning one elbow on the desk, his long forefinger demonstrating the point —"remember what has been proved that, as the ecclesiastical Zion was a type of the New Testament church, so the political Zion was equally an emblem of the central nation in New Testament times—that is, America." And clearly does the preacher apply the prophecy to the instantaneous secession of the South.

"Turn again to Daniel twelfth, seventh." And Brother Barker finds the place and reads— "'When he shall have accomplished to scatter the power of the holy people, all these things shall be finished.' Now, who are the holy people?" asks he. "America, of course, the Christian Israel. What was their being scattered? Secession evidently. And what was to be accomplished then and thereby? Look at the seventh chapter going before: the establishment of Christ's last and most glorious nation—these Confederate States! Can any thing be more conclusive?" And Brother Barker goes over the passage and his comment thereupon several times to impress it upon the minds of his hearers. Very fixed is the attention of those hearers.

"Once more, if you please. Isaiah twenty-seven, twelfth." And the preacher reads—"'Ye shall be gathered one by one, O ye children of Israel.' The exact manner of Secession! No co-operation, no movement out of the Union in a body; 'one by one' do the States secede!" And on this point also Brother Barker dwells at length.

"Let us turn now to the eleventh of Zechariah." And the preacher reads the chapter. "By the breaking of the staves therein—'Beauty and Bands'—was prophesied the dissolution of the Union. The three shepherds alluded to in the passage, and all that is said of them there, how manifestly it refers to Missouri, Maryland, Kentucky, and their temporary exclusion from the Confederacy!" And the interest is thrilling as Brother Barker shows from the passage how the North, in its awful destitution and self-division, are to "eat the flesh of one another!"

But the enthusiasm of the preacher overflows all bounds as he turns to the fourth chapter of the Prophet Micah, and paints therefrom the millennial splendor of the Confederacy. Over and over again does Brother Barker read it. "'In that day, saith the Lord, will I assemble her that halteth, and I will gather her that is driven out—driven out!'" cries the preacher, "'and her that I have afflicted; and I will make her that halted a remnant, and her that was cast far off a strong nation.' Observe, brethren, 'cast far off,' 'a strong nation!' 'And the Lord shall reign over them in Mount Zion from henceforth, even forever.'" And so to the end of the chapter, at which the speaker arrives entirely exhausted.

"Matthew twenty-first, forty-third," resumes he, his handkerchief almost dripping in his hand from its service upon face and neck. "'Therefore say I unto you, The kingdom of God shall be taken from you, and given to a nation bringing forth the fruits thereof.' In the verse before is allusion to a rejected stone," reasons the preacher. "You will remember we saw this stone all through Scripture; cut out of the mountain of the old Union; destined to destroy and supersede all other nations is the Confederate States; 'become the head of the corner' it there says. Why? Because the Union, the old Christian Israel had failed—verse forty-three—to bring forth fruit—fruit which the Confederacy will bring forth!" And closing the Bible, Brother Barker describes at length the awful apostasy of the North, its universal infidelity and abominable wickedness. "Ought I not to know?" he asks, in conclusion. "Am not I a Northern man? born there, raised there? It is sometimes asked by people," continues the preacher, with both hands clenched upon the ledge of his pulpit, and leaning as far forward as possible between them—"sometimes asked why we Northern born men make the strongest of all Secessionists. I will tell you, brethren. It is because we who have lived at the North know the North so much better than men at the South. From long, personal, close observation we know the North!" And what intense loathing did the preacher infuse into the word! Strange that his audience should have such a sense of distaste at hearing this from the lips of one born there! True, of course, but they did not like him to assert it. The Brother is conscious of this, and falls back a little disconcerted upon the thirty-

BROTHER BARKER.

fourth chapter of Ezekiel, the eighteenth and nineteenth verses.

"You need not take my word, friends; see what Scripture says of the conduct of the North." And he reads—"'Seemeth it a small thing unto you to have eaten up the good pasture, but ye must tread down with your feet the residue of your pastures? and to have drunk of the deep waters, but ye must foul the residue with your feet? And as for my flock, they eat that which ye have trodden with your feet; and they drink that which ye have fouled with your feet.'" And the minister illustrates this prophecy of the tyranny of the North over the South by its course in regard to the Tariff and the Territories, consoling himself with the speedy righting of the South, prophesied so clearly in the verses which follow.

"Some of you have been rather trying to joke me about my last sermon here," the preacher says, by way of digression. "True, I did believe then that M'Clellan was defeated and captured. Suppose it was not so complete a defeat as we then supposed; and where is that one of us that had any doubt on the subject then? Look again at my text of that sermon: 'I will remove far off from you the Northern Army, and will drive him into a land barren and desolate, with his face toward the east sea, and his hinder part toward the utmost sea, and his stink shall come up, and his ill savor shall come up because he hath done great things.' Is there a man that does not see that Scripture refers here to Lincoln's army, by its very name, too? I need not enter into this passage again. If it has not been fulfilled entirely yet, it certainly will be, and that soon. But let us turn to Daniel again, seven, eighteen, this time. 'The saints of the Most High shall take the kingdom, and possess the kingdom for ever, even for ever and ever.' Now what does 'saint' mean when applied, as Scripture means it should be here, to a government? Why, it means a mild, a gentle government. Friends, contrast the Confederacy with the old Federal Government. That bound the States together strong and hard; ruled them with a rod of iron; the most despotic Government, as this war shows, that ever disgraced the earth. But our glorious Confederacy! How perfectly mild and easy it is! The States are free to go and come under it as each one pleases, no restraint, no coercion. The North is invading us—does our Confederacy invade them? No, brethren. It only asked to be allowed to go out of the Union in peace. It did not want a war. It never dreamed of a war. This day it is the gentlest, most peaceable, most lenient; the lightest, easiest government the world ever saw. No wonder Scripture speaks of it under the name of 'saint.' Ah, if the North could but come up to the true idea of all government in this nineteenth century; the millennial, the Christian idea of government—States free as air to vote themselves whichever way they like! Instead of that, what do we see? Why, the old heathen ideas of permanent rule, coercion, war! I tell you, friends, Secession contains in itself the very essence of Christian freedom; it is a Gospel doctrine; it is the very germ and substance of all human organization in millennial times!" And largely did Brother Barker expatiate on this theme.

"Bear with me, brethren," he continues, as he searches the pages of his Bible. "I want to show you another—ah, here it is! Zechariah thirteen, from the seventh verse." And here the pen recoils from recording in such connection the first, at least, of the verses quoted by the preacher. By "the man that is my fellow" Scripture meant, according to him, the "one like unto the Son of man" referred to in Daniel; in other words, the Confederate Government. "'And it shall come to pass, that in all the land,'" continued the preacher from his Bible, "'saith the Lord, two parts therein shall be cut off and die; but the third shall be left therein.' When we seceded there were thirty-three States, you know," continued the preacher, holding his finger upon the passage for after use. "Three classes there were among these thirty-three States. First, the Border States; second, the Coercion or Northern States; third, the Confederate States, eleven, you observe; just a third of thirty-three. The two parts cut off from God's new and glorious nation, our Confederacy, shall die, you see, be defeated, destroyed, perish—the Border and the Northern States. The third—our Confederacy—shall be left in the land in permanence and prosperity. And look how our trouble from the blockade and the war is further prophesied—verse nine—'And I will bring the third part through the fire, and will refine them as silver is refined, and will try them as gold is tried: they shall call on my name, and I will hear them: I will say, It is my people: and they shall say, The Lord is my God.'"

But it is impossible to follow Brother Barker. Only the intense excitement attaching to every syllable said by any one on the one topic enabled the audience to sit so patiently under his eloquence. Less than twenty minutes of a discourse from his lips on any other topic would have wearied them out. There was a force, too, in the glowing enthusiasm of the speaker. Whoever else did not he at least did believe in his interpretations of prophecy. Need we say how he described the impending convulsions at the North from the sixteenth chapter of Revelation, the nineteenth verse? Or the rout at Manassas and in all the other battles of the war, as foretold in the forty-eighth Psalm, fourth, fifth, and sixth verses? Or the future influence of the Confederacy over the world in the nineteenth chapter of Revelation, the fifteenth verse, the "rod of iron" referring to its commercial, and "the sword out of his mouth" referring to its moral influence? That Secession was the act of God himself, He setting up the Confederacy with his own hand, Brother Barker proved from the second chapter of Daniel, the forty-fourth verse. The peculiar estimation set by Heaven upon the same Government, from Isaiah the twenty-eighth chapter and fifth verse. And that the Almighty himself was fighting for them the prophet Zechariah has left beyond question in the fourteenth chapter and third verse of his prophecy. Let those who wish to study the theological aspect of the insanity of the times refer to the chapters and verses specified at their leisure. Let them remember in doing so that there were men who sincerely believed in Brother Barker's application of them, and a new insight will be had into the depth and desperation of that insanity.

But the preacher has reserved some of his most telling texts to the last.

"In my previous discourse I showed you," said he, "that in Scripture the number seven refers to the seven States that first seceded. Permit your humble speaker to give you a few more illustrations of this most striking fact." And so he drains the last drop of water from the pitcher, full when he began, pulls down his waistcoat by the lower edge, moves pitcher and glass out of his way by placing them on the bench behind him, and resumes:

"Micah, brethren, fifth, fifth. 'Then shall we raise against him seven shepherds and eight principal men.'" And clearly is it proved that while the seven principal men means the seven States which first seceded, it is Virginia, seceding when the Federal Government had become "Assyrian" in its attitude toward God's chosen, which makes the eighth.

"Once more, brethren. Isaiah fourth, first." And transfixing the passage with the forefinger of his left hand, with the other hand he entreats special attention. "'And in that day seven women shall take hold of one man, saying, We will eat our own bread, and wear our own apparel; only let us be called by thy name, to take away our reproach.'" Dull indeed must his brethren be if they do not see the singular and striking meaning of this at a glance. The seven women are the seven States in a desolate condition when they first seceded. Instantly they all lay hold of one man. "You see it, brethren! They take the Confederate Government to be a husband over them. Each is to remain, you observe, an independent State; insists on feeding and clothing itself; they only want the Confederate Government as a sort of protector. The reference of Scripture to our new nation is as minute as it is abundant. Who can doubt, then, the peculiar regard had for us by the Almighty?

"Once more, but once, though you can not but observe how exhausted I am. Jeremiah fifteen, nine. 'She that hath borne seven languisheth: she hath given up the ghost; her sun is gone down while it was yet day.'" The old Union is this unhappy mother; and its fate, after the departure of the seven seceding States, its utter destruction in mid career! Brother Barker surpasses himself in the delineation thereof. When he ceases at last it is solely because he is physically unable to articulate another syl-

lable. And then he holds forth his long arm, his heavy-lidded eyes almost shut, and stands for minutes exhausted but triumphant, in the attitude of a conqueror over his captives.

Fanaticism? It has nothing to do with sect merely as a sect; it is temperament. Look at Brother Barker as he stands. That narrow forehead, that lank hair, those restless gray eyes, those incessant hands. Had that man been cradled in Rochester and Mormonism he would have been Danite, apostle, leader of the delusion. Had he come into the vortex of Spiritualism, no man would have whirled more madly on its rapid error. Only let him have had a hint in time of Father Miller's theory of the end of the world, and no man alive would have been more positively certain than he that the world was to end on the second day of June, 1843, at precisely half past two o'clock in the morning. The Scripture for it? The Bible for this, that, and the other, whatever the fancy be he flies off upon? He could find you passages innumerable, passages clear beyond all skepticism, passages so perfectly convincing of his theory that, it pains him to say it, but you are an infidel if you hesitate to believe. Or place a red conical cap upon that small, narrow head; strip off the suit of rusty black, and wrap Brother Barker's loins about with a cow's skin instead; give him a twirl by the shoulders, and no Dervish along the Golden Horn would revolve more frantically on his heel, or yell with greater strength of conviction and lungs than he.

But the evil is, Brother Barker is not content to revolve and howl himself; he is for war on all the world if it fails to spin and scream with him. Riding one's hobby is an innocent amusement enough. Did not Uncle Toby ride *his* hobby? Only Uncle Toby never rode his hobby over any one else; and that is nine-tenths of the pleasure of the ride with Brother Barker.

Dr. Warner had once remarked to his wife that Brother Barker was afflicted with a species of moral "cutaneousness," by which he meant, as he explained to his wife on demand, that the Brother was forever breaking out all over in a sudden rash of spirit and tongue whatever heat happened to be in the atmosphere. It mattered not a straw the nature of the heat; from the first the hottest of the heated was Brother Barker.

At the time Mrs. Warner entirely agreed with her husband; and the defect of character being her own also, so repeated and deplored the fact as to lose the Doctor nigh a score of patients, the members of the Brother's church. To do her justice, however, when the preacher went in for Secession with Mrs. Warner, that lady retracted in every circle this injurious opinion of him, and mournfully ascribed such an impression on the mind of the Doctor to "his abominable Union notions."

Nadab and Abihu? Alas, the censer of *this*

minister never glowed except with "strange fire." Most of his ministry had been spent in onslaughts upon other denominations, and it was wonderful the skill with which he platted detached passages from Scripture like so many separate thongs into scourges for his foes; for all who did not agree with him were foes, actual and active foes to be met and defeated as such. Neutrality? No more than moderation was there an atom of it in his character; therefore he could not conceive of its existence in that of any one else. And when Brother Barker did preach the Gospel, it was in tones so vehement, so unlike the gentle accents of his Master, that the very Gospel heaven, and Gospel hell, and Gospel salvation savored too strongly of the minister himself to have their due influence. Even the wind which bloweth as it listeth never blew at all in his estimation save as it blew exactly when and where *he* would have it, and in a hurricane at that.

"Just one thing more, my friends," says Brother Barker, as soon as he has recovered voice enough for the purpose. "When I was explaining just now that prophecy from Daniel about the saint-like character of our Confederacy, its being, in other words, the mildest government the world ever knew, so mild as to be almost no government at all, just there, brethren, I saw a gentleman in this congregation shake his head. I ought to have stopped and spoken of it on the spot. The truth is, I was under such headway I could not stop then. Let us now ask the Brother *why* he shook his head?"

There is instant and intense excitement in the audience, the deep stir within the heart of war. The minister stands silent for some minutes, but no one stirs or speaks.

"I believe you are the friend that shook his head," the preacher remarks, and his long finger indicates a man among the congregation. An unusually large and tall man it is, a conspicuous object on account of towering above those around as he sits. A large sun-burnt face, plenty of black hair and whiskers, butternut coat and pantaloons, no waistcoat, hickory shirt, copious use of tobacco in the way of chewing—nothing else noticeable.

"Paul Brooks, I think," adds the preacher, all the St. Dominic and the Torquemada stirring in his veins.

"Me!" exclaims the gentleman designated, after a torrent of ambier. "Did *I* shake *my* head?"

"Yes, Sir, you did," says the inquisitor, solemnly, and in the discharge of a painful duty.

"I did, heh? I didn't know it. But I know I thought *No* very strong just there. Now I come to think of it, I dare say I did." The speaker says this coolly enough, but he knows the peril he has incurred, feels it creep along his bones, Kentuckian as he is, even more than he acknowl-

edges it in his mind. There is breathless, painful silence.

"May I ask why—may this intelligent audience of Southern citizens ask *why* you shook your head?" The preacher speaks as to a criminal condemned. He will let him say why sentence of death should not be passed upon him, however.

"When I shook my head, though I didn't know till now that I did it," replies Paul Brooks, "it was when you made Scripture say this new movement was the freest and mildest Government on earth. What I meant by shaking my head was—conscription and martial law."

The preacher hears him in silence; then only draws together his lips to restrain unspeakable words, shakes his head in the deepest sorrow, and takes up his hymn-book.

"Forty-sixth Psalm, second part, long measure," he begins.

"Will you excuse me one minute?" says the Kentuckian. "I don't like to mention such things seeing it's Sunday. You won't object, I suppose; and I think a good many of us would be interested."

The preacher pauses, hymn-book in hand, with the air of a martyr at the stake, assaulted but patient.

"You say Scripture speaks plainly of this new movement?" asks the Kentuckian.

The preacher assents with a low bow of the head. There is something indescribable in it. It is as of a Judge on the bench to some unreasonable prisoner whose fate is already settled.

"And we must take exactly what Scripture says of this movement—that is, what Scripture may *seem* to say about it?"

Brother Barker smiles a sad but patient assent.

"And we, as good Christians, must obey what it says in reference to this movement to the letter?"

The Kentuckian retains his seat, but spits copiously between each question.

"By movement I suppose you mean our glorious Confederacy," replies the preacher, appealing with both hands to the audience in sorrowful deprecation.

"Yes, Sir," says the Kentuckian, very mildly, even persuasively.

"You have some intention in your question, I see *that*. But yes, Sir, yes. What Scripture says of our Confederacy—and it alludes to it continually and pointedly—we must do. Of course." And the preacher loses a little of the martyr as he stands on the defensive.

"There are one or two texts in Scripture," begins the Kentuckian.

But "Brother Barker was sharp as a steel-trap," as was afterward remarked by some then present. "Exactly as I thought," he interrupts, at the same time closing his Bible and pushing it away from him. "No, Mr. Brooks, I will not read those passages. For one, I can not, I dare not make such mockery of the word of God."

"Nothing more to say," remarks the Kentuckian, and so expectorates and subsides into his former indolent position on the rude seat he occupies.

"Forty-sixth Psalm, second part, long measure!" says the preacher, briskly, and with some emphasis, hymn-book in hand.

"Hold on a moment, Brother Barker!" It is an old man seated, with a staff between his knees, near the pulpit. "I don't like this way of doing things on a Sunday, and in meetin'. But now we are at it friends present would like to hear you read them passages; every thing bearing on the pint is interesting."

The preacher acknowledges the movement of assent among the crowded audience. But he can not comply.

"No, Brother Robinson, if I would I could. As a minister of the Gospel, standing here in this sacred place, I can not, I dare not make mockery of God's blessed book."

"The shortest way is, let me read them then. Friends present want to hear. No danger of Scripture hurting any of us whatever part it is. Name the texts, Mr. Brooks." And Brother Robinson, the patriarch of the neighborhood, is standing before the pulpit, the minister's Bible in hand.

"I had no intention of disturbing the meeting," began the Kentuckian.

"Passages, Mr. Brooks; you name them passages," interrupted the patriarch.

The Kentuckian names the eighty-third Psalm, the first five verses. The patriarch is a long time finding the place. Brother Barker leans, with a patient smile, on his elbow, rested upon the pulpit.

"'Keep not thou silence, O God: hold not thy peace, and be not still, O God. For, lo, thine enemies make a tumult: and they that hate thee have lifted up the head. They have taken crafty counsel against thy people, and consulted against thy hidden ones. They have said, Come, and let us cut them off from being a nation; that the name of Israel may be no more in remembrance. For they have consulted together with one consent: they are confederate against thee.' Humph, confederate against thee!" The patriarch has read the passage very slowly.

Brother Barker groans.

"Hold on," he says; "Brother Barker has just told us how one-third of the States—eleven, that is—are the Confederacy Scripture speaks of. I see the ones confederated together in this place are mentioned lower down. Let's count." And the patriarch transfers the Bible to his left hand, while he counts aloud with the fingers of his right upon the stand: "Edom, Ishmaelites, Moab, Hagarenes, Gebal, Ammon, Amalek, Philistines, inhabitants of Tyre, Assur, chil-

dren of Lot—by jingo, eleven exactly!" Deep sensation among the audience.

"Any more places, Brother Brooks?" he asks, after a long pause, during which he is counting over again to be certain. "Out with it, Brother—yes, eleven exactly!"

"Isaiah seventh, second, third, fourth, and seventh verses," from Paul Brooks. Breathless attention.

"'And it was told the house of David, saying, Syria is confederate with Ephraim.' Confederate? Yes, well. 'And his heart was moved, and the heart of his people, as the trees of the wood are moved with the wind. Then said the Lord unto Isaiah, Go forth now to meet Ahaz, and say unto him, Take heed, and be quiet; fear not, neither be fainthearted for the two tails of these smoking firebrands. Thus saith the Lord God, It shall not stand, neither shall it come to pass.' Humph, queer!"

There is a movement of interest in the congregation as the reader ceases.

"My friends," begins Brother Barker, holding up his right hand.

"In one moment, Brother Barker," the patriarch interrupts him. "Any more passages, Mr. Brooks?"

"I was told Mr. Barker found a good deal about the Confederacy in the Bible. I happened one day in Somerville to come across a Concordance, and hunted out the places where the word occurs. Our preacher says the Jews were emblems of this country, so I thought the word in their history might teach something. However, only two passages more. Let me study a moment. Ah, yes—Obadiah, seventh verse," says Paul Brooks.

"Chapter?" asks Brother Robinson, turning over the leaves.

"Ain't any chapter, seventh verse."

"'All the men of thy confederacy have brought thee even to the border: the men that were at peace with thee have deceived thee, and prevailed against thee: they that eat thy bread have laid a wound under thee: there is none understanding in him,'" reads the patriarch. The very slow manner in which the passage is read is itself almost equal to a running comment upon it. The interest in the congregation deepens.

"Only one more: Isaiah, eighth chapter, ninth verse," says Paul Brooks.

"'Associate yourselves, O ye people, and ye shall be broken in pieces; and give ear, all ye of far countries: gird yourselves, and ye shall be broken in pieces; gird yourselves, and ye shall be broken in pieces. Take counsel together, and it shall come to nought; speak the word, and it shall not stand—' But there ain't any thing about the Confederacy in this," says the patriarch, looking up.

"Go on," says the Kentuckian, with a copious expectoration first.

"'For the Lord spake thus to me,'" the reader continued, "'with a strong hand, and instructed me that I should not walk in the way of this people, saying, Say ye not, A confederacy, to all them to whom this people shall say, A confederacy; neither fear ye their fear, nor be afraid.'"

"That's all," said Paul Brooks.

The reader closed the volume, laid it on the pulpit, and took his seat, resting his chin again on the staff between his knees. Dead silence.

"And do you, Sir," said the preacher, severely—"do you, Sir, say to this intelligent Christian, intelligent *Southern* congregation, that those passages have reference to our glorious young nation?"

"I say nothing about it. You all bear me witness *you* attacked me first. I only say, if all *your* places in the Bible mean as you say, what do these other places mean?" And in the silence that follows the splash of the Kentuckian's indignant expectoration is distinctly heard.

"I have read, I have heard of awful perversions of this blessed and sacred book, brethren," says Brother Barker, after a pause, and in deep and measured tones; "but such an awful desecration and wresting of Scripture I never heard in my life. On Sunday! In this holy place! During the very hour of divine worship! Only this one thing I've got to say, brethren"—and the preacher leaned over his pulpit toward his audience, and spoke in low, significant tones—"I've been told before Paul Brooks is a Union man; now I know it from his own lips!" And the brother drew himself back, as with a calmness awful to behold. "Forty-sixth Psalm, second part, long measure. Brother Stevens will please raise the tune, my bleeding lungs will not permit."

GOING HOME FROM CHURCH.

## CHAPTER XV.

At the same hour in which Brother Barker is preaching the Gospel—according to Jefferson Davis—at the Pines, Edward Arthur is preaching another Gospel—that according to the Lord Jesus Christ—in his church in Somerville. And he and his comparatively few hearers know that he has got such a grasp upon the very substance and essence of that good news to men as he never had before. Yes, he, and multitudes like him at the South, in ever deepening despair of things human in these days, are looking to the Gospel and to the living God, of whom that sacred paper is but the transparent drapery, with an ever-increasing singleness and intensity to which all previous experience is tame indeed.

"It's the last time, the very last time, you catch me a-hearing him," Mrs. Warner had remarked a few Sabbaths ago as she walked her portly husband home from church. "Yes, I know it, I did say before this I never would go again, and I haven't been, you well know, for ever so long. But I thought that to-day, Thanksgiving Day for our glorious victory over M'Clellan, he certainly would come out for the Confederacy, and be down at last upon the Yankees. And look at it. All that sermon of his to-day only a-trying to prove what terrible sinners *we* are instead, telling over all our sins. Not one word about the vile wickedness of the Yankees."

"Why he said, Helen," ventured the Doctor, "that, whatever were the human instruments of chastisement employed, the Almighty would deal in strictest justice with them as with us. You see he wants us to look more at that for which we are being punished than at the punishment itself; he says that if we do not we will be more and more punished by Him until we do. For one," added the Doctor, rashly, "I agree with Mr. Arthur entirely!"

But the Doctor never would have said this save from the warmth of just having heard that sermon.

"It's his influence has ruined you; he's a traitor, a Yankee, a vile Abolitionist!" says Mrs. Warner, and so decidedly that Alice Bowles, walking home alone from church, can not choose but hear. "Always insisting and insisting upon our sins," says Mrs. Warner, "as if we are not a million times better than the Yankees. Talking, too, about the Almighty, as if *He* had any hand in this wicked war upon us—it's awful! Look here, Dr. Warner," adds his wife in a sudden change of tone, as a light breaks on her, "I've got it now! The one great sin the South is being punished for is Slavery. That's his idea. Ah, hah. Yes, oh yes, I see! The Almighty is so angry with us because we own slaves he is using the Yankees to chastise us—*chastise* us, as if they could do it!—for that."

"Has he ever said so?" begins the Doctor.

"Hah, I remember now. That's why he has never preached a sermon—never, on the Bible command to us to hold slaves. Brother Barker—why there's not one preacher I know of but has done so often. Exactly!"

"I am astonished at you, Helen," says Dr. Warner, a new light, of somewhat different hue, breaking on him also. "You well know he has often urged on us—taking the institution for granted—to instruct our negroes—"

"Wants us to see to it that they are actually married and all that—as if a negro ever does more than take up with a husband or wife for a while; and as if virtuous white ladies were going to meddle in such things! Catch me! Something about the duties of negro parents to their children too. Parents! I tell you, Dr. Warner," adds his clear-spoken partner, "all such stuff is inconsistent with the institution. To preach it is to preach Abolitionism, that's all. It may deceive you, but it can't deceive me, so I tell you. And that he, a Southern man, that has lived here so long—"

Dr. Warner walks with drooped head beside his wife while she is exhausting herself upon the subject. Not that he hears a word she says. That Sunday morning when his pastor announced his settled purpose to confine himself exclusively to his Spiritual duties comes up before him. People agreed that was a pastor's only true course then—now it is disloyal. Mr. Arthur's is a peculiar position. Once, at least, during the week, the bell of every other church in Somerville summons the congregation to a special prayer-meeting for the success of the Confederacy; alone of the churches Mr. Arthur's remains closed, his bell silent. The only exception to the preachers in and around Somerville, and there are a great many of them, one never sees him on the streets laughing and shaking hands over the last glorious news, or clapping and stamping at the public meetings. Not once has he even been seen at the aforesaid prayer-meetings, where Sam Peters prays till he can only gasp for the swift and utter destruction of the Yankees. "By the sword, Lord, by the yellow fever, Lord. Like Gideon's foes, by one another, Lord; any way, good Lord, any way, every way, so that thou only out of thy unwasting fullness speedily destroy them!" Where Brother Barker, too, rises in prayer to such heights of expostulation as well as entreaty as he had never dreamed of even at the climax of the most successful of camp-meetings. All the "putting down, O Lord," Brother Barker clamors for these days is the "putting down of our thrice fiendish foes!" All the "saving" he supplicates is the "saving our new, our young, our great, our glorious Confederacy, even thine own peculiar people, O our God!"

Yes, it is a trying time for Mr. Arthur, these days.

"He's a liar, it isn't a political matter at all," Sam Peters says in reference to this speckled bird in the flock, "the very existence of Christianity at all on this continent is involved in the success of the Confederacy!" and that is the first article in the Creed—ah, you may deny it now; you know it was then—of every religious Secessionist at the South. But, in the rising tide of the times, friend after friend has been swept away from Mr. Arthur, some fled North, some gone to the war in reality, some gone to the war, from him at least, in heart.

His congregation wanes from Sabbath to Sabbath. In pastoral visits among the few that remain, even among some as heartily opposed as he at the outset to Secession, he hears, "Well, I was opposed to the thing at the beginning as much as a man could be, but now that we *are* in it"—and so on to the "last ditch" with the "black flag" waving over it! Such a forgetfulness of all principle in the matter, such an utter abandoning yourself to the current simply because it *is* a current. And that current is Lethe itself as to the Past. It matters not a straw how sincerely good Mr. Ellis, and thousands like him, once believed it to be a great sin; "now we are in it; now, you see, we *are* in it!" is the magical formula, and, presto! off you are gone, soul as well as body, with the movement.

A trying time for the man. There are many as clear and as firm, too, as he, but, unlike them, he can not shut himself up in his office, bury himself in the furrows of his farm, occupy and conceal himself behind his counter. He is before the public every Sunday, peculiarly before them on the often recurring Thanksgiving and Fast days. Somerville has forgotten a good many people, but he is too much before it for that. An annoying Elijah, who will not even hide himself away in the seclusion of Cherith and Sarepta, but is perpetually in Ahab's path.

By slow degrees, keenly as it hurt him at first, he is becoming used to people passing him without speaking, to the cold words and colder manner of those who were once his friends. On what pretext resign? Where go if he should? What occupation can he, a man under ban, follow? He has no capital to become a merchant, no farm to be a farmer, as objectionable a teacher as he is a preacher. Let him resign to-day, before to-morrow Brother Barker will himself see to it that he is conscripted. All he can do is to continue in his present line of duty. He wonders, Is the delusion in myself or in the mass around me! Ignorant and educated, sanguine and phlegmatic, silent and talkative, violent and mild, the avowedly wicked and the devotedly pious—the fermentation is seething all men into oneness of opinion, feeling, speech. Alas! for Edward Arthur, he is only petrifying in his isolation.

Look at good Mr. Ellis. There is almost nothing left in his store these days for sale. His last calicoes went off at two dollars a yard. Mrs. Bowles bought his last bolt of domestic at one dollar and seventy-five cents. He did have shoes at ten dollars, none now. His shelves display only empty boxes, bottles of hair oil, stone jugs, patent medicines, and an amazing number of mouse-traps. Any quantity of coffee-mills, but they are only a mockery, coffee selling at two dollars a pound. But not a cent cares Mr. Ellis. His main object in opening his store in the morning is to hear what people—dropping in during the day to ask for articles they won't get—have to say upon the one topic, while, leaning against his empty shelves, he exchanges instead of goods his own freshest hopes in return.

"Goods? No, Sir; and, for one, I intend getting few or none from abroad hereafter. I hope to sell nothing that is not made within the Confederacy. In a short time, Sir, we will have achieved our independence in every sense of the word."

Piety develops in a man the faculty of hope, and the vigor of Mr. Ellis's hope has reference to the Confederacy, and is amazing. His son Henry writes gloomy letters from the army and he rebukes him therefor, ignoring to every one and to himself every thing not encouraging to "the South." The paper he reads several times over on its arrival, with what heated unbelief in its discouraging items, with what magnifying fervor in its encouraging ones. The least thistledown of a rumor of the latter kind is a solid satisfaction for, at least, the passing moment. He eagerly repeats it to customers calling in on vain search for axes or nails or pins. An iron-clad navy arrived at Wilmington for the South, a civil war already broken out at the North, European intervention—his sincere belief in the news satisfies all who hear it from him that it must be even so. Whoever else is absent from any war meeting Mr. Ellis is not; his sincere face giving moral sanction to the proceedings otherwise rather vindictive, not to say profane. It is singular, though, that he is not a more regular attendant on the prayer meetings; there is a spirit in the remarks and the prayers thereat from which, in spite of himself, he winces and shrinks. The religiousness of Mr. Ellis's belief in the Confederacy disquiets his pastor more than any thing else—all Mr. Ellis's piety running so swiftly in that one channel in these days.

But the two rarely meet now. "He knows my sentiments perfectly well; how can he be so cordial with me—not cordial—so full rather of a struggling respect and esteem for me still?" the pastor asks himself, wondering whether he will see his former friend at church next Sunday or no. Is it possible deep down in his soul he knows I am right? Mr. Arthur muses upon it, till one Sabbath Mr. Ellis disappears with his family from church.

Perhaps Robby Sorel may have had an unconscious share in this last step. Not a more modest, quiet, sober little fellow than Robby; but, to say nothing of his mother, he has by this time become exceedingly attached to Mr. Arthur, who teaches him at home, and makes a companion of him in all his excursions, his heart yearning doubly over Robby in his state of banishment, and being repulsed from almost every one else. As with the children of all Union people, Robby has a great deal to bear in the way of abuse. That his mother and Mr. Arthur are Yankees, Abolitionists, and traitors he is told almost every time he is sent into Somerville on an errand. But when Charley Ellis, about his own age, becoming rapidly the very bad boy which the children of pious parents sometimes do become, heaps cursing and abuse upon him, about this time, as a "whitewashed negro," with a great deal more in reference to Mr. Arthur and his mother, Robby's wrath bursts forth, and, as much to his own surprise as that of Charley Ellis, he gives this latter a sound drubbing. Of course Mr. Ellis bears only his son's, or rather his son's mother's version of the matter; that, with Charley's blackened eyes, settles the matter. Only he will not put it on that ground with Mr. Arthur.

"The prayers he offers are precisely those he might put up in a Boston pulpit: I can not stand it," says Mr. Ellis. Not that he has any more fancy for Brother Barker and the like for all that. For the present Mr. Ellis and family, his children withdrawn from Sabbath School, are adrift upon the world.

"I wonder whether I would be as dumb upon political matters in the pulpit if I was where I could speak?" said Mr. Arthur to himself, next morning as he rode home from his bath, feeling fresh and strong. "And is it an hypocrisy for me to put my position on the ground that it is the duty of ministers to abstain from politics?"

"You and your fellow-preachers of the same sentiments are in somewhat the same case here at the South that the preachers of the Democratic party are at the North," says Mr. Ferguson, to whom, in Guy Brooks's office the same day, Mr. Arthur propounds his case. "Were you and your like at the North they at the South, to say the least, the temptation upon you as upon them to speak out would be tremendous. Eh? I dare say you would be among the loudest, most violent of them all—a perfect Barker. It is only human nature, man," says the Scot.

"My convictions," means the minister, "are so very clear and strong; so very much to so many is at stake; and, then, the question is so largely a moral, in fact a religious, one! Yet surely a minister should be exclusively—"

"Oh, never mind about that," breaks in the lawyer. "You are occupying the only position you can now;" and Guy Brooks continues an interrupted denunciation of the new Stay Law.

"And there is conscription," begins the Scotchman.

"The most awful violation of State Rights—the most unconstitutional thing!" burst out the lawyer.

"You must not say that; you know our Supreme Court is unanimous against you. By-the-by," continues Mr. Ferguson, "I had a visit last night from a man on land business—wanted to buy land—as if I would exchange my solid acres for his worthless paper-money! He was telling me about a District Judge in our sister State—a long story. Being a Yankee and in office he decides instantly, eagerly, that conscription is constitutional. They wanted to argue before him the question of Martial Law, as now existing in every village over the State. 'Not one syllable, gentlemen,' he said; 'my mind is already made up—Martial Law is constitutional also.' And if that gang at Richmond had enacted Polygamy it would have been the same. Poor fellow! I know all about it: at the beginning of Secession, too thoroughly informed in head and heart not to know its diabolical nature and consequences, he winced and shrank. In, however, he went at last, under the terrible pressure, desperately; now he stops at nothing, of course. My land-seeker told me the poor fellow is thinned to a ghost—you can read his misery in his face—he can not sit still a moment —in and out of every group he comes upon, seeking consolation and finding none. Like Milton's Satan he can not fly himself, however. I've put my man's information in my collection, adds he, laying his broad palm on the vast volume in question lying on the table beside him; "and you mark my words, Sirs," continues the grim Scot, "if I do not have to complete that person's history with an account of his suicide I am more mistaken than I was ever before in my life."

"I suppose you have that printed list of those who have not paid their War tax," asks the lawyer—"the one pasted up in the Court-house?"

"In my collection? Yes, Sir, my name leading the list. There has not been a matter relating to Secession in my reach that is not there. That collection, Sir, is nothing to laugh at—it is

material of profound philosophical study. The regular steps of Secession toward despotism are perfectly beautiful, illustrating the invariable working of moral law as the rainbow does the natural laws of light. Stay law, exemption of the rich from military service, martial law, conscription, prostituted press, terrorism—we will soon get on to currency utterly depreciated, then impressment of property and negroes, terrible military executions to prevent desertion, State militia passed into the hands of the Richmond gang—"

"What raving madness!" breaks in the lawyer, rising from his seat in desperation. "We seceded for what?"

"For our share of the Territories, and they are gone; for State Rights, and they are gone."

"For Slavery, and it will soon be gone, too. *Quem deus vult perdere*—a hackneyed old proverb, Mr. Arthur. You cut loose from the Union," continues the Scotchman, "and sail off on the one bottom of Slavery! Beautiful experiment, *experimentum crucis*, as Bacon calls such; Faraday, with a broad, clean counter before him, never tried a neater, completer one in Natural Philosophy. The idea, you see, is to eliminate Slavery from all that has hitherto been mixed with it, to see how the thing itself and by itself stands. Well, not a Power in the world dare recognize your Slave Government; at home corruption and despotism and ruin until you sicken of it—to say nothing of the awful judgments of Heaven upon you by the hands of the Federals! Being from Scotland, I am impartial, of course. And such men as you two, Dr. Warner, Paul Brooks up there at the Pines, and all like you at the South, why, born and living at the South, it is no wonder you are coming so slowly to see. But you are on the road—three years hence the Union men of the South will be the most hearty emancipationists on earth, without a spark of Northern fanaticism!"

It was an awful sentiment; but dry Mr. Ferguson stated it simply as a scientific fact. He was canny Scotch enough, however, to lower his voice as he made the atrocious statement. "And it is the hand of God," he added; "you good people could see no harm in Slavery. Very well, Heaven is putting that very cup to your lip, pressing it there bitter and long, to see how you like the taste. The Jehovah of Moses still rules, an eye for an eye, *lex talionis*—retributive justice the old Covenanters call it."

Neither of his friends would have endured such language a few months before. Yes, an immense amount of thinking was being done in the South those days, and in the mind of every reasoning mortal there, Union man or Secessionist, it all bore upon that one thing—Slavery.

"And so you had to march up, too, and take your medicine?" the lawyer asks Mr. Arthur, after a long silence. And that gentleman needed no explanation. He *had* stood before the Provost Marshal, and, under oath, renounced all allegiance to the United States Government, swearing fealty to the "Confederate States of America" instead. Medicine? Yes; and the bitterest to him, and to thousands like him, their manhood had ever taken. Certain zealous females of the Secession persuasion had even offered themselves to the Provost Marshal of Somerville as a committee to administer the same oath to every one of their own sex in the county. Unfortunately the Provost Marshal declined the offer; acknowledged its importance, but plead absence of instructions. Not one of the Secession females but would have died or succeeded. Not even the feeblest of the Union ladies but would have endured first a thousand deaths. Who can conjecture the issue? And, alas for Poesy, Bellona, dread goddess of war, being the muse, that such an Iliad should not have been enacted!

"Tim Lamum Provost Marshal? Oh, come now, not Tim Lamum!" had been the universal remark in Somerville when that fact was announced.

Wait one instant. For it takes very little expenditure of colors—water colors—to paint Tim Lamum. A suddenly shot up youth of nineteen was Tim, oily as to hair, sparse as to mustache, feeble as to stamina, profane as to speech, loose as to morals, good as to only one thing on earth—and that one thing is poker. All the rest of Tim's full length is on the canvas when it is added that Tim had "plenty of negroes," and was nephew of the editor. An exceedingly vaporous existence had Tim led up to Secession. With his hat perched, tilted well forward, upon the top of his head, a cigar in the corner of his languid mouth, nothing on the surface of this planet had Tim to do. And he did it; that is, during the day. At night it was poker.

Tim was off to the war from the first, was in one fight in which a bridge was much mixed up, and came back. Forever on the point of leaving to "rejoin his command," somehow he never got off. But as a private? No, Sir. No man readier than he to go as an officer. Not attaining to that, Lamum, editor and uncle, discovers that he can not dispense with Tim from the office of the *Star*. So Tim is compelled to smoke his listless cigar a fraction of every day in that dreary and very dirty den until his uncle can get him something as Commissary, Quartermaster, Contractor from Richmond.

So, when Martial Law is established in Somerville, Somerville finds it embodied in Tim, cigar in mouth, hat on head, heels on the little table before him, ready to perform all the duties of Provost Marshal in the empty store employed for the purpose. And very easy Tim took it. Bob Withers acted for the time as his clerk on the dusty counter near by, entering the names and administering the oath. All that Tim has to do at present is to smooth down his incipient mustache in the hollowed fore-finger of his left hand whenever he takes his cigar from his mouth with his right. Medicine? Ay, the bitterest on earth.

"An oath under duress has not the least obligation," reasons Guy Brooks and hundreds of thousands at the South. Ye who seriously revere an oath as the most solemn of appeals to God, is or is not the taking of an oath on the basis of such reasoning about as cool, as deliberate a taking the name of God in vain as a man can be guilty of? If the whole moral law, in every possible inflection thereof, were but as explicit and invariable as the Multiplication Table now!

A pitiful sight it was to see old, white-headed men, who had not had time yet to realize the possibility of Secession, the very imagination of which they had abhorred all their lives, suddenly hurried in from their homes, stood like children before this beardless puppet of the hour, driven there to do so under peril of property and life, calling on God to witness they renounced the Government they had up till that instant regarded as the noblest and firmest on earth! Solemnly pledging themselves to what? To the suddenest and wildest and windiest—

Strong men came sullenly forward too. Heaven help us! not a man in Somerville failed to come. Many swearing, as they took the oath —ah, how solemnly!—by the God that made them, to take full vengeance for this their deep humiliation. Yes, it *was* an oath—not to Secessionists—it left *them* as it found them; to Union men it was the awful pledge and sacrament of hatred and vengeance. Before that oath their purpose was merely a resolve; henceforth it was a vow.

In the establishment of Martial Law and Conscription Secession rolled up into its zenith, subsiding thereafter—but oh, how slowly!—to its nadir.

"I call you to witness, Mr. Lamum, and you, Mr. Withers," Edward Arthur, as he stands before Tim's boot-soles displayed on the little red table, remarks, "that I take this oath only on one ground. Were it not for that I would perish first."

"Ah, and what ground is that?" asks Tim, with languid curiosity, clasping both hands together behind his head and tilting his chair farther back as he speaks. He manages to ask the question, too, with his cigar in his mouth.

"Solely because I am commanded to obey, by Scripture, every ordinance of man for the Lord's sake. I obey as part of my submission to the Powers that be, yielding not to those Powers but to the Providence that permits them present might, and to the express command of God in

THE PROVOST MARSHAL'S OFFICE.

such a case as this. I submit to this as I would endeavor to do to every affliction He pleases to send, however painful. I have nothing more to say."

"I'm afraid you do not like my Government," says the Provost Marshal, with pitying dignity. And if Tim used the expression once during his official career he used it—shall we venture to say? —one thousand times. He had met with it in the corner of some newspaper as the language of some other high and distinguished official in diplomatic correspondence. "I have no choice in the matter," he afterward remarks to those whose houses he has had searched for conscripts, or who are up before him for using disloyal language; "it is my Government which directs me to act as I do. If my Government did not consider it necessary they would not have made it my duty," he replies, when any one attempts to argue the matter of passports from county to county. Yet there is something, as peculiarly pleasing to Mr. Arthur as it is distasteful to Mr. Ellis, in hearing just such an individual as Tim Lamum mention the Confederacy as "my Government."

"I regarded the act of Secession as a wickedness, from voting for which I abstained exactly as I would abstain"—the Minister *will* add in a steady tone and looking his beardless hero in the eyes—"from the wickedness of swearing, gambling, or lewdness. Every hour I live I more firmly regard it as part of the great crime against God and man for which we are enduring and will continue to endure an awful punishment. I am submitting to it, meanwhile, only as to the afflictive Providence of Heaven, in obedience to its express command to that effect."

The old store is full when he says it. Of course he ought no more to have said it than ought irate Paul to have made that unpleasant remark about a whited wall when on *his* trial. His own ideal Minister would have quietly taken the oath and ridden back again to Mrs. Sorel's, thinking and feeling as much as he pleased, but breathing no syllable aloud. He was surprised at himself, for he had no intention of saying a word. But he felt more deeply than he knew, and in the anguish of the moment could not refrain from bearing testimony against the Baal of the hour if he died for it.

At least no other man in Somerville did any thing of the kind. It would have been a too dangerous experiment in the case, say, of Guy Brooks, Ferguson, Dr. Warner, and the like. But Edward Arthur was so well known in Somerville, had married so many of the couples there, buried so many of the dead there, his purity of life, his acknowledged piety, the evident sincerity of the man, as he stood there before Tim Lamum, erect, earnest, utterly fearless, took the crowd too much by surprise. Besides, just then, it was Tim who presented the majesty of Secession in his person—the contrast between the two was too striking.

"Oh, said he hated and despised the Confederacy with his whole soul! Said he obeyed it only because the Bible made him. Acknowledging, you see, the Bible is on our side. Said the Secessionists were worse than adulterers, liars, and thieves, and murderers! Got so mad he was white with rage. Had his right hand in his bosom all the time, a revolver there I've no doubt. Would you have ever thought such a thing of him, Mrs. Bowles? I used, myself, to think the whole world of Mr. Arthur, have said a thousand times Brother Barker was not to be compared to him. Now just look at those two men! Brother Barker, a true patriot, a strong Secessionist, and Barker a Northern man, you know, while he was born at the South and

lived all his life there. I tell you what, Mrs. Bowles"—Mrs. Warner it is, she has been in Mrs. Bowles's parlor for the last hour or so, her eyebrows wide apart at the inner ends—"if we only knew we'd find out he's a bad, bad man. There's nothing I can lay my hand on, it's true; but if we only knew! I always was doubtful about him, there's a sort of pride— My little 'Ria is a child, I know; but if she was old enough, and I but imagined Mr. Arthur had any idea of her—"

"I can not imagine what you mean, Madam," says Mrs. Bowles, more in reference to Mrs. Warner's mysterious manner than to her words.

"I mean, if my 'Ria was as old as your Alice —I say it as a friend—"

"You will excuse me, Mrs. Warner," Mrs. Bowles interrupts her visitor in her stateliest manner—some ten inches lower, forty pounds lighter than Mrs. Warner; but it is South Carolina in contrast with Mississippi, and she towers above her as did Marie Antoinette above the *canaille*—"we will not allude, if you please, to my daughter, Alice Bowles, in this connection."

How the said Alice managed to bring in Mrs. Warner's name that same evening, as mother and daughter sat sewing together at those perpetual haversacks, is not known, but Alice suspended her needle and looked up surprised at the vehemence of her usually quiet and refined little mother.

"Do not mention her name to me again, Alice. I did suppose our acquaintance with her was ended by my reply to her impertinence in reference to Lieutenant Ravenel's visit. It is not so much her loathsome snuff-dipping, that she should bring her filthy yellow bottle with her into my very parlor, actually converse with me, her filthy mop-stick in the corner of her mouth! It is her quick eyes and her incessant tongue. I do believe the poor creature *is* a sincere Southern woman; but much as I dislike the Northern people, she has a venom in speaking about them that is exceedingly unladylike."

"That is one thing I dislike Secession for, mother. Those— Mrs. Sorel, and the other Union people—with whom we used to associate most we have been separated from. Mrs. Warner is only one of the new class of people the war has thrown us among. Dr. Peel, for instance, daring to speak to you in Mr. Ellis's store yesterday; that intoxicated old oddity, Captain Richard Simmons, Bob Withers, and Mr. Lamum actually acting with you as a Soldiers' Aid Committee. That odious Yankee schoolmaster, Mr. Neely, too, actually visiting here almost every week. He never dreamed of doing so until he had the war news to talk over with you. For one, if it were not for you and Rutledge, I would almost hate Secession! And to think it is Slavery we are fighting for! it never did before, but it seems odd to me now—*Slavery!*" adds the young lady, with—like Mr. Arthur before Tim Lamum—a great deal more depth of feeling than she before knew herself to be possessed of.

"Aristocratic little old fool, putting on her Charleston airs with me!" says Mrs. Warner, snuff-stick in mouth, that same moment at her fireside. "And that Alice of hers, so polite and reserved, as if she was a queen or an heiress. Plague take them! They say that that Rutledge Bowles the old goose is so everlastingly talking about is going to the dogs there in Charleston. I hope so with all my soul! It's a heap she needs to bring down her abominable pride." And a good deal more to the same effect, Mr. Arthur being intermingled therewith, she said that night in bed to Dr. Warner, like a veteran in the trenches, asleep by her side.

Nothing since his elevation to office pleases Tim Lamum more than Miss Alice Bowles's bearing toward him a few evenings after at a party given by Colonel Ret Roberts. Tim has long since given up Miss Alice as—"beautiful as you please—yes, Sir—but too"—a heated expression here—"proud for me!" It is his new position, of course, which causes Miss Alice to pause near him in an incidental way that night with such a smile as emboldens Tim to inform her that it is a pleasant evening; with great dignity too, the Provost Marshal's hollowed forefinger smoothing down his mustache.

"You are quite busy these days?" says Alice at last, and with an interest in Mr. Lamum as flattering as it is novel.

"Yes, Miss Alice. Well, only tolerably so. The Secession people among us are so very willing, and those poor Union chaps are so frightened, I don't have as much to do as I supposed I would," says Tim.

"It is such a new thing among us, Mr. Lamum. Do tell me what the duties of a Provost Marshal are?" asks Alice.

("Not a bit proud these days. It is really amazing how the girls are taken by a fellow's being a Government official. Gloriously beautiful!" says Tim afterward to Bob Withers, and a dozen or so more, as opportunity offered, and not without expletives.)

"Well, it is a new business to us also," he replies to his fair questioner. "Yes—oh, well, we just do, you know, what turns up to be done. Make every soul null take the oath, say. Haul people up if they hesitate about taking Confederate money. A funny thing happened before me about that only to-day, Miss Alice. Joe Staples, the hotel keeper, you know, he has that Scotch Ferguson, grizzly-bearded, positive chap—oh, you know him—up before me, you see. Ferguson had lent Staples some thousand dollars, gold and silver, you know, on interest when Staples was fixing up his hotel, you see. Staples has a trunk full of Confederate money, taken in, you know, from people stopping with

him. Staples wants Ferguson to take it in payment. Ferguson refuses. However, he says he may do it under protest, and steps out to consult Guy Brooks as his lawyer. Just as he steps out in comes Colonel Juggins, outs with a bundle of Confederate money—he had heard, you see, that Staples was up at my office, and had followed him—outs, you know, with a bundle of Confederate money as big as a small baby, and wants to pay Staples some—well, I don't know how many hundreds, Tom Juggins's board bill; you know he used to loaf a good deal about the hotel before he went to the war. What do you think? Staples said he would take it only under protest; steps out to see his lawyer if even that would secure him."

"And what did Mr. Ferguson decide to do?" asks Alice, with interest.

"Came back with Guy Brooks; said he would not take the money in that shape at all. Fact is, people don't like, you know, to take the money. We have the case under advisement. If I could only know," adds Tim, with the dignity of an embassador, "what my Government would have me do—"

"You have assistance in determining?"

"Assistance? Oh yes; plenty of that. My uncle, Dr. Peel, Captain Simmons when he is sober enough, as for that, and when he is not sober, never is, you know. Fact is, I leave it pretty much to them. I only sit there, you see. We always have a detail of a dozen or so of soldiers to haul up people. The worst bore is making out passports. We let no man go out of the county, and it is so all over the State, but we have him to tell where he is going, what for, how long, and all. However, we have blank forms. Bob Withers fills them up; all I have to do is to sign my name."

But that was just what frightened Mr. Neely. After incredible exertions for office that gentleman had been offered the post of Provost Marshal before Tim. At first he was immensely flattered. But the Yankee, though steadily smothered and trampled down in him with his own hands and feet, was too strong there for that. One night's sleep over it, rather one night's tossing wide awake over it, and Mr. Neely, with a thousand reasons, declined, exactly as he would have done any other speculation in which he might make hundreds, yet, possibly, might lose thousands; for the inner Mr. Neely was not exactly as confident of the certain success as was the outer Mr. Neely. His signature to bills for tuition, in other days, was not so glorious, but safer.

"Mr. Lamum," says Alice, after a while, in lower tones and playing with her fan, "you know how curious we ladies are; there is one thing I would like you to tell me: you have sent some of the worst of the Union men out of the country, have you not?"

I

Government official as Tim is, he could no more refuse those eyes! Besides, he has an increasing sense of his new importance, and does not care to diminish it.

"I ought not, perhaps, officially, you know, to tell it, Miss Bowles; but you will not mention it, we have. My Government—"

"And in every case they were hung by the road-side?" Alice is paler, but more erect, too, as she asks.

"I'm afraid so," says Tim, not quite so erect, and forgetting his mustache. "My Government is prosecuting a war—"

"It is very close in here," interrupts Alice; "a little nearer the window, if you please. Thank you!" and Tim has a deep consciousness of his importance. It is more painful, however, than pleasing just now.

"You were mentioning Mr. Barker just now, or were you not? He has taken the oath?" she asks at last.

"Parson Barker? I don't remember."

"I must have mistaken. That is—" Alice says, with a stammer and a blush.

"It must have been Mr. Arthur I spoke of," says Tim; and adds: "But it is this conscript business is beginning to make us work. It would look, you know, as if it will take all the volunteers we've got to hunt up the conscripts. In hiding, you see. And when one does catch them, their wives and sisters and old fathers and mothers crying there in my office, you know—"

"However, it relieves you that no one refuses to take the oath—"

"Oath? Oh no! Who cares for an oath, you know? There was Mr. Arthur—but of course you've heard about that?"

"Not clearly. Mr. Arthur? What was it?" It is amazing, considering their long acquaintance, how indifferent Alice is. But Tim tells the whole story very nearly as it occurred—truthful fellow, Tim, except at poker. Besides, he likes to talk, and it is a feather in his new cap to be seen by the company passing and repassing around them talking with her.

"Spunky chap, Miss Alice," he adds at last. "I haven't much use for preachers myself; but one can not help liking that man. He seems really to believe our revolution a wrong thing; shakes his head over us as if we were all out on a spree. Singular! but he really believes so! You won't mention it, Miss Alice, but fact is, of the two men, Mr. Arthur and Brother Barker, as they call him, I can't stand Barker. As to being a good Secessionist, that is all right, you know; at the same time we outsiders don't like to see a preacher mixing himself up in things of the sort too much. It's like a woman outside her sphere. It's that distinguishes us from the Yankees. There's a holy, I mean a pious, or

rather a religious—oh! I don't know what you call it," says Tim, making vague gestures with both hands, "a sort of Sabbath-day something one likes to have in a parson. The hardest case among us don't like to see a preacher leaving his sermons to mix up— Men are doing, you know, a good deal of cursing and swearing and worse these days; and a parson hail-fellow in that sort of crowd, you know— And on Sundays, you know, and in churches, too. For one, I hate—we all do—to have Brother Barker everlastingly in with us, discussing and suggesting—"

"Only trying to moderate you leading officials," explains Alice, in wonderful good-humor.

"Not a bit of it, Miss Alice! Moderate? Why, the parson is the most ultra of the whole lot. If we had actually done half the things that parson has urged on us, and from the Bible— You mustn't mention it," continues Tim, who, never ice, is thoroughly thawed under the young lady's influence, "but he was for having us send Mr. Arthur out of the country. His Union influence, he said. If we had! But we won't speak of blackjacks along the road any more; excuse me, I see it doesn't agree with you. Parson Barker, his hair combed back, his sallow face, eager eyes, always at a white heat— Fact is, I can't stand Brother Barker!" says Tim, with considerable disgust. "Only you won't mention it, Miss Alice, he always puts me in mind, that man, of the Abolition preachers we read about. Mr. Arthur is mistaken, of course; but no fanaticism about him."

The question, as an official one, weighed, however, on Tim's mind. "I declare something ought to be done with Arthur. I believe my Government would justify me—"

"Oh, play your poker, and let Arthur alone," interrupts Bob Withers, frank and honest Bob, to whom the remark is made that night over the cards. "No, Tim; no, Sir-ee; you, by George! let the parson alone. I believe I've got hard sense when it isn't my own good is concerned, and I've proved right, by George! more than once in differing from your red-mouthed Secessionists, Simmons, Barker, and such. For my part, I tell you this provost-marshaling business won't do; you'll see yet if it will. The whole thing is only a tremendous spree the South is on, a mag-nificent bender and blow-out, see if it ain't. Smash up, too, some day, by George! But never mind all that; it's poker we are at now.

"I'm an awful wicked scamp—swear, drink, do things worse still—but I can't lie, by George!" says Bob in general, and he says true.

"And, my dear, I was almost shocked," Mrs. Bowles was saying to Alice the same night at home, "at the way you flirted with that Mr. Lamum. You forget that his uncle is a Yankee. Don't do it any more, dear."

TOM IS DEAD!

## CHAPTER XVI.

"Weary? Yes, even unto death, but that is it. Yes, let us ride up to the Pines and spend a week or so with Paul up there. A plain, rough man is Paul, but a sincere and thoroughly sensible one. He lives in rude fashion, but will give us a hearty welcome. We will try to forget for a while there the very existence of Tim Lamum— we shall have to get a pass from him, by-the-by— Dr. Peel, Secession, and the Somerville *Star*."

It is Guy Brooks who makes the suggestion, to which Mr. Arthur eagerly consents.

"I never was in better health in my life," he adds, standing erect as a grenadier, and slapping his hands upon his breast. "When I get fairly into my studies I take to them with keener zest than I ever did before—to get into them from Secession is the thing. If one could only get away for a while, off say among the Esquimaux, I could shout there 'Down with Davis!' till the blue icebergs rang again. Since, like the starling, I can't get out, I could roll myself up like a hedgehog and sleep for six months— such weariness, such intense anxiety, and for so long now."

"Ah, that is a weakness!" remonstrates the lawyer. "We are at our post, and must stand manfully there!" As if he himself did not require to be often rebuked by his friend—the Federals are so long, so very long in coming—for despondency and impatience.

"I know it, since I say it to myself several dozen times a day, but the flesh is weak; Country. Church of God, Civilization even, so suddenly swept from under one. Truth, Justice, Providence itself, gone. Only, all of it my own miserable lack of faith under trial. One will lapse a little when the weather is gloomy, when some special wickedness comes to mind, when Secession gains some great victory, when the North seems to halt, perhaps fall—who knows out here?—in its work, the greatest work, Guy Brooks, Esq.," adds Edward Arthur, boldly, "ever given a nation to do since the world began!"

And this is astounding language for even a Union man at the South to use at this period; think it he may, perhaps, but say such a thing aloud? No. "If one," he continues, "was only where one could *do* any thing."

"You are doing something," placid Mrs. Sorel had said to him months before, when he had ventured a like remark to her over the supper-table. The truth is, one *must* have some one to unbosom one's self to, especially in periods of great trial, and by this time Mrs. Sorel had become to her guest as a mother.

Robby has left the table before this. They would not mind speaking before him, however, for he rarely goes to Somerville except on Sunday with his mother; and when he is there he has learned, from experience, to evade the attempts to draw information from him in regard to his friends—attempts which not only Mrs. Warner but even Dr. Ginnis and Brother Barker have not disdained to make. You can teach a child silence on a given topic sooner than you can teach him to read—try it. Besides, Mr. Arthur and Mrs. Sorel had thoroughly instructed Robby in the whole quarrel. No more devoted Union man in the world than Robby.

"If we only knew it," she had then replied, "we would see that the silent influences are ever the most powerful. What so powerful as light and heat, yet what so utterly without sound! You have quietly, but from the outset, occupied a position of solemn protest against the rebellion — sermon, prayers, conversation, very existence in Somerville, all an influence unswervingly against it."

"I have tried to urge in every way I could," Mr. Arthur then said, "the supremacy of Heaven in this matter, as in every thing else; that we are being chastised for some great and good end of God."

"That angry prayers are never heard, that trust in men is vain, that violence of speech and feeling is unchristian. I have never said so before, nor would I now but to encourage you," adds quiet Mrs. Sorel; "but your very contrast to Mr. Barker all the time is an influence in Somerville for good."

"Could Christian men outside the South, at

the North, in England say, know my course, I think it would meet their cordial approval; I do think I would have the sympathy of the wisest and best of my generation. In any case," added Mr. Arthur, "I have the hearty approval of my own conscience, though deserted by so many who once esteemed me."

The fact is, he pursued the course he did because any other was simply impossible.

"I do not make my conscience a law to any other man living," he reasoned with Mrs. Sorel; "but neither can I make the conscience of any other a law to me. My own deliberate conviction I *must* follow, even though it leads me to 'a traitor's rope,' as Mrs. Warner says."

More than he knows it, too, is there growing up in him one great hope. From the hour she had first burst upon him in her mother's parlor a glowing school-girl, swinging her sun-bonnet in her hand by its long strings, his love for Alice, very foolish in him as it was, certainly, had grown up into an absorbing affection. None the less that he rarely met her. He was a Union man; Mrs. Bowles knew it, and was of opinions exceedingly contrary: not for worlds, not for Alice even, would he intrude unwelcome. When he did visit Mrs. Bowles, too genuinely a lady to allude to the war save in general terms, she confined herself to Rutledge Bowles, whose letters few and far apart was the food of her mind and the fountain of her speech. Rutledge Bowles, to Mrs. Bowles South Carolina incarnate, was very often in trouble in these days; his letters were full of it: eternally seceding from Secession right and left, east, west, south—almost, in times of peculiar injustice to him, north even, rather than stand it.

Mr. Arthur often met Alice when at her mother's, never alone, however. Sewing beside her mother, on some one, generally, of the war garments so perpetually demanded in the Somerville *Star;* or playing old music, or reading old books—there were no magazines or new books now. He had a fancy that a blush tinged her smile at their meeting. Did he not see her also as a teacher in the diminished Sabbath-school? Alas, poor human nature! his chief happiness on these Sabbaths is to meet Alice at Sabbath-school, even though mere sight and casual greeting was all.

Her mother never attended church now, for Mr. Arthur would *not* pray for the Confederacy. But the preacher was aware all the service through of one sweet face down the aisle, down too far away toward the door. The solemn fact is, he selected his weekly text, and wrote every line of his sermon almost as much for her as if it had been a letter. Had not Alice become a communicant just before Secession? How much or how little through his means he never dared ask himself.

Long ago, if Secession had not come in, would

he have learned his fate at her hands. Yet he believed—that is, he hoped—I mean, he felt assured— However, for the present, wait. Perhaps when the end comes she will see how right I was all along—even her mother may. Not without terrible apprehensions meantime of the young gentlemen in gray clothing and brass buttons who frequented Mrs. Bowles's hospitable parlor, rode with her, took her to parties. But if a man is not to be governed by his own intuition of the wisest, happiest course, what is left him to do? So far, his unwavering intuition is —wait. But it is for something considerably more to him than the re-establishment of the Union that he yearns in looking to the end. Besides, he says, if I was to learn certainly that I have no hope with her, this, with the other trials, will be too great a blow to bear. Let the hope live, if only to sustain me through these dark days.

Perhaps it is as well he does not know of the letter Alice receives these days from her brother. It is soon after his ordeal before Tim Lamum— the first but not the last of that dynasty. Rutledge Bowles writes his sister that he has received a letter to the effect that she is being addressed by a Mr. Arthur, a Union man! Could it have been Mrs. Warner? Surely not Mr. Neely? For these are, both of them, too sharp not to know the kind of epistle Rutledge Bowles will write to his sister, with the effect upon her of that epistle.

He can conjecture the possibility of some such letter to her from her brother weeks after, however. He, too, is favored with one from the young Carolinian. Such a letter that, after reading the first few lines, he refolds it, places it again in its envelope so redirected as to go back to its author, and drops it in the letter-box of the Post-office. This does not diminish the pride of his attitude toward the one he loves most of all the world. Not without a medicinal virtue is that letter, a counter-irritant to the other inflammation of Secession.

And thus does, even on this fair young girl, the great question press heavier every day. No neutral ground between the old era and the new. One opinion or the other. And to the opinion you adopt must be given your whole heart also. The past is forever gone; as to the future, choose!

But by a determined effort Edward Arthur throws every painful thought from him down upon the west wind, blowing full upon and past him, as he rides away from Somerville this August morning beside Guy Brooks, on their way to the Pines. Riding avowedly away from Secession, conversation, however, on all other topics droops and dies before they have got ten miles out from Somerville.

"One of my old clients that was that stopped me as we were mounting," said the lawyer at last. "He was telling me that he had escaped the ranks by working in a powder-mill. I told him he had better have gone into battle at once. At least a dozen of their trumpery powder-mills have blown up in this section. Villainous—"

"My dear Sir," remonstrates his companion, "do let us forget Secession for a while. We must, or we shall lose our wits. If a cow gives a shake of her bell at night lying by the calf-lot at Mrs. Sorel's, it wakes me instantly out of the deepest sleep to imagine it the Somerville bells over some great victory. I am perpetually fancying I hear the sound of distant cannon on the west wind. If I hear a shot-gun, I say that man has heard some news. The distant crowing of a rooster has been to me more than once the far-off yelling of somebody for victory. I am positively reluctant to open the *Star*; it is like opening a letter with a black seal. In fact, I never ask the news of any but a Union man, because I know he will break any disastrous tidings to me in the gentlest possible way." Mr. Arthur laughs as he says it. "I never knew," he adds, "so well before what the command means to pray without ceasing. I never wake at night, never recur to the subject during the day, but it is with a prayer for the Union on my lips. You may laugh at me, but I never catch glimpse of a leading Secessionist, nor the house, child, or dog of one reminding me of him; never see a war-poster on the walls; never see a Government wagon, postage stamp—any thing that reminds me of the great crime, but what theologians call ejaculatory prayer burns on my tongue for its swift and utter destruction."

"Yes, may Heaven speedily crush the rebellion and give us back law, order, civilization, society, country, religion, ourselves. With all my soul, Amen!" adds the lawyer, to such lengths of disloyalty has he arrived. "However, don't tell the Provost-Marshal I said so."

And it is note-worthy the manner in which Union men risk their lives in each other's hands in these days. Meet a stranger casually in a store, fall in with a respectable traveler along the road, the one topic is introduced as soon as the salutations are over, and, almost from the first syllable on either side, by tone, manner, bearing—the subtle Freemasonry which causes people who feel alike—lovers included—to be aware of the fact, especially when they feel very deeply, in half an hour the stranger and yourself have mutually placed a life in each other's hands if you both be Union in sentiment. Because there is no longer neutrality. The gulf has so deepened and widened by this time between the two opinions that there can be henceforth no passing and repassing. If you and your chance acquaintance are not Secessionists now, both of you are to the centre of your souls the opposite to that, and opposite to that forever.

"That client of mine," adds the lawyer, "was telling me the various shifts to escape conscription. Some have gone to tanning, and the sort of leather produced is a sight to see. Others have rushed into the making of salt, nitre, sulphur, shoe-pegs—any thing. Others are flying desperately around to get the required twenty scholars, to be exempted as teachers. One man, to my certain knowledge, exposes himself purposely to keep up a sufficient rheumatism. People suffer with rupture, neuralgia, and every other disease under heaven, to a degree unheard of. Many a man has suddenly proved to be many years older than his own wife ever imagined. I have heard of Campbellite congregations of late which have mutually ordained to the ministry every male member on their books—how true that is I don't say."

"What a mercy the comic *will* slip into even the most tragic!" puts in Mr. Arthur.

"There is that client of mine," continues Guy Brooks, "a poor, honest, hard-working man, with a wife in wretched health and a swarm of white-headed children. Jewet is his name—Silas Jewet—a fair specimen of really the most virtuous class in the country. All his life he has regarded Disunion with as much horror as a man can regard any thing which he considered impossible; Washington's Farewell Address, framed and glazed, is the only ornament there, hanging up against the wall of his cabin. A Democrat from his pine-wood cradle, idolizing Jackson for whipping the British at New Orleans, the United States Bank, and Nullification. This man wakes suddenly up to find Disunion a fact, and Jackson's alternative with South Carolina actually upon us. And *he* must leave bedridden wife and helpless children, a few rags of clothing, a little corn in the crib, a few pigs, perhaps an ox or two, their only supply, to be gone—he has no idea where nor for how long, and to fight for —Disunion! No alternative but to take his shot-gun, strip himself almost to the skin for the use of his suffering family, and march off in a cause he abhors. Silas Jewet fighting for Colonel Ret Roberts, Tim Lamun, Colonel Juggins, and the like, that they may retain their negroes, slaves which they have jeopardized by their own mad folly in Secession!"

"And this going before board after board to be examined, displaying your hidden sores, concealed diseases, to move their pity and secure an exemption—tasting slavery ourselves to the very dregs to see how we like it, as Ferguson says. And all this the insolent triumphing over us of men, at least the most active and prominent among them, grog-shop politicians, bullies, and ruffians, the very sediment hitherto of society—" And the clergyman emphasizes his remark by stopping his words in full flow lest he should add what he ought not.

"The woods around his house, Silas Jewet says," adds the lawyer, "swarm with runaway negroes. Twice they have broken in, while he was away, upon his helpless family and stripped the cabin of all the little food there was in it. I couldn't advise him to run the country; he will lose every stick of what little he has got if he could move his family even. The woods are full of runaway whites as it is, naked, starving. That we should be brought to this—*we*, and for what?"

"I tell you, Sir," says Mr. Arthur, more calmly, "at first I regarded the deadly principle of Secession as the great sin, the cause and source of our suffering.—Slavery I was born and raised with, and I never had any very definite idea in reference to it before. I have now. It is the accursed root of this accursed upas. Could any other than a wrong thing have destroyed our country as it has? Slavery is a sin, Sir; the judgments of Heaven now on us are God's wrath against us, North and South, just for this great sin. And to think that in the Church of God itself this sin has its last and strongest citadel; God's great institution for putting down sin in the land itself the most active and powerful engine for its establishment! When Heaven's only instrumentality for good to a people is thus not only powerless for good, but is actually the most efficient means in the land for the sin, no wonder He drops it as his instrumentality and draws the sword instead. And nothing less than God's awful judgments could open our eyes to the truth."

"See those two women in that field on your left?" asks Guy Brooks, interrupting his friend as they ride by a road-side cabin with its improvements. "Don't seem to notice them, but look at that largest one in the big yellow sunbonnet—one with the hoe. Any thing remarkable about her?"

"Not that I can see—why?"

"Well, nothing, only the one in the blue bonnet is Mrs. Peter Hook, and the other is—"

"Her sister, lately from Carolina. Yes; I stopped here to get a drink a few weeks ago. Mrs. Hook told me," says Mr. Arthur.

"You saw the sister—talked with her?" asked the lawyer, with a smile.

"N-n-no; she had just stepped out, Mrs. Hook said."

"Yes, and always has just stepped out, whoever calls. It's her husband, man!"

"Why, I asked after her husband," says astonished Mr. Arthur. "She told me she had a letter from him, in some regiment, somewhere. Was shot in the leg, or something of the sort. I remember I tried to encourage her. She said she hoped so, but feared not. And that other woman—"

"Don't look back. Not five people besides them know of it. Dare say he is used to the women's clothes by this time. Delightful state of things, isn't it?"

And while the friends ride thoughtfully on let us in this connection turn for an instant to Colonel Juggins's household, type and emblem of hundreds of thousands of households throughout the land.

"We ain't goin' on to *their* lot to interrupt them," had been Mrs. Juggins's reasoning in regard to the Yankees. "Why can't they stay at home? If they don't like ownin' niggers, well jest let them *not* own them. Our havin' hands is none of their business."

And very cheerfully indeed had Mrs. Juggins equipped Tom, when the war broke out, to go and help drive the Yankees back home. But news comes, months and months afterward, that Tom has been killed there in Virginia. Now Mrs. Juggins is a mother; Tom was her son, her only son. And a very ordinary youth, gawky, freckled, stolid, was Tom Juggins; but to his mother he was all the world. When the Colonel, coming back that disastrous afternoon from Somerville, after a dozen efforts to break the news to her, at last takes out the soiled and blotted letter from Henry Sorel, who was in the same company with him, and reads it out, breaking down a dozen times in the attempt, Mrs. Juggins's hands fall with the knitting in them into her lap with a first feeling of profound astonishment. Such a thing had never been entertained in her mind for an instant. Then follows the burst of grief, till all the negroes flock into the house from cabin and field to know what is the calamity. It lasts in all its bitterness for weeks; loud weeping when it is the theme of conversation with friends; silent, steady weeping, the tears rolling for hours down her cheek and sparkling upon her half-finished stocking as she knits. Tom as a baby, Tom as a little boy, Tom at school, Tom a grown youth, Tom as she last saw him leaving for the war.

But now a change is coming over Mrs. Juggins which perplexes her husband wonderfully, smoking his cob-pipe on long afternoons with old age suddenly fallen upon him. With everybody else, long before Tom's death Mrs. Juggins has come to know that the war is, at last, a struggle for slavery. And since, as her grief loses, so to speak, its first personality, she is thinking the slavery question steadily over as she knits—no Tom to knit for now, but only from habit.

"You may say what you please," she remarks to Brother Barker, whose condolences are, somehow, singularly unacceptable to her, "but my Tom was more to me than all the hands *we've* got. I'd give up every black one *we've* got, God he knows, an' glad too, to get our Tom back. Yes, every one of them, from old Cudgo, that waited at my mother's wedding, and can only tend the young turkeys, down to that last little thing born in Sukey's house last night. It's them this fight is about. In my 'pinion one white man like my Tom is worth all the niggers in the world. The Colonel there, he says I mustn't say it; but I've always said, for one, all my life what I think, I don't care who knows it; and if any body else thinks slavery is worth all the men bein' killed and all the other ruin brought upon us for it, I don't. As to what you say about the Bible bein' for it, may be so; there's a sight of things connected with it. Many a time ever since I could remember I've asked myself— However, no matter, that's neither here nor there; but it seems to me a curious sort of thing for God to be for. For our Jesus Christ, say, to be for. Or I wonder if Tom's death is makin' me kind o' unsettled in mind, this slavery 'pears so dif'rent. An' you believe it is of God, wise an' certain, now?" she asks of Brother Barker with such eyes, as her hands fall with the knitting in them into her lap, that even that Brother, eager to reply, has queer sensations up his spine as he does so.

For his wife's practical sense Colonel Juggins has ever had the highest esteem, and her remarks to him when they are lying side by side under the dingy old tester, or when he is smoking his pipe, have opened a totally new train of thought in his mind. You see at the South we all took the institution as a matter of course from our birth. But many thousands are smoking the same thing in their pipes now. Is slavery worth the ruin it has caused? Could any other than a thing essentially bad have produced such ruin? Up to that date, however, very rarely did the universal thinking utter itself in words. Ah, it is too vast a result to be reached by other than much thinking, even though that thinking be quickened by swift-succeeding and tremendous events.

It was generally, though silently, agreed that it was not a good idea Brother Barker preaching that sermon on the Exodus from Egypt. True, an anonymous admirer requested it by note; he was hardly well through the discourse but Brother Barker suspected a trap, and he rages inwardly over it these days like a caged fox. For Mr. Arthur has been urging of late that the Almighty is pledged against all wrong as it exists in the world, now as ever, and has used, is using, and will use all elements and agencies for its overthrow.

"I confess I am uneasy in regard to Paul," Guy Brooks is remarking to his companion as they ride along, and after a lengthened silence. "I fear trouble is brewing up there in the Pines. There are many Union men living there. They have kept very quiet all this time, never expressing their opinions, at least except to each other, violating no law, staying as closely at home as possible about their business. As many as could have fled the State from conscription, and are scattered about wherever they can go, unable to hear from or assist their families. For myself I don't want to go into the Federal lines if I can help it! If I did I might be tempted to take

the stump and tell those people, If you care so much for the slavery of the blacks, at least care something for the worse slavery of the whites among us, your own flesh and blood, and come and help us. I do think I could stir them up to move a little faster, to tell them of the accursed despotism under which we perish. But then I hate to leave, and I hate to go, on every account. Many Union men about the Pines have been shot from behind trees, hung along the roadside, sent out of the county in irons, Heaven knows where. This is the main reason of my going up now," adds the lawyer—"my anxiety in reference to Paul."

"That accounts," said his companion, "for those three columns of abuse of the citizens up there in the last Number of the Star. It is the most ferocious thing I have yet seen in the paper."

And it was. Mrs. Warner, who had fallen into the habit of reserving the strongest "documents" met with during the day to read to her unhappy husband at night, had accomplished two objects on the Doctor by the reading to him of that article, curdled the very blood in his veins, and convinced him that it was the production of a more frantic pen than that of Lamum—even Brother Barker's.

It charged the objects of its rage with being Abolitionists banded into a conspiracy to murder and rob in the pay of the Federals—describing its leader as the avowed infidel who had recently disturbed a peaceful congregation gathered together for the worship of God by intruding his blasphemous atrocities. "More hereafter." The paper added, "That a single one of these miserable traitors has escaped so long does little credit to the undoubted loyalty of the country. These are no times for the regular processes of the law; let the rifle and the rope do its just and speedy work upon them!"

"And Amen, say I," added Mrs. Warner in conclusion; "and I wouldn't wonder, Dr. Warner—ah, you needn't drop that head of yours, if you are one of this band of traitors, President of them, for what I know; you are a Union man, and you know it!" Viler abuse than is intended by that epithet even Mrs. Warner can not use.

For the last half hour the travelers have ridden along in silence, Guy Brooks with his head declined in thought—thought evidently so deep and painful that his friend hesitates to break in upon it by a syllable.

"Mr. Arthur," says the lawyer at length, looking up at his companion with an expression of deepest anxiety, yet almost childlike supplication, "you are my spiritual guide, now what do you say? You know Lamum has often urged upon the mob to murder me; I am as liable as any man to be shot, as so many have been, from behind a tree; besides, they are sure, sooner or later, to force me into the ranks, even if I escape that. Now what ought a man to do? 'It isn't that my business is broken up, that so many of my old friends have become personal enemies, that I sacrifice every cent I have on earth by going, that if I am caught on the way my life will be taken. What I hate is to desert the South, wrong as the South is. Then the idea of actually enlisting in the Federal army and systematically killing my own— If they would only let a man alone. I am not disobeying a law they have made, am doing nothing against their Confederacy. But the idea of actually fighting for this thing, and I know they'll force me in at last. I have fifty hands down on my place; but as to fighting for slavery! I don't say slavery is a sin or any thing of that sort, but as to fighting for it I can't, and I won't. God Almighty seems to be against it—any way I'm not going to fight for it or for the ruin of the South, which I know Secession to be. I hate, too, to leave you to struggle on, matters in the church getting worse every day. What do you say?"

The Kentucky lawyer has spoken with energy, turning in his saddle as he rides, and looking his friend full in the face. And it is not the first time the minister has been·applied to for advice of the kind. Mothers and wives of members of his church, young men members also, had come to him: "What is my duty, Sir, as a Christian man in reference to escaping or enduring conscription—risk it, or escape, if I can, North, which?" Ah, how fervently had the pastor sought divine instruction in order to instruct others. What can he say? seek the guidance of Heaven in Scripture, prayer, and—Providence.

"It seems to me," he now said to his friend in conclusion, "that you should wait the plain indications of Providence. Don't act an instant before it is essential you should act. The fog opens only as we advance into it. Wait. Let your hand lie in that of your Heavenly Father. He will make it so plain you will not even hesitate when the time comes. 'Wait on the Lord: be of good courage, and he shall strengthen thy heart: wait, I say, on the Lord.'"

We all know the Ruler of all uses devils in all their degrees to accomplish His purposes—devils damned already for centuries, and those not as yet in hell, as much as He does the angels in heaven, and those not yet arrived thither from earth. In fact, when you consider it, so far as things now are, it is of all His human instrumentalities the diabolical ones He most uses, these being so much the most numerous—ay, and energetic.

But the travelers have by this time reached a creek within a mile or two of the home of Paul Brooks. It is a wild and barren spot. The road runs along through deep sand and under pine-trees rearing their heads far above, inter-

mingling their boughs there in unceasing whisperings; only the tapping of the woodpecker upon the dead branches relieving the steady murmur, now rising, now falling, overhead, with a surge as of the sounding sea. Riding slowly along through the solitude, conversing in low tones, they come immediately, and by a sudden turn of the road, upon the creek, which, running for a time parallel to the road, now rushes, swollen by late rains and quite a torrent, across their and cones of the pines swept away in its course through the forest. For some minutes past there has been the roaring as of falling water, and they now observe that, on the left of the road, and not a dozen yards off, the creek suddenly falls over the edge of a deep and circular chasm.

They say the hazel wand bends in the hand toward water flowing far underground. Certainly the iron filing blindly obeys the attraction of the magnet. And whenever, you must have observed it, there be an object near you charged with that which will waken within you to excess joy or sorrow, like or dislike, love or loathing, the very object itself would seem to exert a power upon you direct, and through none of the five channels by means of which objects of lesser interest flow in upon the mind.

Certain it is both travelers at the same instant, and swayed by the same unaccountable influence, turn their horses and ride to the edge of the chasm. Horror! Do their eyes deceive them? The water has washed out a round pool some twenty feet across, falling into it down the bank of the gully with a fall of ten or fifteen feet, and now runs in the hole it has made round and round ere it finds its outlet under a fallen log, and so down the slope. Runs slowly round and round, bearing upon its surface, half-discernible among the floating pine leaves, cones, and trash, the bodies of murdered men. A bearded face turns up full to view—One. Discerned by the naked knees floating only just above the drift—Two. Next it, the bushy top of the head of some one—Three. No doubt about the next; the body is stark naked and floats at full length, swollen, ghastly—Four. Yonder is only a hand, barely distinguishable among the trash—Five. Another in the corner there, the hairy chest broad and full above the water—Six. Yet another, the naked shoulders and back above the water, look—with long and livid streaks laced across from right to left, from left to right— Seven. And that is all.

No. As they gaze in speechless horror another dead body rises suddenly up from under the water, forced up by the current, in an erect posture, the breast toward them; they can only see the bottom of the bearded chin, for the head has fallen back from the hideous gash across the throat—Eight.

Bear witness, O heart-searching God, that

THE FATE OF UNION MEN.

herein no syllable is written not in exact accordance with truth ; bear witness, for Thou didst see it ! Eight men, poor men, honest men, well-meaning, hard-working men, torn at midnight from their shrieking families, borne off into the silent forest, scourged, stabbed, shot, gashed, killed—no man of the murderous gang but had his hand on each victim in some way.

And for what? Simply for doubting whether the destruction of their country was a wise thing, a good thing. Simply for being unable either to change their convictions or to lie and play the hypocrite in regard to those convictions. Only for what they are supposed to think and feel; with having *done* or intending to *do* any thing no man charges them. "Union men, damn them!" that was indictment, sentence, death warrant. During less time than we have been narrating this the two friends gaze upon the scene. Then, by the same simultaneous impulse, they turn their horses, standing back snorting with terror and struggling from the spot into the road again, and gallop on as if for their lives. The lawyer guides his animal with his left hand, holding his revolver cocked in his right. Not a syllable between them as they ride. On through the creek regardless of its swollen depth, on along the heavy sand; the road winds here, winds there, up declivity, down into hollow—will they never reach Paul's place?

Here it is, at least the field, every rail inclosing it cut, split, and built into its place by Paul's own hard and honest hands. Another turn of the road. There is the spot. Only a chimney or two, a heap of smoking ashes and charred logs lying between! As the lawyer glances around him, his panting horse reined up in the gap of the torn-down fence, his companion points him to two men standing a hundred yards off. The lawyer is upon them in a few bounds of his horse.

"For God's sake don't shoot, stranger!" one of them yells, falling on his knees on the muddy ground. The other, a negro, has turned to fly, but it is an open field before him, he fears being shot as he runs, and thinks it safest to halt and fall and implore for his life. A trembling, yellow-faced, copperas clothed white man, and a ragged negro, these are all.

"For the Lord's sake don't shoot a fellow till you can hear him. I ain't no Union man. No, Siree. May God Almighty—" and here the shivering wretch lifts one hand to Heaven and imprecates the most awful curses upon himself if he is. A perjury; he *is* a Union man: whatever of mind and soul he has is invested to its last particle in that direction.

"I no Union man nudder, Lor a massy don't shoot dis yer chile. I Suvern man, Suvern man, Massa! I mighty willin' you hang Massa Brooks! Suppose he alive I help you hang him ef you say so. He Union man, he—" and the negro heaps oaths upon the head of Paul Brooks to a degree which would have satisfied even Dr. Peel, perhaps Brother Barker.

"You hush!" says his companion, angrily, lifting a hoe in his hands. "You hold yer ridiculous tongue, or if the stranger don't kill you I will!"

"I'll tell you all about it," continues the man, in hurried tones, and greatly relieved as the lawyer lowers his revolver. "You see, it looks queer to leave the dead body out that way in the open field," he says, rapidly and deferentially. "The smell, you know. Them buzzards, too. Besides the man is *dead*, bad as he mought be. A fellow couldn't know any body would object to *buryin'* him, you see. I live near by, up the creek. No Union man—Hol Robbins, you may have hearn the name. Ev'ry body about here knows Hol Robbins, Catfish Robbins they sometimes call me, mouth like a catfish's, you see. Well, I says to Hark here to-day, 'Hark, you take the spade, I'll take your hoe, we'll go over an' bury Brooks.' Not that I approve them sentiments of his, gentlemen, not one bit of it, but he was a sort of neighbor, you know, close neighbor. Fact is, a kind neighbor in sickness, lendin' a fellow a day's work now an' then gettin' in his fodder an' sich like. A few dollars p'raps 'casionally. And then them buzzards an' the smell an' all. Besides, my ole woman, she says—"

"Lor, yes, Massa," broke in the negro, "dars de grave yonder to show fur it, jest finishin', Massa Catfish an' I, when you come up," and the negro points eagerly to a spot beneath the nearest tree, evidently a grave just filled up. The eye of the lawyer catches at a glance the rope hanging from the lower limb. Instinctively he rides nearer to read what is written on a leaf, evidently torn from an old ledger, fastened with wooden pins to the bough just beside where the rope is tied:

A. UNION: MAN

he makes it out, rudely scrawled upon the paper with a bit of charcoal.

Silently the two friends sit upon their horses, gazing upon the superscription, understanding the whole story almost as well as if they had witnessed it all with their own eyes. The unlatched cabin door burst suddenly in at night; the sleeping man overpowered in his bed by a dozen men upon him before he is well awake; the desperate struggle amidst execrations and yells; the sturdy form of the Kentuckian dragged at last beneath the tree, bound hand and foot, by men insane from strychnine whisky, drunk abundantly for that very purpose; the rude cabin plundered and fired behind its owner; the sublime bearing of the man, as of Another Man in like situation before him; the rope hurriedly fitted around the sturdy throat under the bushy beard to stop his words before they can move them from their purpose.

A kind of paralysis is upon the two friends as they sit, and grow years older as they gaze. They as liable to the same death at any instant as he.

Yet, let the plain truth be told, they were less affected than you would have been if you live any where in the civilized world outside the Southern States of America. It would have been strange, indeed, if these two had not long since grown accustomed to men dying by violence. No event more familiar to them than that. Men falling dead from their horses by a bullet through them from behind as they ride along the highway; men called, by day or by night, to their door by a halloo from the front fence, and shot down at the feet of wife and children; men killed in a "fair fight" in the streets after having gone armed for months, the one aim of each being to kill his foe before his foe can get a shot at him; men killed accidentally, by-standers in a store or along the street, by some one of the bullets generally distributed plentifully around during the settling of some such "difficulty." In all their varieties such deaths had formed a large part of the practice of the lawyer, of the death-bed visitation of the minister. Pity if they had not got somewhat used to such things by this time. Murder? Nothing more thoroughly familiar to them than that. But in all their double experience, except in the case of a negro or two, and that by a mob, not one single murderer put to death by law for his crime.

Let only the truth be told. Not for money were men killed in the South, or very rarely at least before the war. Very rarely on account of seduction, that crime being almost unknown; whether or no the abundance and the perfect accessibility of females of a darker hue prevented the attempting of seduction who shall say? Anger from any one of ten thousand causes—anger in first flash, or anger cooled into the steel of revenge: this is the grand cause. But neither of these two had ever stood so near the hanging of a man before. They had often, of course, heard of the hanging of Abolitionists and horse thieves, but for murderers there was only the jail, out of which they soon "broke;" in particularly atrocious cases the Penitentiary, from which a pardon sooner or later released them.

Not that law at the South was an inactive thing. The unsleeping vigor and vigilance of the law of the land in regard to negro property, for instance; its eye upon the slave, and upon any one even suspected of entertaining doubts upon the institution, was as that of the Eumenides. As to its grasp upon the murderer, the hold of an aged crone, toothless, blind, deaf, paralytic, palsied, were comparison too flattering to the law.

Years ago Edward Arthur, and ministers like him, had urged the Scriptures of God on the subject, and the certain judgments of God, too, upon the land. Even if slavery be a divine ordinance, insuring the protection and peculiar fa-

vor of Heaven, murder is not. He urged the sin and its certain national consequences as earnestly, fresh from the civilization of Scripture, as if he had just arrived from the civilization of Edinburgh; and with what result?

"By George, parson, you're right; only nobody minds at last," said Bob Withers.

"For my part, Mr. Arthur, I really can not understand, *can not* understand how you can bring yourself to speak so of your own section!" And much more from Mrs. Warner, snuff stick in mouth, to the same effect.

It is a Southern hand writes this, a heart true in every fibre to the South prompts it: If ever Nineveh needed the threat; if ever London needed, in its great plague and great fire, the execution of the divine wrath upon it for its sins, then did the South need the tornado of war rushing over it for its sins. "The earth was filled with violence." That it was that brought the Deluge; and, chief among its causes, this, too, it was which brought upon the South its deluge of fire and blood. Not that the slave-holding States are, or were, the worst in Christendom; as much piety there, in proportion to the population—as much of many an excellence—as in any part of the world: certain virtues, even, as peculiar to and characteristic of the South as is the magnolia and palmetto to and of its soil. None the less is all this true. They say that the percentage of illegitimate births is larger in Scotland than in any other part of Europe — for which Heaven's justice will be meted to *it* at last! It is one human nature every where, in some form of weakness and wickedness in each of us. "The whole world lieth in sin," but it is of the South we happen now to speak.

During the few moments Guy Brooks has been gazing upon the superscription over his brother's grave, as true a superscription as that other the world wots of, Hol Robbins, peering anxiously, then curiously with his small eyes at the lawyer from under the flapping brim of his old wool hat, has come upon another idea.

"Look here, Squire," he begins rapidly to say, "you *are* Squire Brooks, ain't you?" The expression of the lawyer's face has satisfied him of that, however, and with keen reference to the revolver in the brother's hand he proceeds rapidly:

"Look here, Squire, don't you go and believe one word I said about my not bein' a Union man—" And at this point Hol Robbins takes off his old hat, throws it on the ground, and with both his yellow hands above his head proceeds to such imprecations upon himself if he is a Secessionist, such a throwing his entire soul into the matter as puts his assertion beyond all doubt.

"An' I never knowed about it till next day, Squire," he says at last. "But ef I had a knowed what could I a done? One man, you know—only Catfish Robbins. S'pose they'd not a come by an' killed me, too, ef I'd been any 'count? Day's been, Squire, when I could a done somethin'. What with hard work, fever an' ague, an' the whole country almost agin a fellow. However, there's one thing I *kin* do." And turning toward the ruins of the cabin he proceeds with hands, arms, feet, every fibre of his body as well as his tongue, to curse the murderers in such a lava of heart-felt execration as to bring down upon him the stern rebuke of the lawyer and minister even in that moment of horror and hate.

Catfish Robbins lets falls his outstretched arm, and, ignoring the minister, looks at the brother with perplexity in all the lines of his yellow and withered face.

"Why you ain't no parson, Squire," he says at last; "any rate you ain't piouser than God Elmighty Himself, an' He is a cussin' sich devils as them in hell an' onter hell all the time. Yankee Secessionists a'most all of them devils were. Jest what a cotton-mouth moccasin in August is to a chicken snake at Christmas a Yankee Secessionist is to a Southern-born one—pis'nous! Don't matter," he adds, brightening up after a pause and replacing his old hat, "I'm a cussin' them men all the time, any how, and keep my boy Hark here at it too. It's my prayers when I first wake up of a mornin', between the tails of my plow, hoin' corn, eatin' dinner, dreamin' at night, under my breath when I'm among them sort of scoundrels—never stop. You couldn't a knowed this Paul Brooks as well as I!"

Meanwhile, in consequence of an order to that effect from the lawyer and with lively remembrance of his previous remarks and the lawyer's revolver, the negro has climbed the fatal tree with the agility of a monkey, obtained the paper, and given it to the brother. Folding it up carefully as if it were a bank-note he places it securely in his breast-pocket.

"Now blaze the tree with your axe," he adds to the negro. "Not that side, this side toward the cabin. That will do, thank you." His voice is so gentle Catfish Robbins and the negro both glance at him with surprise.

"Stay," he adds; "Robbins, I thank you for your kindness to the dead. I can't talk now. Another day, when God pleases, I certainly will repay you. Now go."

"Wait a moment, Squire," says Hol Robbins.

"Not now, go!" says the lawyer, impatiently.

"About his property, you bein' the heir—"

"What do you want?"

"Oh, nothin', nothin' at all. What I was tryin' to say is, you needn't go an' distress yourself s'posin' there was so much plunder burned up or tooken away by them devils. Fact is, there was almost none. You see he'd been strippin' himself, givin' first to one an' then to another till a'most nothin' was left. Families of people whose husbands had gone to the war,

you see: other families, too, whose men folks had run away to keep from goin' to the war. I see his last blanket down at Widow Maxwell's only last week."

"Well, go now!"

"Hold on, Squire, you wouldn't mind a poor fellow havin' some of these yer old rails?" says Hol Robbins, coaxingly; "maulin' rails ain't so funny with me as it used to was, fever an' ague—"

"Take any thing you wish of what is left on the place. Stop. Roll two or three large logs over this grave."

"Count of them hogs an' things. It was rather shaller, that is the fact—"

But what consolation can the minister use as they ride off at last from the spot? He says what he can, but to deaf ears; his companion is too deep in thought to yield attention. He ceases at last, and they ride along the way they came in silence. Crossing the creek, whose turbid waters are hurrying on as if they had heard of what is in the gully below and are crowding there to see, by one impulse they both urge their unwilling horses to the brink again, and sit gazing upon the murdered men circling round and round below. They gaze upon the ghastly sight; and at the same period, if not at the same instant, millions throughout the South are aware of men assassinated in like fashion, for like cause, here and there throughout all the Southern States. Millions? All men, women, children at the South are more or less cognizant of, and are thinking upon, like tragedies; beneath whatever outer bearing, thinking, thinking.

The solemn pines put their heads together far above the pool with incessant whisperings of horror, parting and swaying themselves hither and thither if so be they may cast off from their branches the foul birds drawn from leagues away to the spot. The waters babble garrulously to each other as, having seen and borne tenderly up in their turn the mutilated dead, they rush away to bear the tale to river, and so to the broad sea. And over all bends the great God so patient, knowing that events are converging now so rapidly, and by the inherent force of their own nature, to their appointed end. Yes, thank God, no stone falls, no planet turns, no comet flies with motion more certain than that by which every Judas goes "to his own place."

The two friends are miles off along their road before the silence is broken.

"You won't object to camping out with me to-night, Mr. Arthur?" says the lawyer, at last. "We've done it together before now on our hunting excursions. I know a place up the creek where I camped once with Paul a week while he was getting his cabin ready. I can not enter a house to-night—I could not endure to see any one. And, besides, we've enough left of our lunch for supper and breakfast."

The night has fallen by this time, but the spot is not far off—a secluded and grassy knoll under the pines. To dismount, tether their horses where they can graze, build a fire, and arrange themselves before it upon their saddle blankets, is the work of a few minutes.

"Thank you, I can not," said the lawyer, when his companion pressed him to share in the food put up by Mrs. Sorel in lavish abundance for their lunch. "You eat, and listen. We may not meet again soon, and I've much to say. First, I want to tell you about Paul.

It is a long story, as Guy Brooks tells it, that night under the pines, the light from the camp-fire flickering upon his broad face as he speaks, revealing therein a new expression altogether. Mr. Arthur is almost surprised at the calmness of his friend. Guy and Paul were the two only children of a Kentucky planter. The lawyer lingered long upon even the trivial incidents of their boyish attachment to each other—like a boy again himself while he recalled them. The parents had died. Carrying out a long-cherished scheme, the brothers had sold the old place, bringing the negroes southward to their new home. "I am just beginning to understand Paul in reference to those negroes," said the lawyer. "Just before leaving Kentucky he joined the church. I am a professor too, as you know. Not as Paul was. We were very different. He had a hundred times my depth. I don't think it was his religion only. Our father was a good man, but our mother was an extraordinary woman for intelligence and piety. I remember her as if I saw her to-day, erect, beautiful, the finest-looking woman I ever saw in my life. For years before her death she —through her I suppose—my father also, both were uneasy about the negroes, used to be often speaking with us, especially with Paul, who was justly the favorite with them, on the subject. Vaguely, perhaps. I don't know—never mind. As it was, Paul turned over every soul of them to me. He said very little to me on the subject. So far as I know he never spoke a syllable about slavery to a human being. He was a silent man on all points. He had a queer idea that he would prefer to be independent, to work with his own hands for his living. I used to think him a kind of dumb Daniel Webster—superior to me in every respect. I used to tell him how wrong it was to bury himself in the woods. He would say, 'I don't know, Guy—I've got odd notions. I'm before my times, or behind them. People are not ripe for me, or I am not ripe for them: we are too far apart somehow.' It seems to me now," continued the brother, musingly, "Paul did not feel prepared to bring his ideas to bear on other men, or despaired of succeeding with them if he did. He resolved that his opinions should, at any rate, be a rule for *him*. I think he had a hope, too, the time was coming

when he could do something; a great believer in the Future Paul was—a deep, serious, joyful faith in what is to be among us all right here. And so he lived meanwhile up there in his cabin, and worked hard. You see, after paying the estate debts, nothing was left us but the negroes, and he would neither sell them nor work them, nor take from me one cent more of what I got from their labor than he could help. He hunted a little; read, especially his Bible: helped his neighbors, and the like. Yes," added the lawyer, suddenly, "I *am* Paul's heir, as Robbins says, and I intend to take full possession of my inheritance—all of it. Never mind that now. You told me to-day to wait—Providence would show me what to do. You were right—Providence *has* shown me my path at last."

Immediate departure from Somerville, enlistment in the Federal army, life-long war against every foe which holds the South in bondage—the lawyer tells his friend his whole plan.

"And your property?" begins Mr. Arthur.

"I will write from the next town to Ferguson. I gave him a power of attorney months ago in case of accidents; he did the same to me; as for that, we did not know what might turn up. I owe no man a cent, except yourself, and Ferguson will arrange all that. You will not be dependent on Mr. Ellis or Mrs. Warner in any sense, I've fixed *that*," added the lawyer with a smile. "When they go to work, if they get time to do it, confiscating my property they will find they had a lawyer to deal with, even if he isn't a Yankee. What to *do* with them?" he added, after a pause, in more anxious accents.

"Do with whom?"

"I do believe it was that which staggered Paul," continued the lawyer. "You can not free them at the South. You'd have to sell half of them to pay the expenses of the other half to Liberia. The North won't have them. Well, all Egypt is being stirred for them just now. When they get to the very edge of the Red Sea perhaps the waves will part in some way before them," he added, musingly.

"Halloo, I never thought of it!" he suddenly exclaimed, with brightening face, "why not go with me?"

"No," adds his friend, promptly; "I agree with you, your path is plain. Mine is not. At least not to go yet. I know I seem doing nothing in Somerville, less and less apparently every day. As your brother said, the people there and I are too far apart. I am worn down in struggle with evils there, mightier than my puny hand to do more at least than point out. But not yet. My heart is not ready to go; I would feel too much like Jonah. We must be governed by our conscience. You won't thank me, but I would feel almost as reluctant to go with you as I would to go with good Mr. Ellis in his way—it is right for you, but not for me."

It is long after midnight, the camp-fire often replenished before they ceased from their earnest conversation. Then, with a fervent prayer for divine aid, they fell asleep, each on his blanket, their feet to the fire, under the pines making mournful lullaby over them. But before doing so, the lawyer had scooped out a hole into which he drew the coals, lest they should attract any one to the spot while they slept—"To say nothing about your life"—he said as he did it—"my life is very precious to me from this hour. I have so much I want to do."

When Mr. Arthur awakes next morning after such a sleep as people enjoy only under the free air of heaven, he finds his friend cooking the remains of their supper at the fire.

"Up, man: it's late breakfast! I could hardly wait till you woke. I'm going to eat such a meal as people never make except in camp!" he says; and the minister joins him in the repast, wondering in the change which has taken place in the Kentuckian's manner.

Yes, the gloom, hesitation, doubt which has darkened over that broad face since Secession, darkening deeper and deeper as the slow days roll by, is gone as by a charm. There is trace of the sharp distress of the night before, but distress out of which has broken a new light. He moves, speaks, laughs like the frank-visaged, plain-spoken, warm-hearted Kentuckian he was that day, years ago, when the young parson stepped, the day of his arrival in Somerville, out of the stage and, as it were, into his very arms. A less care-worn man you would not wish to see and shake hands with. He is almost jovial now, in sudden reaction from long uncertainty and indecision. Out of the brambles at last, a broad, clear path stretches away straight before him.

"And you hold to your decision?" he says at last to his friend, as a voyager, flushed and eager for his journey to some happy port, might speak to one who lingers behind on a deserted shore.

"Yes, my mind is clear as well as yours." Mr. Arthur endeavors to rally and to speak as stoutly as he can, cheerfully even. "Somerville is my post of duty still. For me to leave would be desertion; my flag, you know, yet flies there, as well as whither you are going. I stay bound in the spirit in Jerusalem, not knowing the things that befall me there."

"God forbid the rest of the passage should come true of you!" adds his friend, hastily, and with blank face.

"I know nothing about that; I only stand to my post. As to the rest, why, God's will be done!"

"Oh, well, I dare say, only, Mr. Edward Arthur, don't be too sure that your duty is all that keeps you in Somerville. Unless I tremendously mistake, there is a certain something vastly more attractive. Never color so, man," he adds, heartily; "all our motives are terribly mixed up. And I tell you, Sir, you are right. Leave my mother out of question, and the one you think of is the finest specimen of a lady, that is, will be, she is so young. Go ahead, man, go ahead!"

"I'm afraid," begins his companion, gravely, "there will have to be a very great change before—"

"Change!" breaks in the lawyer, who is in highest spirits; "and there will be a great, a glorious, a most magnificent change. Not in a moment, in the twinkling of an eye, perhaps: but we shall all be changed—I don't mean any irreverence—even in Somerville. I have all Paul's faith—not the Apostle, my Paul's—in the Future, only I stand nearer to it, understand it perhaps better."

It is an hour yet before they part. But when they do Mr. Arthur rides back alone toward Somerville at last, not as sad a man as when the two friends passed over the same road the day before. Thank God for our memory of the Past! thanks be to Him for our enjoyment of the Present! but threefold thanks be to Him, above all, for—the Future!

---

## CHAPTER XVII.

"O HAPPY day!—O glorious and blessed day! —O day for us to celebrate with joyful hearts as long as we live here and throughout all eternity! No room for hesitation now. Many a time you have laughed at your humble speaker—said, 'Don't be too fast, Brother Barker'—hah! was I not right? From the first whisper of the great news I believed it all, every syllable. Shame upon you who held back, who wanted confirmation, as you call it. There was your sin. Men standing high like among us, too—like the lord on whose hand the king leaned that our text— Second Kings, seventh—speaks about. You wouldn't believe me any more than they would the lepers when they came to tell of the invading army fled. Like them, it is faith you need. You may despise me, but you can't take from me my faith. You hesitated. You said, Louisville taken? May be so. Cincinnati captured? Perhaps; only there's a good many people living in that town, railways to bring more, and the like. But Washington captured? you asked. Don't know about that. You all believed about the second battle of Manassas which went before all this glorious success; you hemmed and hawed about the rest. Only let me have the humble satisfaction of calling you all to witness this day that I believed it all from the first—second victory of Manassas, capture simultaneously thereafter of Louisville, Cincinnati, Washington —yes, and of Philadelphia and New York City, too, which will soon follow. Is it because I believe in our glorious Davis and Lee and Stonewall Jackson and our gallant army? Not one bit of it. What I believe in is God. From the first I have said, Brethren, here's the only ground to stand on. This whole war is a war for slavery. God teaches plainly in His Word slavery is a divine ordinance. In all the world we are His peculiar people, being the only people on earth who believe in the institution as such. An infidel North, an infidel world against us, but God for us! You have trembled and said, 'Oh, the North is so populous, so rich, so united, so determined—the North is so this, and the North is so that.' All I said is this, Very good, if the North is all this and a millionfold more so, what do I care? The God of this Bible is for us. But the whole civilized world is against us. Who cares if all the devils in hell were too? If God be for us, who can be against us? I, all the brethren in our denomination, almost every preacher of every denomination has said the same here at the South—if you would only believe it when you hear it. There in that ninth verse—'We do not well: this day is a day of good tidings; and we hold our peace;' what the lepers said to one another. As I said in taking that text, this being a day of good tidings, I don't intend to hold *my* peace!"

And Brother Barker did not. It was on Sunday morning in his pulpit in Somerville, to his church crowded to its utmost capacity. For a week the news he specifies has been pouring in, increasing in magnitude and being more fully confirmed every mail. Some rejoicings had taken place from its very first arrival; but last night the news was so entirely confirmed that even the most prudent Secessionist in Somerville abandoned any doubt as to its authenticity. Hurrahing until hopeless hoarseness, bonfires, firearms from cannon down to the feeblest pistol, bells from the big bell of the Brick Church down to the weakest tea-bell in the hands of baby assisted to hold and shake it! Shaking of hands till exhaustion. Somerville has rejoiced before, but Somerville outdoes Somerville this time. Very properly, the news being by far the most glorious ever received.

Around Mr. Ferguson, sitting grimly aloft in his room, Somerville sweeps and roars like a maelstrom, all the county around sucked into the vortex of rejoicing. Like a hunted lion in his brushy lair, the Scotchman broods in defiant scorn behind his grizzly beard. His only care is to secure each and every dispatch or other printed fragment in relation to the news as it appears, and before it can be whelmed in the torrent of later and fresher tidings, give it a permanent place in his Scrap-book according to its exact date and sequence. It is a very Daniel Lambert of volumes. No easy matter to handle it now, as it lies on a table in the Scotchman's room devoted expressly to it; and it is growing rapidly in these days. Mr. Ferguson has no children, not even a cat, and this is his pet. Mr. Ferguson has no visitors beyond Dr. Warner, Guy Brooks before he left, Mr. Arthur, and one or two more; his business is destroyed for the present; the collection is at once his only business and recreation.

Yes, on this Sunday morning, while Mr. Arthur is preaching the old, obsolete, utterly uninteresting Gospel to quite a small congregation, both he and they none the brighter from a night from which sleep had been routed by the bells—at the same hour Brother Barker actually outdoes and altogether eclipses the Brother Barker of any previous occasion. No wonder. Is not the North now finally defeated? The war is over, as Brother Barker very justly reasons in his sermon. Washington being captured, there is no longer any Northern Government existing to fight. With tears in his eyes he confesses in sermons, and in conversation which fills up all the space between sermons, to a feeling even of deepest pity for this misguided and infidel but now utterly wrecked and ruined people. As he refers to it in the pulpit he has broken down, has turned himself to one side to wipe his eyes and blow his nose. Friends must excuse him, he was born among that infatuated people who have so madly rushed upon their ruin; and so, with a hasty swallow or two and a twenty-fifth sip at the tumbler of water beside him, he tucks his wet handkerchief under the edge of his Bible.

"I know your magnanimous souls, dear friends. Even in this hour of your final triumph you pity your fallen foe. In view of their awful overthrow we all feel to sorrow over them. It was an inscrutable Providence that caused me, no will of my own, to be born there. You will excuse—you know how wicked Jerusalem was, yet you know who wept over it!"

Pardon the hand which records this, but shall not that time be set down as it actually was?

"I have heard from my earliest infancy many, very many sermons; in fact, in the earlier portion of my existence I never heard any thing else," Captain Simmons remarks to a group of friends in the grocery next day, "but I never heard a more brilliant discourse—a more affecting one, parts of it, in my life. My nature revolts from a Yankee, even when a Secessionist, yet I must do Parson Barker justice to say that."

"Bear in your minds, friends, this one thing," reiterates Brother Barker, speaking the almost unanimous sentiment of his denomination South at that hour. "The success of our glorious Confederacy, the destruction of the old United States and the infidel North is the doing of the Almighty. And why? Because he could not be a just God and act otherwise."

And it is a little singular that the sovereignty

of God is the theme, far from the first or the last time, of Mr. Arthur's sermon at the same hour, the grand doctrine, not the same inferences. Though he, too, is dreading this morning in secret lest the will of Heaven may be at last as Brother Barker interprets it—dreading it, rebuking himself for any pain at what Heaven decrees, yet oh that acute, bitter, sickening dread! "Not my will but Thine!" he repeats a thousand times, but oh that it would throb in his very heart as well as on his tongue!

"You observe my condition, friends," says Brother Barker, half an hour later in his discourse. "My bleeding lungs will not permit—I must close. Only I find on the desk a note making request that I will explain a little Scripture before we part. With pleasure will I do so." And that thin, sallow-faced fellow-creature—his lank hair combed back off his forehead and tucked behind his ears, the centre and soul for near two hours now of that crowded church, enjoys, as he leans forward over his cushion, note in hand, a degree of self-satisfaction intense beyond the ordinary allotment of the rest of us.

"I find here," he says, "some questions to answer. I have had no time to examine them. I trust my general knowledge of this blessed Book is sufficient. 'First, What does prophecy mean by the stars of heaven?' An easy question to answer," with a smile: "as I have often told you, by the stars of heaven is meant in prophecy governments, particularly the States which once composed this Union. 'Second, Has prophecy a meaning when it speaks of a third part of the stars of heaven?' Whoever wrote this note could hardly have attended the preaching of your most humble. I've explained it often in the Sunday-school. The smallest child there could tell you the reference is to our Confederate States: thirty-three States at the time of Secession; eleven seceded States. Yes, if there be, as I've often explained, any thing certain, positively certain, in Scripture," says the preacher, slowly, "it is that by a third part of the stars of heaven is meant these Confederate States of America. Very good. 'Third, When Scripture speaks of the great Red Dragon what is meant?' Really, friends," says Brother Barker, smiling, "these questions are too simple; I'm wasting your time. By the Dragon is meant, of course, the Devil, the Adversary, Satan. He is called great because of his terrible power over men. He is called red—the great red Dragon—to show that he burns like fire with fury, and because he accomplishes his dreadful purposes against men very often by bloodshed and war. 'A last question: Please say, then, what is meant by Revelation, twelfth chapter, third and fourth verses.' Revelation, twelfth, third—twelfth, third." Brother Barker has his long forefinger on the place in an instant, and reads, without a pause: "'And there appeared

BROTHER BARKER IN A TRAP.

another wonder in heaven; and behold a great red dragon, having seven heads and ten horns, and seven crowns upon his heads.' All this emblematic," the preacher pauses here to say, "of the devil's terrible power over men; but let us go on: 'And his tail drew the third part of the stars of heaven, and did cast them to the earth—'"

Total silence in the vast audience. Then a perfectly distinct "by George!" from the direction in which Bob Withers is seated, with a tittering among the younger portion, first at Brother Barker's aspect of sudden and total discomfiture, swelling as the meaning of this most unexpected Scripture breaks upon them according to the explanation yet ringing in their ears! The whole congregation at last catch the joke, and join in. The thing comes upon it so suddenly. The reaction of feeling also. The sympathy of a crowd of laughers likewise.

Brother Barker has closed the Bible, very sallow indeed, and leans himself over the desk with deprecating hand for some time before he can make himself heard.

"Brethren," he begins, at last, in his most solemn tones, "an enemy hath done—" But the congregation has at this instant a fresh sense of the joke, and go off together in another peal of laughter, as audiences sometimes will, as much at Brother Barker himself, the victim, as at the sudden Scripture.

"An enemy, an enemy hath done this," he says at last. "Once before, in my humble labors in the cause of the South and the God of the South, an enemy attempted to wrest Scripture at church in somewhat the same way. I foresaw then and told friends he wrested Scripture to his own destruction. You have all heard the fate, the just fate, of the traitor who did it—the double vengeance of God on him as a traitor both to his country and to his Bible. Like Uzzah, he laid his hand on the Ark of the Lord, and, like Uzzah, he perished for his sin."

But there is laughter breaking forth yet, here and there, among the most thoughtless. Brother Barker grows more livid, his hair seems blacker, his eyes like those of a serpent, his head projected nearer his audience, his long arm shaking a prophetic finger at them.

"I have spoken of the fate of that miserable man's body," he adds; "but what of his immortal soul gone to the Judgment? I tell you, friends, disloyalty to the Confederacy is a sin against God, a great sin. He will damn a man for that as well as for any other sin. The Powers that be are ordained of God; and it goes right on to add: Whosoever therefore resisteth the power, resisteth the ordinance of God, and they that resist shall receive to themselves—Damnation!"

But it is impossible to describe the force and zest with which the word passes the speaker's lips.

"As to the person who wrote this"—the preacher holds out the offensive note at arm's-length—"let him look out for himself. He may be here this instant. I tell you, Sir, whoever you are, we have your handwrite. You can not escape. Has it come to this!" wails Brother Barker. "Is it possible there can exist among us men so desperate! Men who can yet cling to our vile foe, cling to it in the very hour that Heaven has finally crushed it beneath its awful wrath! From whom," continues the speaker, after a pause, and with a lower leaning of his body to his audience, as he asks the question, in confidence, of them, "did the writer of this get his Bible passages? The Concordance by which this note was got up belongs," shaking the paper almost to pieces in his extended hand as he speaks, "to a minister of the Gospel now living, this moment preaching, preaching without one prayer for the Confederacy, in Somerville!" And the speaker's silence is more eloquent of meaning than any words could be. Not a grown person but says to himself—Mrs. Warner is not the only lady who whispers it to her neighbor then—"Parson Arthur."

"I will say this much more"—the preacher has worked himself by this time into a frenzy, the projection of his lean body, long arms, small head over the desk, with the hiss of his words resembling him, even to Tim Lamum, who sits on one side of the pulpit, crowded there by the stress of the occasion, and has the preacher

in profile, to an enraged serpent—"this moment our brave boys, your own husbands, brothers, sons, lovers, friends are far away there, enduring hunger, cold, intense toil for their country, lying in their heart's gore, being this very instant butchered by a fiendish foe; pouring out from every vein their rich, warm, Southern blood! And for what? Doing the Almighty's work on their and His hellish foes. Yes, pursuing and slaughtering and burning the Louisvilles and Cincinnatis and Washingtons of your defeated tyrants as those other slaveholders and peculiar people of God did the Canaanites! Our dear boys are this moment slaying such of our cruel foes as come in their reach; and here are we at home, the same foes right among us, people sitting deliberately, insultingly down to write such a paper as this"—a deadly shake to it—"while we are exulting in our great victories. Men right at our firesides! Adders doubting the news on the very hearthstones which warm them. I tell you what, friends and fellow-citizens"—and the preacher, lower down over his desk, two-thirds of his body toward his breathless congregation, suits eyes and lips, long arms and convulsive hands, face livid and teeth set, to the words—"you should this hour seize the wretches and crush them like vipers under your feet!" and the stamp with which he dashes his heel upon their shattered heads thrills every heart.

But not without the conscious uprising in his own bosom, ay, and in the bosom of every Christian man there, of a something adverse to all this, not without that, no not without that!

Only human nature, and that nature yours, dear reader, as well as his. Our common nature; in this instance dizzied in and by the raging of such a whirlwind as never befalls twice a century. Let Him decide the degree of guilt who only can.

Reaction, however, being thus established, Brother Barker draws himself back again into the pulpit and takes up his well-worn hymn-book.

"Sixty-eight Psalm, first part, long measure:

'Let God arise in all his might
And put the troops of hell to flight.'

Brethren, please sing."

Yes, the case of Mr. Arthur grows a more painful one every day. Many of his members, once his warmest friends, cease to attend church; even those whom he knows most cordially to approve his course are very rare indeed in their attendance there, exceedingly shy of being seen conversing with him, even for an instant, on the street. So many whom he once knew pass him on the streets, refusing to speak to him, that he now takes the initiative in that matter, and never himself first salutes any one of whose friendly feeling he entertains the least doubt. The very children are, in more instances than one, prompt-

K

"YOU BLACK-HEARTED ABOLITIONIST!"

ed to call after him as he passes along. The week after Brother Barker's sermon Mrs. Warner's little son salutes him as "A black-hearted Abolitionist." It is on record that the same child receives, for the first time in many months, an exceedingly severe chastisement from Dr. Warner, followed by a much more severe scourging of the Doctor himself by the tongue of his wife; but who dare raise the sacred veil of their family privacy to explain matters?

In fact, Mr. Arthur's apprehension of the exact standing of a leper in Hebrew society is clearer than it ever was before, with all his reading. But let only truth be told; with all his bitter unpopularity in the community he enjoys a sweeter, more solid peace than ever before.

"It reminds me of the story of the prisoner whose dungeon was curiously constructed to contract around him every day," he says to Mr. Ferguson, who has just read aloud from his portly scrap-book a furious onslaught upon "the miscreant ministers yet lingering among us who refuse to pray for the Confederacy," from the last Somerville *Star*.

"They do their utmost to drive you away. Only go, and they will publish you as having deserted to the Federals, being a hypocrite and a spy all the time you were here," added the Scotchman, upon whom quite a change has passed, by-the-by. Rough, cross, an old bachelor, and a tough Scot, since Guy Brooks has gone—"fled in a base and cowardly manner to our dastardly foes," as the *Star* had it—Mr. Ferguson, whose regard for Mr. Arthur has, since Secession, steadily increased, is now, to him at least, more gentle than he was ever known to be to man before. There is the spirit of John Knox in Mr. Arthur which he can not resist.

"Yes, if you were to go you would leave an odor behind you proving you to have been all along the vilest of wolves in sheep's clothing, just as the smell of brimstone proves a departed visitant to have been the devil." So he comforts his friend.

Heretofore he scarcely ever visited any one. The truth is, he was afraid to leave his collection. Now he lugs and crowds that ponderous volume into the iron safe in which he keeps his land-titles and money, and frequently visits Mr. Arthur in the study of the latter. If busy when his friend enters the minister merely returns the dry Good-morning, and waves the Scotchman to a chair till he gets through. Often Mr. Ferguson mounts his horse, a scrubby, obstinate hack, the very counterpart of his owner, and visits his friend out at Mrs. Sorel's. He has even been known to pat Robby, when out there, on the head—the first time he has touched a child for many, many years. True, the conversation is upon the one topic until Mr. Arthur wearies of it, yet he experiences a pleasure in having his grim and taciturn friend with him. It is somehow like the having a rocky barrier for the time between him and the roar and dash of the ocean—for, very broad, deep, dark, and clamorous is the phase of Secession just now.

"I know dozens of cases in which they have made preachers take the oath even though they furloughed them to preach; resign this morning, and before night Simmons and Tim Lamum will be after you," says Mr. Ferguson, perpetually.

"None of the interest in religious matters among even the best of our people, which I counted on to make up for other things," moans Mr. Arthur. "The Union men flying the country or giving up all heart, despairing of the purpose or the power of the General Government. So many who abhorred Secession have gone into it from a deeper hatred still of Abolition. But oh, this spiritual apathy!"

"Quite a contrast to the fervent praying, preaching, singing, crowding, at that fellow Barker's Sunday services and weekly prayer-meetings!" says his friend. "But the inspiration of all that is purely the Confederacy. It lives with it, will die with it."

"They ignore, for the present, every Gospel doctrine, so far as urging it is concerned, I fear," replies Mr. Arthur. "God is feared principally as the One who may help the Federals; believed in, and invoked, and clung to, mainly as the One who must and shall help the Confederates. It does seem as if their chief affection for the very Saviour now is, because he sanctioned, or, at least, did not expressly condemn, slavery. At heart the truly pious are better than all this, but this is the outer seeming. And I, perhaps, am as fanatical—only the other way."

"The Almighty," puts in the Scotchman, reverently, "is simply witholding his gracious Spirit for the present, leaving men, for the time, to their own ways. There is now a lull in that Divine wind which bloweth as it listeth."

"And, the analogy of Nature, will it prove true here?" says the minister, eagerly, "the strong blowing which seamen know always to follow a calm."

"When His other instrumentalities have got slavery out of the way. Even that man Barker has some blind idea toward the truth. Before this last ridiculous news, they tell me, he had a vast deal to say about some Jonah or other being under deck of the Ship of State—some wedge of gold and Babylonish garment being hidden somewhere in camp which prevented success."

"I fear he refers to the Union men still left unhung in the land—not to the institution; but who can tell? How often I wish I could catch a glimpse of some men's *hearts!* Alas, I do not even know my own!" says Mr. Arthur. "I don't want to speak of myself; but I do feel as if I was actually in jail—my feet in the stocks."

"And midnight upon you; then do as Paul and Silas did, in like case: pray and sing praises to God. The earthquake will come in due time," is the consolation of the Scotchman.

"But so many really good men have gone into this thing—men who hated it at first as much as myself! Some from the influence of others, especially their wives or sons; some because money is to be made in it; some from despair of the success of the Federal Government; some because they are led to regard Heaven as being at last, by its favor, on the side of the South. What pains me most is, that ministers, ministers of our own denomination—men older, wiser, more devoted than I—men superior to me in every sense, should be so thoroughly persuaded and zealous for the Confederacy." And Mr. Arthur's head as he walks his study, wherein this conversation takes place, sinks upon his bosom in deep and painful thought.

The Scotchman sits at the table, apparently turning over the leaves of a Ridgeley's "Body of Divinity" in search of something. Really he is far away in Scotland, standing beside a grave wherein he saw laid, years on years ago, a fair young form, whose blue eyes and flaxen locks are parts of his memory forever. The plumed Hamlet, the white-bearded Lear, the swarthy Othello you see upon the stage are not the only heroes of drama. This grizzly old Scot was not driven apart from men and so deep within himself, more a hermit than if fled to desert and cave, without his tragedy too.

What divine finger touches his heart this morning? Astonished that he had never thought of it before, a new purpose, as his eye rests upon his friend, suddenly blossoms upon him, like the almond bud upon Aaron's dead rod. A new purpose! And like the arrival of the time for the putting forth of buds, it brings a spring and a joy with it even to the wintry old Scot. A purpose, and a substantial one, too, as we shall yet see.

It strikes him—the change in this once enthusiastic young divine, who came to Somerville to accomplish wonders—that is long ago now. The long gallops before breakfast, perhaps. Say it is the plunges the year around into the cold pool. Maybe it is because, in intervals of study, Mr. Arthur toils in Mrs. Sorel's garden so with hoe and spade. Because, once too reliant on others, circumstances in these days have thrown him altogether on himself, perhaps. And it may be for the reason that he has been swimming very long now against a current broad and deep. All the providences of Heaven, from without and from within, have wrought together to make him, bodily, mentally, spiritually, a thousand times the man he once was. Men will turn to look upon him as he passes them hereafter, saying to themselves, "There is one who has had a history." Ay, and one, please God, who has a history before him also.

The Scotchman removes a tumbler of fresh flowers from off an old volume of Shakspeare on the table; and with the sight and smell of the flowers is mingled a fair face he sees at Sunday-school and church. Yes, yes, if God will, there shall be a story, yet unlived, as pleasant as any Winter's Tale or As you Like It in old Shakspeare or out of it: a story of love through years of trial, and, at last, union just the sweeter and more perfect for all that. Not that Mr. Fergu-

son is perfectly confident; he knows too much of this sorrowful world for that. If it is in my power, he says.

But Mr. Arthur is thinking as he walks of that last visit good Mr. Ellis made him the Saturday before Mr. Ellis's last appearance at church. "I do not ask you to take an active part," Mr. Ellis had closed a long entreaty with his pastor by saying. "I confess there is much in Mr. Barker's temper and manner which I can not approve. But people tell me every day that you wish the defeat of the Confederacy, the success of the Federals. Assure me this is not so. This is all I ask."

Mr. Ellis had been urging the waning influence and usefulness of his pastor with tears in his eyes; most sincerely is he attached to his pastor and to his church. If he possibly could he would cling to both.

"Being born at the South, it is impossible for me, as for you, to desire any thing other than what is for the welfare of the South. As to the rest, I can only say, God's will in regard to the South be done. He knows what is best for the South; let us leave it to Him."

And Mr. Ellis can by no means be satisfied with that. If Mr. Arthur could only have told him that he can not regard either Secession or slavery as things for which Heaven is likely to fight.

Dark days these for Mr. Ellis. True, the Confederacy has been most wonderfully victorious of late; its ultimate success is a certainty, of course. But then Henry is off in camp, terribly exposed body and soul. The demoralization even among Christian men is frightful. And Mr. Ellis, his expenses becoming heavier every day, is making nothing there in his empty store. Strange to say, there is a love of property developing in Mr. Ellis's bosom which surprises men—an altogether peculiar love. The new emotion surprised himself at first; but he is past that now. In fact, Mr. Ellis is becoming known as, of all Secessionists in Somerville, that one whose feelings are most involved in it. He is nervous, sensitive, quick to take offense, petulant exceedingly when bad news is coming. Far from as liberal, however, toward the object as he was at first. He has been so drained, you see, and doubly drained by its perpetual appeals.

"Who knows, Mr. Ferguson," says Mr. Arthur at last, "but Providence may permit the Confederacy to be established—a Christian nation of slaveholders, off by itself from all intermeddling—to show what Christianity within it can effect on slaves? The world may thus get a new idea of the power of religion; and the slaves may thus be in an admirable training for freedom, if such they are to have at some future period."

"Visionary!" growls the Scotchman. "God works according to laws inherent in the nature of things. We have no Scripture warrant to calculate upon miracles in our case; and this requires a double miracle. Only by a supernatural restraint would the world be held back from such intermeddling. Only by a miraculous increase of the Christianity at the South will owners do more for and with their slaves than heretofore. Did they not *know* that marriage is an ordinance, the relation of parent and child is an ordinance of God, even if slavery is, as well as slavery? Did they assert *those* ordinances for the slave? They have had the opportunity; it is gone from them forever. Christianity? It demands the observance of the parental and marital relation in the case of every disciple, white and black, and that is utterly inconsistent with the very existence of slavery. Let a Christian owner try any improvement upon the culture of his slaves; like a dog with a tin kettle tied to his tail he would be run out of the country, with Abolitionist! fastened to him in no time."

"Well, then," says his theorizing friend, "Heaven may permit the Confederacy to gain its independence, to set up for itself, isolated from all the world, as a nation peculiar in this—that it claims to be Christian, yet on the basis of slavery. The Ruler of all may permit this that said nation may work out its own ruin apart from all the world by the law of self-destruction inherent in every wrong thing ; or that, as a distinctively slave yet nominally Christian nation, it may be the object of His swift and direct vengeance."

"I prefer," grumbles Mr. Ferguson, "to take a plainer, more common-sense view. By Secession the South is at arm's-length from the National Government, and Heaven is giving that Government both will and power to scourge the South out of Secession and slavery, and back into civilization, Christianity, the Union, and the nineteenth century. That is the way Providence has worked from creation till now—by means."

But Mr. Arthur's attention is rambling. He has lived all his life at the South; and as he walks up and down there come up into his mind the many instances of oppression, cruelty, corruption, awful sin, which have passed under his own eye in connection with, and the direct and, as human nature is constituted, the necessary fruits of just such an institution. How many, many there are! Were he outside the South he would not mention one of them to a soul. He would not narrate a single instance of them all even to Mr. Ferguson. He almost blamed himself for recalling them to memory. He an Abolitionist, even in thought! Perhaps ten years hence people even at the South will hardly appreciate the horror with which such a man as he shrank then from the thought. He ventures now only this far:

"People say I am not sound, Mr. Ferguson. They are right in a sense. I am very much apart from them. If I could only stand up and speak! I am no true Southern man, they say.

As if the believing in and urging on the men and the things which have destroyed, are destroying, my own native soil, as I *know* they are, constitutes that! And here I am gagged, tied hand and foot, not permitted to do or say one thing for my country, dearer to me now than ever. Make a gesture even to save it, and I die. Running daily peril of death for even thinking and feeling—"

"Patience, man!" interrupts his cooler friend. "You can at least preach the Gospel."

"Not all of it. Not the many parts of it bearing directly on the times. No Sunday passes that there are not those at church expressly to see if there is a syllable in sermon or prayer upon which they can lay hold. More than once I have had persons throw themselves, as if casually, in my way, who spoke in denunciation of slavery and Secession expressly to trap me. But if it was not for this spiritual apathy into which we have all fallen! I pray, I strive, I can not move it even though as with the finger of an infant. I can not even grapple with it in my own bosom. Powerless, absolutely powerless!" and he falls into a chair and covers his face with his hands.

"Only mortified pride," says the Scotchman, with the promptitude of a surgeon. "Heaven would use you if it needed you. Who knows? You may be in training for future usefulness. And then you may not be : only an atom, any way! When you have learned your own entire feebleness you may lean upon Heaven enough for it to use you in the future."

"I feel at times as if there is no future," rejoins Mr. Arthur, after a silence. "That is, as if I had reached the end of my career. No country left me. The very Church of God powerless, or worked as the most powerful of all engines to delude and destroy the South. I will tell you what is about all my consolation just now"—drawing a Concordance toward him as he sits at the table.

The Scotchman patiently listening, the young theologian proceeds, with alacrity and increasing cheerfulness as he makes his points more and more past all doubt from Scripture, to prove conclusively that the world will end, in all probability, in a year or so. He rapidly explains from Daniel and Revelation the twelve hundred and sixty years; no doubt on *that* point. Now for the exact date from which this period is to date. Scott, Henry, Dr. Cummings, Gibbon—Milman says differently, but isn't to be trusted—dozens of books are torn down from the shelves and consulted. The Emperor Phocas *did* declare Gregory universal bishop in 606 A.D. "Can you show me on what ground we are to doubt it?" asks Mr. Arthur, eagerly. "Now add 606—please do it yourself on that slip of paper—to the twelve hundred and sixty."

"For the year in which the world is to end?

I can calculate without ciphering," says the grizzled Scotchman, with amusement under his beard. "Exactly eighteen hundred and sixty-six."

"But really and in good earnest," pleads his friend, as if for a gift. "You know I never indulge in idle speculations in private or in public; but it really does look as if it *may* be the year of the end of all. God in mercy grant it!"

"All stuff, man!" says the callous Scotchman, rising from his seat with a yawn. "You would not say so if you had heard to-day of the final success of the Federals, not even if you had heard of any great victory on their part. Nonsense, man! Of that day and that hour—you remember." And Mr. Ferguson, conscious of the flowers on the table, the fair face he sees at Sunday-school, and the youth and energy of his friend, of his own new purpose too, says, emphatically, "For one, *I* hope not.

"Besides," adds the Scot, in his own room, half an hour later, and with his collection open on its table before him, "it would be the greatest pity," passing his hand lovingly over the pasted pages, "the greatest pity in the world for such a collection as this to be burned up incomplete, even if it is by a world on fire!" and thereupon Mr. Ferguson falls into meditation as to what kind of binding will be good enough for said collection; and which of the Edinburgh public libraries most worthy of it at his death—all when the Confederacy is exploded. "My only fear is *it* will not last long enough!" he adds.

---

## CHAPTER XVIII.

Of late Mr. Neely—a beef-contractor now, and getting rich much more rapidly than when he taught school; no man striving more desperately than he to keep himself in the very van of Southern sentiment—finds himself suddenly mystified and left behind. For several weeks now he has observed posted up from time to time on every dead wall about Somerville a mysterious placard of red paper, sword-shaped, bearing mystical letters:

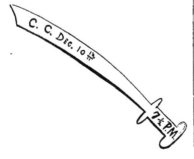

THE MYSTERIOUS PLACARD.

Turning whithersoever he goes to keep Mr. Neely out of some unknown Paradise, blazes this awful portent, until the contractor for beef can stand it no longer. He has questioned others in vain. Why had he not thought of it before? Tim Lamum!

Even after he found Tim, in the bar-room of Staples's Hotel, industriously engaged—Tim is a commissary agent these days, by deputy, his sole business by day being to smoke, with poker added at night—it is some time before Mr. Neely can get through with Burnside's repulse on the Rappahannock. This is the last news; and to Mr. Neely fighting it over again with terrific slaughter Tim only puffs a languid assent. In fact, the war has become a bore to the ex-provost marshal; for *that* bubble of blood has burst before this, at least until another and more regular one can be blown. The Yankees being so invariably and utterly routed in every fight, the independence of the Confederacy being beyond all question, very tired indeed is Tim of the whole subject.

And now, when Mr. Neely at last arrives at his point, and desires admission to whatever secret society lies behind the mystic sword, this Dragon of the Hesperides has that one fatal question to ask:

"Where were you born, Mr. Neely?" though he already knows perfectly well; and on Mr. Neely's reply assures the applicant that his admission is therefore an impossibility, and walks off.

That matter of birth—it clings to Mr. Neely as to Œdipus clung *his* curse. No child born out of wedlock, no offspring of one who dies by the hand of the hangman, so unfortunate. Yes; if his mother had been a harlot kenneled in a brothel, if his father had been a criminal whose last dying speech and confession had been published in all the papers, Mr. Neely could have concealed the blot and shame upon his name in some distant region, and lived and died respected and in peace. But his New England birth! The "damned spot" will not "out," nor can it be concealed. New England training will not permit him to tell a point-blank lie in the matter, even if he did not know from bitter experience that a certain Yankeeism clings to him in spite of unceasing and long-continued exertion, an ointment of his right hand, which bewrayeth itself do what he can. Cruel misfortune! and he so little to blame for it, too! Was it he or his parents who sinned, that he should have been born—in Connecticut? He would not have insisted on South Carolina, if that were too great a boon; if he could only have been born on the northernmost edge of Maryland, or the southernmost possible coast of Florida! Better have first seen the light even in the most desperate county in Arkansas.

In the name of Reason and St. Logic what is it constitutes one a Southern man? What the very essence and marrow of the thing so much more desirable to Mr. Neely than was the being a Roman citizen of old? Surely, Mr. Neely reasoned, it must be in the actually owning a negro. Yet, while many a man who enjoyed the enviable blessing of being Southern born, either could not or would not own a slave, Mr. Neely both could and would and did. The first moment it was in his power, with money industriously made and hoarded for that one end, Mr. Neely bought a negro. Not a negro man; Mr. Neely was not sufficiently acquainted with owning of the article to venture that at first. He bought a negro woman, of the jettest black he could get for the money.

Language fails to describe Mr. Neely's feelings on that eventful night when his woman Ceely, paid for and delivered, made herself at home in the kitchen of his residence, while he sat in his room and thought it all over. He went back to the happy hour he came into possession of his deceased father's huge silver watch, had it actually ticking in his distended fob, his *own* watch. He recalled the day he put the first horse he ever bought in the stable, and stood without in the snow listening to it munching its hay; his own animal, hoof and hide, from the tips of its ears to the end of its tail; his own quadruped, to ride, harness, plow, swap, sell, exactly as he pleased. But here was something far superior to all that. A woman, a living, breathing, speaking, working woman. There

was the "help" at his old home, Keziah, but she could drop her work, place her arms akimbo, and give Mr. Neely's mother just as good as she got—could, and on the occasion of a final spat did, hurry her things in her trunk, slam to the lid, snap her fingers in the face of the Neely household, and depart, leaving them cookless and in the middle of a heavy washing. But here was a Keziah, only of another shade of complexion, who could cook, wash, iron, ay, plow and hoe, and his own, own property. His own woman to keep or to hire, to sell or to swap—from the crown of her head to the sole of her foot as much his own article as was his watch or his horse. And then, all her children as they might come into the world his also!

That eight hundred dollars had bought him more gratification than he had ever dreamed it lay in the power of money to purchase; it gave a value to money which it had never had even in Mr. Neely's eyes. Mr. Neely sat up late thinking it over, not unconscious of how much elevated he was thereby above any of his old acquaintances still resident in his old village. He would like to be there—they knowing of his purchase—if it was only for a few days to enjoy it. He woke a dozen times that night with the thought. He even went out once or twice during the night to the door of the kitchen to make sure she was there, heard her deep breathing within and returned satisfied. You who own merely houses, lands, bank stock, railway scrip, and the like, wait till you own a human being before you can claim to understand the pleasure of property. Only we at the South got so used to it!

With Mr. Neely there was at first the flushed eagerness of a school-boy with a stolen watermelon; the sense, too, of having achieved a kind of moral impossibility, which added to the excitement of the purchase.

But these weeks, up to and after the date of the sword on the walls, roll by very slowly; wearily, too, with the burden of heavy hearts. A vast and increasing difference between Union men and all others. Business, ruined with the Union people, was never more thriving with good Secessionists. Hardly one of these last in Somerville but has an office, a contract, an agency—something or other which pays. If Tim Lamun has bought one fine horse in the last year he has bought twenty, the best to be had in all the land. Captain Simmons also. Hitherto it was with utmost difficulty he was able to pay his board bill at Staples's; in fact, Joe Staples, his hair standing a thousand ways with indignation, extailor as he is, has been loud in comment upon the Captain's delinquency, fearless of consequences. During the last few months, however, the Captain has "settled up like a gentleman," as Staples himself proclaims; has bought several new negroes, drives a splendid pair of blacks—

not, of course, of the last-mentioned race—and is now habitually drunk, and therefore habitually the most Chesterfieldian in his intercourse with others of any man in Somerville. Bob Withers expresses only the experience of many thousands like him the South over.

"As for me, gentlemen, what's the use denying the thing among friends? Secession has put me on, by George! *my* legs for one?" Only a tax-collector is Bob; yet in some mystic manner he has got capital from *some* source, with which, ceasing from drinking even for the time, in the eagerness of a new excitement, he has speculated in flour, salt, and whisky, until, if we may credit his statement, he is "Rich, by George! You can always count on returns trading in the actual necessaries of life, gentlemen. Yes, rich; you'd better believe so. Don't pretend to say how long it will be before Tim Lamum there wins it all from me at poker; but until that or some other providence happens to relieve me of it, for the first time in *my* life, by George! rich, yes, Sir, rich!"

There is Smithers, the postmaster, as ordinary a little sandy-haired man as you have in all your circle of acquaintance. A strange article wherewith to fill a post-office is sugar; yet Smithers has several rows of hogsheads thereof and therein. Seven cents a pound Smithers sells it at? No, paid for it. It is forty-five cents a pound wholesale, fifty cents a pound retail, he sells it at. Smithers's intentions are—negroes. In fact, he is always in the market for a woman to do the housework. An unfortunate man he invariably is in his perpetual purchases of the same. As fast almost as he can buy them do they run away—owing to Mrs. Smithers, whom even Mrs. Warner has described as being "one of those women who will not have a moment's rest herself, nor let a soul on the place have it either, day or night. Deliver *me* from such creatures!" unconscious that that respected lady is as much like herself in that as is a pin to a needle, a thorn to a splinter.

If Smithers has one woman "lying out" he has half a dozen. And where is the use of having the dogs to trail them? You have to pay more than the woman is worth to catch her. And when she is caught and whipped, Smithers doing it with his strap, Mrs. Smithers with her tongue, the first thing Mrs. Smithers finds when she wakes of a morning is the kitchen hearthstone cold, and Polly, Molly, Cynthy, Aggy, whatever it is, gone again. And thus does Smithers's sugar dissolve away.

Look at Joe Staples. Happy day for Staples when he laid aside shears and goose, leaped from his counter, rallied to himself the other eight parts of manhood, and went to keeping tavern! With money—gold it was—lent him by Mr. Ferguson, he provisioned his house so thoroughly when prices were low, and charges so enormously now when prices are high, that he too is getting rich. Since he has straightened his crossed legs he has actually grown inches in height, feet in circumference, beyond all admeasurement in the estimation of his household and himself. His very hair is more electric than ever with increased life at its roots.

As to little Joe Staples—the forward, dissipated, little offspring—under the new hotel régime, "he has money in great rolls, you'll bet," is the touching plaint of other boys to their parents; "buys game-chickens, candy, cigars, and a new pony whenever he wants to!" He is not quite nine yet, but already disdains the hotel gong on the arrival of glorious news. Generally he is the first, after Bill Perkins has announced it, at the Brick Church, holding on with the grip of a cray-fish to the knot on the end of the rope, rising high from the floor into the air at each semicircular sweep of the great bell.

And there is good Mr. Ellis. Four daughters has Mr. Ellis, and two sons. Henry, his eldest, is back home now, a hero from the repulse on the Rappahannock, but a cripple for life with a shot through the hip, and dreadfully emaciated by months in the hospital. Charley Ellis, his brother of twelve, no longer an attendant at Sunday-school or at church—it being impossible to go to Mr. Arthur's church any longer, since he will not pray for the Confederacy —shows terrible evidence thereof in marks; is, in fact, a distress to his father. A care-worn, haggard, stooping man now, from whom collectors of the perpetual subscription-lists for war purposes shrink most when they are abroad—as, for one such object or other they always are; because they know how Mr. Ellis shrinks from them. He really can not, will not! The money is misappropriated, or the object does not exactly fit his way of thinking. More intensely, bitterly, even fanatically Secession than ever before; yet Mr. Ellis is getting the reputation, justly or not, of being the most penurious man in Somerville. In far shabbier attire than he ever wore in other days Mr. Ellis, from talking at street corners all the rest of the time, is frantic to disprove all unfavorable, and to magnify all favorable news. On Sundays also, discussing Burnside and Lee with lying Sam Peters, Tim Lamum, Dr. Peel, Captain Simmons, and the rest, while the bells are ringing, and afterward too. As to that, the Union people in Somerville are also thrown together these many months now in new combinations. Society, thoroughly broken up from its foundations, is crystallizing into totally new forms.

Mr. Neely is flourishing as a beef-contractor in war times should. Possessing Confederate money in great sheets, he has bought quite a snug tract of wooded land near Somerville, and sells wood off it by the hundred cords. True, it is land belonging to Guy Brooks, Esq., but he being, as is well known now, a Colonel in the Federal service, his property has been confiscated and sold.

It is not in horses, lands, sugar, or even—which he declares in the *Star* to be the best of all investments—negroes, that Lamum, the editor, has placed his money. Cotton is his weakness. Report whispers into your ear that he has hundreds of bales safely to his account in some place over the water—but report says the same thing of most of the Secession leaders; it may all be false. With Government teams an immense deal of cotton is certainly going to the nearest ports, the Government stores coming back on blockade-runners being singularly disproportionate. In fact, a cry of swindling and corruption and favoritism is already begun, which swells every day; only among the people, however, and the power has long ago passed out of their hands.

Dr. Ginnis, big, pompous, spending his money—on all sorts of Medical Boards these days—in improving his place in Somerville, asserts that Dr. Peel, who has half a dozen contracts, has made half a million—but who can say?

"Even an infidel," reasons Mrs. Warner to her husband, "can see the Almighty is on our side by the way He is blessing us. Every mail brings news of glorious victories, and scarce a Secessionist at home—I mean those who took a leading hand—but is coining money. As to those miserable, God-forsaken Union people—look at them! I say, only look at them!"

Well, yes. As a general rule these last have sacrificed to their pigheadedness, to their perverse principles, every thing in the shape not only of popularity, common respect even, but of business also. But their infatuation, their obstinate convictions, like cancers in the bosom, seem destroying their victims; and, like cancers, are incurable—only the more deep-seated as the days roll by and Secession develops itself. Their love for what they still persist in calling their country glows still unquenched, unquenchable.

You who lived outside the South during the war, reading all varieties of papers, speaking exactly what you happened to think and feel, imagine, if you can, yourself to have been placed as these were. You were no more accustomed all your life hitherto to freedom than were these. Your convictions upon the whole matter were not clearer than were those of these men; only, living within the disease itself they knew more of its misery than you could. To them the rebellion is devastating their own soil. Think of yourself as, under like circumstance, not daring to speak your deepest and dearest sentiments at your own table and fireside lest your very children should, by their unguarded babble, betray you to death. Imagine yourself doomed every day of your life to hear read aloud from the papers and -spoken by every tongue that

which you knew to be lies; forced to see the commonest of common sense hourly trodden under foot; compelled continually to hear approved things subversive of all morality, powerless to help yourself; obliged to hear positions assumed by Christian men and women, by Christian ministers and in churches on the Sabbath—positions assumed, sentiments advanced, plans proposed, which, in common with every believer in Christianity outside the malaria of Secession, you knew to be exactly that which Christianity was given to overthrow—principles which you knew, as well as you could know any thing, to be of the devil, fathered upon a holy God! All this, and you required to sit under it all like a statue!

The next time, dear reader, you hear news, glad news, which causes all your heart to leap for joy, oblige me by trying yourself the experiment of wearing thereupon and therefor the saddest of countenances, as if for tidings the most disastrous. On the next occasion you hear news which rings a death-knell to your fondest hopes, be so kind as to assume the appearance of one who has just heard what he most desired. This was only the lot of Union people at the South all the war through. Your son, your husband, off from you in the Confederate ranks, enduring all the privations of a soldier's life, fighting, in spite of yourself and himself, in a cause you abhor; fighting against all of succor that is coming doubtfully toward you! But you can not imagine it as we felt it.

"Never was my poor faith in God as strong as it is now," placid Mrs. Sorel says to Mr. Arthur in these days of the repulse of Burnside. "Because I feel that nothing but his special grace could sustain me as I am sustained. That my boy—*my* Frank—but the other day standing beside me, with his dead father's eyes and hair and very voice, his father's strong sense beginning to beam upon his forehead—my pride, beside Robby—my sole hope on earth—that he should be undergoing all those horrors in Virginia, and for what?" And the tear which trickles down her cheek as she bends lower down over her sewing is, alas! but one of the drops as abundant as rain which, from the same cause, fall over the whole South.

Because Frank Sorel has been trained to be true to his name in all his dealings with his mother, as with every one else, and writes, accordingly, as truthfully as he would have spoken had he been at home. Letters filled, as all truthful letters from Confederate armies these days are, with tales of nakedness, hunger, loathsome food, exhausting marches, cold, and wet; letters telling of filth, vermin, disease, death by hundreds, like that among infected sheep; letters after battles in which valor the most desperate avails as nothing against artillery, and persistence even after frequent defeat, and telling of all the after-horrors of wounded, dying, dead; letters at least hinting at the gambling, hideous profanity, and licentiousness, before which even white-headed Christians give way, even Chaplains not rarely go down; letters written on a blanket spread on the ground, on saddle flaps, all blotted and blurred. If Mr. Ferguson, now, could only have made up a library of volumes of the war letters!

"And we have Davis's assertion that the war may last for years," says Mr. Arthur. "Even after it is over, the Confederacy a success, our young men have still to be soldiers, partly to watch the North, partly to stand perpetual guard over the negroes, then a hundred-fold more in need of being guarded than ever. May Heaven deliver Frank and Robby here from such a country! The ruin of our glorious land, and all this for—slavery." How evident that Mr. Arthur is becoming a fanatic!

"Pardon me, Mr. Arthur," says Mrs. Sorel, gravely, "but we will not speak on that subject. You know all my life-long prejudices on the matter. If our peculiar institutions are displeasing to Heaven, it will do away with them in its own time and way. I would not raise a finger in the matter. Meanwhile, to talk upon the subject—pardon me—is disagreeable to me. You know I am a South Carolinian, and we have been so basely abused by the Abolitionists! I am too old to change my views, too old even to think patiently upon the subject."

Not the only Union heart in the South which at that day shrank from all investigation on that point. We all shudder and turn away when the bandages come to be unwrapped from an ulcer or a wound long neglected. We are so constituted, some of us, we grow pale, sicken, faint—we can not do it. We prefer to let the bandages stay, and hope for the best. Put on the broadcloth over it all, and, for Heaven's sake, let us say no more about it.

Mrs. Bowles is whitening in her hair these days as well as Mrs. Sorel. Not trouble only—bewilderment. Things were so perfectly settled in her younger days there in South Carolina. If Mr. Neely was not born there Mrs. Bowles was; it was a satisfaction to her every waking hour of her life; she escapes as much as she can out of the present which so stuns her into that blessed past.

"Dear Mrs. Sorel, please advise with me, talk with me as you used to do. There is such a difference between the two opinions; they are in such conflict one of them must be victorious over the other before very long. Which is the right one? Won't you tell me something?" It is Alice who says it, seated on a stool at Mrs. Sorel's feet, in Mrs. Sorel's own room. Her friend sews and muses with bowed head, muses almost unconscious that Alice beside her is other than the little girl she was it seems but yesterday.

"You know you have always been another mother to me. You used to advise me in all my little troubles, and always advised me right," pleads Alice. "What do you think—what ought I to think upon these terrible things?"

"Do not think upon them at all, Alice," says Mrs. Sorel. "We are women. Let the men think and vote and fight."

"In so awful a state of things even we ought to know at least which is right and which is wrong," begins Alice.

"It is a theological affair in part; why not consult Mr. Arthur?" asks Mrs. Sorel, with something of the smile of other days as she looks her fair visitor in the eyes upturned to hers. Alice colors beneath the smile, drops the long lashes over her eyes, but answers none the less promptly:

"A minister has already advised me on the subject—that Mr. Barker. You know mamma has not attended Mr. Arthur's church for some time. Mr. Barker has had the good taste to make her a pastoral visit in consequence. But you know mamma. Good Secessionist as she is, she has a horror none the less for such men as Dr. Peel, Dr. Ginnis—especially for Mr. Barker, almost as much aversion as for the Abolitionist preachers. She sent down a request to be excused. He did not understand it in the least, and left behind, with his compliments for mamma, his last printed sermon."

"Well?"

"Oh, I actually read it through!" says Alice. He preached it on one of his visits to the capital of the State, and it was published, as the Preface says, at the earnest request of the Governor and all the other officials there."

"And what is it all about? Colonel Juggins always sends me over Mr. Barker's sermons as fast as they are published, as well as every thing of the kind, but I'm ashamed to say," adds Mrs. Sorel, "that I have never read one of them yet."

"All about the Institution. It is like what I have read about the clergy of Europe preaching that kings rule the people by Divine right. They proved from Scripture that despotism is not of man at all, but exists by Divine ordinance. All who believe in and fight for despotism are God's peculiar people. All who oppose kings are infidels. This combining of the preachers for slavery so earnestly reminds me of the Holy Alliance of Europe. Am I wrong, Aunty?"

"I have been trained from my birth, my dear," says Mrs. Sorel, gravely, "to believe that the Bible does expressly sanction slavery. It is true I have never read but on one side. I may add, that I have at times had some painful doubts on account of some of the things which seem inseparable from slavery, yet you know there is no institution but is liable to be abused. Two things settled my mind: the Abolitionists are a bad, violent, blaspheming people—avowed infidels many of them, running into a thousand isms and errors. With such a people God can not be. And, then, what to do with the blacks if they were freed? But we won't talk about it, dear; there is nothing I dislike more. God will do what is right."

"Only this, Aunty—it does look so much as if men who themselves cared nothing for the Bible were using the preachers as a convenient set of tools to establish their own purposes. And I could not but think," adds Alice, after a long pause, "if the Church in the South—God's own Church—should turn out to be the chiefest instrument in defending a great wrong—"

"My darling Alice," interrupts Mrs. Sorel, nervously, and placing her hand upon the lips of her visitor, "you must permit me; please, don't. How earnest you are! Let us talk about something else. I am an old woman now. You young people belong, for what I know, to a new order of things; but you must let us old people alone in our notions. Did I tell you about Robby's fight with Charley Ellis? I would like you to see how he has grown; but he has gone fishing with Mr. Arthur—no one in the world like Mr. Arthur. And you actually did this transferring yourself—take off your collar, dear, that I may see it better. And what does your mother think of the terrible prices? Mr. Arthur insists on not having any sugar in his coffee. He thinks I must have white sugar for my tea—actually bought up the last fifty pounds in Somerville for me. But just to think: wood ten dollars a cord; meal five dollars a bushel. Not a bit of flour. Molasses four dollars, beef fifty cents, fifteen dollars for the coarsest shoes."

"I make my own, Aunty; you know how independent I am; pretty good for a first attempt, are they not?" and Alice, holding aside her skirts, puts forth the neatest of little feet.

"And Alice, dear, your mother did have to sell Charles?" Mrs. Sorel asks in the lowest of tones, gently as to a sick child.

Ah, how the bright young face at her knee clouds!

"I will tell you, Aunt Sorel. Ma says it is because Charles has been so insolent of late, and she has no one to control him; but we were compelled to, every thing is so very dear. I plead with her to let me sell my piano instead; she would not let me even speak of it. And such trouble we have had with Charles's wife ever since! but what could we do? And, then, she may revenge herself on us."

"Revenge herself, child?"

"You are the only person in the world I would tell," says Alice, her eyes so troubled as makes Mrs. Sorel's heart sick to see. "But I do believe Sally has given that Mrs. Warner a hint already of the—the plain way in which we have

to live. What I most dread is, that Sally may tell of my making things."

"Making things, dear?"

"Making caps—those ridiculous military caps that are so much worn now. You know I can make them before ma is up in the morning, and when she supposed I was reading or writing to Rutledge in the front-yard office. They sell them at the stores for five dollars each, and pay me three. I was obliged to take Sally into my confidence to sell them; and you can't imagine what managing it has taken to keep ma and the storekeepers from knowing about my making them. If she knew of it I do believe it would make her seriously ill."

"And you have sold your pony, Alice?"

"Of course, Aunt Sorel; with corn so high what could I do?" But Alice's assumed gayety is not altogether a success, for Lightning Bug was a great favorite.

"No letter from Rutledge yet?" Mrs. Sorel asks after a long silence, during which she is smoothing down the long hair of Alice, seated at her knee thoughtfully.

"Not a line for months now. Oh, Aunt Sorel, we have so much trouble!" And leaning her head upon knees which have often supported her in infancy, Alice wept silently. "I do believe if it was not that I have to be cheerful and managing in order to keep ma's spirits up, I would —I do not know what would become of me!" Alice adds at last without raising her head.

It was one result of Alice's visit to Mrs. Sorel that, closeted that very night with Sally in the kitchen, she told her all. Ever since Charles had been sold Sally had been sullen, on the usual road to insolence, insubordination, the marshal called in to whip her as a last resort; only the worse for that; next the calaboose; after that disgrace a servant lost to all love or fear; always insolent, always being whipped, always running away, in some instances slipping Jamestown weed or some other poison into the family coffee-pot.

"Why, good law, Miss Alice, why didn't you tell me all dis before?" is all Sally can say for some time, her tears flowing plentifully in unison with those of her young mistress. "Ef I had only knowed it! An' I half suspicioned somethin' of de kind, you carryin' on so with them caps an' things. On'y you telled me so many little fibs, Miss Alice. Bless your soul, you know you did, an' I don't blame you a bit. I don't mind one straw 'bout Charles now. You see he don't hab to leab Somerville. Fact I'd rather your ma did sell him; he was about the lot all de time before; now he comes home on'y at night, sets more by me, an' I sets more by him for havin' him off some. Sollum fact is, I 'serve cowhidin' for not seein' it all before; an' you an' your ma, all of us, from Souf Car'lina too! All ober now," she adds, soothing Alice like a

MAKING CAPS.

child. "You get up in de mornin' de same Miss Alice, proud-like an' strong; need nebber say 'nother word to me."

"I am glad to see that Sally has come back to her senses again," says Mrs. Bowles, profoundly ignorant of the facts of the case, as she and her daughter sit sewing together the next morning; "but it is all in the State they are from. They may talk about their old Virginia servants; at last there is all the difference in the world between even them and our South Carolina black people. As your dear father used to say, it is only in South Carolina that slavery as an institution exists in perfection."

At the moment her mother was speaking, Alice, by some singular association, was thinking of a picnic long ago in the woods, when Mr. Arthur, rolling over an old log to serve her as a seat, had pointed out to her the ants thus uncovered to the light scampering off in every direction for their lives. It happened she had just been reading aloud to her mother from the papers an account of the manner in which the planters of Virginia, Tennessee, Alabama, almost all of the Slave States, were hurrying about with their negroes from the Federals breaking in. "What the Yankees call the breaking in of the nineteenth century upon them, I suppose," said Alice to herself, singularly mingling the incident of the log and the events of the day with feelings of pleasure and pain wonderfully blended together. That Satan should put such thoughts in a heart so pure, so secluded, too, from his usual outward appliances!

"I have been thinking more than ever before in my life as I lay awake a little last night of one thing Mrs. Sorel told me," says Alice to her mother after an account, not a complete one, of her yesterday's visit.

"It is amazing about Mrs. Sorel, perfectly past my comprehension," says Mrs. Bowles, sadly. "She a South Carolinian herself, and after South Carolina had itself seceded and caused the other States to do the same! But what was it, Alice? I know Mrs. Sorel too well to suppose she would attempt to pervert your judgment—"

"She did not allude to it once, mamma. No, she was speaking of the little things that occur to one. She insists that each even of the smallest events happens to each of us by the special ordering of Heaven. That each event is of just such a kind as is best fitted to destroy what is weak or wrong in us, to qualify us to be happier, more useful to God and men here and hereafter. She says that generally even the most painful events have most influence on one in this way for good." But the last words of this Alice murmurs almost below her breath and to herself, with her eyes fastened upon the fire. "God help me to understand and feel and believe this all the time!" is the silent prayer of her soul.

"Mrs. Sorel is a truly pious woman, although strangely permitted to err in regard to her native country," assents Mrs. Bowles. "By-the-by, Dr. Ginnis is a member of Mr. Barker's church, I believe. I trust he will have piety to feel, under his loss last night, the truth of what Mrs. Sorel told you, but which, my dear, I have myself instructed you in long ago in reference to a Providence over us. It is my only hope in reference to Rutledge Bowles, I am sure."

"Sally came back from market by way of the place, and says his whole property there is gone, only the chimneys left," rejoins the daughter.

And this brings us back to the night before.

At the very hour in which Alice was admitting Sally into her secret, the C. C. were engaged in admitting Henry Ellis into theirs. Henry is a wounded hero, and he is hastened—no neophyte fitter for these Eleusinian mysteries than he—into that dread organization, holding midnight conclave in the upper room over Mr. Ellis's store. Though violently opposed to masonry and all secret societies heretofore, the rush of Secession swept him into the new society as into many another position from which he would before have shrunk. Is the heavy expense attendant upon his membership therein the only reason why he rather regrets the step after the first few weeks? Nor has he seemed specially pleased that Henry should be initiated into this modern *Vehme Gericht.*

Consumed with intense curiosity, we follow Henry Ellis as he enters the front-door below stairs, conducted by Tim Lamum, who bears, instead of a lighted torch in his hand, a cigar in his mouth as they grope along the darkness within. There is a tremendous oath in renunciation and denunciation of the old Union, and of intensest devotion to the Confederacy, and especially to Slavery, administered to them when inside the front-door, when at the bottom of the steps, when arrived at the top thereof; nor are they admitted into the door of the innermost arcana without a repetition of the same. And very imposing it all is therein: the members seated along the sides of the room, an elevated seat at the far end, draped with a black flag, while before it burn a certain number of candles, to signify the Confederate States; other unlighted candles among them, to indicate the deplorable condition for the present of Missouri, Kentucky, and Maryland. Dr. Peel, in very remarkable attire, occupies the seat as the Glorious Calhoun, presiding. And very imposing the ceremony is when Henry Ellis has it explained to him, by the Glorious Calhoun before whom he stands, that a certain altar thereby—on which lies a Confederate flag, upon which is placed a Bible—represents that, of all nations on earth, it is the Confederacy which is truly Scriptural. In vivid proof of which the whole Scripture record of Noah's curse upon Cain is immediately enacted before him: Drunkenness of Noah—tent-scene—Shem, Ham, Japheth, and all. The effect is somewhat impaired, however, by Noah, a venerable patriarch with a white beard to his waist, to whom Ham, very black indeed, holds a candle while being duly cursed by Noah from a book.

"'Cursed be Canaan,'" reads a well-known, frank, and honest voice, "'a servant of servants shall he be—' By George! Simmons, hold the candle nearer, can't you! 'Blessed be—' One half inch more, Simmons, and you would have set the beard on fire. If I was too drunk to stand, by George!' adds Noah, with asperity, "I'd lie down." And Ham reels away at last, the curse being endless and overwhelming, in deplorable plight.

Next Abraham, with a voice and gestures singularly like those of Brother Barker, in spite of beard and mask, reads the neophyte brought before him in another part of the room a lengthy lecture, embracing the rest of the Biblical argument for Slavery, closing with a strong intimation that as the South, in obeying the Divine command in this matter, are therefore God's peculiar people, those nations who do not do the same are under the wrath of Heaven. Shall we relate how George Washington, risen from his grave in the person of Dr. Ginnis, rehearses—in bag-wig, knee-buckles, and portentous voice—the innumerable wrongs of the North and the rights of the South? Nor shall we wholly abstain from referring to a sarcastic Eulogy upon the Union delivered by the Evil One himself, to personify whom the only alterations Tim Lamum thinks it necessary to make in himself are a tail and a pair of horns. After which the novice is instructed in all the countersigns and grips,' and learns also that the mystic C. C. stand for Children of Calhoun, and also for Curse of Canaan, and the red sword to be pasted so as always to point North—but that needs no explanation.

Next follows the arrangement of certain moneyed matters relating to the widows and orphans of soldiers, in which the sums specified bear ludicrous proportion to the grandeur of their distribution.

"Children of Calhoun. Business," says Dr. Peel at last.

Whereupon, to the astonishment of Henry Ellis, the lights are put out and the conclave left in perfect darkness, during which the entire membership are evidently employed in changing their seats.

"Business!" says the Glorious Calhoun, at last.

"Glorious Calhoun!" A voice from the darkness.

"At my post!" replies that individual.

"Silas Jewet, conscript, sought for. Fled!" says the voice.

"Isaac Smith, over conscript age, but disloyal. Warned to leave. Fled!" says another voice from the other side, which Henry Ellis has heard before from the lips of Joe Staples.

"Glorious Calhoun!" from the far end of the room.

"At my post!"

"Hol Robbins, known as Catfish Robbins, exempt on account of sickness. Very seditious in language, *disappeared!*" The voice is evidently disguised. "His boy, Hark, actually

fought for his master—soon settled *him*," the speaker adds, in a lower tone for the information of his near neighbors. But, after this, name after name is called out, now from one side and now from the other side of the darkness, with comment like the above. Then there is called one name more which makes most sensation of all.

"Parson Arthur!"

"Make charge!" from the presiding officer.

"Opposed to Secession from the first, and persists in his crime. Silent but influential for the Union."

"Business proposed!" from the Glorious Calhoun.

"I move he be regularly warned to leave:" the speaker carefully disguises his voice, but is loud and dogged. Whereupon rises a hubbub over the whole hall, some urging with violence, some opposing the suggestion. One voice has at last obtained the mastery; it would seem in the darkness as if its owner had mounted upon his seat.

"I tell you, fellows, you'd better not; by George, no! No man *can* regret the parson's course more'n I do; but that man has buried too many of our dead, nursed too many of our sick, married too many of our couples for that! I ain't a Christian, but I know one when I see one, and precious few they are. Parson Arthur is *not* favorable to the Confederacy, I know, but you all know he is a Christian, a Christian gentleman. We can't afford it, fellows; and, by George, we won't!"

"One word more, gentlemen"—another voice from the darkness—"I'm Henry Ellis, you may know that by my crutches, there!" and a double knock is heard upon the floor. "You all know I have been fighting for the South in Virginia. Well, for one, the man that disturbs Mr. Arthur, unless he breaks some law, has me to disturb too. I say no more!"

A vote is taken. According to the Ritual of the C. C. on any thing moved for the benefit of the Confederacy the vote is South instead of ay, and North instead of nay. On this occasion a voice in the darkness, evidently the original proposer of the motion to rid Somerville of Mr. Arthur—a thing often before done by the C. C. in the case of other obnoxious individuals, and which has landed said individuals in a clime exceedingly unlike Somerville and very far above it, or in still another place not so greatly unlike Somerville though below it—on this occasion, we say, the original voice votes South, with an emphasis which makes up for its being the only vote to that effect. Most of the C. C. do not vote at all; but enough vote North, and with emphasis of their own, too, to decide the question for Mr. Arthur's further stay in Somerville. Let it be distinctly recorded here that we do *not* assert the first-named vote to have been given by the Patriarch Abraham; for the sake of sweet St. Charity let the matter at least remain in doubt.

This matter being disposed of:

"Glorious Calhoun!" from the darkness, which, like that of Egypt, is both intense and swarming with angry spirits.

"At my post!"

"Mr. Ferguson." We all know Joe Staples's voice.

"Make charge."

"Against the revolution from the first. Bitterly against it still. Won't touch Confederate money. Won't give the least belief to any good news. Always says it's a lie."

Joe Staples, who is deeply in debt to Mr. Ferguson, has never probably read Sallust, and imitates unconsciously those of whom that historian records that they joined the conspiracy of Catiline to get rid of their indebtedness. Not Staples only, no more eager Secessionists in all the South and from the outset, and a little before, than those owing heavily, especially to Northern creditors. But—

"He ridicules all the good news," adds another voice.

"And pastes it all in a big book," contributes a third from the darkness.

"And won't give one single cent toward the war," adds a fourth.

"A cross-grained old Abolitionist, heart and soul against us!" cries still another.

"Business proposed!" from the chair as soon as the Glorious Calhoun can make himself heard.

"Frighten out of his boots!"

"And to-night, right away!"

"Those in favor will say South!" Overwhelming vote.

"Those opposed will say North!"

"North"—only one voice, Henry Ellis. "One word, men," he adds. "You all know I have fought, will fight as long as I can pull a trigger for the South; but only on the open field, and where I can see. I resign." And the speaker is hobbling on his crutches toward the door as well as he can guess at it.

"Children of Calhoun," says Dr. Peel, promptly.

"At our posts!" from the members, evidently part of the Ritual.

"Because, not fighting for the South in the field, we must work for it at home!" In full chorus, after Dr. Peel.

"Well, it's a sort of work I won't do for one. And I tell you, gentlemen, just this. I find here among all you stay-at-homes a sort of ferocity, a kind of devilish bitterness there isn't the least spark of in the army, and you know whether it fights or not. You must excuse me, your secrets are safe with me, but I am gone;" and a stumble and slam announces that the speaker has managed to find the door and leave

—those nearest the door not unconscious that several seem to be leaving with him.

It is a singular fact, but from that night the C. C., notwithstanding the immense amount of work yet to be done, and the appalling oaths binding upon the organization to do it, steadily wanes to extinction. In vain Brother Barker especially exerts himself; for by his powerful appeals, not without tears, he has brought about, from outside, such an alteration as admits him and Mr. Neely and others of Northern birth. It may be the very violence of these hastens its end. Even the dullest Secessionist knows that Union men have been initiated, at least men who were once Union, and that these have been foremost in ultra propositions therein. The sincere Secessionist sees afterward how these Union men thus kept the proceedings of the C. C. fully known to all their own kind outside, and, also, by putting on too much steam from within hastened the explosion. But the genuine, sincere, Southern-born Secessionists did the Northern-born members of the C. C. great injustice when they afterward charged the same treachery upon these.

"For one, gentlemen, I am firmly persuaded," said Captain Simmons, afterward, "that there was not a Yankee Secessionist in all the South, whoever he was, and whatever he said or did as editor, private, general, quarter-master, mere citizen, or what not, but went into Secession, and acted as he did during it with the full though secret determination thereby to defeat Secession and overthrow Slavery. In fact, gentlemen," continued Captain Simmons, with a firm grasp upon the pillar of the porch in front of Staples's Hotel, peculiarly dignified because particularly drunk: "I have become fully satisfied that Secession was got up and carried through by Yankees, South and North, expressly to procure the destruction of Slavery and the triumph of the North over the South. Hypocrites, gentlemen, every soul of them. Their bended eyes salute the skies, their lifted knees the ground, as the hymn has it; abhorrence of such was among the deepest sentiments instilled into me by parents now saints in heaven, where one day I hope to rejoin them. This whole thing has convinced my mind, gentlemen," adds the Captain, with a wave of his left hand, "being a Southern-born man myself I am none the less free to say it, that the Yankees are what they claim to be—the smartest people on this planet. None the less does my soul loathe them; to the last degree are they offensive to me."

Whether any of said Yankees who afterward claimed any thing of all this for themselves individually spake truth or not who can say? Oh if we could but read the heart! Alas! he who pens these lines can not read his own. Enough for us that He who has the final settlement of all things can.

"Secret and Special Committee of Three will

meet here to-morrow night at twelve. Be vigilant, Children of Calhoun, much and great work remains to be done." This from the chair, after the candles have been again lighted.

"France, what from you?" The editor, Lamum, who is thus addressed, sitting in his place under that flag, is silent.

"England, what from you?" Jem Budd, gunsmith, seated opposite France, under the Cross of St. George, is compelled, by the painful facts of the case, to remain silent.

"Ourselves," says Dr. Peel, with enthusiasm, rising from his seat broad and jeweled as midnight, "what from us?"

"Rappahannock!" prompt and loud from the whole C. C.

A fervent prayer from Brother Barker in closing, as there had been one from the same source in opening, and, with certain mystical signs gone through, the C. C. adjourn. A Federal Flag being first spread before the door, each of the C. C. in passing out tramples it under foot, stamping and grinding their heels and spitting upon it in a manner in strict conformity with the Ritual and the feelings of—some of them. Only let it here be written that the faculty of dissembling in some men, and during some epochs, is vigorous beyond all estimation.

"Oh yes, do what you please to old Ferguson!" is heard in the noise of departure. "We are at *war*, by George! We've got into this mass, and all we've got to do is to fight out of it if we can. But not Parson Arthur, by George! not the parson—"

---

## CHAPTER XIX.

It is not long after the adjournment of the C. C. that Mr. Ferguson, seated in his room reading the well-worn little Bible which, while yet a youth, he brought over, a genuine fragment of Scotland, with him, preparatory to going to bed, hears a noise as of the gathering of a crowd beneath his windows.

It is the upper room of a large stone building which he had built, by far the most substantial edifice in Somerville, to rent as a store. And it had brought Mr. Ferguson in a good rent until Secession closed it up, as it had closed up almost the whole legitimate business of the South. "The temporary inconvenience," Colonel Ret Roberts remarks in his public and private speeches, "which precedes independence and unparalleled prosperity; and he who bewails it is," adds the Colonel, coming down upon the stand with clenched fist, "either a fool or a Union man and a traitor!"

Very true, of course; yet it *will* sadden one. To say nothing of the vast tracts devastated by actual war, the appearance of the country far from such scenes is mournful. Fields, as you ride along, with broken-down fences, and acres wholly given up to sunflowers and cockleburs, or making but faint fight against them. Nor did you ever before see white girls so young carrying water, or boys so very small driving oxen, or females, not African, cutting wood and hoeing. The desolation looks worst in the little towns through which you pass. The homes are there still, but in painful need of glass and palings and paint. The shops are all still there, but almost all shut up—no sound from within of hammer, plane, or saw. Nor have the offices emigrated; they are all there still, with their rusty signs of lawyer or doctor; but the lawyer, generally speaking, is colonel now, speculator, or quartermaster; while the doctor is killing more rapidly than before in the ranks, or practicing wholesale surgery in the distant hospitals. And the stores remain, but mostly shut up, their enterprising proprietors gone into battle, or, most likely, into cotton. The shut-up doors and windows of the towns may, like the closed mouths and eyes of those in a swoon, be only temporary; but it looks, all the circulation stopped, very much like death. Not that there is not in every village at least one shop, store, grocery, gathering-point of some sort left, whereat clusters together the whole male population on the arrival of the stage, to get the papers and to hear the much more diversified and thrilling news brought by the passengers. An hour is spent by the neighbors so assembled in anticipating what the stage will, and should, and "has to" bring before it drives up; then two hours, after it has gone, in discussing what it actually does supply them. Blessings on these, the mass, the more virtuous and industrious portion of the people, the country, in fact, yes, Heaven abundantly bless these, even though it be in ways they dream not of! But upon the leaders—editors, military magnates, political preachers most of all—upon these rest the justice of Almighty God!

But Mr. Ferguson. He listens a while to the noise growing louder beneath his windows, then kneels for his evening devotion, remaining perhaps longer upon his knees than usual. Rising at last, he listens and considers. All the doors and windows of the building, for fire-proof purposes, are coated with sheet-iron and securely fastened. The truth is, Mr. Ferguson has long calculated the possibility of an attack, and is not unprepared. He glances at his iron safe—yes, his Scrap-book, to say nothing of other valuables, is secured therein, and the Scotchman deliberately hides the key in a crevice to which he has called the attention of Mr. Arthur long before. As the noise below increases into groans and yells he coolly produces from their hiding-places and lays upon the table, cleared of every thing for the purpose, two of Sharp's rifles, a pair of revolvers, a claymore brought from Scotland; the two Derringers he secures about his person, with the handles ready to his hand.

"Twelve and twelve," he says aloud of the provision on the table for his coming guests, "are twenty-four; two in my pockets, twenty-six; claymore at least one to that—say thirty in all." And so he snuffs the candle, takes his seat, and listens. Yes, it is the night of the C. C.—he remembers that. But then it may prove a false alarm.

He listens. Yells, oaths, blows upon the door, cries for ladders and axes. Not the C. C. only; there is a Camp of Instruction some dozen miles from town, and stray soldiers therefrom drop in to take a hand—good practice for actual war.

"Oh, nobody's going to kill the man; only going to give him a good scare," is the remark made to Dr. Warner, who, plucking himself out of the coils of his wife wound about him in night-gown and hysterics, has come down to see what is afoot, and that physician is tossed off from the crowd like a straw; and while he catches desperately at the attention of this and that individual, meditating a stump speech in defense of his friend, the tumult increases until he is fairly drowned and washed away.

"Now, then, what do you want?" hails the Scotchman, who has raised a sash, opened the leaf of a shutter, and looked out.

The pressing necessities of the mob thus appealed to are various.

"A hundred dollars for the soldiers!"

"In gold, old hoss, mind!"

"And holler hurrah for Jeff Davis!"

"And down with old Lincoln!"

"Promise you will leave in twelve hours."

"And never come back." It is Joe Staples, this last; it will be several thousand clear gain to him if the Scotchman complies or is killed. And thereupon follows a perfect storm of suggestions from the many-headed. The Scotchman waits patiently till he can be heard.

"Men!" he begins, at last.

"Stand firm, mon!" shouts a powerful voice from over the way; and it is followed almost instantly after by the awful blasphemies of Dr. Peel, in the centre of the crowd, upon the man who said it.

"Men!" continues the besieged, "you are half of you deranged, the other half drunk. On that account I don't want to kill you. Do what you please. Only put my life in danger, however, and I will kill some of you. Howl away!"

And the Scotchman draws in his head, closes and fastens the shutter, lowers the sash. Not an instant too soon, for the missiles rattle upon it like hail.

Considering within himself, the Scotchman drags a large desk so as to fortify himself in a corner commanding windows and door, upon which he disposes in easy reach his weapons, having first carefully examined the caps of his fire-arms and unsheathed his claymore.

"Yes, I maun not forget it," he says, relapsing for a moment into a dialect the very burr of which has almost worn from his tongue; and taking the key from its crevice over the mantle, he unlocks the safe, takes out a written paper, dates and signs it, with a line under in explanation.

"It's not as regular as a mon can wish, but it's the best a mon can do. Ah, yes!" And he lugs out his ponderous collection, writes a rapid bulletin of matters up to date of siege, pastes it in from his mucilage apparatus and with the dexterity of long practice in its place in the volume, and replaces it and the paper in the safe, relocks it, puts the key in its place, and is comfortable once more.

"What fules men are about their Wills," he says as he takes his place behind his abatis, "and I as great as any," he growls.

Meanwhile the uproar without is enough to appall the stoutest heart. If yells and curses could have beaten down walls it would have been "all over" with Mr. Ferguson. What next?

Towering on the horse-block in front of the store, Dr. Peel, with terrific profanity, announces to the C. C. present that, having splendidly accomplished their project of frightening the old scamp, the next thing is to adjourn in quest of drinks.

But Alonzo Wright, being already supplied on that point, most strenuously objects, his thirst

L

is now for blood. "Our own boys far away to-night," he shouts from the horse-block, "fighting for us, pouring out their blood in rivers. And here in this house is an insolent old scoundrel worse than the worst of Yankees. It is time to make example of these Union men, sneaking scoundrels, traitors, abolitionists," and a deal more to the same effect. Furious curses, ardent appeals, passionate entreaties—there is splendid eloquence in the raving of the man, and the audience are in the mood to appreciate it. In fact Joe Staples is making a free thing of it at the bar of his hotel near by, is even pressing his liquors upon all who come in perpetual relays from the crowd and back again. The ex-tailor sees a chance of his making the happiest hit of his life; he even dispatches a negro with a demijohn down to the crowd.

"Axes, men, axes, and our cry to-night is Rappahannock!" And the speaker springs from his rostrum among an excited crowd of kindred spirits. Some little time is spent in obtaining axes, those near by having unaccountably been mislaid. Next, it is slow work trying to peel the iron sheeting off the stout doors, especially in the rush of the crowd, each thinking he can do it better than the other, Dr. Peel as active among them as Alonzo Wright.

Meanwhile Mr. Ferguson within ponders his course: "Had I not better fire on them from above? If they get those doors down they'll be upon me in such numbers—wait on the Lord till the last moment before you take to your pistols. God forgive me, I *have* been too cross with these poor demented bodies all along! Too close in business matters, mon. Not meet to be partaker of the inheritance of the saints in— It is good," he continues to murmur to himself, "both to hope and"—arranging the weapons to his hand —"quietly to wait for the salvation of the Lord. Forgive my contempt for these fules, Lord, but Thou seest they are *such* fules."

The blows rain fast and heavy on the doors. Stop! They must have given up the axes, and are now using a ram of timber. The Scotchman has known of too many similar atrocities, has dozens of them in printed form and written in his Scrap-book, not to know, specially since he has heard Alonzo Wright among the crowd, that his own death is about as much a speedy certainty as any thing human can be. The flaxen hair, the blue eyes, the bonny smile—it seems nearer, clearer to Mr. Ferguson than for many a long year now. Heaven! But unfortunately he can not think of heaven without a grim remembrance of the Secession of angels therefrom, and the fate of said angelic Secessionists, too. Pity the one great gulf should swallow us all up so completely these days.

But the bells? What can they be ringing the bells so for? That begins to be an inquiry among the excited mob, pausing a little to listen and ask.

Fire! An illumination upon the sky, dark shadows beginning to fall from the houses that way across the street. Fire! fire! And falling upon the excitement before Mr. Ferguson's doors, as when the sun shines on the hearth-stone, the greater glow extinguishes the less. Fire! fire! fire! and even Alonzo Wright, disabled some time ago by an accidental blow upon the shoulder from the axe of Dr. Peel in the intense energy of the Doctor, after cursing for a time the rapidly-diminishing crowd, is compelled to limp after it. In little more time than it has taken to record it the assault on Mr. Ferguson has begun and ended.

"Dr. Ginnis's! Dr. Ginnis's!" is the cry into which that of fire has now subsided.

"Dr. Ginnis?" Then, as we too hurry on to the spot, one word about him; it can soon be said, before we've gone more than a square. Low of stature, stout of frame, red of face, puffy of breath, loud of tongue, excitable of temperament, "Secession from the start," of course. From the outset it is with pain that Dr. Ginnis tears himself from the knot at the street-corner to visit a patient. He is hardly in the sick chamber before the topic is introduced. As soon as possible the complaints and the prescription for the patient are got through with as an altogether secondary matter, that the Doctor may get to European dependence on the South, the sovereignty of cotton, the Scripturality of slavery, the religious apostasy and hastening downfall of the North, the untold blessings Secession is to pour from its cornucopia upon our glorious Confederacy, and all the last great Confederate victory, too, roars over again with all its cannon in the ears of the stunned patient. The Doctor is enthusiastic, as even his political friends allow. Secession has taken possession of every globule of his blood, fold of his brain, holds as a rider does the reins every fibre and tendon of the Doctor's gibbous person. A big bubble, Dr. Ginnis, oscillating wonderfully when the wind blows as it often does, glittering in the sunshine of good news. It does Mr. Ellis good to see and hear him.

"Glory be to God!" he shouts, clapping his hands together, snatching his hat from his heated forehead, and waving it with enthusiasm. Then off like a shot, a large one, from the Post-office to spread the tidings whenever wonderful news arrives, as it does almost every mail.

"Have you heard the news?" he cries to people on foot across the street, on horseback, in carriage, whom he sees as he goes, never waiting till he can get near enough to see whether they be acquaintances or not. "Glorious news! Yankees cut to pieces again! fifty thousand killed!" Not apt to be up early as a general thing himself, no man before Dr. Ginnis when the stage is to get in before day. "Wake up, all of you!" he shouts at the doors of the houses as he returns home with the great intelligence. "Wake up!" banging tremendously on the gates and doors. "Great news! Louisville captured! Cincinnati burned! Washington City in our hands! hurrah! Wake up! Glory be to God!" And the Doctor hurries on to stir up the rest, making great billows in his wake, literally *wake!*

"Twenty-seven regiments bayoneted where they stood; cut down and cut to pieces; the carnage tremendous!" And Dr. Ginnis has a peculiar way of drawing his coat-sleeves up his arms, turning down the cuffs of his exposed shirt-sleeves, as he says it, and moving his mouth and eyes as if he was about taking part therein himself, unctuous to behold. Being a member of Brother Barker's church, no man, not even Sam Peters nor Brother Barker himself, more fervent in prayer than Dr. Ginnis—only he begins too violently, runs in fifteen minutes into hoarseness, and ends in wheeze. There is this slight inconsistency in Dr. Ginnis. At the very outset of Secession, in indignant denial of the possibility of war resulting from the same, he had loudly and frequently promised contemptuously to drink every drop of blood that might be shed.

"If you will turn to Psalm fifty-fifth, fifteen, you will see that David said exactly the same thing, 'Let death seize upon them, and let them go down quick into hell,'" remarks Brother Barker when informed that Dr. Ginnis had been distinctly heard to say "Damn him!" in reference to Butler in New Orleans. "You will hardly deny that David was a holy man. And these are most extraordinary times. We can not judge men by the rules of ordinary times; it would be foolish as well as useless to do so," reasons the divine. Nor was he the only professed Christian who used the same reasoning in reference to the intoxication of leading members of the church, even chaplains in the army, on rejoicings over victories. In fact, it was said of Brother Barker, and of many others like him, that, not content with supplicating yellow-fever and death in every form, as well as that in battle, upon the infidel foe, he and others had prayed for something that sounded marvelously like an eternal damnation of the same foe. Let any one who retains to-day clear recollections of what passed during the great delirium say, was this actually so or was it not?

Turning a corner on our hurried way from Mr. Ferguson's we find it *is* Dr. Ginnis's house that is on fire. Upon the whole, the handsomest two-story residence in Somerville, handsomely furnished, the Doctor has not occupied it more than a year. And the Doctor is moved as never the most glorious news had ever moved him before. Consequently the wheeze is upon him almost from the first. He stands now near the fast-consuming remnant of his home, stunned, silent, in utter collapse. For there is this peculiarity about Dr. Ginnis, that he is as much af-

fected by bad news as by good, the elation produced by the last being fully equaled by the degree of depression produced by the first—according to the inexorable law of mechanics whereby action and reaction are equal. Hence it is that while we good Secessionists rather like falling in with Dr. Ginnis when good news is afloat—we couldn't avoid doing that, as the Doctor then pervades every nook and corner of Somerville—we would rather not fall in with him when the news is bad. In this last case, to do the Doctor justice, we are not apt to, however, as he stays pretty closely at home then, if possible.

But Dr. Ginnis is not needed at the fire at all. Dr. Peel has arrived on the spot among the first, and has been hard at work from the moment he arrived. Truth is, Dr. Peel, by sheer force of the man, has come to be the life and soul of Somerville long before this; no public dinner, no war-meeting to receive from or dismiss to the war any distinguished personage or personage going to become distinguished, no ball or tableaux, no public enterprise, of which Dr. Peel is not the grand carrier-on as well as the originator. We have come even to accept the essences, jewelry, broadcloth, and boasting of the man in consideration of his undoubted patriotism and princely liberality of feeling and of funds. It has got to be generally believed that Dr. Peel and Anne Wright are engaged to be married, and Alonzo Wright has risen a hundredfold in public consideration, to say nothing of Anne, frail in form, fair, gentle, and doubly lovable in appearance from her contrast to magnificent and swarthy Dr. Peel as she hangs upon his arm or stands by him in the dance in public assemblies.

And Dr. Peel sustains his well-earned reputation for public spirit and energy now at the fire. He has rushed a dozen times into the house, and returned bearing wardrobes, bureaus, and the like, beyond the strength of other men. Tearing off weather-boarding to get at the flames: on the top of the stable endeavoring to save it; here, there, every where; men running hither and thither like children at his command; his hat gone in the confusion; moving in the heat as in his native element, no man there refuses to feel him to be the hero of the hour, Agamemnon, king of men. But even Dr. Peel can not work miracles. When morning breaks it is upon the chimneys only and a few charred timbers, upon a bed of ashes, the bones, as it were, of the once living home, from which life and flesh are gone. All that is left is for Dr. Peel to start a subscription list, before he has washed his hands for breakfast, in Dr. Ginnis's behalf, heading it with a handsome amount, and canvassing the entire community with it before night.

In his heavy loss Dr. Ginnis accepts the assistance with gratitude, but adds to Dr. Peel: "A thousand thanks, Dr. Peel, for all your noble aid; but if you could only help me to prove it was the work of an incendiary, even if we did not know whom, and couldn't catch him—just to know that certainly would be a great satisfaction to me!"

He does not say it, but to have it known that his house had been selected out of all others in Somerville as that of the most prominent patriot there for destruction, would have gone far to console the Doctor.

"That was my full belief at first," says Dr. Peel, with oaths, "until I happened upon that pipe I showed you lying near the stable among the straw. Some careless old negro woman. If I was you I would examine into it; and if I was to know that any negro of *mine* had lost *me* so splendid a property—" And the friend describes, with awful profanity, the vengeance he would inflict.

And Mr. Ferguson? It is full compensation to him for the insults of the night that it has, at least, yielded him one of the most interesting pages for his collection. With more than the neatness, precision, blue ink, red ink, and black, with which he keeps his own land and other accounts does he prepare the bulletin for posterity, date, events, results in full.

The second day after the fire Dr. Peel rides out to see Alonzo Wright. No man could make a handsomer apology for having accidentally lamed his friend's shoulder, which is badly hurt.

"I was opposed to going on at first, you will remember, General Wright. I only wanted to frighten the old scamp. But I got excited by your eloquence; it would sweep away a stone. When I got hold of that axe I was in such a desperate hurry, too, to get at the fellow—"

"Let us say no more about it," interrupts Mr. Wright. "I am sorry for that man Ginnis, of course, but I am very glad the fire happened just as it did. When I am drunk I am a perfect fool, rather a devil incarnate. If any thing had happened to that brave old man I could never have forgiven myself. What an old Trojan he is! I will make a point to speak to him the next time I see him on the streets. It was the same way with Mr. Arthur. I made myself a perfect blackguard with him once—you may have heard of it—at the old gin. He will bear me witness I went in next day and apologized. I've told Anne here nobody ties the knot if she ever marries but that man, if only he was not an Abolitionist, or Union man, which is the same thing. True as steel he is, for all he is so quiet. But let us talk about Burnside, any thing. I made a fool of myself that night in Somerville, am ashamed of it, and have made Anne a half promise never to go to the place any more." This, with a good many strong expressions between, from Mr. Wright sober, a person bearing no resemblance to Mr. Wright drunk.

So Dr. Peel, taking another cup of the coffee —"the genuine article, Doctor; no rye, barley,

okra, sweet-potatoes, or other trash in it"—of Miss Anne's making and another slice of Miss Anne's sponge-cake—only blondes like Anne can ever make real sponge-cake; brunettes succeed in pound, preserves, and the like, not in sponge—Dr. Peel, we say, changes the topic to our bright prospects now of speedy success. At which point, Colonel Juggins having ridden over to trade certain oxen with Mr. Wright, Dr. Peel is left to be entertained by Miss Anne.

*Petite* Anne! A canary-bird is small, we know, never so small as when in contrast with an eagle. Very quiet is Anne; low-spoken, too. Blushes also coming and going on causeless errands to and from heart and cheek. No one plays better on the piano—not concert music, you know, but exactly the kind for a parlor. Anne sings, too, as a canary-bird ever should, and very sweetly; not the operatic style either, yell, squall, inarticulate; you are not deafened by Anne, and can make out as distinctly every syllable she sings as if she spoke it. Dr. Peel standing behind her, turning over the leaves of her music as she plays, joining in with his splendid voice, stooping to say this and the other nothing in his lowest modulations.

"I had no idea it was so late!" she says, with an instant thrill at the impropriety of saying so with such simplicity, when, at last, Dr. Peel sees by his massy gold watch that it is time for him to go. Mr. Wright, done with Colonel Juggins by this time, urges his guest to stay to tea. Dr. Peel would do so with great pleasure, he could ride in to town by moonlight, only he has "an appointment to keep."

"With some fair lady, I'll bet," says Mr. Wright, good-naturedly, as he shakes the Doctor's hand on parting.

"Wrong this time, General—*not* with a lady," replies Dr. Peel, Anne's little hand in his as he bids good-by.

No, not with a lady. As the Doctor nears the corner of a fence, about a mile from Somerville, he draws rein to speak with a particularly ill-visaged negro man, evidently waiting for him there. Protruding chin, with beard in little knots upon it here and there; retreating forehead; coarse wool tied up in pig-tails, sticking up in every direction from his head; squalid clothing; long, ape-like arms; big, flat feet—a savage. In all New Zealand none more so. Not a more thorough savage that hour in the Africa from which the man's great-grandfather came, save that here Jem is enveloped in an atmosphere of civilization, the chief ingredient gas of which for his breathing is—force. And Jem has lost his ancestral Fetich, the Christianity he has in exchange being too undefined for him at least to put in words if questioned. Not that there are not thoroughly pious negroes at the South; there are many thousands of them—a larger proportion of them pious, perhaps, than of the

DR. PEEL AND JEM.

whites, only Jem was not one of them. Yet, sad to say, when Jem has any special villainy to engage in the negro in Somerville of all others whom he is sure to call upon to assist him therein is Orange, a preacher, a very Brother Barker for singing and praying among the blacks. Beyond this there is not, of course, the least parallel between the two preachers. Only, the remark may, with great deference to everybody, be made, that, if Brother Barker's Scripture views of Slavery prompted him to his most violent courses, by a singular coincidence, it was the Rev. Orange's views, too, of Slavery from the Bible—read, doubtless, upside down—which prompted him to his most objectionable courses; *his* evil courses being, however, all underground. So very sly is Orange that it is hard to speak certainly; yet, if the fact was known, it is rather Orange who employs Jem in deeds of darkness than Jem who employs Orange. Just now both are in the hands of a greater than either.

"Splendidly done, Jem; you couldn't have done it better," says Dr. Peel to Jem standing before him. Great contrast between the broad-clothed, bejeweled, perfumed, highly-educated, perfectly-accomplished, and powerfully-influential Dr. Peel and the savage beside him! Civilization and Barbarism embodied and in strongest contrast? Apparently. Only there is not another white man in Somerville to whom Jem does not take off his hat when he speaks to him, but the relic of a head-covering remains untouched on Jem's head now, though no man can express in word and manner greater respect, even affection, for a companion.

"On'y Orange an' me," he says.

"I told you boys before I don't think it is safe the money should be in your hands; you are sure to let it out," begins Dr. Peel, taking a canvas bag, apparently quite heavy, from his bosom.

"Me an' Orange think so too, on'y we is out of tobacco. A few dollars for our women-folks, too," pleads the savage as humbly as a child.

"Very well, certainly," says Dr. Peel, replacing the bag in his bosom, and giving the man a few coins of gold from his purse. "You may have that over and above, and welcome. The rest any day it is safe for you. You and Orange can't be too careful, Jem. You know how to get it to me if you hear any thing. When I need you boys I'll let you know."

But what would have struck an eves-dropper in all this interview most was the singular bearing of these two very different villains to each other. It can not be expressed in words, but it was very singular—very singular indeed.

———◆———

## CHAPTER XX.

THERE is a certain manner—the nautical name for which the writer has clean forgotten, though he assures the reader he once knew it—by which a vessel is advanced upon its way when steam or tide or wind fail it. Its anchor, with a stout cable attached, is carried forward in one of the ship's boats and hooked on to some rock or iceberg ahead, the other end of the hawser being fastened to the capstan on board. With many a heave-ho the crew then ply their strength,

as in a slow whirlwind, around the capstan until they and their vessel are drawn to the anchor. The anchor is then again borne forward, and so the operation continued as long as may be necessary.

And in the same way we will bear the anchor of this our bark ahead, and grapple it with this first day of March, 1865, and endeavor to—yes, warp, that is the word—warp ourselves up to that point; for, though all the world else moves, Somerville has seemed sorely to lack, so far as advance is concerned, of steam and tide—not of wind, only it has been perpetually shifting.

Great events have befallen since Dr. Ginnis's house was burned—many of them.

Vicksburg. The Somerville *Star* had acknowledged, after the fall of New Orleans, that the Mississippi River, Fort Pillow and Memphis having fallen, was open along its whole length to Federal navigation. Only a few days after its article in proof that this, so far from being an advantage, would be, like the capture of New Orleans, a positive disadvantage to the Federals, Vicksburg and Port Hudson are known to have suddenly arrested the navigation of the river, at which, with singular inconsistency, the *Star* greatly rejoices. Then follows the long story—oh, how long and weary in the slow telling!—of the assault upon Vicksburg and the repulse. The episodical capture of Arkansas Post, though Somerville has accounts for weeks after that event of the escape on their way up the river, and their march across Tennessee to join Bragg, of the prisoners there taken. Next comes the wearisome digging of the famous canal, and its failure, proving that hydraulics and hydrography are greatly neglected parts of civil engineering as taught at West Point. Great rejoicing in Somerville over that. Then comes Grant's desperate march around and regular investment of Vicksburg, at which also Somerville greatly rejoices.

"With Johnston in front of him, and Pemberton in his rear cutting off his escape to the river, we regard the annihilation or capture of Grant's entire army as a positive certainty," says the Somerville *Star* for weeks. "As to starving out Vicksburg, we happen to know it to be victualed for a two years' siege."

Then follow tidings of the fall of Vicksburg. This is scouted with scorn. For weeks after, it is amazing how many gentlemen arrive, not in Somerville, but in its immediate neighborhood, who "are known to have left Vicksburg on the tenth or fifteenth of July, the place not having fallen then, nor having the least intention so to do."

Even when Vicksburg and Port Hudson are known to be captured—"We see only cause of congratulation in it," says the Somerville *Star*. "First, because of the tremendous loss—one hundred and fifty thousand is the lowest estimate—

of the Federals in capturing those points; second, because it will occupy a large part of their army to garrison these places; third, in that guerrilla bands will as effectually prevent the navigation of the river as before !"

Yes, there is the singular fact. We Secessionists may attach infinite importance to an Object, may wait in most intense anxiety to know the result in regard to it, deny the capture of it indignantly for weeks after it has fallen, yet the instant it is known to be undoubtedly gone we care no more for it, wonder we should ever have interested ourself so much in New Orleans, Vicksburg and Port Hudson, Chattanooga, Atlanta, Savannah, Mobile, whatever the object is in its turn; can even see now, are astonished we did not see it before, that the loss of each such place is on every account rather an advantage than a disadvantage to us. Not merely in words only or in editorials—to some degree actually in heart it is so! No doubt there is, with the occurrence of each disaster to the Confederate arms, a secret undermining going on in the understanding and heart of each even of the most rabid Secessionists, but it is unacknowledged at this period even to themselves. In exactly the same way, Dr. Ginnis, swelling and bursting to-day with some wonderful news of Foreign Intervention, Confederate Victory, and the like, abandons it to-morrow when it is known to be false, not only without much regret, but scarcely remembering even that he ever heard, much less believed, in any thing of the kind.

"But who," says Mr. Ferguson, "can reason in regard to lunacy, or analyze infatuation? There is something even awful in it," he adds; "a supernatural folly at which ,I shudder, as at the direct doing of Jehovah."

At which point Mr. Arthur corrects his friend by drawing distinction between the positive and the permissive providence of Heaven—a distinction lost upon the Scotchman, who quotes the case of Pharaoh and the children of Israel to a frightful degree in these days.

But even while we are scouting the lying rumors of the fall of Vicksburg all Somerville is electrified by tidings of the glorious victories of General Lee in Pennsylvania. The bells can not ring enough after the dispersion of the Pennsylvania militia and the capture of forty thousand prisoners at Gettysburg. Brother Barker has been entrapped by false news so often by this time that he is far from being as credulous as of yore, yet, "Do you imagine General Lee would have crossed the Potomac if he did not know what he was about? Believe it; yes, brethren, with all my soul!" For who can resist, if it was only the big bell of his own church, to which little Joe Staples clings, with brief relays for refreshment, for hours at a time? And so, when he can have the bell stop long enough for him to be heard in special prayer, as on Sabbath,

Brother Barker leaves all doubt in regard to his patriotism far behind.

It was a singular coincidence that Orange, plowing in his master's field, and Jem at work with his axe in the woods near Somerville, both paused from their labors at the first sound of the bells with about the same exclamation upon their lips.

"Dar's bad news for me!"

They, and, of their colored friends, not they alone, had made about the same remark once or twice before at the sound of distant explosions, taking them to be cannon for victory. These reports, however, had turned out to be only the blowing up—quite a common incident—accidentally, of powder-mills and all therein—no mistake about the bells, however.

Not that, returning his visit, Mr. Barker, his has been an altogether unruffled course. Like other eminent confessors in all ages he has had his troubles also. Many, among the best of his church, have long ceased to attend thereat. There is Mrs. Juggins.

"No, Brother Barker, I can't do it. It was bad enough to see you, a preacher of the Gospel of peace, marchin' along, as I see you that day in Somerville, with a gun on your shoulder, member of a company, practicing, too, with them at a mark, I'm told! But for a disciple of the blessed Jesus to preach and pray as you do is more'n I can stand. Not only it is nothin' but politics, politics all the time with you in the pulpit and out of it—.    . ut, then, you're fiercer than Staples or Lamu..., actually bloodthirsty an' bitter. God, He knows I love my country. I gave Tom for it, didn't I? Please God, I hope the Yankees may be whipped back where they come from. If they ain't, it won't be for want of prayin' for it here South !"

"All the Union people have ceased to come to church long ago, and to support the ministry," begins her spiritual leader.

"Can't help it, Brother," says Mrs. Juggins, firmly ; "the Colonel and I is getting old ; since Tom was killed, too, I've seen things diff'rent. The Confederacy gaining its independence is a great thing, I dare say ; but religion here, the reachin' a better world after this, is a better thing still. Dare say you have no idea how you've stopped preaching and praying any thing but the Confederacy. And look at it. The Sabbath-school there in Somerville is broken up, they tell me. Except on some grand political occasion, they say you've only a handful to hear you. Then you know better'n I how many of the very pillars of our church, ministers even, some of them, has taken to drinkin', cursin', and swearin', swindling, and all manner of wickedness. As to sinners, they are farther off than ever; and who's to blame ?"

Yes, Brother Barker has a hard time of it as well as Mr. Arthur. Somehow his salary is very slow in being paid, what little is promised, the reliance he placed upon his Secessionist admirers in this matter being exceedingly mistaken ; ready enough they are to crowd his church on every political occasion to hear, and to inflame and inflate by their presence the violence of, sermons and prayers for the South.

"If the Almighty does not give victory to General Lee in this his march upon our wicked foes, the very angels of heaven will be ready to revolt," he had remarked one Sabbath morning in a sermon. Who could say more than that ? Yet the subscription paper circulated the very day after on his behalf was far from as successful as it should have been. "We all greatly admire, esteem, approve Brother Barker's course—no man in all Somerville more patriotic and useful than he—yet the war has cut our means down so, and we have really so very many calls every week connected with the war, that we can not say at this moment what we can give, Brother ; we will think upon it, however, and let you know."

"No, Sir, you must excuse me," Captain Simmons remarked when applied to. "True, I was early instructed to worship in the sanctuary, and I could at this moment repeat to you, sing to you to its own tune, the hymn 'Away, away ; away, away, away to Sabbath-school.' True, I do drop in to hear the parson when he gives us a red-hot sermon, prayers, and all the trimmings, on the times. But I can not disguise the fact that he is a—Yankee. My soul revolts at a Yankee and—you must excuse me."

There was the shameful way, also, in which Brother Barker was treated on his last visit to the Pines. The preacher is exceedingly averse to speaking of it, but it seems a camp of soldiers stationed there have varied their monotonous routine of slaughtering such fat beeves, and stealing such poultry and honey as they can lay hands upon, by insulting, hustling, throwing clods at Brother Barker on his last appointment. Not on Union principles at all—from sheer contempt of a religion which has ceased to awe them in reference to things spiritual in its superhuman exertions to instruct and excite them in reference to the Confederacy.

Very slowly, indeed, the truth comes out in regard to the Gettysburg affair. Somerville has placed all its hopes on a long succession of heroes, dropping them in turn as easily as it has done great cities ; for the time, even General Lee lies shattered on the earth from his pedestal. The ebb and flow of feeling during these days among Secessionists and Union people—the one class being in the trough exactly at the instant the other is on the crest of the sea—who can describe!

Neither can be described the intense eagerness of Mr. Arthur, Dr. Warner, Mr. Ferguson, and all other Union people—it is amazing how many of them are left in Somerville still—for Federal papers. Colonel Guy Brooks, not a written line from him since he left, contrives to get papers to friends in Somerville. Isaac Smith, painter, too, little he cared for literature of any sort, still less his big and butter-making wife; now the zeal with which Isaac Smith, from within the Federal lines, pours in letters and papers upon his wife is wonderful. Mrs. Smith's little parlor sees, and sees very often too, visitors it never dreamed of before. Let fat Mrs. Smith get a package as large as your hand at night—and her mails almost invariably arrived at that period—before noon to-morrow she had a dozen applications from friends to know the news. And a great deal of news Isaac Smith managed to smuggle in ; only, alas ! Isaac, from long use perhaps of his brush, gave too much—so little proving to be true. For, let the truthful record be made, we Union people in Somerville are almost as credulous in regard to the news we wish to be true as are the Secessionists—not quite, but almost.

But, ah, the eagerness with which we clutch a paper from the North ! We get it as a great favor, to be read as rapidly as possible, to be returned exactly at such an hour to such a place. We button it up in our breast-pocket, and hurry home, for we dare not be seen with it on the streets. Arrived at home, we arrest all the household work, turn the children ignominiously out of the room with terrible threats in case they come in again, which, by-the-by, they are sure to do a dozen times during the reading on pressing emergencies which can not be postponed a moment ; and so we carefully unfold and read the precious paper aloud to wife or sister, to say nothing of all the Union people in the neighborhood cautiously summoned in to hear. The editorials, dispatches, items, advertisements of hair oil, and the like—with greedy hunger we let no morsel or crumb of the paper escape us. In spite of all the effort we made, a dozen readers or two have had the document before us, as dozens will, eagerly wondering why we can not remember that others want the paper as well as ourselves and get through with it after us. In consequence of this, the paper is painfully illegible at the folds ; we have, in the centre of the most interesting articles, to stop and puzzle around the chasms, often to take a flying leap over them and proceed. The little scraps of patriotic poetry, here and there, we often memorize even. And so the paper circulates till it is read, literally read, to shreds.

There was Everett's speech at the Dedication at Gettysburg. Could the orator have imagined the zest with which his words there spoken would have been read from soiled and worn-out sheets by thousands at the South his soul would have burned with sublimer enthusiasm than any wakened in him by the audience then visible to his eye. Who of us forgets the keen enjoyment with which we read our first fairy tales in childhood's sweet hour—not so keen, so delicious that gratification as the reading, during the war, of all thoroughly American matter oozing in to us, parched with thirst, from abroad. The circulation through Somerville of one good paper of the kind did all the Union people—for if one individual thereof read it, every soul did or had it repeated to him—evident good for weeks to come. Perhaps the shortness of the allowance—as with food doled out to the wrecked at sea—increased its value, months often elapsing between the rations. Let us keep secret the absolute faith even Mr. Ferguson placed in the least assertions of a Northern paper, his belief herein as absolute and sweeping as was his unbelief in reference to the Somerville *Star* and all its kind. And, as men build a mural tablet into the wall of an edifice with due inscription, permit the insertion here of this profound truth, that in very much every sense of the word human nature at the North and the South is exactly the same; with superficial differences we are at last One people.

The fall of Vicksburg and Port Hudson and the victory at Gettysburg send the Union people of Somerville quite up upon the crest of the ever-rolling sea, and—Mr. Ellis, Dr. Ginnis, lowest of all—the Secessionists down into the trough thereof for months to come.

"I tell you, Lamum," Dr. Peel says to the editor of the Somerville *Star*, toiling away cold, pale, steady as ever in his business of lying by power-press, ever consistent in falsehood whatever news Bill Perkins brings in his budget—"I tell you, man, one screw loose in the machinery of the Confederate Government is the way the Post-office is managed. What avails all you say in your paper so long as there is a perpetual stream of private letters coming in to the contrary? Federal papers, too, these Union people are constantly getting them; letters, also, from friends in the Federal lines—such things provision them, so to speak, to hold out. If a few more of them could be hanged—!"

But this last remedy has been so thoroughly tried—not actually in Somerville, as yet, but all around it. There was Mrs. Isaac Smith's brother, John Jennings. Who did not know him? Gray-headed with fifty years of farming—farming with his own hard hands alone these days, his boys being in the Confederate service, and he owning no negroes.

"You see, Mr. Arthur," Mrs. Isaac Smith says to that individual, who hurries to see her—is she not a member of his church?—on hearing of the catastrophe, "they knew John was a Union man. He tried to help its being known, but he couldn't. Not that he said any thing. He made a point to stay close at home—never opened his lips. But he was my brother, you know, and my husband being gone that was enough. Every once in a while he'd come down from his place—fifteen miles, you know, it is from here—to bring me a little butter, or cheese, or wheat, whatever happened he could spare. Ever since Jim Boldin waylaid and shot down his own brother-in-law, Mr. Tanner—they do say Mrs. Tanner, his sister, who is a bitter Secessionist, actually put her brother Jim up to it—ever since Tanner was found lying dead in the road with a ball through his head for being a Union man, John has been careful as a man could be. Letters from Isaac! How *could* John get letters from Isaac? As God hears me, Sir, John never saw one that I didn't show him. But you've heard the story; I have no heart to tell it, hardened as I'm getting to almost any thing. A party of a dozen of them broke into his house at midnight: said to his daughters, poor things! screaming around, they only wanted to take him to Somerville to be conscripted. Sarah, the eldest, knew better; she clung to him till they tore her off, some of them holding her to the wall while they tied John's hands. As they was dragging him out, Sarah she begged and screamed only to be let give him—her gray-headed old father—one last kiss; they wouldn't let her do even that, the man holding her saying things— Can you make yourself believe, Sir, that such a thing *can* be true in this Christian land?" says Mrs. Smith, speaking more slowly, exhausted with weeping till not a tear is left, emotion itself worn out from exercise so intense and so long. "Sarah here in the next room could tell you herself. They dragged that unoffending old man—lived fifteen years in the neighborhood—out of his house, mounted their horses, and rode off at full speed, holding the end of the rope. Of course when he couldn't run he was dragged. Sarah tracked him next day by the bits of his clothes on the brush till she lost the trail over the rocks. No one but her, and she not twelve years old, near night she finds her father at last. They had hung him by the neck from a blackjack. God knows whether it was because they intended it, or because they did not know how to tie the rope so as to strangle, but he was warm yet when she came upon him. He had been hanging there in struggle and agony full fifteen hours. Sarah she had never thought to bring a knife—just think if you can of that poor young thing working there—"

But here there is loud crying from the next room of the little house—Sarah has been wakened from her slumber of exhaustion by her aunt, who has forgotten in her excitement that her niece is asleep there.

"We must get used to it, man; like things, in all varieties of hellish wickedness, are taking place every hour," says Mr. Ferguson, to whom Mr. Arthur has been telling the story. "The National Government will not or can not help us. For His own wise purpose the Almighty is leaving us to ourselves."

"But to me the strangest part of the infatuation of these men around us," says Mr. Arthur, walking the floor of Mr. Ferguson's room like a caged leopard, "is that they do not seem to understand exactly where Dr. Warner and you and I and all other Union men of Somerville—and I know of more and more of them every day—actually stand. Do you suppose Mr. Ellis, Captain Simmons, Bob Withers, Ginnis, the Lamums, and the rest *know* that there is not an individual at the North, in the Federal army, in the Cabinet at Washington—not Lincoln himself more thoroughly, utterly, absolutely—"

"Sh-sh-sh, man, not so loud!" says cautious Mr. Ferguson.

"And expect me actually to pray for the success—"

"We must beware of becoming too excited. It is our duty to exercise the patience and meekness of the Gospel," remonstrates the Scotchman at some length, whose feelings never assume the form of wrath, only of intense bitterness and contempt. "Beware of becoming a Brother Barker, only on the opposite side," adds this grizzled mentor.

And it strikes this Telemachus that night, ruminating, Testament in hand, in his room at Mrs. Sorel's, that he is sliding down into a condition to be alarmed at. He blames Mr. Barker, Mr. Ellis, and the rest — for what? For leaving the Gospel and the moderation of the Gospel behind them; for ceasing to have main reference to things spiritual, and becoming far too intensely interested in things of this world. Wonder if I am not doing the very same thing? he thinks. If they are too excited for what they call their country, am not I for what I regard as mine? True, theirs is a wicked rebellion; my interest is in my country, in which is involved civilization, freedom, the Gospel itself— And all he can conclude is to set more vigorous watch upon his heart, out of which are all intemperate deeds, words, thoughts, feelings—the issues of life. For grace to do which he prays here and there. Only there is the same sense of exhaustion in prayer that there is in reading the Scripture and in preaching. Leading the life of a pariah with most in Somerville every day, so little encouragement, every emotion in such perpetual and intense play—thought, forever on the strain—insufficiency of actual labor to give relief—exhaustion.

And Alice? If she was a thousand miles away now! God forbid—she is all of hope he has. Yet, like the Princess of Fairy Tale, alive to her lover in all her charms, yet inclosed beyond anything but mere sight in adamantine crystal.

Oh yes, yes, of course, the writer knows all that fully as well as the reader; but Mr. Arthur, though he ought to have done so, doubtless did not. It is the easiest thing in the world for you to say how you would have gone boldly to her like a man; how you would, and long ago, have had a perfectly frank and full conversation with herself, and, if necessary, with her mother. You have a contempt for this Mr. Arthur for waiting, hoping, fearing so long. Very well; better despise him for cowardice in the matter than that the one who pens these lines should despise himself for telling a falsehood in the matter. "If I was Alexander I would do so and so," said Hephæstion. "And so would I were I Hephæstion," replied Alexander. You have, dear reader, first to be Mr. Arthur, defects and all, and then to be exactly in Mr. Arthur's rather peculiar position, before you can decide how he should have acted.

"We so-called Union people here in Somerville are like— By *we* I do not mean to include you, Miss Alice," says Mr. Arthur to her one day. He has made his semi six-months' call at Mrs. Bowles's, and finds that lady away from home assisting down-town in the preparations for a supper in behalf of the sick soldiers—the proceeds somehow never reaching them in its transit through so very many hands—very little at least—and that paper-money into which the specie paid in has become singularly transmuted. We dare not stop to ask whether, before calling at Mrs. Bowles's, Mr. Arthur knew or not of that lady's absence. How could he, in that case, have conscientiously asked Miss Alice if her mother was at home?

"The Union people in and around Somerville," he repeats, having corrected himself from daring to class his fair friend among them, "are like the early Christians."

"In purity of purpose or in degree of persecution?" asks Alice, looking up—what beautiful eyes! thinks her visitor—from her sewing. Was ever woman lovelier? demands Mr. Arthur of himself, warming himself in her presence after long dwelling among winds and frosts and icebergs without.

"It was of their kindly feeling toward each other that I spoke," says he. "Not a day I do not hear of some charitable and generous deed. You have long heard of old Mr. Adams—"

"Is it not strange that so large a slaveholder should be a Union man? You know he openly avows it," says Alice.

"He is far from being the only slaveholder—" begins Mr. Arthur, but prudently halts. "He has had the reputation heretofore of being rather—rather—"

"A penurious old gentleman," supplies Alice, demurely. "Proverbially so, I fear."

"Well, his corn-cribs, fodder-stacks, smoke-houses, grain-bins, poultry-yard seem to have ceased to be his own this last year. He gives away as freely as water. People send out their wagons, and help themselves as a matter of course. Provided, you know—"

"The applicant be thoroughly disloyal—to the

Confederacy I mean," says Alice with, did ever woman have so sweet a smile since Eve was created? says Mr. Arthur, to himself. "Oh, yes," she continues, "Mr. Neely was telling me of it when he was here last night; no, it was when he was here last week. He tells me the Union people are more like one family dwelling over town in different houses—what belongs to one belongs to all. I happened to pass Mrs. Isaac Smith's this morning, and I noticed no less than three wagons unloading sacks of something—pigs, turkeys, chickens, corn—almost every thing, and met two immense ox teams going in that direction with wood as I came away."

Like one family? More loving with each other than the members of families generally are. Those of the Union people in Somerville who did not even know of each other's names or existence had long now become well acquainted. Long before this had old quarrels between such of these as had been at variance ceased. No distinction of occupation, denomination, property between these any longer. Treated with contempt, at least coldness, by all Secessionists, Union people can not even pass each other on the street without stopping to shake hands. On the most frivolous pretenses, and on none at all, they are visiting each other, specially when "disastrous news" is afloat, all the day. The very children of Union parents confidently expect now, when they pass him on the street, as much of a smile as Mr. Ferguson ever manages to radiate through his beard. As to that, more than once or twice has sober little Robby Sorel come home laden with gifts from men he has met in town of whom he only knows that they asked his name.

And how Mr. Arthur cherishes, hidden among his sermons, letters of encouragement, anonymous, honestly signed, drop-letters from persons in Somerville, long letters from strangers living far away. Letters in which the writers venture decided opinions in reference to current events in guarded language, but with such an air of being arrived at on the part of the writers after much thought, and as original and remarkable discoveries as makes Mr. Arthur smile. The plain country people that take Mr. Arthur cautiously to one side when they meet him, and break to him, in exceedingly prolix and roundabout way, their views, or ride out, introduce themselves, and spend the night at Mrs. Sorel's to do the same, each displaying his devotion to the Union and his execration for the Confederacy from within a hundred wrappings, like a precious jewel peculiar to the speaker's self. And the delight, too, mingled with fears that he may not be prudent as he should be, of the new friend when he finds Mr. Arthur, with exactly the same opinions, so very decided and clear.

Not plain people, obscure and quiet only.

"Parson Arthur, hold up a minute, I want to say a word to you," says Bob Withers, whom Mr. Arthur meets face to face on horseback in a sequestered spot near Somerville. And Mr. Arthur complies, but with very cold manner, for, like almost every man of his class in Somerville, Mr. Withers is very shy of Mr. Arthur in public; Mr. Arthur, therefore, is doubly shy of him. But Bob's open, cordial face is irresistible.

"I've wanted to speak to you for a long time. But in strict confidence, by George! mind—in strict confidence, Parson. You look pale and worn, and go about Somerville looking as if you didn't have a friend there. I wanted to tell you it's a mistake—you've plenty, only we don't like just now, by George! to show it. You just hold out, Parson; that's what you've got to do, hold out! I ain't a professor myself, as you well know, though if I don't get to heaven at last it's a poor chance for most Christians, by George! I know. When this thing came about, do you suppose I didn't know as well as you and Brooks and the rest it was a piece of the most in-fer-nal folly? What could a fellow do, by George! We were in it, you see. But it's worse than I ever thought it could be. Worse? The lying, swindling, shirking, stealing, murdering, un-i-ver-sal scoundrelism! Oh, never mind, by George! You only hold out—that's what I say, hold out! And if you think I don't know as well as you that this whole thing is hurrying, like every other spree, slam bang to eternal smash, you are just, by George! mistaken. Yes, Sir-ree!"

And Mr. Arthur does not see his way clear to refuse the double eagle Bob Withers insists upon leaving with him as a token of regard when they part at last. As to that, no one can write a letter or speak a word, "in confidence between us, Sir," without doing something of the same kind. Though Brother Barker even would have been almost satisfied with the coldness with which Bob Withers and Mr. Arthur pass each other on the street the very next day.

In fact Bob Withers is very far from being the only prominent Secessionist of whom Mr. Arthur could have told some singular things if he had wished. But who dare say what is done toward this by Vicksburg, Port Hudson, and Gettysburg?

Even the grand old Major seems to look down more benignantly than of old from his frame, this spring morning of eighteen hundred and sixty-four, upon Mr. Arthur thawing himself in the society of the Major's daughter. Very dignified and reserved indeed the visitor intended to be when he found, so very unexpectedly, that he must be entertained by the daughter instead of the mother. It was, after all formal inquiries in reference to Rutledge Bowles, at whose name both color simultaneously; after being fully informed in reference to Mrs. Bowles's health, whom he already knows to have become grayer, thinner, more nervous than ever from what he has casually heard and seen of her; after Alice has volunteered to speak of the school she is intending to keep, after all this and a little old music too, that Mr. Arthur, slipping from sheer force of habit, permits himself to speak of politics by the reference to the kindliness among Union people.

He ventures, Mrs. Sorel and Robby being mentioned, to tell how the latter is advancing in his studies. Nor can he resist the inclination by this time to relate how Robby was assaulted for about the hundredth time on his last errand into Somerville by Joe Staples. But Mr. Arthur refrains from mentioning the artillery of Yankee, free negro, Abolitionist, traitor, and a good deal worse with which Robby was assailed. That he and every child of every Union parent had long ago become accustomed to, though it took a long time before Robby could endure being cursed as an Abolitionist, that being something ingrained into him as far worse than any other epithet in the world—the quintessence of all abuse. But when Joe Staples actually seized upon the bridle of Robby's pony, and would not let the child pass till he had been sufficiently cursed, nothing being left for it, Robby slipped off his pony, left him to his fate, and pitched in, demure little

A SMALL SKIRMISH.

fellow as he was, with his neat jeans suit and his hair fresh from his mother's brushing, and, with the sudden ferocity unknown to his mother and himself under surface of his sober sense,

gave Joe Staples such a drubbing as increases tenfold Staples Senior's hatred for the Union people, and causes Mr. Ellis to caution his Charley that night at table against ever associating with a boy so desperately depraved as Robby Sorel.

"And she to set herself off from every body, and pretend to be so very strict with her children!" says Mrs. Ellis from her bed in the next room. "You hear what I say, children? If ever I know of your associating yourselves with them—" And so on, and so on.

"Do you know," says Alice, at last, "that Mrs. Warner and Mr. Ellis, and the others who have withdrawn from the church, are greatly offended that you never have called even to see them since they withdrew?"

"And when they have urged me so often to do so, too," adds her visitor, reflecting her smile. "Would you have me do so, Alice—Miss Alice?"

What a nameless charm in the very parting of her hair, in the plain collar around her neck, in the flow of her calico dress—one she has had now four years if he only knew it—a divine grace, a heavenly sweetness! After so long, long a period, too, of anxiety, disappointment, alienation from a hundred friends! Of course he exaggerated her, idealized, apotheosized—just as we must not trust what is said of Italy by travelers fresh from long and bitter travel in crossing the Alps. So rapidly and thoroughly has this lover thawed, beyond all his resolves when he first bowed to her, on principle not even shaking hands with her on his first coming! Five minutes more, and, having lost all resolve to the contrary as if it had never been, Mr. Arthur will have learned his fate. A discourse infinitely more impassioned and eloquent than he had ever favored her with from the pulpit already burns on his lips, when—the big bell of Brother Barker's church first, then, clamoring in as for their places in a procession, one by one, every bell in Somerville! Really and truly it was the great, hidden, unacknowledged movement, from the recent Federal successes, which had thrown these two thus so close together. At the first blow made by Joe Staples—yet stiff from his drubbing but a martyr to the cause—upon the big bell, these two are far asunder. His fault, his, not hers!

And here are Mrs. Bowles and Mr. Neely. Great news, glorious news! From the States west of the Mississippi this time. Banks is repulsed at Mansfield, eight hundred wagons, fifty cannon, innumerable prisoners, all the gun-boats and transports; not the least doubt but the next mail will bring accounts of the capture or destruction of the last vestige of the Federal forces.

Slight, pallid, enthusiastic Mrs. Bowles! She strives, even in the excess of her joy, to be quiet from habitual refinement, but fairly radiates with exultation. And Mr. Neely! Getting quite fat, physically as well as pecuniarily, upon his contractorship, he is rosy as morning, rubbing his hands, pulling down his waistcoat, jubilant in every curl of his hair, in every motion of his body, for he *can not* sit still! If any thing was needed to brim his cup it was meeting Mr. Arthur in just that parlor on just that occasion. Even the old Major overhead beams upon them in grander proportions, struggling in his frame to speak.

And just at this juncture it is that Brother Barker makes that fatal mistake of his. The Somerville *Star* is full of the news. Tim Lammm and Bob Withers shake hands over it—alienated during three months before from something rising out of poker. Dr. Peel has read the dispatches aloud in a dozen crowds, with running oaths of confirmation. Even Bill Perkins, fallen back into a mere stage-driver on account of Confederate disasters he has been bringing so long, with vague sense on the part of the people that he is somehow to blame for them, is treated till he can not stand. Dr. Ginnis, inflated, from the shabbiest collapse, in five minutes, by the news, to his fullest former proportion, is up and down every street, in and out of every store in the place, slapping his hands together, drawing back his sleeves, wheezing but irrepressible, gesticulating though he can not speak.

There is Mrs. Warner; from some sudden whirl, given by the Confederate disasters, she has been prophesying defeat and ruin to the South for weeks on weeks now. Not a bit less vituperative. She plies her snuff-stick as energetically as ever, denouncing the swindling, stealing, lying officials of the Confederacy, their cowardice and inaction! She does not stop with, "We are whipped—whipped, I tell you!" but even adds, "And I'm glad of it, because I hope the Federals will catch and hang these miserable fellows loafing about with their stripes and ambulances and things, when they ought to be off at the front, as they call it, fighting!" All of which falls incessant upon Dr. Warner, who droops his head and takes it, conscious of being in some general way guilty of it all himself. Even if he is balder these days, what he loses in hair he makes up in flesh—a storm-beaten mariner, but used to the squall and gust. The instant Dr. Warner could tell his wife this last news, before he had got it half out of his lips, his wife had snapped her forefinger and thumb, and thrust the former within half an inch of his nose.

"Didn't I tell you so, Dr. Warner? I want you to tell me that this instant! Didn't I tell you so? Didn't I tell you, over and over and over again, we would whip them yet? Always croaking!—telling me about your Gettysburgs and Vicksburgs till I was sick of the sound! And you a pious man—at least, pretend to be, and doubt that God is a just Being! Wanted me to laugh at Brother Barker."

Which brings us back to the fatal mistake made by that clergyman when the news comes of Banks's repulse.

"I hope so, I hope so!" he says, having hold of Mr. Ellis's hand, with peculiarly mournful intonation of the word "hope;" "but I fear not. We have been so often deceived—I myself, on one occasion—by mere idle rumors. You, as a Christian, will understand me when I say I see the hand of Satan, the Father of Lies, often put forth these days. For some inscrutable purpose, always against the best and holiest of causes; but," adds Brother Barker, with a sorrowful shake of his head, "we are not ignorant of his devices. I *hope* so, Brother Ellis, but I fear not, fear not."

Even Mr. Ferguson, pasting the dispatches as they come into his Scrap-book—with grim unbelief upon the surface of his beard, though sincerest apprehension is tugging at its roots—even Mr. Ferguson might have admired the sorrowful, not to say morose, disbelief in the glorious tidings by Brother Barker, as he shakes himself away, with boding head and sorrowful hand, through the crowds upon the streets.

Long ago, like all his class, his chiefest associations have been, especially on the street, with striped officials and brass-buttoned heroes. He may be talking with Sam Peters about his bad fall from his horse, awfully exaggerated by Sam; or with Smithers, about a member of his church, about Mrs. Smithers's last worthless runaway of a cook; even with Mrs. Warner, who regularly attends his church now, and always bewails Mr. Arthur's course in conversation with her new pastor—whoever it is with whom he is speaking, let Brother Barker but catch sight of a military man passing, or over the street, and, with a hurried excuse, he is off to speak to the son of Mars, or to get an introduction—oftener to introduce himself, if unacquainted.

But when this news of our glorious victory over Banks in Louisiana arrives, Brother Barker fails to render to Cæsar the things that are Cæsar's.

"I hope so, Captain Simmons—ho·p·e so," he says, steadily resisting the universal Faith and Joy, gently deprecating it, with open hand, as a father among his thoughtless children—"but I fear not, f·e·a·r not!"

And this illustrates just what Mr. Neely so bitterly bewails—the deep-seated, utterly incurable want of faith in even the most thorough-going of Northern-born Secessionists on the part of Southern-born men.

"Gentlemen, you see that person who has just left us," says Captain Simmons, full of solemn joy, and something else, over the news, his left arm around a friendly post; "Rev. [hic] Mr. [hic] Barker, resi-resident clergy-clergyman of this commun-munity. Did you ob—[hic]—observe the statement he imparty-imparted to me

"DIDN'T I TELL YOU SO!"

[hic]? We having ful-fullest dispatches of a glori-glorious achey-y-achievement, he, that [hic] individual, doubts it, gently-gentlemen, *doubts* it!" (Intense scorn.) "But do you conjr-con-jecty-conjecture the reason? A Yankee! I ady-admit he toils hard [hic] to hide it—very hard. It *will* come out. Not a Yankee in [hic] the whole Confedy-Confederacy this day [hic] but is

a double traitor—traity-traitor to his own sick-sack-section, and a traitor to [hic] us. My earliest inf-infancy was, I may say, sat-sit-saturated with reverence for the cloth. But that Yankee, Bub-Barker, I revolt from. To those of his birth I apply the language of the—the hymn : 'Touch not, taste not, handle not !' "

Is it reasonable, therefore, to wonder at the frantic effort made by Brother Barker to right himself, when it is established beyond all doubt that Banks has really been repulsed ? Eager as Mr. Ferguson and the rest of the Union people are to stave off that conviction, strange to say, the fact of the affair breaks at last upon them not more against their wishes than it does upon the preacher against his ! Frantic effort ? Brother Barker finds Prophecy which bears direct upon it. In the course of a sermon on the golden image which Nebuchadnezzar set up, after proving that the erection of the Washington Monument at Washington City, being as palpable an idolatry as in the case of the Babylonish king, was doubtless the grand sin for which the South was chastised, Brother Barker gave in his painful experience as an unbeliever in reference to the late news. With tears he made a clean breast of it :

"As lack of faith, brethren, in Kirby Smith, it was no sin ; as lack of faith in Heaven, pledged by all its attributes to the cause of the South, it was a great sin. Pardon your most unworthy speaker"—bowed head, wet eyes, handkerchief. "And at this very moment, while I stand here before you"—handkerchief dropped on the desk, arms extended at their full length upward, eyes upon the ceiling above the pulpit, lank hair falling back from the head bowed backward—"the angels in heaven, seraphic Stonewall Jackson towering among them, all who have gone thither by mill—thousands from our glorious battlefields, all heaven !"—extended arms farther extended to take it all in—"from innumerable harps rings Jubilee over our victory at Mansfield !" Speaker stationary for a moment in thrilling tableau ; then slowly-falling eyes, then hands, then head.

"But"—handkerchief, sip of water, tone fallen from ecstasy to commonplace—"let us note, in the fourth place, who are destroyed by the Furnace Flames." Which proves in some way to have been the Federal Government.

If we think we can depart when the sermon is over we are mistaken. Brother Barker—very hoarse—has been, as we brethren may be aware, in attendance last week at the regular semi-annual meeting of our Church in the State. A full attendance, as we are happy to know. Subject of the support of the ministers ; fully dwelt upon this by the preacher. One or two other matters before we come to the main business done by said meeting, brethren.

And here Brother Barker proceeds to read in

his best manner a Whereas, with ten resolutions thereupon, passed unanimously at said meeting, in enthusiastic eulogy, exultation, prophesy, in reference to the Confederate Government in general, and one or two Major-Generals in particular—the well-known morals, or rather immorals, of said individuals causing their names to have an odd sound, as of Saul among the Prophets, in that connection.

One thing more—the collection for Brother Barker's support.

"Not that you do not mean well by putting in Confederate money, dear brethren," the preacher mildly expostulates as the hats go around ; "not that I will not gladly do all in my power to sustain the currency. But you know as well as I that it rates only at twenty for one. Even at that, people, I grieve to say, will not touch it when they can possibly avoid it. Of their *gold* and *silver* Scripture invariably represents the generous as contributing ; it is surely of our *best* that we should give to the House of the Lord. Understand me, brethren, not that I—"

THE YANKEES HAVE COME.

## CHAPTER XXI.

IT came upon Somerville at last. Came the very week of the Sabbath upon which Brother Barker had exulted, with the angels in heaven, over the repulse of Banks on Red River. Came at the very time the Secession element of Somerville was glittering upon the very crest, the Union element glooming in the lowest trough of the ever-rolling sea. Came to Somerville as comes upon the pit of his stomach to a pugilist an unexpected blow when he has just warded off another from his eye. So occupied were we all in Somerville with the defeat of Banks that we had completely forgotten about ourselves. It was like that ball in Brussels of which Lord Byron has issued such extensive tickets: no marriage bell went merrier than did Somerville, when, like the roar of the coming Waterloo, dimming the sparkling eyes, paling the glowing cheeks at said ball, comes the rumor of an advance of the Federals upon the town.

How the rumor first reached the place who can tell? Rumor at times seems to be, indeed, the living goddess the Romans made it, and to move with lightning rapidity in and by itself without the intervention of any means whatever. It was exactly at nine o'clock Friday night that Dr. Warner threw Mrs. Warner into strong hysterics by the announcement that the Federals were coming. When that lady ventured to steal forth after a night spent in hiding her silver and the children of her negro woman, lest the mother should run away, her jewelry and other valuables, refreshing herself occasionally by abuse of alternately the Confederates and the Federals, her husband being most to blame of all, the first object she beheld was the Federal flag flying from the roof of the Court-house, near which Dr. Warner had his home.

We have the authority of Sir Walter Scott that the bugle blast of Roderick Dhu possessed the double power both of causing the instantaneous appearance and the as instantaneous disappearance of bodies of men. Whatever wizard blew the blast in this case, the appearing of the Federal force was not more sudden than was the disappearance of the male Secessionists of Somerville. For reasons which will appear in the sequel, we abstain from saying any thing more in reference to this raid than the actual fact of its having taken place just at that time in Somerville compels us to record. Closed stores, upon the walls of which the enemy have posted bills informing the citizens that, so long as they are themselves quiet, the invaders will scrupulously avoid molesting any other than Confederate property; deserted streets, every individual peeping from behind doors and through the slats of shutters with curiosity swallowing up all other feeling; the marching hither and thither of blue-coated cavalry; the sound of martial music—a dream come and gone before we know it.

That Friday night Mr. Arthur was in the very act of kneeling with Mrs. Sorel's household at family worship when an halloo makes it necessary for Robby to go down to the front gate to quiet the dogs and find out what is wanted. He

is gone so long that Mr. Arthur himself goes out. He meets Robby returning, and only hears some one shout, "Tell them exactly what I told you!" as the one shouting gallops off in the darkness. Repeating his message on the way back, Robby repeats it yet again when he gets into the house. A most remarkable message it is.

"Colonel Brooks says, 'Be prudent, don't commit yourselves!'"

"Colonel Brooks?" asks Mrs. Sorel—"Colonel Brooks, Brooks?"

"Nothing else?" asks Mr. Arthur, bewilderment giving place to the sudden joy.

"As soon as I could get old Cuff to stop barking I asked, 'Who's there?'" says Robby, soberly, but not without some vague sense of new importance. "One of the men—"

"There were two, then?" asks his mother.

"Yes, ma, on horseback, two—Dr. Peel and Mr. Brooks. Colonel Brooks says, 'Be prudent, don't commit yourselves!' That is exactly what Mr. Brooks said. 'Is that you, Robby?' he asked, when I first got to the gate— 'Is that you, Robby?' so eagerly. Humph," adds Robby, "I think I ought to know Mr. Brooks's voice. Didn't I used to see him every day? Wasn't he my Sunday-school teacher? Colonel Brooks says, 'Be prudent, don't commit yourselves!' And then they galloped off."

"But how do you know the other was Dr. Peel?" asked Mr. Arthur, while Mrs. Sorel has sunk again in her arm-chair, as if unable to stand.

"Oh, I knew that before I got to the gate. He was cursing old Cuff, you know," adds Robby. "Oh, I know Dr. Peel. I've heard him cursing and swearing ten thousand times. Colonel Brooks says, 'Be prudent, don't commit yourselves!'" Robby repeats the words as he had before done quite other words, verses and the like, from Mr. Brooks's lips in the Sabbath-school.

"I really and sincerely think you had better go," says Mrs. Sorel, suddenly, to Mr. Arthur, after half an hour of wondering and questioning.

Mr. Arthur lifts his eyes in mute inquiry, though he sees at a glance that placid Mrs. Sorel has been reading his thoughts all the time.

"By the Federals you know I shall be respected," she says, rapidly but quietly; "if any of the Secessionists should endeavor to molest me, it would be none the better, all the worse, if you were here. Go, Mr. Arthur, go!"

"I can not think of leaving you. None but you and Robby," begins that individual. "The negroes—"

"They would not harm their old mistress. No—Mrs. Sorel is safer without you," she adds, with a smile.

"I can not think of going. I will not leave you exposed," says Mr. Arthur, throwing on the table his hat, which he has, most unconsciously, got from the hall, and has had in his hand all this time. And he takes his seat, and draws Robby to his accustomed place between his knees.

"Mr. Arthur," says Mrs. Sorel, very erect in her chair—as thoroughly from South Carolina at the moment as Mrs. Bowles ever was—"I am mistress in my own house—No, I don't mean that. I am old enough to be your mother. I will do to you as I would to Frank if he were here. I command you to go!"

Even as he gallops along through the darkness toward Somerville his conscience smites him; but he gallops on, leaving the casuistry of the case to be settled when he has more time.

A busy time he finds it when he reaches town. He had met more than one vehicle on the road thither; he now hears the roll of wheels, the galloping of horses in every direction; slamming doors, running feet, sawing, hammering, glancing lights in the windows, lanterns in almost every stable. Few voices heard, but an exceedingly busy time.

Not until he has alighted at Mrs. Bowles's gate does he ask himself how he is to arrange matters with that lady—what he is to say. The front-door is open, a light streams from it, and, as he opens the gate to go in, the beams fall full upon the face of Brother Barker, of all men in the world. And very much excited indeed is Brother Barker.

"Ah! Brother Arthur," he says, in an agitated manner, seizing upon, and—from sheer force of general habit—shaking the hand of the other in the long, and altogether indescribable manner peculiar to Brother Barker after a warm meeting in church or arbor. It is the first time he has even spoken to Brother Arthur for years now. Generally he has avoided him on the street, or, when compelled to pass him, it has been with a nod greatly colder than no recognition; the repulsion—moral, religious, intellectual, every way—the repulsion between these two men being really greater than that between any other two men in Somerville.

"Your horse, I believe, Brother Arthur?" pointing to the animal from which Mr. Arthur had just alighted with his left hand, while he retains his friend's hand, still shaking it, in his 'right.

It is Mr. Arthur's horse.

"Would you be so kind? Some unprincipled person has stolen my animal from the stable within the last hour. The fact is—I presume you may know—it is believed the Federals—I would not wound your feelings for the world, Brother Arthur"—another shake of the hand—"but I have reason to think that I may be singled out"—greatly agitated.

"What can I do for you, Sir?" asks Mr. Arthur, to close the interview, endeavoring in vain to extricate his hand.

With many hurried words Brother Barker at last asks and obtains Mr. Arthur's horse, and rides off, and faster than its owner had come. The fact is, just before, Brother Barker and Bob Withers had been thrown together at Staples's hotel, in the universal jumble of the confusion and hurry.

"Oh, is this you, Mr. Barker? You here yet?" Mr. Withers has found time, in the rush, to stop and ask of that gentleman, with astonishment, even terror, depicted on his face. "Why, my dear Sir — by George! You here still? Don't you know they have sworn to hang you? You must have heard of it; it is you they are coming to Somerville after! Colonel Brooks commands the force. It was you, you know—don't you, by George!—who had his brother Paul hung. From your own steeple they'll hang you, man!" But here the two are separated in the confusion, and for several days after Brother Barker has disappeared, with multitudes of others, from the streets of Somerville.

Mr. Arthur finds himself in Mrs. Bowles's parlor, and in company with that lady and her daughter, before he has at all arranged what to say. He had not supposed Mrs. Bowles could be as cold and stately as she now bears herself, frail as a shadow, the silvered hair so smoothly arranged under the neat cap, the refined face as sorrowful yet as stern as Antigone. Mr. Arthur has a general idea, in the hurry of the moment, that so far from being in undress Mrs. Bowles has on her very best attire, dressed even with unusual care. With coldest politeness she barely endures Mr. Arthur. Alice sits with drooping eyes after the first salutations. No wonder he can not read her thoughts, she is far from knowing them herself.

"Will you pardon my intrusion?" he asks, without taking a seat. "I happen to be in Somerville to-night, and come to beg, if altogether convenient, that I may be permitted to sleep in the front office to-night."

"If you desire to sleep there, not being able to go out to Mrs. Sorel's," begins Mrs. Bowles, with coldest dignity, and as ungraciously as she can force herself to be.

"A gentleman has just borrowed and ridden off my horse," Mr. Arthur remarks, Hannibal like, his ships burned behind him, that having been not the least motive with him in permitting Brother Barker to take his horse—not without a mounting color in his face, and conscious of the appealing eyes of Alice upon him.

"We do not need your protection, Mr. Arthur, nor do we desire it—Alice, my servants, and myself," Mrs. Bowles proceeds to observe in her coldest and most measured manner. "Were there no one else, Rutledge Bowles being absent, Mr. Neely has kindly sent word that, as soon as he has secured his negroes and other property, he will endeavor to call. I think that was the substance of his note, Alice, my dear?"

M

"Mrs. Sorel and myself thought—"

"I am aware that the enemy which has desolated other parts of our country is expected," continues Mrs. Bowles, still more measuredly. "Excuse my interrupting you, Sir. I am perfectly informed also of the outrages and atrocities to which we may and probably will be subjected by them. It is not impossible but they have heard of my son, Rutledge Bowles, and may seek to visit vengeance on Alice and myself on that account. Nor will the place of my known birth be a protection to me, nor my known horror of the flag they bear, nor my unspeakable aversion to their country—"

"Dear mother," begins Alice.

"Permit me, Alice. I admired your spirit in sending word, as you did, to Mr. Neely that we would not need his presence. Alice will tell you also that we do not need yours, Mr. Arthur. You will pardon me. Alice and myself are prepared to suffer whatever the fiendish foe may see fit to inflict—to lay down our poor lives, if need be, on the altar of our country. We are quite poor now. They will find but little to rob us of. My husband—Major Bowles's portrait I have already caused to be removed." Sure enough, their visitor, who had missed something, he could not tell what, from the room from the time he entered, glances over the mantle, and sees only a blank space where lately the grand old Major used to sit enthroned.

"You *must* permit me to add, Sir," continues Mrs. Bowles, dignified as ever, but excited by her own words, "that of all the gentlemen in this community you are the last I would look to for protection. Passive as you have been, to use no harsher phrase, in this the struggle for the land of your own birth, withholding even your prayers for its success, associating exclusively with, and encouraging to your utmost, those in our midst who are traitors to their country, vipers upon its hearth—hush, Alice, you will permit me to speak in my own house—you, Sir, are the last man in the world to whom I would wish, above all, whom I would have Alice my daughter to look to for protection. Though he has been at one time even insolent, I would prefer my—the boy Charles, who was once my servant, as a protector. That you are here now, instead of at Mrs. Sorel's, is the result, I presume, of secret communication with the enemy. Besides"—all in a quiver from head to foot, her hand wandering about her brow.

"You *must* permit me, Madam," interrupts Mr. Arthur, quite conscious of Alice's eyes in mute entreaty, not without color in his cheeks, but never speaking in sick chamber or to dying friend in gentler tones, "to withdraw my request. I should not have intruded. I will do so no more. I trust you will one day do me more justice."

With a bow to the ladies in leaving, carefully avoiding Alice's face with his eyes, yet reading more meaning in them none the less than ever before in his life, the visitor is gone. And Alice, though she never looks out at the window during the rest of the night, is perfectly aware, amidst all the noise of wheels and hoofs and feet, that Mr. Arthur is keeping watch and ward about them.

"I have ever esteemed Mr. Arthur a gentleman; I have often wished Rutledge Bowles could have known him; but that he should have pursued the course he has amazes me. Mrs. Sorel, too, positively bewilders me. And I am told that Mr. Brooks is actually a Colonel in the Federal forces. It can be nothing," said Mrs. Bowles, with her hand to her head, "but insanity, raving insanity. Either they are deranged"—her hand wandering about her brow—"or I am," added she, with the use of the strongest metaphor in her knowledge. "As I have told you a thousand times, Alice, my dear, I wish you to have no farther acquaintance with this Mr. Arthur. You have known him for years, but I wish you always to class him in your mind with Benedict Arnold—remember, dear."

But Alice is thinking, by some strange coincidence, of the night of the insurrection—how they three sat up together on the front porch all night waiting for what did not, like millions of other things expected in Somerville, take place at last.

And so the night wears away, neither mother nor daughter caring to lie down. Mrs. Bowles, poor lady! at one and the same instant blaming herself severely for having spoken so to Mr. Arthur, and regretting that she has not been even more bitter to him; wondering that persons like Mrs. Sorel and her late visitor—so good and calm and firm heretofore—so calm and firm and gentle now—wondering, wondering! And Alice, too, so silent and quiet.

And so she comes back with a start to the fact that the Federals are coming, and that she must meet them with the dignity and quiet scorn which behooves South Carolina when Yankees are in question.

And Alice? Conscious all along of Mr. Arthur keeping watch around the place; now glowing with her mother in heroic resolve; now mourning that it is such things as Secession and Slavery that we must be heroic about; imagining to herself one Great Republic rending these twin curses out of its bosom, and lifting itself free, strong, one People henceforth! But it is we, the South, who are being whipped, subjugated. And so she wanders about in the same brambly, marshy, darksome theme, treading in thought now to the right, now to the left, as upon tufts of turf in a morass, upon the innumerable yeas and nays of the matter, but with firmer foot, in straighter course than before, not unconscious of broadening light ahead.

Had it actually been Colonel Brooks himself Mrs. Sorel would have been less surprised than she was when Brother Barker, not two hours after Mr. Arthur's leaving, presents himself before her, after most violent protestations on the part of old Cuff at the front gate and along the walk—even Cuff scenting trouble abroad to-night, and vigilant accordingly.

"Ah, Sister Sorel!"—and he has her hand in his before she can believe her eyes—"hope you are well? And the family too? And this is your little boy, Robby, I believe!" Retaining Mrs. Sorel's hand with his right, he takes Robby's with his left, and so establishes double *rapport* with the household.

"What a fine little fellow—sober as a judge! The truth is"—another shake of both the hands in his own—"I met Brother Arthur in town, and have returned his horse for him. Please have him put up; and it would be well to tell your servant—how are you, girl?—not to let the boy give him too much corn. Mr. Arthur rode him rather violently." Another shake of the hand for both, and releasing them. Then the visitor, placing his hat upon the table, takes a seat, and adds: "From long experience, Sister Sorel, I have learned never to feed a horse when too warm. All are well, you say? Pleased to hear it. Excuse you a moment?—certainly."

For it is Mrs. Sorel's first thought to have Robby out of the room, and impress upon his youthful mind these two things: First, not to mention the strange message given him; nor to allude to it in any way.

"Why, mother, do you think I don't know?" says Robby, with as much indignation as is consistent with respect.

"Yes, mother," to the next injunction—to be polite to their new visitor, and to keep silence generally. "But the best way is for me to go to bed." Which, with a kiss to his mother, he forthwith does.

Immediately on her re-entering the room, her emotions, singularly like those of Mrs. Bowles with her visitor, Brother Barker informs her where he met and left Mr. Arthur—for whom, it seems, from words and tones of voice, the new-comer has an affection rather more than merely fraternal. And so, with briefest possible allusion to the expected raid, Mr. Barker requests and obtains a bed—Mr. Arthur's—for the night.

"In case any armed men should visit the house during the night"—he lingers behind with his candle to say to his hostess, who has hardly opened her lips—"I know you will not mention the fact of my being concealed here. As a minister of the Gospel, Sister Sorel, an humble preacher of peace, I desire to hold myself utterly aloof from all scenes of violence and strife. My life is in your hands, my sister; but I am not a Sisera, I am pleased to say, nor are you a murderous Jael."

Nor does the sudden guest, over "the dish of butter and milk," furnished him by his harmless Jael next morning—the night having passed without event, save the uninterrupted barking of Cuff, assisted by all the other dogs on the place, at the perpetual passing of travelers—have any thing to say except to dwell upon the horrors of war in general, the absolute inconsistency of the same with Christianity. The eyes of Brother Barker, sunken as by long illness, to say nothing of sallowness of visage, show how little sleep he has found that night in Mr. Arthur's bed. However, we were all of us wide awake that night in Somerville.

Robby, with lips visibly sealed, places the Bible upon the table after breakfast is over, from force of invariable habit; the decent servants gather in as usual; Mrs. Sorel, with fewest words, requests their guest to take Mr. Arthur's place, and lead in worship.

"We will omit singing, if you please," says Brother Barker, after reading the first Scripture which comes up; "my voice might attract—ahem. Let us pray." And having prayed for every possible blessing upon that particular household, with general supplications for delivery from war, Mr. Barker hastens through that exercise.

"If it is not too great a favor, Sister Sorel: if you will give your servants some charge to keep silence: if you will allow me to occupy Brother Arthur's room for the present—I observe it to be his by the books there—I will be obliged." And the guest disappears within that room, the curtains of which he has carefully put down, but appears again at the sound of a galloping along the road.

"Sister Sorel," he says, bending, with ashy face, over that silent lady as she sits at the table washing up the cups and saucers, "I have reason to know that my life is in great danger; even now the foe may be on my track. I am—am" —the galloping outside louder and louder—"not a soldier, I am"—white lips and trembling voice and sallowest of faces—"a poor, humble preacher of the blessed Gospel of peace. My life is in your hands, my blood will be upon your skirts."

"Mr. Barker, go to Mr. Arthur's room and remain there. Any thing an old woman may be able to do for you I will do. You have no cause of apprehension."

And in his room Brother Barker remains, trying to read, trying to pray, tucking the curtains so as to conceal himself from any one passing, listening, trembling, enduring such agonies of fear as waste him like a spell of sickness.

Mrs. Warner, peeping forth that morning, finds the Federals in quiet possession of Somerville. We can not be mathematically accurate, but Mrs. Warner has said, a very great number of times, that she only wished the entire Yankee nation had one neck that she might break it; one throat that she might cut it; one heart that she "might drive *this*," holding up the knife wherewith she is carving at table as she speaks, into their heart to the hilt. Touchstone's complete destruction, in words, of his foe; Dr. Slop's exhaustive curses upon the knots in the string of his bag; Romish anathema in full, so far as her knowledge of the language furnishes her with the words, her intellect with the thoughts, her imagination with the possibilities, her heart with the zeal, has Mrs. Warner long ago equaled in imprecation upon the Federals. No Mrs. Partington has ever swept away the Atlantic more vigorously, in anticipation, than has Mrs. Warner; yet now that it is actually over her threshold the mop fails her wearied hand. She has so exhausted herself before their arrival that she can scarce even feel any thing, except curiosity, now they have actually come. Probably this is the reason why she does not burn her house now, as she has so often said she would do. She has ample opportunity of shooting at them from her windows, she has almost sworn she would, yet she merely peeps at them instead.

Friday night they take possession. All Saturday and Sunday they are in possession. Not one male Secessionist visible. Union men quiet as mice. Guy Brooks need have sent no message to that effect.

The stores are all closed. Somerville has long ago learned to do that when even Confederate soldiers are in the neighborhood. Over and over again have squads, half-naked, two-thirds starved, four-fourths desperate, helped themselves from the stores in Somerville to exactly what they wanted, a good deal more than they could consume. It shocked us terribly at first, but Mr. Ellis and the rest of us have become used to it. Only three days before the raid of the Federals, Mr. Ellis was speaking of it to Colonel Ret Roberts in his store, on a visit to his family from his duties in Richmond.

"Three times, Sir," said Mr. Ellis to that distinguished Senator, "has my store been sacked by ruffian soldiers."

"And very probably will be a dozen times again," said the Colonel, very coolly indeed. If Colonel Ret Roberts was a splendid blackguard, a brilliant bully, an eloquent, unprincipled, thoroughly plain-spoken scoundrel before the schooling of the last few years, tell us, oh whichever of ye daughters of Jupiter and Mnemosyne is the Muse of History, what Colonel Ret Roberts is now!

"And my taxes!" says Mr. Ellis; "look at it, Sir. I pay two and a half per cent. on my sales every three months; one per cent. more for soldiers' tax; five per cent. on all real estate; eight per cent. on all the wool, tobacco, cotton I had on hand in '63; ten per cent. on profit on sales. Let me see! Yes, I am taxed as a retail merchant, taxed over again as a wholesale merchant. And all this while my Corporation, County, State taxes are at least one hundred per cent. heavier than they were before the war."

"Certainly. But you may rest sure the taxes now are nothing to what they will be next year," says Colonel Ret Roberts, as coolly as if stating a desirable fact, with a soft of pleasure even.

"But have you nothing encouraging to tell us?" asks Mr. Ellis, nervously. "Your opportunities at Richmond—"

"I know nothing but what you read in the papers," remarks the Senator, elaborately paring his finger-nails. "You have heard me from the stump, Sir. If you people at home will sustain the currency, the South will succeed. If you do not, it won't. You know as well as I whether they will sustain it. We are, *in* this thing; all we can do is to—do what we can. Hold on, Lamum!" to that editor, who is passing, and the distinguished Senator is gone.

An exceeding, scarcely disguised, contempt Colonel Ret Roberts had for the people before Secession; his contempt now is so great that it is not at all disguised. He is elected for years to the Confederate Senate, entirely beyond the favor of the people. They stand so astounded by his cool insolence in public and private that he has left again for Richmond before they have time to recover themselves.

And Sabbath dawns upon Somerville still in Federal occupation, the quietness of death upon the population peeping from behind doors and shutters upon the Federal cavalry passing and repassing. After full conference with friends, a Federal chaplain desecrating Brother Barker's pulpit, the only church beside his own in Somerville open that day, Mr. Arthur fills his own pulpit, his sermons being exactly the same they would have been had there been no raid. Quite a large congregation too, to Mr. Arthur's surprise; almost all ladies. Mr. Ferguson sings bass, as grave and cold in manner as if war were confined to the Crimea and like distant regions. And the Federal officers and men, whom the ladies came to see, are there, quiet, orderly.

"Nothing remarkable at last, every thing exactly as usual," Mrs. Warner, at church for the first time in many months, remarks, as she and the Doctor walk home. And, beside a little abuse of the men who have tamely permitted the Yankees to come here, Mrs. Warner is strikingly silent to-day.

"If I knew Colonel Brooks was not coming to church I wouldn't have gone, I can tell you. Have you seen him yet, Dr. Warner? Mighty shy you Union people are of your Federal friends, and they of you! As if I don't know the reason why. You all had better be, I tell you; if all our men are gone—miserable cowards that they are!—there's plenty of women left in Somerville to watch you. Did you notice that fat Mrs. Isaac Smith at church, she whose husband has gone over to the Yankees? I watched at her sitting there on a side-seat near the pulpit expressly to look at those Federal wretches, looking wistfully at them—expected to see her husband among them, I suppose. As I live, there she is this moment going into that Jem Budd—even 'Ria could tell what *that* is for!"

It was true. Mrs. Isaac Smith had never made a visit since her husband fled. She has only a general invitation made her years before by poor, pale little Mrs. Budd, the gun-maker's wife; yet there she is this moment, in Sunday finery long laid aside, entering the door in question. Sharp Mrs. Warner sees it all at a glance. Jem Budd's little one-story house is right on the most public street in Somerville; its front porch is as good a place as any in the town to see all that can be seen of the Federal troops.

Besides, Jem Budd and Jem Budd's harmless little wife belong not only to the one side of the great question which rends Somerville asunder but also to the other. Secessionists say of Jem: "Oh! Jem Budd is a quiet sort of fellow, but he is all right at heart. He doesn't talk much, but he has said this, that, and the other exceedingly severe things about the Yankees, and especially about the Union people. And then Alfred Morgan, Mrs. Budd's brother, who left for the war years ago, we all know that he is a good Secessionist, in dangerous and efficient service for the Confederacy in the North. Jem doesn't say much about it, but he has shown letters from Alf to that effect. Oh, Jem is all right!"

"You can't change a man's nature," Union people say to each other of Jem Budd. "Of course it's his interest to keep well with the faithful; it's the only way to hold his detail to fix guns and stay out of the army. As to Alf Morgan, Jem can't help *that*. But we all know Jem. He's told me in confidence a thousand times a vast deal about the madness of Secession." There were disadvantages in Jem's course. Neither party were thoroughly cordial with him. Besides, for Jem is making money these weapon-using days, he can not refuse to give when called on to assist Union families suffering for the necessaries of life in the absence of their husbands. Far more impossible to refuse his mite when called on, as he is about every other week, to contribute to some war purpose or other. He has to pay for his position, but he holds it and his tongue quietly, firmly.

"I took a lunch just before coming to church, ma'am; please excuse me. But you know my house is out of the way, and I am dying to see the Federals. If you have no objection," Mrs. Isaac Smith says to little pale Mrs. Budd, who lives in her own house as closely as a snail, and keeps no servant, and who, a good deal astonished at the apparition of stout Mrs. Smith,

whom she has not seen for so long, invites her from the parlor in to dinner.

It is all very well when, dinner over, Jem Budd smoking his pipe in one corner of the fireplace for the convenience of spitting, Mrs. Budd opposite him in her easy-chair, Mrs. Isaac Smith filling with her portly person the chasm between, the three fall into a quiet, confidential chat. At least Mrs. Isaac Smith, greatly freshened up by the blue shirts she has seen at church, talks, and the others listen.

First, she tells all she has seen and heard at church, for Mr. and Mrs. Budd haven't entered any church for years now; Jem Budd, a member of Brother Barker's church, too. Next, Mrs. Isaac Smith, by natural transition, speaks of Mr. Arthur; to all of which, Jem Budd, on one side, saying "Exactly" when Mrs. S. appeals to him; pale little Mrs. Budd, on the other side, says, when she is appealed to, "Just so, ma'am." By natural transition, too, Brother Barker is next on the carpet. Mrs. Isaac Smith waxes warmer as she recounts some of that divine's violent remarks in and out of the pulpit. To this, also, Mr. Budd, when directly appealed to for his sentiments, says "Precisely," and Mrs. Budd, "Just as you say, ma'am." Next, Mrs. Isaac Smith asks in general terms after Mrs. Budd's absent brother. She has heard what a bitter Secessionist Alf Morgan is; how actively and terribly at work for the Confederacy he is at the North. So she asks after him as under a sort of protest. At the North somewhere, and well, when last heard from, is all Jem and his wife can inform her on that point.

Her entire being, day and night, flowing in one channel, her husband who is away, Mrs. S. tells for the ten thousandth time that Isaac would never have left if it wasn't they were forcing him into the army. Isaac has his faults—who of us has not? Isaac is a peaceful man—didn't want to fight on either side if he could help it. But Isaac could *not* fight for what he believed to be a wicked—rebellion. Mrs. S. rather hesitates before bringing out this last word, but Mrs. Budd only replies, "As you say, ma'am," while her husband merely puffs another cloud of smoke, and adds, to the tearful eyes of Mrs. Isaac directed to him, "Exactly so."

Like other large bodies broad Mrs. Smith does not easily get started; but once started, momentum being in proportion to weight, it is very hard for her to stop.

"Of course you have heard of how they murdered my brother John Jennings?" she asks of Mrs. Budd.

"Goodness gracious, what's that?" she adds in the same breath.

"That? What?" asks Jem, nervously, while poor Mrs. Budd is several degrees paler than before.

"Ha! must have been mistaken, of course;

thought I heard somebody under the floor. But I am so nervous!" says Mrs. Smith.

"Thought you heard somebody under the floor!" and Mr. Budd exclaims this in singularly loud tones, as if addressed to some one at a distance, and resumes his pipe.

"Your brother, ma'am? there are so many murdered, you know, one can not remember exactly," says pale, little Mrs. Budd, eagerly, quickened a good deal by the overflowing warmth of her visitor by this time. Mr. Budd smokes with inquiring puffs. And so Mrs. Smith enters on the murder, describes it minutely, tells the destitute condition of the family left—all with such a natural eloquence that even stolid Jem Budd is affected. So much so that when Mrs. Smith says at last, suddenly, "You knew John Jennings well, Mr. Budd; you know I've only told you the truth; now what *do* you think of a cause which permits, even justifies such a thing as that?" Mr. Budd removes the pipe from his mouth and begins :

"So sure as there is a God in heaven, ma'am—"

"Jem! My dear?" interrupts his wife from the other side with a cry, and holding up a warning hand.

And well it is for Mr. Budd. Though his wife does not know it, there is a tap upon the door, and in walks—of all persons in the world—Mrs. Smithers.

Mrs. Smithers! We write the word reluctantly, knowing how hopeless it is to portray her upon the page. Let us see what our recording that she was a very tall, a very long and red in the face, a very violent female in temper and language will do. Mrs. Smithers's brothers are known, all six of them, as desperadoes who have long ago killed their men. Mrs. Smithers is said to be a good shot with rifle, double-barrel shot-gun, revolver. The way Mrs. Smithers is known, with her own bony hands, to cowhide her erring negro women, has wakened even Mrs. Warner's reprobation. Her nearest neighbors are exceeding respectful to, and shy of, Mrs. Smithers, not knowing what instant a chicken from their yard into her garden, or a quarrel between her children and theirs, may bring her down upon them with some deadly weapon, or more deadly tongue. As to her having hurled, in a paroxysm of rage, that negro babe which *would* keep crawling in upon her recently-scoured floor, down the hill back of the house, we reject all that story of course, knowing, as we all do, that negro testimony is no evidence.

But we knew we could convey no adequate idea of Mrs. Smithers, the postmaster's wife, when we began. Mr. Jem Budd had such an idea, however, and the instant she entered the room he uttered a "Whew!" none the less intense from being altogether internal. Publicly, meeting them on the street, had Mrs. Smithers refused and resented the salutation of more than

one Union man of her previous acquaintance. The Union ladies, met by her casually in stores and at funerals, she had not contented herself with refusing to speak to, but had looked at them in a way which had sent more than one of them from shopping and visiting home and to bed. Being of a fighting stock, Mrs. Smithers was true to the breed—even her brothers, with many an oath, admitted that.

As Mrs. Smithers entered, offensively ignored the existence of Mrs. Isaac Smith, and took the hand and the seat which poor, pale little Mrs. Budd offered her, Mr. Budd saluted her and withdrew; remembered in the hall the feeble state of his wife's health and returned; really could not risk it, when back in the parlor, and retired; feared, when half-way out of his front gate, that his wife might faint, perhaps die, and so returned again. He has an inspiration, he will effect a diversion.

"Bad news I hear this morning," he begins, after the usual salutations are over—Mrs. Isaac Smith will not, Mrs. Budd can not speak, nothing left for him. As the husband of his wife, the head of the household, the only chance is to keep the conversation in his own hand till one of the visitors shall depart—any subject on earth rather than of the Federals just arrived.

"What news is that, Mr. Budd?" asks Mrs. Smithers, reserving, "It's a lie," in the corners of her eyes and upon the tip of her tongue.

And having mentioned it simply that, being uppermost in his mind, it came first in the hurry of being compelled to say something instantly, Mr. Jem Budd narrates the fact of the suicide of the District Judge of a Southern State. Nor had Mr. Ferguson been so interested in the occupation of Somerville as not, that very day, to have entered the same in his Scrap-book. Had he not foretold it?

"Drunk or crazy," is the verdict of Mrs. Smithers, relieved to know it is only that.

Jem Budd, toiling more vigorously for another topic than he ever does upon gun-lock or barrel, stumbles upon the case of the refugees. Tells how they are pouring into the region about Somerville; how poor they are, how sorry they all seem to be that they ever abandoned their old homes; thinks it a great shame people should receive them so coldly.

"Serve them right. Why didn't they stay where they were and fight the Yankees?" is Mrs. Smithers's opinion, who gives only half attention to her host, casting about in her mind how best and soonest to assault Mrs. Isaac Smith.

"Have you noticed, Mr. Budd," asks Mrs. Isaac Smith, advancing her skirmishers, "how all the papers agree about the swindling going on by Government officials? Every single paper! Charges made by judges, findings by grand juries and by little juries, every body knows it, universal corruption and swindling. From the highest to the lowest, all the officials at it, the papers say." Because the lady speaking has heard very often of the remarks made in reference to herself by the tigress at her side—infinitely more than that, the very often expressed wish of Mrs. Smithers has come to her ears, to hang that red-headed painter, Smith, abolitionist and traitor, with her own hands. Nor does the least doubt linger in the mind of any of Mrs. Smithers's circle of friends but she would do just that thing if she had but the chance.

"I have noticed it, ma'am," says sorely-perplexed Mr. Budd, "but have thought"—with special reference to Mrs. Smithers — "our papers ought not to publish such things at this time."

"I suppose you notice, Mrs. Budd, how sick even the Yankees are, from their own papers, with that vile Lincoln? All we have to do is to keep whipping them till his term is out; they'll be only too glad to make peace with us then, if they don't have a revolution among themselves before that," says Mrs. Smithers.

Mr. and Mrs. Budd retaining their seats on opposite corners of the fire-place, the two visitors between them, Mrs. Isaac Smith being next to Mrs. Budd, Mrs. Smithers to Mr. Budd; Mrs. Smith having addressed her remarks in reference to the refugees across Mrs. Smithers to Mr. Budd, in contempt of that lady, Mrs. Smithers addresses, of course, her conversation across portly Mrs. Smith, and in utter ignorance of her existence, to Mrs. Budd. Conversation *will* become platted together in this way, even in ordinary times and under friendly auspices all around. Even then it is hard at times for the couples thus engaged to keep their threads of talk untangled. It is peculiarly difficult to-day in Jem Budd's parlor.

"As you say, ma'am," pale little Mrs. Budd replies, across Mrs. Smith to Mrs. Smithers..

"But isn't it strange, Mr. Budd, people won't take Confederate money? It's the most miserable trash, no better than brown paper!" says Mrs. Smith, across Mrs. Smithers.

—"and they actually force the miserable people to take their greenbacks at the point of the bayonet!" continues Mrs. Smithers to Mrs. Budd, heating with indignation at Mr. Budd's bare "Precisely, ma'am," in reply to *his* interlocutor, disregarding the "So I've heard, ma'am," which she gets from hers.

—"could hardly believe what I hear every day of how poor people are getting among us. A good many can't send their children to Sabbath-school, nor day-school either, for want of clothes. Can't even put their foot out of their own yard themselves. What a terrible condition we are—"

—"universal infidelity there now, ma'am," from Mrs. Smithers, drowns Mr. Budd's "'Tis, indeed!"

—"that, of course, is worse. Backsliding? Worse than that, Mr. Budd! Open gambling, drinking, swearing, stealing, and worse. The preachers themselves—"

—"can you wonder at it? Only wonder, ma'am, is they haven't left, all of them long ago, wretched traitors to their country! Anxious to leave! *I'd* help them in a shorter way than they ever—" But Mrs. Smithers's remark only lies across, by no means extinguishes.

—"because the Union people among us know the awful times which are coming. I'm told, Mr. Budd, the people driven off are sworn to kill every—" from Mrs. Isaac Smith, while the "As you say, ma'am," from Mr. Budd and the "I fear so, indeed," from Mrs. Budd are made no account of by either belligerent as the strife grows hotter.

—"even to the last drop of our blood, ma'am, and if the war should last ten thousand—"

—"said it was kept up only by the women, and especially the Secession preachers at home. The army is sick enough of it, you may be sure. Why, Mr. Budd, I got a letter, I mean a person told me—"

—"for of all things in this world, ma'am, a traitor to one's own soil they were born on, and a she-traitor is a thing I do—"

—"always so, Mr. Budd. Yankee Secessionists are the craziest, just as Yankee masters and mistresses are the hardest upon their poor negroes."

The conversation becomes more tangled as it becomes more personal.

Mr. Budd has firm hold of the pipe between his teeth, long since gone out, and only repeats his "Precisely so, Exactly, ma'am," from mechanical habit. Poor, pale, little rabbit of a Mrs. Budd, with firm hold upon the arms of her easy-chair, fascinated by Mrs. Smithers's terrible eye, no more hears what that fiery visaged lady says than if she was deaf, only is conscious of a steady rattle of words, and gasps her affirmatives at regular intervals.

But the conversation becomes more closely welded together as it heats.

"Quantrel."

"Beast Butler."

"Wretched Repudiator."

"Despicable Gorilla."

"Who wouldn't get fat as a beef, ma'am, when one is rid of a drunken husband?"

"Six, Mr. Budd, six brothers, murderers."

"Used to lie dead drunk, ma'am."

"Has swindled with sugar speculations until—"

"Abolitionist, who ought to be."

"Actually whipped her, Mr. Budd, until the bones—"

Mr. Budd closes his teeth harder on his pipe-stem, Mrs. Budd clutches firmer hold of the arms of her chair, the catastrophe *must* be near—

A long clear bugle blast out of doors! Mr. Jem Budd sees his only hope.

"The Federal cavalry, ladies!" and hurries out of his front-door, in a manner washing with extended arms his angry visitors before him upon the front porch, leaving Mrs. Budd utterly exhausted in her easy-chair behind. And if the company had not made so much noise and been in so great haste in leaving the room they would have heard a distinct sound from beneath the floor upon which they were. It may have been a mouse or a bat. It did not sound like hog or dog. Perhaps a parrot had made his hole there, for it sounded exactly like the words "Good! Thank God!" What makes it strangest of all is, that Mrs. Budd, the instant she is alone, is on her knees on the floor, and, with white cheeks, says in low, sharp tones, "For God's sake, Alf, be quiet," her lips almost touching the carpet.

The Federal cavalry coming up the street at a slow walk, and so very many, apparently, rough, bearded, powerful-looking men, too; moving in much more of a military manner than such Confederate soldiers as we have seen. Mrs. Smith and Mrs. Smithers stand, side by side, upon the elevated porch, both thrilling with deepest feeling, but of quite a different nature. Guy Brooks—erect, sad-visaged, more powerful in appearance than ever—rides slowly and at the head of the column. As he approaches, his eye catches that of Mrs. Isaac Smith. So far he has carefully avoided speaking to any of the Union people, for the best of reasons. There is something in her broad, earnest face, something so wistful in her eyes, that he forgets himself, and salutes her. Just a scarce-perceptible lifting of the forefinger of the gauntleted hand to the cap.

It is the drop too much. Bless you! Mrs. Isaac Smith has not been in the School of Prudence all these years since Isaac left, for nothing. She had resolved to be prudent before she left home; she had told Sarah Jennings over and over again, "Oh, I'll be careful, Sarah, you never fear." She had even made a special prayer, kneeling by her bed that morning, after she had put on her best bonnet and all, that she might be prudent. But perhaps her late engagement with Mrs. Smithers has "overhet" her, as she afterward explains the matter. As Colonel Brooks touches his hat she rushes back into the parlor, snatches from prostrate Mrs. Budd her handkerchief—she had left her own, to avoid the temptation, at home—and, standing beside Mrs. Smithers, waves it to the Federals, continues waving it vehemently!—the tears running copiously down her unconscious cheeks.

But if she waves her handkerchief at the Federals, Mrs. Smithers, advancing to the extreme edge of the porch, shakes her fist at them; a long arm has tall, red, hard-featured Mrs. Smithers, and a fist that has knocked many a

negro child over, as well as her own, for that matter. Handkerchief and fist so energetically flourished, side by side, send a peal of laughter down the column—even Guy Brooks laughs outright.

But Mrs. Smith has bid farewell to her wits "They've murdered Hol Robbins, Mr. Brooks! they've hung John Jennings! you knew him, Mr. Brooks—old John Jennings, my own brother! For God's sake don't march away and leave us!" she cries, with the cry of anguish peculiar to a woman beside, say, a drowning child. Handkerchief hard at work. .

"Tut-traitor! Tut-traitor! Tut-traitor!" screams Mrs. Smithers, with the yell of fury peculiar to a furious female in her fiercest fury, fist shaken almost to dislocation.

"May God bless you!" cries Mrs. Isaac Smith, her entire soul as well as body in each separate word.

"May the devil—" But the rest of Mrs. Smithers's wish, though in the highest and shrillest of screams, is drowned in the cheer for Mrs. Smith, which rings once again, again, down the column, every man of whom by this time enters into the spirit of the thing.

It is full half an hour after both their lady visitors are gone that Jem and his wife can realize it all.

"That it should have taken place of all the houses in Somerville at my house!" said Jem Budd to himself over and over and over again; "and when I've worked so hard ever since the thing began to keep well with both sides. It is too bad!"

Mrs. Budd has long since gone to bed seriously ill.

"But I don't blame her a bit, not one bit either," adds Jem just as often, strictly to himself however, glancing around even then to be sure no one is by, though it is midnight, and Jem is in his own chamber. His reference is to Mrs. Isaac Smith.

He then falls upon his knees, although not, it would seem, for devotional purposes. With his lips to the floor he says,

"Had plenty of supper, Alf?"

"Plenty, Jem," from below. It must be a parrot.

"Good-night, old fellow! Fun, wasn't it?"

"Guess it was. Good-night!" from below again.

"Remind me, Mr. Smithers, to take my Derringer with me whenever I go out," says Mrs. Smithers to her husband that night in conclusion. "If ever I meet that woman I'll spit in her round old moon of a face, as sure as my name is Araminty. If she says a word to that, I'll put a bullet just as deep into her old carcass as the Derringer can carry!"            •

"Needn't talk to me, Sarah Jennings, child. I didn't intend it when I went to church this

THE HANDKERCHIEF AND THE FIST.

morning. I couldn't help it. And, what is more, I don't care one single cent. Let them hang me if they want to, like they hung your pa. It's in a good cause, God knows. I'm tired of my life any way, Isaac gone so long. Humph, but only let *her* try it! But oh, won't we settle with these people when the old flag is here again for good! Not that I want their life; may the Lord forgive me, no!"

As to Mr. Ferguson, when, on Monday morning, he lugs out the Scrap-book from its Sabbath rest in the iron safe, to the bulletin of the arrival of the Federals on the previous Friday night he has to add their leaving during Sunday night. It is a week or two before he can make an accurate statement of the number of negroes and Confederate stores they have taken away with them. One thing he knows, grim and silent during the whole raid as the Sphinx at midnight—no one can touch him for it; not a word, gesture, wink to found any thing upon.

But it seemed strange to Robby, riding a week after upon his pony past Staples's Hotel, to hear the way in which Dr. Peel, absent on pressing business from Somerville a fortnight now, curses the Federals, and Guy Brooks especially. Yet Robby only seals his sober face into still more sober silence, and rides about his errand, earnestly hoping he may not have to engage in another fight this time.

And so Somerville gets past *that* point in its history.

---

## CHAPTER XXII.

It really must not be indulged in, this tendency to loiter along the way—a tendency caused by birth and long residence under Southern skies. We must quicken our pace over these pages to keep up with events falling in rapid succession.

There is the march of the Federals upon Atlanta. The Somerville *Star* has kept all of us in Somerville fully aware of every thing relating to that. It is a thrilling narrative as told us from *Star* to *Star*. Let us think. We give up Chattanooga, a place of no use to the Federals, and the abandonment of which is a positive advantage to the Confederate cause in every way—there is a motive in it. That motive we all understand and exult in when we have the *Star* and all the bells in town triumphant over the total defeat of Rosecrans soon after, and the reoccupation of Chattanooga, capturing therein stores and munitions of war enough to supply the whole South for two years.

Captain Simmons, standing in Jem Budd's shop, is full, as Jem, in paper cap, dirty face, leathern apron, files and tinkers away at his gun-making and mending, of it. During two hours he discusses with Jem the splendid strategy of General Bragg, and his complete success; to all of which Jem says, at intervals, "As you say, Captain." "Exactly so, Sir." "Just what I say." "Precisely." "Yes, *Sir;* of that we may be sure."

Yet when, not a week after, Dr. Warner, in attendance upon poor, pale little Mrs. Budd, upon whom he is always in attendance for that matter, says to Jem, sitting in the room, by the fireside for the convenience of spitting as he smokes: "And so it turns out that the Federals were *not* driven out of Chattanooga, Mr. Budd. Having read the accounts of the way in which they had fortified themselves there, I really did not for a moment suppose that other report was true, did you?" Jem spits and replies, "Certainly not," and weaves in his habitual affirmatives to all that Dr. Warner has to say.

"Eighteen months!" the Doctor ejaculates a moment after. "People at the North wouldn't believe it. And the way you have managed to keep it close, too! I have feared a hundred times—"

"See, Doctor," breaks in Jem, taking his pipe from his mouth in order to lower his tone, "Alf couldn't get shet of conscription any other way. You know how we hammered at it for ever so long before we could fix it up. The cellar was Mrs. Budd's notion; we laughed at it, Alf and I, at first. Then we all thought, when Alf first hid there, the war would 'a been over long ago. He's *there*, and there's nothing else to do but *stay* there that I can see;" and Jem resumes his pipe.

"Why, he's making a fortune in shoes, man, if your wife does get the credit of it. But what preposterous letters he writes! Dr. Ginnis was giving me all the contents of that last one from New York," says Dr. Warner, with glee. "I could hardly keep it in."

"Oh, that's Alf's fun; only recreation he has, Doctor," pleads Mrs. Budd, whose whole existence is invested in Alf and Jem. "But you can't tell how comfortable he is down there. Often comes up after night. Alf's got as fair as a girl there out of the sun. But oh! if the war would *only* end! I am *so* tired, tired! And Mrs. Isaac Smith came so near finding Alf out that day. It would kill me if they was to get Alf," adds poor little Mrs. Budd. "And he won't go with the Federals now he has a chance. Says he wants to see it out here in Somerville; as if he sees any thing!"

"You see, Mr. Budd," says Dr. Warner at last, perfectly grave as he rises to leave, "we Secessionists are pursuing a masterly policy. You will not forget to give Mrs. Budd the powders; those last bells were a little too much for her."

"And you really, really do think—" says pale little Mrs. Budd, smiling through the borders of her preposterously beruffled night-cap. With clergymen, sea-captains, and physicians women are always confidential.

"I really, really *do*, ma'am," replies Dr. Warner, with unctuous energy. "Just wait a little. Yes, a masterly policy. We are retreating toward Atlanta only to draw the Federals deeper into the country, away from their base, their gun-boats, and all that. Oh, don't let any fear of that keep you sick; we are bound to whip them. Your husband will tell you the same."

And Jem Budd, with a responsive grin upon his usually sedate countenance, says, "Exactly what I say, Lucy. Oh, we'll whip 'em, we'll whip 'em!"

Only there is more smiling all around than the conversation, apart from its peculiar tone, would warrant—a degree of cordiality, too, among the parties.

"And Alice Bowles is actually teaching school?" asks Mrs. Budd as Dr. Warner is drawing on his gloves.

"Hard at it, ma'am. You mustn't think badly of her when I tell you, with her absurd raising, it was death almost to her to do it. She always was a noble girl. They are very much pressed, you know we all are now, but *very* much pressed *indeed*. The discipline she is enduring is the very thing for her, be the making of her," says the physician.

"I always thought so much of Alice," says weak little Mrs. Budd, "because she is so pretty and strong. She often comes to see me. She knows all about Alf. How she laughed when I told her! Ah me! Doctor, I never was very strong; but once, years ago, Jem there, at least he said so—"

"Thought you were very pretty, ma'am," interrupts the Doctor, "and was perfectly right, ma'am. Only wait until you get your health again, Mrs. Budd—until our glorious independence is secured, you know!"

"Just what I tell Lucy," adds her husband, with a smile. Mrs. Budd is not the only pretty girl whose beauty gives place to ill health within a very few years after marriage in southern climes—fair, frail creatures, whose day is like that of the butterfly in more respects than one.

"I tease Alice about Tim Lamum and Mr. Neely and all her other beaux," says Mrs. Budd, whom Dr. Warner's visit has greatly enlivened, "but I never dare mention Mr. Arthur to her."

"Such a traitor, you know," adds Dr. Warner. "Pity, pity!"

"Exactly so!" says Jem Budd, reflecting the Doctor's smile.

"Not much worse than Jem here, I'm afraid," puts in Mrs. Budd, with the same light upon her face. "He never says a word to me, Jem don't—not to a soul since this thing began; but I'm afraid Jem's a bad, bad man!"

"Exactly as I say!" adds Jem, following the Doctor to the door with a candle and a grin.

And there is many another among the men still left in Somerville, though none so sedate and non-committal as he. Very often have Dr. Warner, old Mr. Adams, and the like been favored with a wink and an aside smile which said as plain as words, "A good joke, ain't it?" by individuals in the very heat of jubilation amidst a crowd over foreign intervention, glorious victory, iron-plated Confederate fleet, Northern sickness of the war, and all the rest. The num-

ber of these equivocal individuals in Somerville is great, is increasing, their facetiousness becoming more undisguised every day.

And so the times roll on. We are not without news in these days in Somerville. Sure enough, the Federals *are* being drawn slowly but steadily away from Chattanooga. With unprecedented folly they persist in walking blindly, madly into the fatal trap. We whip them at Dalton, we rout them with terrible slaughter at Marietta, yet they still have enough left to follow our army, fallen back to entice them still further in. Such a series of Confederate victories we have never yet enjoyed. Full details by the column; little items, like grains of pepper, in all the corners of every paper. "The destruction of Sherman's army is more complete than had been supposed." "We have totally destroyed Sherman's line of communication with Chattanooga." "It is now well known that at Kenesaw Mountain Johnston will spring his trap, the enemy being drawn sufficiently into it."

Then follows the brilliant victory achieved by Hood, now in command, over Sherman at Atlanta; of this we have the official accounts and the—bells.

It is just following this that Mr. Arthur, riding in to the Post-office very early one morning, goes direct from the office to Mr. Ferguson's room. So early, in fact, that he finds that gentleman still in bed. As to Mr. Arthur, he is wide awake, very ruddy and fresh.

"If you please, let me have the key of your safe," he says, in high spirits, to his friend.

"Key of my safe?" And the Scotchman, drawing on his trowsers, hands that implement to his friend, taking it from under his pillow, watching grimly the futile efforts of Mr. Arthur to unlock the safe, or even to find the keyhole when he has the key.

"I wanted to make an entry in your Scrapbook," he explains at last, with boyish eagerness.

"An entry?" And Mr. Ferguson, holding up his trowsers with his left hand, has opened the safe in a moment.

"Atlanta has fallen!" His visitor can keep it back no longer; beginning with enthusiasm, his voice faltering as he says it, though. "Oh, Mr. Ferguson, Atlanta has fallen at last!"

Not a syllable from Mr. Ferguson, not a smile. If possible, more grim than ever. Yet, by a singular coincidence, he remembers, doubtless merely from the safe being open before him, that he is indebted, which he is not, to Mr. Arthur, and pays him two double eagles on account upon the spot. And Mr. Ferguson spends the whole of that day upon the streets—no particular business at all. For there is this peculiarity of the Union men—that while you never see them abroad, so far as they can help it, when the news is good, as it generally is in Somerville hitherto, for the Confederacy, so sure as it is bad, which will happen in spite of the *Star* occasionally, out they all swarm from their retreats, meeting with each other, clasping warm hands and shaking doleful heads, with smiling faces, over the tidings at every turn and corner. Secessionists not unaware of it either.

The very next time Mr. Arthur rides in to the Post-office he is hailed before he can get there from the yard of Dr. Warner's house. Whenever he conveniently could Mr. Arthur rather avoided that residence. He imagined black eyes watching him through the windows, and, from mere sight of him, a terrible tongue set agoing. More than once have 'Ria and Bub, long since withdrawn from the Sunday-school, hailed him in opprobrious terms in passing, saluting him on one or two instances with *their* political sentiments in the shape of pebbles. Until he is safely past the house he is not sure but Mrs. W. may herself rush out and scourge him with her tongue. For he often hears of the frequent and various ways in which she has expressed her ardent desire that he should be disposed of. Truth is, he has a mortal terror of the lady in question.

THE DOCTOR HAS GOOD NEWS.

So that when he is hailed this morning, as he rides by on his way to the Post-office, he nervously starts until he sees it is Dr. Warner. The Doctor, while shaving at the glass in his room, has spied his friend passing, and now comes out in his shirt-sleeves and the soap upon his fresh, good-humored face to say, "Don't be in such a hurry—hold on." And, leaning over the fence,

Dr. Warner does not wait for an answer as to the health of Mrs. Sorel before he says, glancing behind him at the house and in a lowered tone of voice,

"Have you heard the news?"

"No. Some glorious Confederate victory? Where was it?" deeming it best to show the Doctor and himself thereby that he expects and is prepared for the strongest news of that nature.

"Mobile has fallen!" pressing still closer to the fence, and speaking in a still lower tone.

"Are you certain?" Ah, what relief and satisfaction! You at the North supposed you derived pleasure from news of Federal success—you knew nothing about it!

"Oh yes; that is, Farragut has captured the forts which defended it. Of course the city lies at his mercy. We will hear by the next mail of his occupying the place." Which they didn't, nor for long days after.

"All well?" asks his friend, for they both feel that they are standing in point-blank range of a battery, and do not care to protract the conversation.

"Yes; and, by-the-by, I will send out a barrel of sugar to Mrs. Sorel's this morning. I have been owing you"—which here, too, is not the case—"a long time. Well, good-by. Haven't got time to come in, I suppose? I'll see you on the streets in the course of the day." And, sure enough, all the Union people are abroad to-day again, swarming forth in this last burst of sunshine like bees, with scarcely subdued buzz, too, the weather is getting *so* pleasant!

"Thought I didn't see you?" is Mrs. Warner's sarcastic remark as the Doctor resumes his shaving, which the Doctor did *not* think, however. "I'll bet a thousand dollars, when I come to hear it, there's bad news for the South. Running out this cold morning like a great big boy in your shirt-sleeves and half shaved to talk to a man that never enters your house. There's some bad news—you needn't tell me! I saw you laughing when you told him; and I as good as heard him say, 'Thank God, I'm glad of it!' Humph, I know you by this time!"

Which was the solemn fact; but the Doctor, with his head fallen into its old droop, shaves on, making the soap upon his mouth the base excuse for not saying any thing in reply. But, at last, Mrs. W. has not half so much to say as of old, nor half the bitterness in saying that which she used to exhibit.

There is, in fact, this peculiarity about all Secessionists in Somerville—it is only as they are excited that they are confident; the instant they cool they become doubtful. As a large audience gathered to hear Colonel Ret Roberts or Captain Simmons, for the Captain, with a firm hold upon the desk in Brother Barker's church—"Admittance, one silver dollar for the benefit of the soldiers"—makes orations, Brother Barker opening with prayer, these days, we are enthusiastic, and positively certain of the success of the Confederacy. It is when we break up, go home, and are off to ourselves individually, that we, in the ideas if not dialect of Bob Withers, "Are not so certain of it at last. At least, for one, by George! *I* ain't!"

Of one thing we are, thank Heaven! perfectly certain as the days glide by. We do not pretend to understand what Sherman and Hood are about marching hither and thither. Davis has told us at Macon that Sherman's capture of Atlanta is to be to him a Moscow defeat at last. Leaving out of consideration the conflagration of Moscow and the Russian winter, trifling discrepancies in the historic parallel, we only wait to hear of the total destruction of Sherman in fulfillment of this official prophecy. After the first sickening sensation upon hearing of the fall of Atlanta we recuperate, confidently counting upon Sherman's great disaster as only a question of time, for Davis has said it.

Of another thing we are even more certain— the defeat of Lincoln at the approaching election. For months the Somerville *Star* has been filled with articles from Northern papers, themselves so replete with denunciation of Lincoln, so confident of his speedy fall, that we only wonder the North, in its intense and evidently unanimous hatred of Lincoln, is willing to wait until election day to hurl him headlong from his place. We know the despot will endeavor to bring the bayonet to bear upon the polls; there may be a few votes cast for him by office-holders; but there will be one universal fight at every election precinct in the North. We would prefer M'Clellan should be elected on some accounts, yet count a good deal upon neither candidate being elected, but the whole mockery of a government there being utterly broken up, exploded, totally wrecked by the convulsions sure to shake the land upon election day.

Lamum has articles, a series of them, to prove it. Captain Simmons made a description of these approaching convulsions a thrilling point in his orations, the earthquake in Lisbon being the tremendous illustration thereof, himself tottering in the stand as he spake, in a manner exceedingly emblematic. Yet as the day approaches there is a slackening of public certainty somehow.

"I have hoped M'Clellan might be elected," Dr. Warner has said to Mr. Arthur in the security of Mr. Ferguson's room.

"You have!" exclaims that gentleman, with as much surprise as pain.

"Why, yes," says Dr. Warner, rubbing the phrenological organ, whatever it is, immediately behind the ear with his forefinger. "I see no end to the war otherwise. The Democratic party might conciliate in some way, compromise, arrange the thing," continues the fat, slovenly,

thoroughly excellent physician, in a vague, general, undecided manner. "Don't you?" he asks, doubtfully.

"I?" asks Mr. Arthur, with indignation. "No, Sir! May Heaven forbid! There is only one plain road: to carry the war steadily, unflinchingly on till the purpose for which it began is accomplished. The election of M'Clellan I would look upon as the election of vacillation, weakness, the success of the Confederacy, anarchy, ruin! I am really amazed that you, Doctor, could look at it any other way. Don't *you* regard it in that light, Mr. Ferguson?"

"Of course!" growls the Scotchman, in accents scarcely polite to Dr. Warner, considered as being at the moment his guest. "Not a sensible Union man North or South thinks otherwise."

And yet when we hear in Somerville that Lincoln is actually elected, no man sees more clearly by that time than Dr. Warner that the Union men have greater cause to rejoice in this than in any other victory achieved by the nation. Yes, that victory was the Waterloo of the whole war.

"If you can use it, or if you know any person —any person not a Secessionist, you know—who can use it, send out a wagon, send half a dozen wagons," old Mr. Adams says the very day we hear in town of the re-election of Lincoln, to Mr. Arthur, whom he meets, as he might and did meet every other Union man of Somerville, upon the streets. "I've plenty of rye and oats left; you or any body, any body you can recommend, is more than welcome!"

Very remarkable. Thin, and sharp, and cold as a razor is old Mr. Adams. A tough time of it Sam Peters, even Brother Barker himself had of it before the war in getting a cent for any object out of old Mr. Adams, strenuous communicant of that church as he was. All Brother Barker's communion well knew and bewailed Brother Adams's stinginess. It was as well, as proverbially, known to be Brother Adams's sin which did most easily beset him, as was lying known to be Brother Peters's weakness. Only the latter, in times of religious revival, openly confessed, and, in terms so highly colored as to show the old vice ran in the very blood, bewailed his sin, whereas Brother Adams did nothing of the kind. We all knew Brother Barker meant him in all his many hits at the penurious and close-fisted in and out of pulpit—all of us except the individual aimed at himself. Or if he knew it he only gripped his bivalves more closely together, and took it upon his crustaceous sides, like so much mere water.

But all that was before Secession. If any Secessionist obtained, otherwise than by physical force, a horse, or a bundle of fodder, or a stem of oats, or a grain of corn, or an ounce of pork from old Brother Adams, that fact is not upon record. To Union people, on the other hand, he no more thought of withholding any thing he possessed than he thought of going to hear Brother Barker or any other Secessionist preach. Long and thin, sharp, cold, and hard as he was, sour and close, old Mr. Adams had hidden among his bones, like gold among the strata, a pure, strong love of country: the vein once struck was inexhaustible. How can we tell how much it cost his friends to elect Mr. Lincoln there at the North? Millions in the way of bribes, the *Star* said. It certainly cost old Mr. Adams, when over, in pork and corn and potatoes, hundreds, to say the least.

But we have no time in Somerville to reason about the results of Lincoln's re-election, the *Star* exulting in it as the certain means—as hundreds of events have been before—of at last making the South a unit, and thoroughly arousing the people. Ah, how many, many theories were manufactured at the South during the war, each perfectly symmetrical and beautiful! Bubbles? Yes, but then we could blow them as fast as they burst, you know. Yet we have no time to discuss that question in our intense curiosity in reference to Sherman just now.

"Yes, he *has* cut loose from Atlanta," Captain Simmons demonstrates the matter, newspaper in hand, to Dr. Ginnis and Mr. Ellis collected in Jem Budd's shop out of the rain—"cut loose from Atlanta in sheer despair of getting out of Georgia by the way he came; Hood, you see, having got behind him. He is making—you see what the paper says—frantic efforts to escape by way of the Atlantic coast, his only hope left, sheer desperation."

"Oh, Lee from Richmond!" begins Dr. Ginnis, eagerly.

"And the militia of South Carolina!" adds Mr. Ellis, still more eagerly.

"Of course will close in upon him. I have no more doubt of the capture of his entire command than I have of my existence. Davis's idea of his retreat to Tennessee being cut off was good, as every thing from his consummate statesmanship is; but," continues Captain Simmons, "Sherman's case was worse than Davis supposed. Why, gentlemen, look at it, not one man, not a single gun he has but we are bound to get. It is a certainty."

"A special Providence," says good Mr. Ellis. "I love to trace the hand of Heaven in our cause."

"That's just what I say," puts in Jem Budd, as he hammers away at a gun-barrel clenched in its vice upon his work-table. "Exactly what *I* say." Consequently while we are rejoiced thereby still it is only what we expected when we soon read in all the papers of the capture of Sherman. And, to make this good news complete, the same dates give tidings of Hood's capture of Nashville.

"What I always said," Jem Budd remarks to Tim Lamum, dropped into the shop to see, in a languid way, if his revolver has all the silver mountings he has ordered for it; and who, cigar in mouth, legs hanging listlessly down as he sits on Jem's work-bench, gives him all the details of these two glorious events as they have been coming in for two weeks now.

"Seems to me," Jem Budd ventures at last, punching and hammering away, none the less, at his work, "that Brother Barker isn't as chirky as he used to be." He only says this to say something.

"—— old woman!" vituperates Tim, with prompt profanity. For Brother Barker does not occupy the position in Somerville he used to; he has in some imperceptible, incomprehensible manner dwindled and shriveled. Very few, indeed, at church these Sabbaths. Sabbath-school long since suspended.

Even grim Mr. Ferguson almost pities them, his respected fellow-citizens of the Secession persuasion, when the truth comes upon them at last! Comes upon them so suddenly, and with double blow! And herewith a fact, not altogether new but interesting in human nature, is evolved. As thus:

"Any thing new in the paper this morning?" Dr. Warner asks, the very day after Tim Lamum's conversation with Mr. Budd, of Dr. Ginnis, with whom he has professional relations.

"Why, n-n-no. Some rumors, I believe; I have not had time to look carefully over the paper yet. By-the-by, Doctor, what do you think now of that negro's wound? Not lockjaw supervening, do you think?"

"Have you the paper there, Captain Simmons? Any thing in it?" Dr. Warner—easy, good-natured Dr. Warner—frayed as to the edges of shirt bosom and collar, gone as to half-a-dozen buttons or so on vest, neckerchief and hair disheveled and scattered abroad as by gusty winds; yet we all like him in Somerville, as unanimous in opinion about him as we are in sentiment in reference to his wife; being on good terms with—except his wife—every person in town, the Doctor asks the question in an indifferent way of the Captain.

"Nothing of special interest, Doctor; nothing at all," replies the Captain, folding up the paper as he speaks and putting it in his pocket, oblivious, in a dignified manner, of the Doctor's hand extended for it. "The solemn truth is," continues the Captain, seriously, steadying himself, so to speak, by fastening his oracular and admonitory eyes upon those of his questioner, "there is no truth in the world just now. Falsehood? From my infancy have I loathed it. Lying? Next to a Yankee, my soul abhors it. Sainted parents instilled the story of Ananias and Sapphira into my earliest being. Sir," continues the Captain, "it is painful to say it, but men of my standing," holding on to the Doctor under pretense of laying a Mentor's hand upon his shoulder, "should not hesitate to utter at this awful crisis their religious convictions. You may repeat it, Sir, as from Captain Simmons, Lamum is a Yankee, and Lamum is a liar. Never had I the least faith in him or his paper. No, Sir, I was not falling. When I require your assistance to enable me to maintain an upright position I will say so. Nothing new, Sir, in the paper, save foolish rumors—nothing at all."

"Nothing new, I'm told," Dr. Warner remarks to Mr. Ferguson, into whose room he next enters. "I was up all night with one of Colonel Wright's hands who has given himself an ugly cut, or got one some way."

"Nothing at all," replies, concisely, the Scotchman, who is busy with scissors and paste at his collection, "except that Sherman is in possession of Savannah with trifling loss, and Hood's army has been utterly routed below Nashville!"

"Bless my soul! and it must be true!" exclaims the electrified Doctor, his face ablaze with satisfaction.

"I beg you will let me pay you that little amount, Doctor," Mr. Ferguson says in conclusion of their conversation, a very animated conversation.

"Not one cent, Sir; not one cent. I will be positively offended if you ever mention it again," and both offer and refusal are in strict coherence with the news; and the Doctor leaves him a happier and a wiser man.

"I tell you just what it is, gentlemen! Why not say it if a fellow thinks it, by George! You all know I'm not a bad Southern man, but we are whipped, gentlemen, whipped, by George! and well whipped." It is Bob Withers makes the remark that same day in the presence of Captain Simmons and Mr. Ellis, in the store of the latter.

"Only a few days ago, in Jem Budd's shop, I think it was, I said I was afraid about Sherman. You see I didn't see where the troops were to come from to stop him. Besides," adds Captain Simmons, "Georgia is rotten—you mark my words, rotten, gentlemen. That about Hood I don't see into. I can't believe it, and I won't. Sometimes we say of news 'It's too good to be true,' and this"—with heavy swearing—"is too bad to be true!"

"For me," says Mr. Ellis, too nervous about the news to notice with reprobation, as he ordinarily would, the profanity, "I endeavor to trace the hand of a just God in all events. It can't be we are to be subjugated, can not be; it would be unjust, unjust, grossest injustice in—I mean the Almighty will not permit it, should not, will not!" very much excited indeed.

"But look at it, gentlemen," reasons Bob Withers; "we've got our last men in the field, ain't we? You both know as well as I, not a soul goes to the front if he can help it; neither of you gentlemen has the least idea of going, and

you don't catch me going, by George! Details for this, details for that, nothing but details. Then, it wouldn't do to talk this way about things before Union people, but we know how the soldiers are deserting, shoot them as fast as you please; but they will desert, sick of the war, want to get back to their sweet-hearts and wives. Lincoln elected for another four years, being whipped in all the fights, what's the use? they say. And it's more than enrolling officers dare to do, arresting them around here. Six enrolling officers shot down lately in my own knowledge by returned soldiers."

"Mr. Withers," begins Mr. Ellis, excitedly.

"People won't touch the paper-money except enough to pay taxes. Impressment is souring people, by George! a little too fast; they shoot them down, by George! I know one man won't take office as impressing officer!" Bob Withers continues.

"Mr. Withers, you really ought not," good little Mr. Ellis begins again, emphatically. Only more emphatically than he Mr. Withers proceeds:

"You hear it on every side, openly, 'I do this to keep out of the army,' 'do that to keep out of the army.' You may mow them down by whole ranks at a time for desertion, it does no good, not a bit. Then, look at the country people—returned soldiers, I suppose—breaking open people's houses by night, demanding of old men, even of women and children, their money, or blow their brains out, let alone taking every thing they can lay their hands on in open day. Then—"

"But what is the alternative, man?" Captain Simmons breaks in upon Mr. Withers, with energy enough to drown and overwhelm him. "Submission. Submission to wretched Abolitionists. Ab-o-lition-ists! gentlemen, people who make the negro our equal, actually associate with them. There is, gentlemen," adds Captain Simmons, with an air, "a new ism at the North, miscegenation," tucking a thumb in the arm-hole of his vest on each side as he speaks, "they call it, the abominable intermarriage—"

"How any man can suppose a holy God will—" vainly attempts Mr. Ellis to put in.

"Oh, shut up, Simmons!" interrupts Bob Withers, with violence in honest face and voice, triumphant over both. "Who do I see riding to water late of an evening, with a little milk-and-molasses chap on the pommel of his saddle before him? Oh, by George! Simmons, be consistent, man. Tuesday? No, it was Wednesday last—never mind what day it was. Simmons here will tell you who it was I saw driving out a-fishing in his buggy with a yellow woman—and she ain't even pretty, Simmons—dressed up as nice as you please, and that same little half-white chap—fine child, Simmons, as

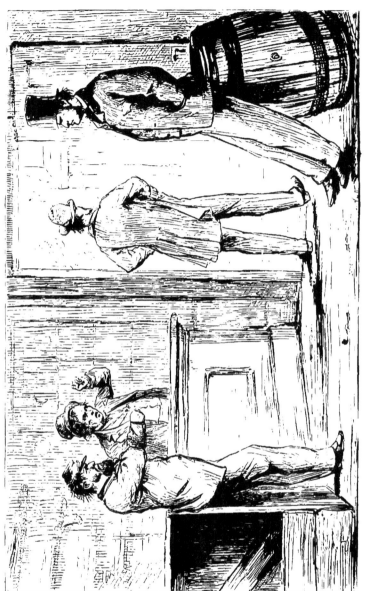

MISCEGENATION ARGUMENT.

I ever saw—in her lap. And it's been so for years—we all know that here in Somerville—does you actual credit in some respects, man. And you know whether or no you *did* send that oldest yellow boy of yours to Oberlin before the war began. But you ain't the only man South, only you are more steady to one, Simmons—steady, by George! to one."

"I consider your licentious remarks, Sir, as personal," says Captain Simmons, reddening and swelling like a turkey-cock.

"Don't intend any offense," Bob Withers rattles on; "but I appeal to Dr. Peel, dropped in just in time. No, I won't; Dr. Peel is one of the sinners, like Simmons and myself. But here's Mr. Ellis—regular church-member and all that, now, Mr. Ellis. Look here! if a man *will* live, it's all a matter of taste; my taste ain't that way myself; but if a man will live for years —you ain't the only one,·Simmons—with a negro woman, raise up a family—no ladies present, I believe—this is the point, Mr. Ellis—is it worse to do that illicitly, illegally, or legally— heh? As to this whole Secession, I always said it was only the grandest sort of a spree—a tireemendous spree, by George! Smash up in the end, see if there ain't."

"I consider, Sir, your whole strain of conversation as unworthy a Southern man," excited Mr. Ellis gets room to say at last. "Your sentiments are dangerous, Sir, dangerous for you to utter in this community, Sir. They will not be tolerated, Sir, not for an instant, Sir—"

There is a nervousness, an excitability of manner, a feverish motion of hands and feet and eyelids with Mr. Ellis which attracts more attention than what he says. But Bob Withers, in the very midst of Mr. Ellis's excited speech, after contemplating him curiously for a while, utters a loud and long-continued Whew! turned violently up in its ending, and with an "Oh, by George!" walks coolly out of the store.

"Pshaw! Withers must be drunk this morning." Captain Simmons explains in a dignified manner to Dr. Peel, after Mr. Ellis's excitement can be got a little under control. "Not a bad fellow poor Withers, only he will find when too late that"—and the Captain says it with tearful pathos—"it biteth like a serpent, it stingeth like an adder."

"The association of the whites and the blacks it was he was talking about?" asks Dr. Peel, magnificent as usual in broadcloth, hair-oil, and jewelry. "Sherman and Thomas have whipped Bob into *that*, have they? By George! gentlemen, we are getting along," says Dr. Peel, in condescending imitation of the person just departed. "How any man," Dr. Peel adds at last, adjusting the gold studs upon his snowy shirt-cuffs, "can look upon an intermingling of the races without loathing unutterable, horror beyond words, I can not imagine. It is done every where else in the world, which is one of the many reasons I have for looking upon our country as the purest and noblest on earth in that it so regards—what is it? — miscegenation." And there is moral force in the solemnity of Dr. Peel's oaths in continuance of the conversation.

"Speaking of marriage," says Captain Simmons, exceedingly malapropos, "come, Dr. Peel, tell us when it is to be?" he asks; for, on the strength of his recent public speeches, with very complimentary notices of the same in the *Star*,

N

Captain Simmons is on more familiar terms with Dr. Peel, splendid Dr. Peel, than of old. "When what is to be?" Dr. Peel brings his full front to bear on his questioner. Yes, splendid is the word, in his fine and perfectly-fitting broadcloth, sumptuous satin vest crossed with massive links of gold, diamond pin, finest and whitest linen, superb teeth, large, authoritative eyes.

"Oh, come, come, Doctor," says Captain Simmons, not drunk enough to be sufficiently a match in dignity with Dr. Peel, "every body in Somerville knows it. We all hope General Wright won't let the war prevent his having a real, old-fashioned, grand time of it. You and he have so many personal friends, too, in all this region. A regular handsome thing of it, Doctor. I haven't sat down to a good table for four years," adds Captain Simmons—who loves eating only less than he does drinking—mournfully and with watering lips.

It was because of the delicacy of the matter. Of course it was that. It could be nothing else, you know. All men about to be married are nervous and diffident. On this occasion Dr. Peel, for a man of his mould and metal, seemed for a time remarkably tensed and taken aback. But he extricates himself.

"Oh, nonsense, gentlemen," waving the matter off with a regal hand. "But I can tell you a little news worth your hearing."

Captain Simmons is wide awake in an instant. Mr. Ellis gets over his counter to be nearer the Doctor, listens to him with eager eyes. Yes, there is a pleasure. Bill Perkins finds more remuneration in that than in his five hundred Confederate dollars a month, in being the bearer of news, especially good news.

"Well, gentlemen," says Dr. Peel, with tantalizing dignity, "a friend has sent me a letter in advance of the mail. No mistake this time— Bragg's official dispatch. The Federals have made an attack upon Fort Fisher by land and by sea. Fort Fisher is the outwork, you know, of Wilmington. I am happy to say they have been repulsed. The attack was under command of Beast Butler—repulsed with terrible slaughter. They won't try that game again in a hurry."

"I knew it!" exclaims Mr. Ellis, with intense delight, rubbing together his almost trembling hands. "Our reverses were only for our trial, you know. The turning-point is reached at last. You will see that we will, from this out, have an uninterrupted career of victory. The loss of Wilmington, our last important port! Why, gentlemen, it would have ruined us! Had it been closed I would have given up our glorious cause as gone. But no; if Heaven be at times against us it is not unjust. The God who rules us could not, would not permit so terrible a wrong." And Mr. Ellis's eyes glitter and roll with an excitement almost painful to behold.

"No, as you say, Sir, they will not attempt that again."

"What will you bet of it?" replies Dr. Peel, suddenly, and with singular inconsistency. "Oh, pshaw! I am only joking, you know. Come, Captain Simmons, I know of course that you are not dry—you never are—but I am. Let us see if Staples has any of that whisky left. Won't you join us, Mr. Ellis? No? Ah, you don't know what is good for you! Good-morning! You will see Bragg's congratulatory address to his troops in the morning's paper. It's well that little sanctified chap don't touch liquor, Simmons," Dr. Peel remarks, with oaths, before they have well got out of the store. "If he did, he would be in the Lunatic Asylum in two months. He's the sort—he and Barker—they make raving Spiritualists, Abolitionists, Free Lovers, and the like, out of up North. Hurrah for old Bragg! he's up once more; wonder how long he'll stay so!"

But Mrs. Warner. The whirlwinds of the last few months have seized upon her, lifted her off her feet, given her the most wonderful twist that can be imagined. Even before the repulse of Banks on Red River she began to insist—inflicting that opinion upon the Doctor like a scourge—that we are whipped.

"We are whipped, Doctor Warner, whipped! and you know it as well as I, only you are too great a coward to say so. Sitting among people who are bragging about our success and all that stuff; going about with those old saddle-bags over your arm, never daring to contradict even that old fool of a Doctor Ginnis!"

The repulse of Banks quieted but did not wholly silence Mrs. Warner. If it did, the fall of Atlanta, of the Mobile forts, the re-election of Lincoln, and the capture of Savannah seized this Cassandra up again as in a Delphic blast. Poor Doctor Warner!

"We are whipped, Doctor Warner, whipped, whipped!" She insists upon it, as if perpetually contradicted by her husband therein—breakfast, dinner, supper, and upon their nuptial couch the Doctor goes to sleep almost every night to the same reiterated assertion.

So that when he ventures, the morning after Dr. Peel has electrified good Mr. Ellis with the Fort Fisher news, to read to his wife at breakfast the official tidings of the repulse of Butler from that outwork, Mrs. Warner justly regards it as a personal insult.

"It's all a lie, Doctor Warner, and you know it. You only read it to me to contradict me. Repulsed! and a man of your sense! I tell you we are whipped, whipped! and if you had half an idea of your own, or half a tongue to speak out like any other man what you really think, you would know it and say it. I've no patience with you! Even that meek, poor-spirited Mrs. Ret Roberts had energy enough to tell me so,

almost in so many words, when I was there last. They do say that brute of a Roberts treats her with cruelest unkindness. I'd like to see any man try that with me. Dare not go to hear Mr. Arthur, her own minister, preach these ever so many years; afraid of her husband, poor thing! Her very boy, with his bold eyes, growing up just like his father. Yes, whipped—if you only had sense to know it!"

So that when, not three weeks afterward, Dr. Warner reads to her, over his forgotten coffee and cold steak, the news, which has burst upon Somerville, almost deranging Mr. Ellis and extorting terrific blasphemy from Dr. Peel, that Fort Fisher has been captured, suddenly, unexpectedly captured, when we in Somerville did not even know that another attack upon it was in contemplation—when the Doctor reads the news in a cheerful tone to his wife what is his reward?

"And now, Dr. Warner, from this time out, I do hope you will hold your tongue. There you sat not one week ago, arguing, disputing that we were not whipped, reading all sorts of ridiculous stories about the Federals being repulsed! Can you look me straight in the eyes and tell me I didn't tell you it was a lie? You know you can't. You tire my very life out with your eternal contradiction. It's enough I take one view of a thing, it's the signal for you to take the other. I tell you, once for all, we are whipped; if you persist in saying we are not, I solemnly declare, if 'Ria and Bub were not here at table—be-have yourself, 'Ria—I could box your ears with my own hands. There's that man Neely; you know he was goose enough to buy up confiscated property right and left. The fact is, he got his hands so full of Confederate money with his swindling contracts he couldn't get rid of it any way. Well, Mrs. Ginnis herself told me yesterday that Dr. Peel had told her that Neely was moving heaven and earth to trade off all his property of that kind. He don't care what for so he can trade it off. As if he could find any body fool enough to take him up! That old Staples, too, they tell me he was a tailor once; any body who ever saw him walking up the street could tell that by the twist in his legs, his hair sticking out in every direction—they tell me he's making desperate efforts to do the same thing. All the rest of them, if the truth was known. You may thank me you didn't buy any. Of course you won't remember it, you never do any thing I say; but if I said to you once, don't touch confiscated property, I told you so ten thousand times. And there's that Brother Barker, too, as they call him. The man looks as if he had seen a ghost. Not that he doesn't richly deserve it; but the way his own members treat that poor creature is shameful. But you ought to see Dr. Ginnis; you know how he swells up sometimes; the man looks—I noticed him close when I was there yesterday—flabby. Always so full of talk too; and yesterday—you know I spent the day there—he didn't have one word to say. But I did. I ain't afraid if you are. I told them we were whipped, whipped! They said Barker and all their other preachers are urging it as a reason why the South should hold out, that, if the Confederacy is whipped, it is all over with their denomination—a blessed riddance I thought, though I didn't say so. The only thing Dr. Ginnis could say was some stuff about peace negotiations going on, as if—What is that you say? Rumored that the Confederacy has been recognized by France, England, and Spain? Stuff! You may be fool enough to believe it, I am not. If we are doing so well as you say, why ain't our money worth more—heh? There was that Bob Withers—Mr. Ginnis told me about it yesterday—went and tacked up a fifty-dollar new issue note on the wall of his office, just to see, he said, if any body would steal it—stealing as they are every thing else. Left it there all night. What do you think? Next morning he finds it there still, and a one-hundred-dollar bill stuck up beside it by somebody else. Oh, hold your tongue, Dr. Warner, I tell you we are whipped! That a man of your sense—"

Ye sparkling stars! Let us run.

Dr. Warner did. At least, did not run, he is altogether too fat for that, walked away in a disheveled condition of hair and attire; but he has the appearance of being blown about rather by gales genial, though violent, than by wintry blasts. And he meets upon the streets this bracing February morning of sixty-five—who does he not meet in fact?—old Mr. Adams, who hooks his long finger into the Doctor's buttonhole to tell him that he is sending a wagon with "a few things"—at least a hundred dollars' worth, by-the-by—up to help Silas Jewett's family, which Mr. Adams has had a hint are in a needy condition. Mrs. Jewett is sick, perhaps Dr. Warner will make out a little bill of such medicines to go in the wagon, as he, Dr. W., may think acceptable. Which the Doctor gladly promises to do, laughing off the earnest offer on the part of thin old Mr. Adams to pay for the same. Fact is, among the Union folks just now each lip is quivering so with Hail Columbia, each heart is so much a Star-Spangled Banner struggling so to unfold itself, that a man jumps at any way of showing his feelings.

He is still engaged with old Mr. Adams when Mrs. Smithers passes them, tall, red, savage, and cuts them both down with her eyes in passing as with a tomahawk—tut-traitors! But the Doctor happens next upon Bob Withers and Captain Simmons, Dr. Ginnis joining them while they stop to chat. Friendly? The most touching affection has sprung up toward Dr. Warner. In fact no Union man can appear on the streets now but some old Secession acquaintance is sure

to stop him with a "Why, how are you?" and a cordial shake of the hand, as if they were friends long parted, which in a sense is nothing but the fact.

Even grim Mr. Ferguson, having posted his Scrap-book up to date, is on the streets. Mr. Arthur, himself respectfully greeted on all sides these days, can not but smile when he sees Joe Staples suddenly recognize the Scotchman with pleased surprise, and, with hands years ago solemnly dedicated by Joe to the hanging of Mr. Ferguson, actually but respectfully seize upon that individual and draw him persuasively aside to "have a little talk." A talk in which Joe takes occasion to bewail the infatuation of Dr. Ginnis, Barker, Lamum, Wright, and others in the past, and to thank his stars that though "a man in my position would not dare openly and violently to oppose them, you know, Sir, I all along regretted their folly, and kept off from the whole thing just as much as I possibly could. And now, Mr. Ferguson, if any man in Somerville, as I have said a thousand times, has hard sense, you have, when do you think this thing is going to end? in confidence, now?"

Truth is, as the scale goes down with the one side it ascends with the other. The joy of the hour thrills every Union heart in Somerville, irradiating even the cellar of Alf Morgan. If things improve at the present rate it will require more vigor than little Mrs. Budd possesses to keep Alf much longer in bounds. Do what she can, he will hum Hail Columbia and whistle Yankee Doodle at his subterranean shoe-making. The foolish fellow actually has a Union flag down there "to feel of," he says, for it is too dark in his hole to see it.

Mr. Arthur can not refrain from going up into Mr. Ferguson's room to have a laugh over matters; for we Union people in Somerville feel a deal more like laughing these days than we used to do. More roses in Mrs. Budd's cheeks now than for years past, as Jem says.

"Every Union man tells me the same," Mr. Arthur says, "and I know it is true of myself. People that haven't spoken to you for years, people that have cursed you, people that have been scarce restrained by the Hand that withheld Saul from the murder of David from killing you, will now hardly let you get along the streets for greetings. You notice how it is at Sunday-school and church, how they are sending back their children and coming back themselves? Others, I dare say, if shame would let them. Not Mr. Ellis though—he is grummer, gruffer, more distant than ever. I don't know how many who voted against Secession, but went into it and became the most bitter, have taken occasion to remind me, and every body else, I suppose, of their original ground; though once they bewailed having voted for the Union as the greatest of their shortcomings."

THE TEST OF CONFEDERATE MONEY.

"It is only because the frogs, lice, flies, murrain, boils, hail, locusts, thick darkness have come upon them, as upon the Egyptians," says the stony Scotchman. "You know as well as I in each interval of disaster these people are as infatuated as ever. I would not be surprised if the hand of God is lifted from them yet again. with the same result. Perhaps when the last plague, the very death of the first-born, has befallen, even Ellis and his like may be convinced.

I never thought that under the New Testament Dispensation—so deep into it too—in such a Christian land as this also—there could be such a revival of the Mosaic Dispensation, as it were. I tell you, Mr. Arthur," continued the Scotchman, solemnly, "when I consider the awful judgments of Jehovah—the same God who sent the Deluge, who destroyed the Cities of the Plain, who slew the Canaanites, who dealt so terribly with the Hebrews, upon this land during this fearful war—I tremble while I adore. Even though He be merciful in Jesus Christ, He is a just God still. This is the new dispensation, I know; but His most terrible manifestation of wrath against sin is yet to be made—the destruction of this globe by fire. The Pope and the Turk are to fall in sixty-six, are they? The Apostle says there are many Antichrists; who knows what awful times may be in reserve for England, and Scotland even, to say nothing of other parts of the world, for who of you here had before supposed that Slavery was an Antichrist which had to go down in fire and blood and earthquake, as well as the Pope?

"Hold on a moment!" Mr. Ferguson adds, to his friend, at last rising to leave. "I want to prove to you that the universal insubordination all through the Confederacy, which all the papers are bewailing so, is an inevitable fruit of the very principle of Secession. It struck so effective a blow at the very idea of Law, Order, Government, as to kill that vital thing even for their own use. Besides, I want to show you from my Scrap-book that no two men South, however devoted to Secession, can agree on any one thing under Secession. Truth, you observe, is one; while Falsehood is as millionfold as the shifting clouds. So sure as one man advances his opinions upon foreign intervention, employment of negroes in the army—whatever it is, another is sure to start up and vehemently dispute it. It is like the contentions of infidels—"

But if Mr. Arthur can listen to such treason we can not.

---

## CHAPTER XXIII.

If ever a man was justifiable in flying to the flowing bowl to-night surely that man is Alonzo Wright. True, he has made solemn oath not to take another drop, Christmas having witnessed his last awful frolic, with the death of a favorite negro man somehow mixed up in its frantic festivities, until next Fourth of July, unless, Mr. Wright most carefully stipulates in his vow, we gain our independence before then; in which latter case he, Tim Lamum, Dr. Peel, Bob Withers, and a few other like spirits, are solemnly pledged to each other to have about the greatest time of it yet known on earth; Captain Richard

MR. WRIGHT AT HOME.

Simmons moving and assisting unanimously to carry said proviso.

A dozen times has Mr. Wright assured Anne, hanging with silent importunity upon his arm on this as well as every other occasion of his leaving home for Somerville, that he will not taste, touch, smell a drop, not even go on the side of the street where the grocery is. For Mr. Wright is far from being an austere father. Anne has grown up in his eyes the fairest and loveliest and most thoroughly accomplished of women. There is a droop in her large blue eyes, a wave and fall in her fair hair, a mould of her form, an altogether indescribable sweetness in manner and tone which would attach any father in the world. In addition to her being his only child and chiefest companion, she is her dead mother over again. Very often, indeed, of evenings, when Anne sits at the piano, her fingers straying over the keys from one piece to another, singing half a song here, another half there, breaking out in some brilliant bravura, or idling through the tangles of a schottiche, does her father sit, cigar in mouth, looking at and loving her with all the admiration and love of his soul. A rather small, light-complexioned man is Mr. Wright, but your big burly people never feel most. It is in the slight-built organizations you find fire and force; leanness and ferocity are coupled in the wild-cat, vivacity and venom in viper and rattlesnake.

In fact, this Anne at least is "all the world to" her father. At the head of his table; her graceful form about the house all day in diligent housekeeping; persuading and remonstrating with the servants, who serve the family wondrous well under the double impulse of mortal terror of "Mas 'Lonz," on the one side, and devoted attachment to "Missanny," as they call her, on the other; even when Dr. Peel or other company are being entertained in the parlor, Mr. Wright, proudly conscious of Anne from the moment he awakes in the morning till he kicks off his boots at night, can join in whatever denunciation of the Yankees is going on between him and the gentleman with whom he is conversing, and he keenly alive all the time to the ever-varying loveliness of Anne on the other side of the room.

Why conceal these bitterest pangs of remorse which give such intensity to Mr. Wright's paternal affection? Yes, Anne is like her mother, most like that mother when at her loveliest; and there were hushed whispers in the community in which Mr. Wright lived at the time of his wife's death, vague rumors from family servants, and from friends who prepared the body for burial, of bruises and marks. Let us say no more about it where nothing certain is known. No man knows better than Mr. Wright that he is a devil incarnate in his cups, and the demoniac love of liquor which possesses the man is restrained only by his love for his daughter, and mortal dread of what he may do to her in some moment of intoxication.

And yet, reasoning with thousands of other Secessionists at the same instant, if ever a man was justifiable, every thing to the contrary notwithstanding, in drowning his sorrows in the bowl to-night that man is Alonzo Wright. As an almost universal rule, even those of the Secession leaders, in the army and out of it, who never drank before, are taking to drinking now. As to those who have drunk hard all along, these do nothing else now at all.

"Why, look at it, gentlemen," says Captain Richard Simmons, who sits to-night on the counter of the grocery, his left arm around a pillar, from which hang the fly-specked festoons of red, white, yellow, and blue paper cut into meshes adorning the ceiling, expressing, for Tim Lamum, who sits dead drunk in an adjoining arm-chair, and for Bob Withers, who smokes in silence, and for Dr. Peel, whose speech is exclusively oaths, and for Alonzo Wright, who is brooding over the times, seated on the card-table, his slouched hat down over his eyes, the painful feelings of all.

"Only permit your eyes to range over the situation, as Lamum says in the *Star*. A Yankee, gentlemen, Lamum is," adds Captain Simmons, impressively. "It may be a weakness inherent in my nature; I've tried to master it again and yet again. I will be frank with you; I can not. My soul abhors a Yankee. Never

mind about his professed devotion to the Confederacy. A lifetime spent in fiercest ardor for it would not satisfy me. My nature revolts from a Yankee. There's old Neely—a Yankee schoolmaster! Who so loud and strong for the South? Insisting on shaking my hand every time we met over our glorious victories. I pledge you my word of honor, gentlemen, I always went straight to my room at Staples's and washed my hands with soap every time. Natural antipathies? For one, gentlemen, I loathe, abominate, detest, execrate—"

"Oh, hold your horses, Simmons, by George! who knows? You may be one yourself. Peddled tin ware for years for what we know. Very likely all your talk only a Yankee trick to throw us off."

"If it is by such buffoonery, Bob Withers, you seek to divert our minds in this dark hour of our country's distress your remarks are beneath, because doubly beneath, my notice. Charleston fallen, gentlemen!" continues Captain Simmons, dismissing Mr. Withers from existence by a slow wave of his hand. "I can not realize it. The fact is, it is a thing which can not *be* realized. I can imagine Wilmington fallen. I do not deny that Petersburg and Richmond are polluted by feet I never dreamed would tread them. That General Lee has surrendered, though it was infinitely worse than death to me, I can because I must believe. Nor do I refuse to acknowledge that Mobile is occupied; that Johnston, whom I revered next to Lee and Davis, has also surrendered. Dick Taylor's surrender smites us to-day like the hand of fate. But Charleston! From every other consideration my soul reverts to Charleston. I can *not* realize it, gentlemen. I may succeed in some degree by the time I have retired at night, but the first thing I know I find myself sitting bolt upright in bed, during the silent watches of the midnight hour, in a cold sweat, and exclaiming, 'By Him who made me, it is not, must not, shall not, can not be so! Charleston? C-h-a-r-l-es-ton! Impossible!'"

"Why not get up a theory, Simmons?" says Dr. Peel, scrupulously neat in attire, while the rest are disordered in apparel to the last degree; in the highest spirits, whether from liquor or not, though he does not show any signs of intoxication other than that, while his comrades, Bob Withers excepted, can not drink enough to float them even to ordinary water-mark. "You proved to us, Simmons, in this very room that Charleston, Wilmington, Petersburg, and Richmond, if evacuated, would only be so in pursuance of Lee's new plan of abandoning the seacoast and concentrating in the interior—a new plan, splendid plan. When Lee surrendered you were ready for that. Lee always had a reason for what he did. Lee had sent all his veterans to Johnston, and surrendered as a consummate *ruse!* Come, Captain, you have never wanted for a theory before; make haste. Where is your inventive faculty? Some brilliant scheme, if we only knew what it was, behind all this news you are wailing over." And Dr. Peel flashes his white teeth upon him, in singular spirits considering the times.

"Sir," replies Captain Simmons, with oracular dignity, "I wait to hear from President Davis. I can see deep meaning in the consummate silence of that Washington of our glorious revolution."

"You can? By George, I can't! What is the use of being a drove of geese *still*, gentlemen?"

It is Bob Withers who propounds the question, rising from his seat to do it. Very much inflamed is Bob's face these trying times, from excessive weeping, perhaps. But it is an honest, sensible, good-humored, Bacchus-like face, too.

"I always looked on the thing as a big spree, and you know I always said so. I knew it was all wrong from the start, ruinous and wrong as any thing gets to be in this world, a tremendous frolic. We all went into it. Of course I wasn't the man to stay behind. It was the wildest, most expensive, biggest spree you ever saw, and I pitched in. Yes, and would do it again tomorrow if it was to do over again; never backed out when half a dozen fellows invited me to go in. When the whole South got drunk, think I'm going to keep sober? But the smash up has come at last—it *will* come. Broken windows and crockery and tables to pay for, headache, empty purse, black eyes, men killed. But wasn't it the grandest blow out! But I knew all along it *was* a spree, always said so; they could never humbug me, by George! with their lies. No, Sir-ree, bob!"

"There is this one consolation, gentlemen," remarks Captain Simmons, more Chesterfieldian the drunker he gets, with a solemn air, and waving gracefully aside the volatility of their Mercutio—"one consolation which fills my nature in this hour of darkness with profound satisfaction—the killing of Abraham Lincoln. Had I an offspring I would have him baptized Booth Simmons. Even in my pangs of bitterest mortification at the failure, if failure it is, of our beloved Confederacy, I say to myself, 'Captain Simmons, Captain Simmons, you forget that Lincoln the tyrant is at this moment in eternal perdition. Like the balm of some place of which I was instructed by pious parents—Gilead I think is the name—the reflection soothes, at least for the moment, the anguish of my spirit."

"The last place I would think you would wish Lincoln to go to, Simmons," remarks Dr. Peel, with great surprise.

"Exactly what I was going to say, Doctor, by George!" puts in Bob Withers.

"May I request an explanation, gentlemen?" asks Captain Simmons, with his stateliest air.

"'I would think you would much rather he had gone to heaven. You have hated him so much here one would suppose you would regret being associated eternally with him hereafter," replies Dr. Peel, with Mr. Withers's cordial assent.

"If there be a thing which disgusts me more than all besides with inebriety," says Captain Simmons, with slow and unspeakable scorn, "it is the reckless impiety and irreligion too often connected with it. No merit in myself, seeing my early advantages, my inculcated habit of worshiping from earliest infancy in the sanctuary. Be drunkards, gentlemen, if you must," adds Captain Simmons, with impressive solemnity, "but not scoffers—no, not scoffers. ''Tis the voice of the scoffer, I hear him complain.' Not exactly that, but something to that effect was instilled—"

"We respect your piety, Simmons," interrupts Dr. Peel. "It *is* fully equal to that of Parson Barker, at least; he told me to-day that it was not so much the hand of Booth as the hand of God. His only regret, he says, is that Booth did not kill him on the day of his inauguration. Dozens of church-members—lying Sam Peters, Dr. Ginnis, and the like—say they are glad of the assassination, regret that it failed in the case of Seward, hope the good work will go on. Even that little saint, Ellis, the sincerest and best of them all, got almost drunk with joy over it." From this statement, however, the writer of these lines distinctly withholds his belief.

Let us step out of this choice set of companions, only for a moment, to say a word as to the way in which the killing of Mr. Lincoln was received in Somerville.

There is Jem Budd. When Staples, every hair on end, rushes into Jem's shop and announces the glorious news, that dirty-faced artisan pauses long enough, with suspended file, to say, "Ah!" with genuine surprise; to add immediately after, as he continues his filing at the gun-barrel clenched in the vice before him, "Just what I always said." It is but history to record, however, that when Dr. Warner drops in a moment after to ask after Mrs. Budd's very precarious health, and to tell Jem—of course that was altogether a secondary motive—the news of the surrender of General Lee, which comes by the same mail, but which Staples had neglected to mention, the gun-smith stops altogether from his work, and, adding largely to the darkness of his nose by a long reflective rub thereof with his forefinger, has genuine joy in his eyes while he says, "Precisely so, Doctor; what I always thought."

The fact is, no sentiment, whatever it was, whether Union or Secession, has ever been advanced in Jem's hearing since the war began which has not met in Jem a ready assent. Like hundreds of thousands of others at the South during this period, Jem has but put in practice Talleyrand's famous maxim—that words were given to us to enable us to conceal our thoughts.

There is Mr. Ferguson, too. Very eagerly he pastes in the dispatch announcing the assassination, with every thing relating to it, but as the grandest of all the lies, the very blossoming and perfection of the lies of the period. Only his sincere affection for Mr. Arthur will afford him patience with the unaffected belief that gentleman. gives to the news from the outset. He even condescends, the Scotchman, to argue with his friend. Mr. Lincoln would have been assassinated in Richmond if at all. How could he have been killed in a crowded theatre, and the murderer escape? Besides, it is known that Mr. Lincoln is a member of the Presbyterian Church, and consequently no attendant at theatres. Can not Mr. Arthur see that the news is manufactured to accompany and neutralize the tidings of Lee's surrender? The trick is too transparent.

A tremendous amount of evidence it took to convince us Secessionists that Vicksburg had fallen, and all the rest; we do not want to believe it, you observe, therefore we won't. Alas, we should all be descended from the same Adam! But the amount of evidence it required to satisfy us Union people that Burnside was repulsed on the Rappahannock and the like is incredible. If the heart would not get so dreadfully in the way of the head!

As wide apart as Heaven and Hades are the brutal rejoicings of red-faced Mrs. Smithers and the sincere regrets of Mrs. Bowles over the same event. Not even Mrs. Smithers's deliberate and permanent sentiment, let us hope.

"I regret it, Alice dear, even more than I would deplore the fact of General Lee's surrender, if such preposterous news should prove true, which I can not for one instant believe. I thank God the miserable wretch who did the dreadful deed was no South Carolinian—a Yankee, I am told, or from some State bordering thereupon. For Mr. Lincoln you well know my unspeakable loathing, but I would rather be even his wife than the wife of his assassin. Read on, Alice." For Mrs. Bowles has stopped her daughter in her reading of the paper to say that much.

"Poor dear Mrs. Bowles! Heaven knows I never loved her so much in all our long, long knowledge of each other as I do now," is Mrs. Sorel's frequent remark of her to Mr. Arthur. "She has not been in my house for years, nor I in hers, lest I should distress her with my presence, as you know. She regards me with—with aversion, or rather horrified amazement, because I can not believe with her in Secession. I have no feeling for her—how could I have?—but one of love and pity. Alice told me about her when she was here last, reduced to a shadow, pale and

fragile as a flower, her hair all white now with mental distress, yet quiet and refined and still. I tell you, Mr. Arthur," adds placid Mrs. Sorel, herself the counterpart of the one she is describing, and with warmth, "I am an old woman now. I once lived in as elevated though plain a circle as this country possesses, but I never saw a human being who came so near my ideal of a perfect Christian lady as Mrs. Alice Bowles. I see what you are thinking about," she adds, with a smile, to Mr. Arthur, who flushes over face and ears at her glance. "Yes, and you will be a most fortunate man, as the phrase runs, if you succeed there. Alice has something of her father's obstinacy—willfulness you would prefer having it called; is of stronger character than her mother; will have all her mother's sweetness if she has all her mother's amount of trial. discipline, sorrow."

"Do you think, Mrs. Sorel," begins Mr. Arthur, eagerly—"do you imagine there is any hope for me? Her mother has such horror of my Union opinions I no longer even enter the house. Alice, you know, has long since ceased to attend church. She is so engaged in her school, too, I never see her."

"I have never asked Alice," says Mrs. Sorel, with a smile. "but I do not think you need despair. Wait till the war is over. You two are undergoing discipline which is good for you both—"

"That abominable school," breaks in her impulsive friend. "The idea of a woman who would adorn a throne teaching! And teaching such children as we have in Somerville! Wasting her health."

"She is doing no such thing. I never saw her looking more beautiful in my life than when she was here on that last Saturday. Propriety requires that, under all the painful circumstances, painful and peculiar circumstances of the case, she should cease to attend your church. Besides, you do not realize, Sir," adds Mrs. Sorel, very gravely indeed, "how poor, how very poor Mrs. Bowles has become. Alice is doing, and doing eagerly and well, her simple duty in supporting her mother. And it is just the discipline Alice needs to qualify her for the new times before us."

"New? Yes, the bran-new, the happy, the glorious times before us!" says Mr. Arthur, with almost boyish enthusiasm. "I tell you, Mrs. Sorel, we are entering on such an epoch in the history of America as even that blessed old Bishop Berkeley never dreamed of when he prophesied of the star of empire centuries ago. Slavery and Secession forever rooted out, one glorious flag from the Arctic circle to the equator, purified by our terrible ordeal, who can tell? That poor Mr. Barker may be in part right at last—ours may be the great millennial nation! I tell you, Robby," and Mr. Arthur; excited by his national, and of course without reference to his individual prospects regarding Alice, claps that sedate young gentleman on the shoulder, "we will have grand times, won't we?"

"When Mr. Brooks is back for good? Yes," adds that sober youth, "and I know the time ain't far off. People don't ask me these days how that Abolitionist Arthur comes on, nor yell at me and throw rocks. Only last time I was in town Mr. Staples stopped me to shake hands and ask after you all. He was as kind as you please, told me just to let *him* know if his son Joe ever said a thing out of the way to me, that was all. Humph, I saw Dr. Ginnis go all the way over the street to stop Mr. Ferguson, and insisted on shaking hands, which it ain't easy to get Mr. Ferguson to do with any body; and I've heard Dr. Ginnis tell Jem Budd, long ago, that that old traitor of a Scotch Abolitionist ought to be hung high as Haman."

"That will do, Robby," interrupts his mother, checking with uplifted hand Robby's eager experiences. "I am too old for all this, Mr. Arthur. It bewilders me. Charleston and Columbia, the whole of my native State, in fact, so terribly scourged! You must excuse me—we South Carolinians can not help it. I smile at Mrs. Bowles, and am just as foolish about the State as she. I don't like to hear or talk or think about it. The Judge of all the earth will do right."

And it is just this that more than bewilders good Mrs. Bowles too. The long holding out of Charleston elevated it and South Carolina to even a degree above her already-intense idolatry of them. She regarded the arrival of Sherman at Savannah, and his setting out upon his march into South Carolina without one particle of apprehension; with joy rather. Napoleon never had, in the fullest tide of his victories, so calm, so confident, so absolutely exultant a sense of approaching success in a battle. So surely as the sun shone, so surely as South Carolina was South Carolina, would the insulting foe meet on its soil with terrible defeat. Mrs. Bowles could see the hand of God in it:

"Your dear native State, Alice, and mine began this great revolution, and will end it. Heaven has permitted a Federal army to get to the State by an unexpected military movement, by almost a miracle, for this purpose. How little does that man Sherman think it! I thank God from my soul. Who of us could have arranged, or even have imagined it all so well? People will flock for generations to South Carolina as they now do to Waterloo, or as I am told they sometimes do to Yorktown there in Virginia. That the Thermopylæ of our revolution should be there! I loved the State before; henceforth every grain of its sand, the leaves of its every tree are dear to me; every one born on its dear surface is to me dearer than relatives. Remember it, Alice—henceforth let your own South Carolina—how musical the very name!—be next with you to heaven and God!" and the thin, pale, classic face glows with enthusiasm. "You know I told you, Alice, all the two weeks during which we had those rumors of the capture of Sherman in Georgia, I knew—hoped, at least, it could not be true. South Carolina, I felt, was to be the hallowed spot."

"The people of Savannah do not seem to be as patriotic," begins Alice.

"Actually admitting the Federals without burning their cotton, receiving food at their hands. That illustrates what I am saying," Mrs. Bowles interrupts Alice, with enthusiasm; "do you not see it is as a foil to Charleston? The very contrast between Georgia and our State, between Savannah and Charleston, will show the world what South Carolina is. To think the two States are actually contiguous!"

How can Mrs. Bowles's eager expectation of the news of the great battle be described? Most seriously did Alice tremble for her mother's very mind. No other topic was on her mother's lips when they are sewing together on Saturdays and by night. No other thought in her mind while alone, Alice teaching in the little front office. Waking often during the night at every distant sound, fancying the arrival of the news in every distant cry, in every footstep passing. Even Rutledge Bowles is comparatively forgotten, though in every prayer for him—and they ascend as from an ever-burning altar—more than for his health, more than for his life even, is it her supplication that, if it please God, Rutledge Bowles may have part in the great victory. Better, far better his death on that glorious field than that he should be absent from it!

How describe the steady arrival of the news of Sherman's unopposed march across the State!

"They are gathering, concentrating the army somewhere further north in the State to make the victory complete and final!" she explains to Alice, repeating it over and over. Alice breaks the fall of Charleston to her tremblingly as she would the death of a dear friend.

"Only evacuating it, child, for a few days, so little do you understand of military matters. You see, they wish to swell the army with its garrison, so as to leave not one man of the Federal army to escape death or capture—yes, capture. I pray God our army may be merciful in the hour of its great triumph; their awful wrongs are enough to exasperate, Heaven knows; but in the moment of victory the brave are ever merciful. Only a few days, dear, and we shall hear of the reoccupation of Charleston after the victory. Let me see the map again. Columbia? Yes, Columbia—see if I am not a true prophet—Columbia is about the centre of the State. I would like the victory to be there." And Alice almost shudders at the light in her mother's eye, the spot of red in her cheek, the uncertain motion of her thin white hand about her forehead.

Ah, that wandering of the hand about the edges of the smooth white hair, rubbing the brow, with the thoughtful eyes fixed absently on book, or sewing, lying neglected in the lap. As Dr. Warner has told Alice and Mrs. Bowles herself many, very many times, the poor lady is wearing herself literally to a shadow by her intense excitement. Alice and the Doctor do all they can.

"Thank you, Dr. Warner; don't be foolish, Alice. I need no medicine or rest. I never felt better in my life; hardly ever felt so well. When it comes, Alice, bring me the accounts of the victory—that will be the best medicine in the world; next to hearing it from Rutledge Bowles I want to have it first from your lips, Alice." But the poor frail hand wanders about the forehead, and Alice clasps it in hers, and kisses her mother there, and bursts into tears.

"What a fond, foolish creature you are, Alice?" says her mother, half indignantly. "You are getting positively nervous and morbid, confining yourself so to that odious school. You sew too steadily."

"But mother, dear mamma," ventures Alice, Dr. Warner being there to back her, "suppose, after all, the Federals should not be whipped?"

"You cowardly croaker," says Mrs. Bowles, gently but pityingly. "But I don't blame you, at least in this case. There has been no battle upon the soil of South Carolina yet—a skirmish or two, perhaps, but no battle for you to judge by. I can not say," remarks Mrs. Bowles, with displeasure, "that your conduct, Alice, has at all satisfied me since this revolution began. I regret to speak so in the presence of another, but it is so. I can not, I do not understand it. It probably is your sewing too closely, the confinement in your school, the absence of Rutledge Bowles, our altered fortunes. Wait, you poor spirited thing, till our independence is secured." Her mother adds, with loving hand on her daughter's head: "If Rutledge Bowles consents we will then return to Charleston. The change will do both of us good."

Poor Alice! Only the day before, seeing from the window of her school-room Mr. Ellis going up the front walk, apparently on a visit to her mother, in the impulse of the moment she had run out and arrested his steps.

"Oh, Mr. Ellis!" she said, "how are you? And how is Mrs. Ellis and the children?"

"As well as usual, Miss Alice," replies Mr. Ellis, somewhat surprised at her manner, and perceiving that she has something more to say.

"Will you excuse me, Mr. Ellis?" she adds, the color flushing her cheek; "but mamma is very much excited and nervous. Please say nothing to confirm her in her delusion. I do not exactly mean that. Please try and prepare her for any disappointment in store for her." And,

in her affection for her mother, Alice looks at him with the imploring eyes of a child.

"Delusion? Disappointment?" Mr. Ellis repeats the words, the strange light kindling in his eyes. "What can you mean?" And seeing her mother at the door, Alice can only murmur no explanation at all, and retreat to her school-room, leaving Mr. Ellis to proceed upon his visit.

It is as she expected. When she joins her mother a few hours after, it is to find her flushed with fresh certainty and enthusiasm of Confederate success, rather South Carolinian success.

"You are always croaking so, Alice," says Mrs. Bowles, with sparkling eyes, "as almost to affect my spirits. Good Mr. Ellis has spent an hour with me to-day. He confirms my utmost expectations of the speedy success of our cause. You can not tell how perfectly he has explained away all our late reverses. He has been informed beyond all question that Europe will intervene very, very soon now; by next mail we will hear. It is official, he says. Why, Alice, you know what a devotedly pious man Mr. Ellis is; and he told me that it was as impossible, if we do our duty, to defeat the Confederate cause as it was to dethrone the Almighty himself." And a vast deal more to the same effect.

Who can describe it? Steadily as the footfall of death to the dying comes the news that Sherman has swept across the State of South Carolina, is in possession of Fayetteville, North Carolina. No glorious Confederate victory in South Carolina. No serious fighting. Not the consolation even of a glorious defeat.

With positions singularly reversed, Alice watches and cares for Mrs. Bowles almost as a fond mother with an ailing child. Never more respectful and reverent to that mother than now. Mrs. Bowles has less and yet less to say with each passing day, bewildered, exhausted.

"Whatever our Heavenly Father thinks best," she says, with the hand, thinner every hour, wandering more frequently about the sunken temples, smoothing continually the hair whitening toward the hue of the garment of the saints in light. With what infinite affection does Alice minister to her wants, careful to conceal her assiduity, weeping during the watches of the night. For her mother's sake she could almost wish the Confederate cause to succeed; almost, not quite.

"Would you not like Mrs. Sorel to call and see you? She would like to so much, mamma; and you were girls together, you know," asks Alice the day she has read to her mother of the fall of Richmond. Perhaps the moment was ill chosen.

"No, my dear," replies Mrs. Bowles, decidedly though slowly, and with the trembling fingers hovering about her forehead. "We differ so widely upon the matter of deepest interest to me on earth. I love Mrs. Sorel dearly, but would rather not. I care for nothing now but Rutledge Bowles and yourself, for nothing in all the world."

And so rolls away the time with us in Somerville. As each disaster arrives, we indignantly deny and scout it as long as we possibly can; only it is pitiful, toward the last, how we only expect disastrous news, and take it with scarcely a perceptible wince, like an animal used to beating, pitiful to see.

Oh, may the God that rules the eternal hereafter as well as the present, deal out from His just bar fitting penalty to the accursed demagogues North and South who *deluded* the South into its frantic folly of Secession! At least, thanks be to God, that to each one of them will be dealt according to his deeds. Alas, may there not be an unhallowed satisfaction even in knowing and repeating the fact, "Vengeance is mine, I will repay, saith the Lord?" Nearly five years now since we were all steeped in the gall; its bitterness is saturating the very soul.

However, if, like a swamp full of frogs, all good Secessionists in Somerville, Dr. Ginnis, as the biggest of the band, and with the deepest base, leading the croak, we are all croaking in inharmonious concert, there is this refrain in which we all fall back:

"Live under Federal rule? Stay in the country if the Yankees do subjugate it? I will go to Mexico first, live in South America, die first!" And so to the possibility, in any case, of existing as individuals under that accursed flag again, we all fall into full chorus, till earth and heaven ring again, "Never, never, never!"

"What amuses me most in you pious people, Simmons," says Dr. Peel, in continuance of his conversation with that exceedingly dignified and intoxicated gentleman, "is the desperate way you are trying—Barker, Ellis, Ginnis, Peters; in fact, all of you, good, genuine, praying Secessionists—to hold on to Christianity."

Never more carefully dressed in his life, bejeweled until some new light is perpetually flashing, with every motion, from hand and bosom, essenced until even the strong odors of the grocery are subjugated thereby, Dr. Peel's fine broadcloth and snowy linen seem radiant with his own exuberant spirits. Overflowing with life and conviviality, his remarks are almost exclusively oaths of as prolific and varied an abundance as the sparks of a fire-work, and as impossible to reproduce in any description thereof. From his heart of hearts Captain Simmons regards the Doctor as by far the most magnificent specimen of a genuine Southern man he has ever met; proud to be seen with him, never weary of quoting his brilliant speeches. And this is the very general opinion of Somerville. Bob Withers has very often remarked: "Dr. Peel? Well, yes. By George! Oh, hang it! Somehow I can't stand Dr. Peel!" And there is considerable mutual shyness between the two; but nobody minds Bob.

"Yes, hang on to their Christianity. That," says Dr. Peel, with impressive profanity, "seems to be the main business of you pious trained ones these days, Simmons. There is Mr. Ellis, insisting and insisting on the hand of God in this and the hand of God in that, over and over, nervous and trembling, like a school-boy afraid of forgetting his lesson. But Brother Barker's the man for my money. Preach! What a chance a pulpit and a Sunday gives a man, with a Bible open before him, of pitching into the Yankees! Colonel Ret Roberts is tame to Barker. But the praying! Twice every Sunday; two prayer-meetings during the week for the success of the Confederacy; opening every public meeting with prayer; to say nothing of our doings up there in the old C. C. If that poor fellow hasn't done his duty in cursing the Yankees, I'm mistaken. People have said I am a pretty hard swearer: for hard, strong, steady, desperate, raving, red-hot pouring it into the Federals in a religious fashion—blasphemy they would call it in me—I give it up to the Parson. He has got Christianity and the Confederacy so twisted together he can't separate the two to save his life. Hardly a verse in your mammy's Bible, Simmons, but these political preachers have used to prove the success of our glorious cause by. We must *not* permit the disasters of the times to discourage our belief in Christianity, brethren. Christianity is *not* dead, my hearers, Barker is repeating, I'm told, in every sermon and in every conversation, showing how desperately hard it is to believe in any part of Scripture if all it says about slavery as a divine ordinance prove false."

"Now there is Parson Arthur," begins Bob Withers, upon whom any audience to Dr. Peel's exuberant conversation has devolved, for Mr. Wright being apparently asleep under his slouched hat, and Captain Simmons, half-humming, half-hiccuping, forgetful of his usual courtesy, what he can remember of a Sabbath-school hymn learned in his earliest childhood.

"Arthur!" breaks in Dr. Peel, with a sudden change of tone and manner, and even experienced Bob Withers opens his eyes at the unexpected and awful way in which his companion heaps imprecations upon that individual.

Could it have been owing to a visit made by Mr. Arthur to Dr. Peel not two hours before this? The two men had scarcely ever met. Truth to say, the minister had often seen passing along the streets, sitting on counters of stores into which he had dropped to make purchases, swearing and gesticulating in knots upon the sidewalk, the superb Southern gentleman in question. Nor did he withhold a certain admiration we all give to Health, in its full development in any thing, from the noble proportions, full chest, commanding bearing of the man. He had fancied that so Hercules was

imagined by the old pagan poets—the bold pro-
tuberant brow, the massy countenance with its
aureole of curly black hair and beard, and large
black eyes, open and fearless. There was a full
life in the man, a force and a sway; a sort of
Assyrian power, even, in the costly adornments
of Dr. Peel, which wonderfully arrested the attention of the minister, interested, almost fascinated, while it repelled him, himself being
of so unlike a type. But never had they ex-
changed a syllable—Mr. Arthur doubly shy of
one whom he knew to have perhaps as thoroughly denounced him on political grounds as
any one—even Mrs. Smithers or Mrs. Warner—
in Somerville.

It was but natural in Dr. Peel, then, that he
should be surprised, on the occasion alluded to,
when Mr. Arthur, with scarce a preliminary knock
at the door of his room at Staples's Hotel, walked in that evening after supper.

"I have called in but for a moment," remarked the visitor, with his hat upon his head, and
in a tone and with a manner totally unlike his
style of address to any other gentleman in Somerville; "and but to make one syllable of remark to you."

Dr. Peel rises involuntarily from the table at
which he is seated writing, the first astonishment on his bold face giving swift place under
the eye and bearing of his visitor to a manner
singularly like that worn by him during all his
intercourse with Lieutenant Ravenel in the same
apartment.

"You know me, you know my sentiments,
you know my exact position," says Mr. Arthur,
coldly and slowly. "I have been informed by
Colonel Brooks of yours. The instant he learned fully who you were he hastened to this place
at the peril of his life—peril of his life from both
sides. He has left me only a moment ago. I
am here now. I would have got to you to-night,
wherever you were, if I had died for it. I
know your case fully, exactly, completely,"
continues Mr. Arthur, the tone and manner
conveying more meaning than the words. "I
speak to you partly on behalf of Colonel Brooks.
I would have spoken to you on my own behalf.
I came to tell you that I know every thing. I
am the only person in this region that does. I
came to say to you I can not help your being
here. I would give millions it were not so if I
could. Under all the circumstances, I can not
order you to leave. I wish I could. But, understand me perfectly, I intend keeping the
closest watch upon you I possibly can. The instant you step out of your—your place, I will
take necessary means to stop you. That is all.
You must not understand that I do not in a
certain sense—a certain sense," repeats Mr. Arthur, with peculiar emphasis—"pity you." The
visitor is evidently touched by the indescribable
and total change in Dr. Peel's manner as he

stands before him. "That is all. You are safe
up to a certain point. Take care."

And the preacher has left the room as suddenly, yet as coolly too, as he entered it, leaving
Dr. Peel, who has not even attempted to speak,
wilted down behind him. Yes, wilted down is
the word, whatever rallying of passions there
may be afterward; as if some gorgeous palm-
tree were to have the life suddenly withdrawn
from its towering height and tropical foliage.

Whether this were the cause or not, there is
no telling how long Dr. Peel may have continued, on the occasion of Bob Withers's mention
of Mr. Arthur, to have cursed him; nor how
zealously Bob, risen somewhat unsteadily to his
feet to do so, might have wielded his cudgels in
favor of Mr. Arthur, whom never since the war
began has he failed to defend on every instance
of attack, and the instances are very many of
Mr. Arthur's being denounced in his presence:
no telling, we say, how long the altercation may
have proceeded, when a singular diversion therefrom occurs.

"Dr. Peel," says Alonzo Wright, whom all
had supposed asleep, suddenly rising from his
seat, pushing back his slouched hat, which has
all along covered his silent broodings not slumbering, drawing his revolver, cocking it, pressing
it against Dr. Peel's broad chest, with his finger
on the trigger—"Dr. Peel, look here: I want
to know, now and here, what do you mean?"

"Mean?" Dr. Peel is of a ghastly sallow as
he asks the question, not daring to stir a hair's-
breadth; even Captain Simmons stops his maud-
lin chant, and, with Bob Withers, is silent with
amazement, as much at the sudden and peculiar
tone of Mr. Wright as at his action.

"Mean? In reference to what?" Dr. Peel
rather gasps than articulately asks the question,
quailing under the deadly light in Mr. Wright's
small, half-closed eyes, as well as at that cold
peculiar voice.

"In reference to her," replies that individual.

"Oh!" It is but an exclamation from Dr.
Peel's parched lips; but it indicates at least partial relief. "You forget that others are present,
Mr. Wright. I will speak with you alone on
that point with the greatest pleasure," he adds
immediately.

"Humph! That is a fact. I had forgotten
they were here with us. I was thinking. Come
now;" and, slipping his revolver, after uncock-
ing it, into its leather case at his side, Mr. Wright
rises.

"With pleasure. In one moment, Sir. But
one word, gentlemen," says Dr. Peel, pausing at
the door. "You will oblige me, oblige both Mr.
Wright and myself, by making no allusion whatever to this little matter. I beg your promise on
your honor you will not mention it to any one,
gentlemen," adds the speaker, still more anxiously, as some new thought seems to pass over

his mind at the instant. "Do I have it?" he asks, with eager look at each.

"Certainly," says Bob Withers, with a good-humored nod.

"Most assuredly you may rely upon my honor," adds Captain Simmons in his genteelest tones, with a reassuring wave of his left hand, and knowing nothing at all of what is going on. "Permit me to entreat you, however, not to abandon the flowing bowl, which inebriates, though, alas! under our depressing circumstances, it fails to cheer."

But the two are gone. Nor is there any record of their conversation thereafter. Only this—an old family servant testifies to having overheard Dr. Peel remark the next afternoon to Mr. Wright in the parlor at the latter gentleman's house, a few moments before Anne comes in to give them, at her father's request, a little music. The two gentlemen had arrived from town very late the night before. Pretty much all day they had spent in riding out over the plantation in company. At dinner the servants, as well as Anne, had remarked that Mr. Wright, though pale and exhausted as he always was after an excess, was in the highest, wildest spirits, peculiarly affectionate toward his daughter. Dr. Peel, on the other hand, attracted the attention even of the dullest of the servants waiting upon the table. At times he would join in the conversation, lead it in his liveliest manner, full of anecdote and laughter. Again his countenance would fall, he would cease to converse, seem to be buried in deepest thought, sallow, drooping, drinking eagerly and frequently of the wine upon the table, and, after dinner, from the side-board, as if to obtain a supply of animation which had been suddenly cut off from within.

The very servants waiting upon the table and about the house that and the ensuing days compared notes in the kitchen even then, as well as months afterward, upon the singularity of Dr. Peel's manner toward their young mistress. Now addressing himself to her in his easy, bold, sparkling way as of old, although by an evident effort, as if he forced himself to do so against his natural choice. Then glancing at her again furtively, fearingly, with an indescribable mixture of admiration and apprehension, not without quick side looks as of deadliest terror at Mr. Wright himself, playing the host with all the ease of the master of a household toward a favored and welcome guest.

But it was this which the old house-servant Alfred spoke of often after as having overheard Dr. Peel say to Mr. Wright, in evident pursuance of a previous conversation:

"You may rest confident, Sir, that it will not be by my fault. But I have little hope. I fear, greatly fear you are mistaken."

"Stuff, nonsense, Doctor. I will take the chances on you any how," Alfred testifies to his master's having made reply just as Anne entered the room. "Faint heart, man, never won fair lady." And surely father had never cause to be prouder of or more affectionate toward a daughter than did Mr. Wright this afternoon. No wonder he so openly manifests that pride and affection.

You may have observed, Miss, or Madam—you, Sir, certainly have—how the ladies, especially the younger ones, suddenly and surprisingly bloom out upon our planet in the early spring. It may be some cunning alteration in their dress, doing with subtle skill for themselves, in the way of adornment, what the Creator does then for bird and butterfly and flower. Or it may be that nature, in clothing at that season the plains with verdure, the lower animals with freshness of skin and plumage, forgets not to give then a softer light to the eye, a sweeter dew to the lip, a deeper bloom to the cheek, a gentler ripeness to the form in the case of woman, who is undoubtedly the dearest to her heart of all Dame Nature's numerous family. And, it may be, the eye and the imagination are themselves quickened by the stirrings of spring in us men also to view things in a brighter light. Whatever be the reason therefor the fact is so.

And never woman that May morning exemplified it more than did Anne Wright. Clothed in a modest dress of some creamy hue, her fair hair in abundant curls about face and neck, her complexion of a softer glow, and her eyes of a deeper blue, she beams upon her father and upon his guest with a beauty surpassing any thing they had either of them ever before imagined in her. Her every motion and tone even are modulated to a livelier, at the same time gentler, melody. Who knows what presentiments connected with their visitor were not moving in her blood?

When left alone together in the parlor by Mr. Wright, who has to see for a moment to the first plowing of his corn, Dr. Peel and Anne know before a word is spoken that the eventful hour of their lives has arrived. It is the man not the woman who is embarrassed. Quiet and modest and pure as she is, the whole thing is with her so much a matter known and settled as to bring no new, or intensely agitating, thought with it. During the years now of Dr. Peel's visiting at her father's house, though he has made no formal proposals, she has learned perfectly well that he loves her, and that—she loves him.

But it is strange so bold a man as Dr. Peel, one so supremely self-satisfied and independent in bearing heretofore, should seem as if smitten by an ague. His face has grown of an ashen yellow, contrasting badly with hair and eyes so dark. And there is a furtiveness about these latter, a trembling about the large and bejeweled hands, an irresolution and timidity, upon which

Anne grounds her own quietness and composure. In fact, the two seem to have completely changed places, only there is something altogether indescribable in the bearing of Dr. Peel, to which even the words mean and cowardly may be given. To any other than poor little Anne he would have the aspect rather of a condemned criminal cowering under sentence than of a confident lover. The simple fact is, strange as it may seem, Dr. Peel seeks to know his fate at Anne's hands to-day, only because the alternative is to receive it in more serious shape still at the hands of her father.

"But I am anxious you should know—should not be deceived. In fact, if you knew all I know you would—I am convinced it would be useless in me to expect your favor."

It is Dr. Peel who says it, more nervous and miserable even than when, half an hour before, his conversation with Anne began. But Anne only laughs, as composed as he is the reverse, laughs a joyous and confident laugh.

"I am a poor man," continues the lover, and repeats it eagerly, as if it was a sudden and welcome thought—"a poor man, a very poor man, indeed. You may have imagined me to be rich. I confess I have given you false impressions on that point. I am extremely poor, Miss Anne; not at all able to support you as you should wish and naturally expect." And he looks at her with eager eyes.

Anne laughs more than ever. "You have told me that you love me," she says, as if she loved to repeat the assertion. "What do you think I care about whether you are rich or poor?"

Dr. Peel walks the room like a baffled man. Another thought strikes him. He eagerly seizes upon a gilded Bible lying upon the table, advances upon Anne as if to say something, then returns it in haste to the same spot as eagerly, and continues to walk the room in evident distress of mind.

"Dr. Peel," says Anne, at last, a blush burning over neck and face, "I do not understand all this. If you do not really love me, do not really wish—"

But Dr. Peel is at her feet before the words are out of her lips, in passionate accents assuring her of his affection, only there is the cowering, fearful manner over it all, hardly venturing to look her in the eyes even in his warmest protestations. "No, no, no, not that, not that, Miss Anne. I only was anxious to save you from—not to deceive you," he says, hurriedly. "You will see what proof I give of affection." And he goes to the table, gets the Bible, and seats himself beside her as with a desperate calmness. "That you may not blame me I am about to put my life in your hands. Will you swear not to reveal to any one what I tell you?"

Anne laughs, wonders a little, gazes upon the anxious face of her lover, lays her little hand upon the book, curiosity creeping uppermost. "Why, what in the world," she begins.

"What I tell you will shock you terribly. If it were known to your father he would kill me instantly, here in this room."

Anne gazes upon the agitated man with blue eyes widening with wonder, curiosity, and deeper affection for this splendid suppliant. "It will not bind me a bit more than I would have been," she says, at last. "Yes, to please you, I'll swear; and I do wish you and pa would let me do all the swearing." And she lifts the book to her lips.

"Not even to your father?" says Dr. Peel.

"Not to a living soul. Why, what on earth?"

"Miss Anne," says Dr. Peel, in most impressive manner and with lower tones, "you and your father have been greatly mistaken in me. I am—am no Secessionist at all; I am a —a—Union man."

Anne sits looking at him with wonder, taking full note of his, to her, handsome face and form; it is as if an emperor kneeled at her feet. "A Union man! Why, Dr. Peel, who would have thought of it?" troubled, wondering, bewildered for whole minutes.

"I knew you would reject me when you knew it. And I swear to you it is so," continues Dr. Peel, watching her face with painful inquiry.

"A Union man? Why, who in the world! Oh yes," Anne adds, rapidly, half in earnest. "It's a great pity, a very great pity. Pa and I thought you the very best Southern man we ever knew. But then I'll give you pa's newspapers to read. Besides, I could convert you myself. I will tell you all how they treated us, about— wasn't it about Kansas or Nebraska? one or the other; and how they wanted to free our negroes, and what women's rights people they are, and all their terrible atrocities, and the way they have marched their soldiers over our country burning and plundering. Oh, ever so much! I am certain I could convert you"—glowing with beautiful confidence—"positively certain!"

"Never, Miss Anne. Not even you. I always have been a Union man. Will be one for ever and ever," says Dr. Peel, very slowly, and Anne sits wondering and troubled, while her lover watches her with anxiety.

"Ha! I never thought of it. Dr. Warner there in Somerville, Mr. Ferguson, Mr. Brooks; there is Mr. Arthur, too—ever so many in Somerville are Union people, they say," breaks in Anne, at last, "and they are not such desperately bad people either. Besides," and the artless girl puts her fair curls from her glowing cheeks, and laughs with delight, "there is Mrs. Sorel, and the girl I love most in the world, Alice Bowles. I know she is Union; she told me so herself; or, at least, she wouldn't say she wasn't, couldn't make her do it when she was here last week. Yes," added Anne, eagerly, and

THE OATH.

with a blush, "and Alice's own mother, too, is a good Secessionist; and I needn't be Union, must I? Please not. I never thought of that. Yes," she added, with the glad haste of a child, "and then the war is over. Pa himself says we are whipped. Very soon there won't be such names as Union men and Secessionists at all, will there?" And the difficulty has passed as entirely away beneath her artless affection as a cloud before a summer's wind. "If you only say you really and truly love me," she adds, with archness and joy.

"Love you? I love you as the flowers do the light. I adore you as you adore God," breaks out Dr. Peel, with feverish energy, but with the cowering eyes, the shrinking and apprehension of manner as before. And again the baffled lover walks the room, Bible in hand, in deepest, most painful thought, while Anne wonders and —loves.

"Miss Anne," says Dr. Peel, "I have not told you all yet. Remember your oath," and he holds up the Bible in his hand. "My life is in your hands. There is another thing I must tell you. If your father but guessed it, had the faintest suspicion of it, he would shoot me down here as sure as you are sitting there. Had I better not tell you? You will reject me with horror."

Anne looks at him with blue eyes opening again with wonder. But love is fast rallying all other sentiments in her heart, for it is master of all else in a woman, to its support. Here is this man, whom yesterday she loved yet so feared, the grandest and most powerful of all men she ever knew, he is at her feet, has put his utmost confidence in her, will hide nothing from her, places even his life in her hands.

"I have sworn; you need not fear me." She wonders and laughs—"Why, what on earth?"

"Miss Anne," says Dr. Peel, coming near her and speaking in lowest tones, "I am an altogether different man from what your father and yourself have supposed me to be—totally different in every sense. I am not an officer in the service of the Confederacy. I am, really and truly, an agent, have been from the opening of the war an agent, an active secret agent of—the Federal Government. I am one this moment. I intend to be one so long as the Government wants me. There! All I ask is that you only reject me, not tell your father or any one else till I can get away." And Dr. Peel, with ashen face and cowering eyes as before, watches her lips as if for his destiny.

Poor Anne! The matter is altogether too much for such lovely curls, and blue eyes, and roseate complexion, and lithe, childish form. She is bewildered, stunned; passes her hand wearily over her brow, tries to think. Love bestirs itself in her bosom, summons all the sentiments of the soul to its aid. Romance! Anne has long dreamed of a hero of romance as her true knight; if ever woman had such a lover she now has. There is a glory and a grandeur, too, these latter days, in the very name of the Federal Government; it is something very much to be detested, but very powerful and magnificent; and all this vague grandeur now falls like a mantle around her lover. Pity, too. Yes, if my father knew it he would lay him dead on that floor. One little whisper to her father, and—she knows him well—there are the rapid cracks of a revolver, and this stately Prince of hers lies his length on that parlor floor a dead man in his blood. Her lover is in her power, and he deliberately placed himself there—such his confidence in her. Besides, it strikes her with wonderful force: what a brave man! To think of his spending years in Somerville, being here now with a sword suspended over his head—why, it is the very chivalry of romance! Love him? She never so dreamed of loving him. She loves him the more she thinks. Reject him? Reject him now she knows all this? It would be like rejecting the whole universe!

"Dr. Peel," she says at last, lifting up her eyes like those of a little child to his face, "did you say that you loved me, loved me really and truly?"

With singular contrariety between cowering eyes and impassioned words, Dr. Peel renews his protestations vehemently.

"I will marry you," she says, quietly and simply; placing, as she says it, her little hand in his.

The strong man is convulsed with emotions beyond his control. He grasps the little, soft hand, and lets it go. He groans and curses half aloud. He actually weeps. Anne notices the beads of perspiration start upon his brow. He lifts her hand to his lips, and lowers it again before touching it with them. And all through his agony it is with cowering eyes. Anne is astonished. There rises against her love a great amazement, which, like a billow, threatens to overtop and bear it down.

She follows him with alarmed as well as wondering eyes while he, again risen from her side, paces the floor in agonies of perplexity. The tears actually trickle unnoticed by him down his cheeks; he grinds his teeth, and curses under breath.

"Miss Anne," says he, at last, "I have not told you all even yet. The worst is to come, infinitely the worst. Do you think you could love me, be my wife, cleave to me whoever and whatever I am?"—but the emphasis he puts into the words can not be written. "Don't answer yet. Think. Imagine of me the worst possible thing that your imagination can frame—the very worst—the very, very, very worst. Stop! Do not be in a hurry. Think!" And the man ventures to look straight at her, with the look, ghastly and dreadful, of a criminal convicted of the foulest of crimes.

"Dr. Peel, I am an innocent country girl," says Anne, at last, even plaintively. "I have had no mother to guide me since I was a little child. All you have told me this morning has astonished and shocked me. I am so bewildered I can hardly think at all. But one thing I know. You have told me a thousand times this afternoon that you love me with all your heart. I can not understand what you mean by what you now say. But I know that I love you and will marry you. Is not that enough?" asks Anne, like a little child. "Though what in the world you mean—"

"Hulloo, man! did ever a fellow need more than that?" It is Mr. Wright, who breaks in upon them, having opened the door unperceived by either in their excitement. "Why, Peel, you look more as if you had seen a ghost. You little rascal, Anne, I didn't know you could cow and terrify a man so, you little Tartar! Yes, I heard her, Doctor. All right! Kiss me before you go, Anne. The fact is, Dr. Peel, I have taken a fancy to you! I knew it was all stuff what you insisted about Anne's not having you. It was because you had not asked her—and no one would ever have suspected *you* of holding back!" And Mr. Wright rattles on in the highest spirits.

Before night Dr. Peel, after an interview with Anne, has arranged with Mr. Wright that the marriage is to take place almost immediately—for pressing reasons. "Meanwhile we will keep it all, of course, a profound secret. And I must leave the day of the wedding with Miss—Miss Anne: most pressing and important business," the lover says.

Dr. Peel may be a happy man, but he seems to be singularly cold and hard—with always the cowering eyes.

---

## CHAPTER XXIV.

"Yes, Sir, the grandest sort of a spree; and, as you well know, Simmons, I always said so from the start, by George! This is the smash up, Sir, and a smash up it *is*, ain't it?"

"Mr. Withers, I have refrained so far with the very desperation of hope. I can refrain no longer. It *is* as you say; I confess it, it *is*," says Captain Simmons, lugubriously dignified. "Sir," continues he, with the solemnity of a drunken and exceedingly dilapidated Dr. Samuel Johnson, "I casually met that fellow Neely. In reply to a question of mine, he informed me that he had ceased to think at all, that there was only vacuum where once he had possessed brains. Neely is a Yankee, just now the bluest Yankee eyes ever beheld, and, being a Yankee, I can have no sentiment in common with him. But such are my feelings also. Words learned in earliest childhood—I think I once sang them in Sabbath-school—

'Something and systems into ruin hurled,
And now a nation bursts, and now a world.'

Something at least to that effect has been running in my mind day and night. I tell you, Sir, ours"—and Captain Simmons extends his right hand, and says it *oro rotundo*—"is the grandest collapse in the history of the world. Yes, Sir,

the suddenest, unexpectedest, most total and complete collapse of which history, sacred and profane, has any instance."

The same phrase runs its rounds among Secessionists, with a sort of pride, too, as if there was something to soothe and console one's self with in the very magnificence of the collapse.

Yes, it is a collapse; no man in Somerville, no good Secession lady even, doubts or denies that now. There was a feeble attempt to get up a public meeting in Somerville to breathe undaunted purpose to continue the struggle; but a ghastly affair it was, very few present, tremendous resolutions presented by Lamum the editor, and passed on the ground of half a dozen yeas and no nays. Captain Simmons, Lamum, Smithers, and one or two vagrant Colonels, make speeches, in which it is well known they have no faith themselves in private circles. And Lamum publishes the proceedings of this, as of dozens of exactly similar meetings throughout the State, with all the old adjectives of enthusiastic, thronging, harmonious, unanimous, and the weary like, but not a soul now is deceived. The whole thing is worn out. Lamum prints letters from fierce zealots here and there, some sending in spoons and butter-knives for the Confederate Treasury, representing that our hope is in the fact that the United States are disbanding their armies; that Europe must certainly intervene *now*; that a just God—Mr. Ellis writes a series of articles to that effect—can not, will not, ought not, must not, shall not, abandon a cause so manifestly His own; that if we will only hold out a little longer, a foreign war or something else may turn up for our deliverance.

People hardly even read a line of all this. For four long years they have believed with a belief passing all calculation, but even the faculty of belief is wearing out. Nobody has any regard even for Brother Barker these days; people withdraw their children from his Sabbath-school, or suffer them to stay away unreproved, and never go to church themselves; the very best members sunk, for the time, into a coldness, not to say apostasy, which language fails to express. Haggard, restless, sallow, lean Brother Barker, from the crown of his lank hair to the soles of his sorrowful feet, in countenance, apparel, and bearing breathes only desolation and despair. At times even he flares up, however.

"Never," he says to Bob Withers, taking up again the refrain of the general croak—a refrain, however, which, vigorous and unanimous at first, is fast dwindling down to the rare and solitary cry of an individual here and there—"I, for one, will never live under Federal despotism; never, Sir, never, never! I will go to Mexico, to the Sandwich Islands first. Rather," says Brother Barker, with a savage gleam in his eyes, "I will stay here and agitate."

O

"Do what?" asks Mr. Withers, who has taken Brother Barker in his hand and excited him up thus, exactly as a child 'rubs a match to see it fizz and burn blue, only for the melancholy fun of it. "Do what?"

"Agitate, Sir, agitate, agitate! Aid in getting up another revolution, if it is eight years hence."

The fact is, we good Secessionists in Somerville, having duly sown the wind, are now harvesting in our whirlwind, and the crop is terrible.

Mr. Arthur endeavors to promote a certain pity for them in his bosom by summing it up in conversation with grim Mr. Ferguson:

"You can hardly imagine a ruin more complete," he says. "Take Colonel Ret Roberts as an instance. He has proved disastrously mistaken in all upon which he staked his sagacity and judgment. He endures the agonies of defeat, utter and perpetual defeat, military and political. He has lost all his property, especially his negroes. He may not owe debts North himself; multitudes do who have paid them to the Confederacy, and now have to pay them over again. He may not have bought confiscated property; multitudes have invested largely in that, and have to disgorge. Then there is his bitter humiliation in the triumph of the Union men, upon whom he has so trampled here in Somerville; dread of terrible vengeance, even, at their hands. We Union men had, even in our darkest days, at least hope left us; these have no hope—none. He has no future. You can hardly imagine loss to a man more complete."

"Yes, I can," replies Mr. Ferguson, who has stern satisfaction in the ruin of his Secession friends painful to contemplate. "Barker, Mr. Ellis, and others like them, have, in addition, lost their very faith in their religion. In the most terrible affliction men can endure they have not even that to fly to. For the time, at least, their very belief in and use of Christianity is stunned."

"Yes," replies Mr. Arthur, even with enthusiasm; "but you will see, Sir, that in the case of the truly pious among the Secessionists—and many of the most zealous of them, in and out of the pulpit, are among the best and most devoted of Christians in the world—this defeat of the cause in which they had invested all that is dearest them on earth, this most terrible affliction and trial will, like every other chastisement in the case of a child of God, work out in each of them a deeper, more devoted piety. I do believe, Sir," Edward Arthur adds, with earnestness, "this whole thing will be as an ordeal preparing the whole church on this continent, North and South, in all its denominations, for greater devotion to God and power over men for good than we have ever yet dreamed men capable of—instruments made meet by these very times, you see, for the Master's use."

And very clearly, indeed, does this minister see it to be his duty, in and out of the pulpit, to preach conciliation, moderation, and all the kindred Christian virtues; mingling much more with men than for years past, suppressing all partisan exultation, glowing with quiet enthusiasm instead in this direction. But joy in the result? Gratitude to God for it? The feeling is a much more quiet one than he had imagined it would be in anticipating it in dark days, which seem a hundred years ago now; but ah, it is an unspeakable one!

Yet, as these eventful days of May, 1865, sweep along, a new hue of feeling suddenly colors the wide and roaring current. Union men in Somerville had dreaded the rise of a bitter feeling against them which might result in the destruction of their lives and property. They are lost sight of, or thought of only with respect, in the new feeling which suddenly and angrily flushes the surface, especially among the soldiers returning by thousands to their homes. It is a feeling of bitter wrath against their own officers, partly because of individual grievances at their hands, chiefly on account of the belief, deep-seated and universal among the army, that the officers, with scarce an exception, have been engaged all along in such systematic swindling in cotton and commissary stores as no country has ever before known. The feeling has been long growing—growing for years. Military subordination suddenly thrown off, it bursts forth with terrible vehemence. Speculators, too, outside of the army, share the deep hatred of the soldiers. The universal cry is, "While we have been enduring privations for years, suffering and without pay, these have been at home making money. At least they shall share with us!"

Suddenly officers and speculators find themselves in the very camp of enemies more to be dreaded than the Federals, and they, after a moment of bewilderment, are flying in all directions. All Government property in reach is in some instances broken into and plundered. The stores of speculators share the same fate. Demoralized by plunder, the soldiery fall next upon any supplies in reach under the same plea. No house in Somerville and throughout the State safe from their search on the least suspicion, or none at all, of secreted Government supplies. Until, at last, every man in Somerville, the officials most of all, first secretly prays for, then openly desires, ardently desires the arrival of the National forces as his only hope.

"I wish to Heaven they would come!" Dr. Ginnis does not hesitate openly to say the day the soldiers disinter twenty sacks of coffee from beneath the corn in his crib. And yet, only a week before, the portly Doctor, in acknowledging in husky voice that we are whipped, that the war is over, had darkly added, "For the present, Sir, only for the present!" with terrible intimations of glare and gesture of a guerrilla war to be waged for, at the least calculation, forty years to come.

Even after the surrender of Lee Mrs. Smithers has denounced the panic of the hour as a mere panic. Smithers has speculated, in some complicated manner, in paper-money. The postmaster Smithers is, but of course it was not Government money he used, turning the paper into specie, and that into sugar, and that into negroes. Yes, negroes. That is Smithers's weakness, negroes.

"Just as soon as this little panic is over," Smithers demonstrates to his wife, "those negroes will bring twice what I gave. Soon as the war is over, Araminty, one negro will bring more'n I paid for all."

Yet the panic increases rather. Smithers has as much as he can do to secrete about his place what valuable property he has. Colonel Ret Roberts's house is searched by the soldiers on one side of him, and Mr. Neely's on the other, and the soldiers say they are successful, too, for Government stores. Even long, red Mrs. Smithers is terrified. With a tub and cloth ready on the front porch, and a child on the look-out, whenever a squad of soldiers happen to pass, Mrs. Smithers, dropping every thing to do so, is on her knees upon the porch scrubbing the floor for dear life—the idea being to impress on the minds of the soldiers the fact that the house is inhabited only by the poorest of people. Until, at last, even Mrs. Smithers is as wrathful against the Federals for not coming as she ever was against them for coming at all.

"I must do you the justice to say so, Dr. Warner. I have never yet had an intimation, even in this dark hour, of any desire on your part for the Federals to come."

It is good Mr. Ellis who says it, seated in the Doctor's parlor at this critical period. Mr. Ellis has dropped in for medicine for his ailing wife, and in fact has never entirely dropped Dr. Warner on political grounds; the Doctor is so fat and easy and good-natured it is almost impossible to do so on any grounds. Very cold has been Mr. Ellis's manner to the Doctor; very crisp his "Good-mornings, Sir!" in passing; very reticent each to the other during the Doctor's professional visits upon Mrs. Ellis; but both are men too thoroughly good at heart to lose all "elective affinity" for each other.

"Of course," continues Mr. Ellis, in his nervous manner, "I regret you have not been more decidedly Southern, Dr. Warner. I disapproved of Secession as much as yourself, Sir; it was wrong. But when we of the South were actually attacked then I buried all that. Even if your brother or father is in the wrong, would you not defend them if attacked? My country right or wrong, Sir! Your upholding Mr. Arthur in his course has pained me. In fact, I do most

heartily disapprove"—Mr. Ellis always kindles as he goes—"of your lukewarm support of the Confederacy. I think it wrong, very wrong."

Mr. Ellis need not have reproached himself at all for saying that. He was not a bit to blame. Mrs. Warner only used it as a pretext; she had almost fretted herself and Sally, her two hundred pounds' weight of black cook, to death for an opportunity ever since the surrender of Dick Taylor, the last of her hopes, to say it:

"And you think Dr. Warner wrong, do you, Mr. Ellis?" she breaks in, whirling like a gust round from her sewing-machine to say it. "Wrong? Wra-ong? Ha! And you to sit there and say it, after God himself—and you a pious church-member too—has Himself shown what He thinks of Secession. Mr. Ellis, I've known you for years, respected you too, and you are under my roof. But this much I must say to you—you are crazy, as crazy as any lunatic that ever was put in a strait-jacket. And for you to believe in that lying, thieving, murdering—hold your tongue, Dr. Warner!—retreating, boasting, cheating, repudiating Confederacy, the grandest swindling concern this earth ever saw! And after it is actually gone to pieces too! I wouldn't say a word, Dr. Warner, but it is more than I can stand. You are wrong—wra-ong! A quiet, sensible man when it begun. A quiet, sensible man, holding your tongue in all the raging folly when you saw you could do no good, all through these—these four long, long, bad, bitter years. Standing by your minister when he only wanted to be nothing but a minister and let politics alone. Yes, I know what you would say, Mr. Ellis. I am not ashamed to confess it, now I see my error, more shame to you sticking out in what you see now is all wrong. Yes, I'm glad of the opportunity to acknowledge how wrong I've been, specially to my own husband. Not that I expect to turn angel. He married Helen Morris, and Helen Morris I'm certain I'll be till I die. But I am sick in my very stomach of Secession—sick to death. Here you've been telling Dr. Warner it wasn't the Federals whipped us, but the speculating and stealing, from the highest officers downward. Confessing with your own mouth that the whole thing was rotten, needed only a touch to make it crumble of itself like a rotten, rotten old pumpkin. And Dr. Warner is wrong—wra-ong!" intensely sarcastic, in shrillest F sharp.

"I tell you what, Dr. Warner," rising suddenly from her seat, upsetting her sewing-machine in doing so, and crossing the room rapidly to her husband. "I've been burning to say it. I'm glad Mr. Ellis has stirred me up to say it—yes, and to hear me say it sits right there. I'm proud of you, Dr. Warner. You do not talk out as much as I could wish; but all these four years you've had ten thousand times my

RECONSTRUCTION.

sense. There, never throw it up to me I've said it, and I'll be sorry in ten minutes I told you; but it is only the solemn fact, you provoking old thing!" And Mrs. Warner throws her arms about that weather-beaten mariner's neck, as he sits with the old droop of his head lower than ever, awaiting the blowing out of this most unexpected gale, stoops down, kisses him upon his bald forehead, rises again, and confronts astonished Mr. Ellis; the canal-gates open their widest, hysterical but defiant.

And good Mr. Ellis finally leaves the house, having obtained a good deal more medicine than he came for.

Mr. Ellis, wilted, shriveled, bewildered, thrice in age what the past four years should have left him, looks up, as he walks home, to encounter the cheerful face and the hearty good-day of Mr. Arthur riding by. It is as the new era in contrast with the old. Only the minister chides himself for not having worn a soberer manner—nothing he abhors more than any even unintentional triumph over his old friend—chides himself for his aspect, under the circumstances, of cheerfulness even. But how can I help it without playing the hypocrite? he asks himself.

But he rides fast, for he has a letter from Mr. Staples's returned son for Mrs. Sorel. He thinks it must be from Frank, her long absent boy, only he does not know the writing upon the envelope, very much worn and dirtied by being brought so far in the soldier's knapsack. There is a singu-

lar fear thrilling to his heart as from the touch of the letter, taking it out of his breast-pocket when he gets out of town to look at it again—a creeping influence, a crawling cold. As he rides it gathers over him, a fear, a vague apprehension, so that he almost starts to hear himself called by some one from among the corn in a field to his left.

Drawing in his horse he sees it is a rough field-hand, who is hoeing near the fence — a savage of a negro, with his hair done up in little tails around his brow, the woolly beard in scant patches over his face. Mr. Arthur, as the negro takes off his fragment of a hat, recognizes him as Colonel Juggins's Jem.

"Good-mornin', Mass Arthur. Jest one minute. Hope all well, Sar. I want to see you. Any way, I seed you ridin' along, an' it comes upon me to tell you—" the boy says, scratching his head, shifting his hoe from hand to hand, looking eagerly at Mr. Arthur, agitated and confused. "Orange he say, you hold your tongue, you fool, none of your business. Orange is a passon like you, but somehow— Look hyar, Mass Arthur, ebery body say you mighty good man—"

"I am in a hurry, Jem."

"One minute, Sar. Case is dis. Suppose a man owe you money, keep promisin', promisin', promisin'—"

"Really, Jem, any other time. I have a letter for Mrs. Sorel from Frank," begins Mr. Arthur, touching his spur to his horse; for a leading defect in this gentleman's character is hurry and impatience.

"You better hear me!" It is all the boy says, but there is emphasis so peculiar in the tones, as they fall upon the rider's ears rods off, that he halts his restive horse and rides back.

"You know that man—Peel is his name— Dr. Peel? Ha! needn't tell me, Sar; I kin see you know him. I nuffin to say of him, Massa, not one word to say," adds the negro, with earnest deprecation. "He rich, big, splen-did man. Nebber saw him myself in my life. Nebber heard him say one word. Nebber spoke one word to him in my life; may Great Massa up above strike me dead in dis fence corner if I ebber did!"

"What about him?" asks the rider, with breathless eagerness.

"I hear tell he goin' to marry Miss Anne Wright, marry her dis berry mornin'—"

One instant, only one instant, the minister sits on his horse still and cold and pale as marble; the next he has gone at his horse's best speed toward Mrs. Sorel's house, but toward her house only because it is on the road to Mr. Alonzo Wright's.

Arrived there, he throws the halter of his horse over the post, and hurries in; it will take him but a moment. It is sheer force of habit which causes him thus to stop, and hurry to his bedroom to be one moment there, only one moment, upon his knees—if ever in his life surely to-day. Meeting Mrs. Sorel in the passage, he places her letter in her hand and hurries by. Before he has well closed his room door he hears her cry. That cry, peculiar to her sex, never uttered by them save when wrung from the deepest distress, he understands. Frank is dead, killed probably, dead certainly. Yet he stands trembling with impatience none the less when the white-haired mother, in the agony of her grief, casts herself upon his bosom, crying:

"Oh, Frank, Frank! I knew it was coming, but I can not, can not bear it. Help me, oh my Heavenly Father, help, help!"

How strange it seems, how cruel! Mr. Arthur has no word hardly of consolation for her, does not draw her down beside him upon her knees in even the briefest prayer in that terrible hour. With but an impassioned word, a mere syllable, in fact, of consolation, he unclasps her aged arms from about him, puts her by gently but firmly, and hastens past with cold, set face.

Fresh impediment. As he walks rapidly down the front walk, he meets a lady coming up it with hurried step. She is veiled, but he would recognize the form if it were only by the quickened beatings of his own heart. Even then it forgets for one instant all the world beside, and bounds toward her with the truest and strongest instinct it is capable of. And she recognizes him in the same moment, lifts her head bowed down upon her bosom, throws back her veil, reveals her face all discolored with weeping. She starts impulsively toward him as she does so, yet draws back even in the act itself with freshened color in her face.

"Oh, Mr. Arthur, such terrible news!" she says. "Rutledge, brother Rutledge, my only brother! And I fear it will kill mamma. I was in school. They gave her the letter first. A soldier brought it. It will kill mamma. I didn't know what to do. I rode out to see if Mrs. Sorel, to see if you—"

"In there, in there—see Mrs. Sorel! Not now, Miss Alice, dear Alice! Mrs. Sorel, Mrs. Sorel!" he interrupts her, in hurried tones; and Alice, amazed even in her anguish, sees her lover unfasten his horse, hurry past her with cold, set face, mount and ride rapidly off in the direction from Somerville. The next moment she and Mrs. Sorel are weeping aloud, clasped in each other's arms.

Not two hours after Mr. Arthur rides from Mrs. Sorel's gate, Mr. Wright, Dr. Peel, and Brother Barker alight at the gate of the first-named gentleman. Mr. Wright is evidently intoxicated, Dr. Peel is dressed with unusual splendor, even Brother Barker is as bright and fresh as his best black suit can make him. But all seem hurried and heated. Brother Barker is sallow beyond all precedent, which is saying a

good deal, for very ashen and yellow, indeed, has been his complexion for the last two months.

"I told you so when you wanted me to have that man come out here to-day. Devotedly as I am attached to your daughter, Sir, I tell you plainly I would rather forego her hand than have such a fellow officiate."

It is Dr. Peel who says it as they ride up to the gate.

"A Union man, Sir, a bitter Union man. As I said at the time, a regular Federal spy in our midst. A —— hypocrite!" Almost the entire stock of Dr. Peel's profanity interposed between the two words. "You did right to kill him, Sir, perfectly right. Even this clergyman could not object under the circumstances. We will ride in to-morrow and surrender ourselves. Acquit you! You will receive the thanks, Sir, of every Southern man in Somerville. Besides, as a spy, even the Federals could not touch you for shooting him."

"Look here, Peel," says Mr. Wright, seizing upon that gentleman's arm as he is about to open the gate, steadying himself with difficulty as he does so. "I told you I ought not to have drunk a drop there in town. Under the circumstances, you see. Out of respect to Anne. Dr. Peel, look here. I love my daughter. You, parson—what is it? Parker? Barker? I love that daughter of mine there in this house. I love her because I killed her mother, you see; not shot her, you know—it was with a big music-book, I believe. Besides, Anne's a good daughter; best girl, prettiest girl on earth. No, you don't," with a firmer hold upon Dr. Peel's arm, who is endeavoring to open the gate. "Wait. Champagne? How much was it? It's my impression you put something in it. I ought not to be drunk before Anne to-day, told you so five hundred times there in Somerville. Humph, if I only had half a thought you did, I'd—Parson Arthur? Why didn't you hit him yourself? However, I fired at him once myself in the old gin, and missed. Did you ever hear me tell about it, Mr. Parker, Marker—what is your name?" with great indignation at the clergyman present, and copious oaths.

"Not now, Mr. Wright," entreated Dr. Peel, in his most persuasive manner. "We've got the license, Miss Anne is waiting—"

"Think I care one cent?" interposed Mr. Wright. "Yes, I did kill that Parson Arthur; plucky fellow, though, he was. Ought to have seen him that day down there at the old gin. Kill? Why," and Mr. Wright took his revolver from its leather case at his waist, "see this? See how smooth it revolves? All you've got to do is to cock it—see?—point it at your man, one little, little touch on this trigger, and—down he goes. Arthur ain't the first man I've killed, by a long sight; nor won't be the last. Why, gentlemen," continued Mr. Wright, with an air of perfect sincerity, his eyes half closing as he looks at each in turn, and his voice in that peculiar low key which can not be described—"if either of you were to give me cause, half a cause, a shadow of a reason for it, I'd kill you here and now—kill both of you with the greatest satisfaction, rather do it than not. You see I *like* such things. Ever since that day I up with the big music-book—you see I had been drinking—"

"Mr. Wright," interposes Dr. Peel. "We have the license; here is the clergyman, Miss Anne sees us. I ask you as a father if you think it respectful to Miss Anne Wright—"

"Put it on that ground, do you? Well, let us go in. Only, wa'n't it over in a flash?" and he confronts his companions as they proceed up the walk toward the front-door. "Here we were riding along talking about—what were we talking about?—never mind. All on a sudden down upon us comes that fellow Arthur—rides well, rode well, I mean, didn't he? What was he saying? Oh yes, Colonel Wright, Colonel Wright, one word with you, Colonel Wright, wasn't that it? You says, Peel, what was it? Oh yes, Mr. Wright, you say, yonder comes a man I know to be a Yankee, a Federal spy, and my mortal foe, shoot him down! What did you turn so yellow for, Peel? your lips were white, screamed like a wild cat you did, didn't he, Mr. Larker, Parker; what"—a very large oath—"*is* the reason I can't keep your name in my mind? Never mind. What was it? I said. Let's hear what the man has to say, Peel. Then you whips out your six-shooter and fired. Missed, of course. Fellow kept right on steady as steel, didn't wince or draw rein. What did he say? For God's sake, Colonel Wright, one word with you! Then over in a flash, wa'n't it? I had out my revolver and fired. I assure you, gentlemen;" and Mr. Wright brims the assurance with oaths. "It was like that day with my wife. I didn't even know I laid hold, or intended to touch that music-book—you see she was playing on the piano at the time; it was over before I knew it. Something in here," says Mr. Wright, gravely, and laying his hand on his bosom, "not myself. It wasn't there the moment before. It is gone the instant the thing is done. What you would call the devil, parson; wouldn't you? Sing out."

"Really, my dear Sir, I—it is very difficult—" Brother Barker begins, smiling feebly, rubbing his hands together, glancing for aid to Dr. Peel.

"Think I may kill you? you are a coward. Arthur wasn't. Riding steadily up. One word, Colonel Wright, for God's sake, one word! his right hand up that way. Then I fired for his left breast button, last of the row, and—down he went. Never," added Mr. Wright, impressively, "whatever you do, gentlemen, never fire merely at a man. Always aim—I always do—

for some distinct something—a button, a breastpin, something of the sort on him."

And so they turn to go, Dr. Peel foaming with impatience, but afraid to cross the man, Brother Barker wishing that he had been on some distant appointment instead of in Somerville when they came for him that morning. Nor does his dismay decrease when Mr. Wright suddenly turns upon him when they are on the steps of the portico.

"What was that you said at the time, parson? For Heaven's sake let me get down and see if he is killed, wasn't it? I says, I've brought you out to marry Anne and I'll kill you too if you —yes that was it—kill you too, if you try it. You pucker up your face and say, rolling up your eyes, as if it was a grace at table, It is the awful judgment on him of God. It's very curious," adds Mr. Wright, as they enter the door— "in these difficulties I am like a spectator looking on; know all that is done, remember every thing that is said perfectly well, a kind of two of us in the thing at the same moment, a cool one and a hot one, and which is me and which is the devil I never *can* tell."

Only all this is pale and colorless delineation of Mr. Wright's words, the crimson and fervor of his profanity being omitted. As to the facts, they were as he stated.

And the minister lies bleeding, apparently dead, in the road where he fell. His horse, startled by the shots and his rider's fall, had fled from the spot for a few hundred yards, had then stopped to graze, and so had by nightfall found his way to his stable-door, carrying fresh alarm for his owner to a household already sufficiently distressed.

Mrs. Sorel had gone to town with Alice hours before and has not returned. The servants, greatly afflicted by the loss of their "Mass Frank," doubly afflicted by this new calamity—for they are all greatly attached to Mr. Arthur—hasten to inform Robby in the house of the arrival of the riderless steed. A few hours before that sedate little boy was only "Robby," now he is "Mass Robby" with the servants. His mother, too, has clasped him to her bosom, wept over him, and kissed him as her only child. In spite of his anguish Robby is not without a new sense of importance. Sorely afflicted in regard to Mr. Arthur, to whom he is ardently attached, with tears streaming afresh down his cheeks, but with the gravity of the oldest of men, he gives charge to the household to be careful, generally, during his absence, and rides in through the darkening twilight to Somerville, meditating soberly and with a sense of having attained, during the last few hours, years of growth.

Entering at last the house of Mrs. Bowles, so well known yet so long unvisited, he steals quietly, as is his wont every where, into her chamber. But even Robby's sobriety of soul is startled at the deadly hue upon the face of that lady, lying, a mere shadow of her former self, partly in the arms of his mother, who sits upon the bed—all the alienation of the last few years utterly gone, and the two friends more to each other now by far than ever before; while Alice comes and goes silently and gently, not without a pleasure in the reconciliation of the hour, even in her deepest sorrow for her dead brother, and for her mother fast following him. Common affliction has melted every coldness between these two, made keenly alive, ● and during their years of separation, to all they really are to each other. It touches Alice to observe how, in a mutual manner and tone, these two sorrow-smitten and white-haired friends are more to each other, like the schoolmates of years ago, than grown persons.

"Read it yet once more, Eliza dear; just once more, please. Not from the beginning—that passage about his being a high-toned gentleman," Mrs. Bowles is saying as Robby steals quietly in.

"'No officer in the army could have been more ardently beloved—' No, that is the wrong paragraph," Mrs. Sorel says, searching for the passage in the soiled and crumpled paper in her hand, wet with tears, and already known by heart, every line of it, to these three. "Yes, here it is," continues Mrs. Sorel, at last, reading from the letter: "'It has been my lot to be thrown with many officers from the State of our common birth, very many of all grades during the war; but among them all, I am free to say that Captain Rutledge Bowles stood pre-eminent as a high-toned gentleman and most gallant soldier. It was only after Colonel Carrington had frequently expressed his hearty approval of the killing of Lincoln that Captain Bowles spoke at all upon the subject; nor then, until Colonel Carrington had pressed Captain Bowles for an utterance of his opinion. The very strong language used by your lamented son in detestation of the crime in question was but characteristic of the man, as I have already remarked in full. Nor has Colonel Carrington even the excuse of intoxication, which the delirium of his language and conduct on the occasion would seem to indicate. Some excuse may be found for him who slew your son in the intensity of chagrin and bitterness attending the fall of Charleston. But, in the interest of truth it should be stated, so far as any exasperation on this ground should have affected any one, that individual might have better plead it in the case of Captain Bowles, he being a South Carolinian by birth, than Colonel C., who is well known to be a native of Connecticut. And this is the general rule—'"

"'That will do, Eliza," and the pale sufferer places her thin hand upon the paper. "I thank God for it, Lizzie dear. I did hope, even pray, that Rutledge Bowles might fight, even if he must fall there, upon some great field of victory within South Carolina. My heavenly Father has granted my prayer, though not as I thought. He has fallen on that soil—fallen in even a nobler cause—fallen in detestation and denunciation of a dastardly crime; the nobler in him to denounce it, to die for denouncing it, as it was a crime against the man in all the world whom we both—Rutledge Bowles and myself I mean—hold in greatest dislike. An inscrutable Providence, Lizzie"—and here the wasted hand wanders feebly about the sunken temples — "has been against the South. We won't discuss it, dear. I have tried to understand it; tried, and tried. If you only knew, Eliza," said the grief-struck woman, with earnest eyes upon the friend on whose bosom she leaned, "how hard I've tried! I've laid awake long nights through, when Alice here slept sweetly by my side, trying to make it out—trying so very, very hard. I have gone over the whole Bible in search for light, Lizzie. I have wept and prayed so! Don't be offended with me; we won't say any thing more about it; but I can not see how South Carolina was wrong. I know God rules, dear; does nothing but what is right; but we ought to have succeeded, Lizzie. I always feel that—"

"Mamma, please, you know what Dr. Warner—" begins Alice, who sits beside her mother, with the humble pleading of a little child, and moistening the thin hand clasped in her own with tears.

"I was only going to speak about the terrible fall of Charleston, and about those awful scenes in Columbia—but you are right. Only I try and try"—the hand taken from her daughter's grasp, and touching the forehead here and there with fragile fingers. "I do not, I can not understand—"

"But you were speaking of Rutledge, Alice," says Mrs. Sorel, mindful of the daughter's eyes, appealing to her through tears, and in gentlest tones.

"Yes, Lizzie, I know, and you know too, how foolish I have always been about Rutledge Bowles—except Alice here, all I had on earth; but I think even this moment more about South Carolina and its defeat and all than I do about him. You know how we have both been trained to that, Lizzie; it is part of my—my very heart; I can not help it. That Abolitionists should actually conquer us!" and again the frail hand goes to the brow, unspeakable bewilderment in her eyes.

"But I too have lost my son, Alice — my Frank. Let me read you the letter again." And in quiet tones, but with the tears trickling down her cheeks and glittering upon the white sheet as she reads, Mrs. Sorel again goes over the few words of her letter, brought in the same package with her friend's, telling of the death of her boy, after long sickness,·in the hospital at Richmond. The letter is roughly written by a comrade, many words misspelled, but all to the effect that it was the death of a Christian youth fully prepared to die, his last breath filled with messages of love to his mother and Robby, and confident expectations of reunion with them in a world where war is forever unknown. Very peaceful and quiet his death, breathing quiet and peace·even through the first anguish of the bereaved mother.

"And there is this too, Eliza, about Rutledge Bowles," says the pallid sufferer, returning immediately, though after deepest sympathy with her friend, to her own sorrow. "Alice will tell you I told her, when I recovered from my fainting fit it was my first thought, as it is now my consolation. It is better he should have died, Lizzie, now that South Carolina is defeated. Rutledge Bowles could not have endured to see it, dear. To live under the rule of Abolitionists would have been to him a living agony and humiliation worse than death. It is better as it is. Though why our heavenly Father should have permitted—" And as the wasted fingers seek the forehead, Robby can no longer keep silence. He has stolen silently by his mother's side, she aware of his presence there, but too absorbed in the sorrow of her friend and herself for her to notice him.

"Oh, mother, mother!" says Robby, the tears beginning to flow afresh at the sound of his own voice, "Mr. Arthur, Mr. Arthur!" and breaks down.

Alice is seated by the bed, gently drawing out through her hands the long white tresses of her mother, too full of sorrow to speak, but at the name she turns so sharply around even her mother can not but remark it, her lips parted, every vestige of color gone from her cheeks.

"Oh, mother, Mr. Arthur is killed! His horse—" But Robby can get no farther, for Alice has fallen forward upon the bosom of Mrs. Sorel in a faint, and all is confusion.

An hour passes away before, Robby having told the whole story so far as he knows it, any tranquillity is restored. Filled with the most painful apprehensions, Mrs. Sorel, nevertheless, endeavors to reassure herself, as well as her companions, by all manner of hopeful conjectures. Mr. Arthur may have merely alighted somewhere, leaving his horse standing, and it may have left him ; or, he may have been thrown, though not seriously hurt. But she herself and Alice too, hovering about her mother's couch pale, cold, and silent, can not but recall the singular manner in which Mr. Arthur parted from them that morning. All through their deep grief they have both felt vague apprehensions, even painful anxieties, on his behalf. Not on political grounds, for, as they both well know, there are no men so safe just now as Union men, even if Mr. Arthur's course had not been so quiet and without positive offense, as, in spite of his thoroughly known loyalty to the Union, to leave him without one embittered enemy in the world.

But Mrs. Sorel, and Alice also, can not help, even in that anxious hour, remarking the silence and, if possible, deadlier pallor into which Mrs. Bowles has fallen.

"Blind, blind, blind," she says it more to herself than to Dr. Warner, now with her, Mrs. Sorel and Alice having gone for the moment out of the room. "You know it all, Dr. Warner, perhaps have known it for months, and for me, her own mother, never to have more than feared it."

"Feared it, Madam?" says Dr. Warner, with some indignation. "As to knowing it, there are few besides yourself but knew Mr. Arthur was attached to your daughter, has been devotedly attached, I dare say for years. A good many of us have fancied it exceedingly likely his affection was reciprocated."

"He never whispered such a thing. Alice never even hinted any thing of it to me," Mrs. Bowles says, feebly, and in a bewildered manner.

"Because he knew the aversion for him you, and her brother too, might have, Madam," remarks Dr. Warner, warmly. "He did not even know how she herself might regard him, being, as he knew she knew him to be, a thoroughgoing Union man. He was too honorable, Madam, to endeavor to win her affections against your wishes—too proud to desire, even, to intrude where he was not heartily welcome. Had things continued as they were, in my opinion, though most devotedly attached to Alice, he never would have taken a step as long as the world lasted."

"That so many terrible blows should fall upon me at once," moans the invalid, feebly lifting her hand to her forehead.

"You are in a weak state of health, Madam," interrupts her physician, with a good deal of firmness for him, but professional as with a patient, "and we ought not to converse at all. Only I must say this. For all we know, Mr. Arthur is, at this moment, lying dead, either thrown, from his horse or by the hand of an assassin, God forbid! But, if he lives, there is no man living I would so well be pleased to see 'Ria, if she were old enough, the wife of. A gentleman of spotless character, of good talents, of sincere piety—one who has proved himself, during all these years of madness, true as steel, through great and unceasing pressure, to what he knew was right; not a partisan in it either, calm, mild—I declare, Madam," says Dr. Warner, with more spirit than he ever dared exhibit to his wife, "I am astonished at you." And he rubs his bald head with the palm of his left hand impatiently. But Mrs. Bowles only lies with her eyes closed, pallid, silent.

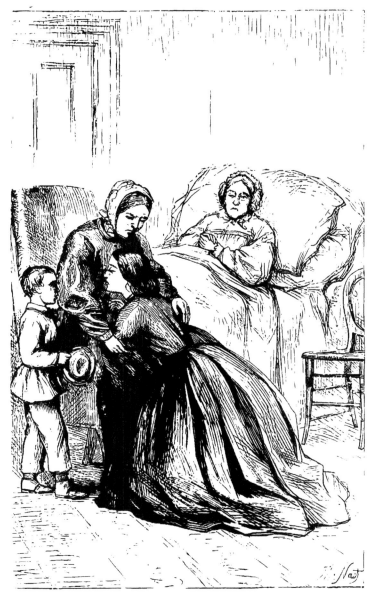

OH, MOTHER, MR. ARTHUR IS KILLED!"

"There is one thing, perhaps, I ought not to mention," says Dr. Warner, after a very long pause, and much rubbing of his brow. "Under these peculiar circumstances, however, and it is of a nature which will make it sacred with you. Mr. Ferguson might not like it—might be very angry with me," continues he, with a very plain and frightened recollection of the character of that person; "but I *know* the secret is safe with you. You will pardon me, Mrs. Bowles, I speak only this once, do it to relieve your mind. You are not as rich—pardon me—Miss Alice will not inherit—oh, forgive me—" in great confusion.

"You are not intending to remind me of our poverty." Feeble as she is, not more than barely able to speak the words, the pale sufferer abashes Dr. Warner greatly by the silent dignity of her eyes fastened with surprise on his.

"You are right, pardon me. As my wife says, I always *am* doing something I ought not," remarks the culprit, feeling himself a huge culprit to the extremities of his disarranged neckerchief in every button-hole lacking its button, and with his head sunk into its shower-bath droop. "I only meant to say that Mr. Ferguson has placed a sum of money, a very large sum indeed, he has no child or relative, you observe—nothing else on earth to do with it," the Doctor adds with a deprecatory gesture, and by way of apology for Mr. Ferguson, "out at interest in Mr. Arthur's name. He intends the papers as a wedding gift to him on his marriage. Besides, he has made a will—"

"Dr. Warner!" Nothing but that, with its accompanying look, but it cuts the physician to the bone. There is long silence, during which he looks at his watch and administers a soothing powder, rubbing his head with vexation, but having nothing more to add.

"I am bewildered, exhausted, can not sleep as you all would have me do," murmurs Mrs. Bowles at last; "but I am still in my right mind. And I never can consent that my daughter should marry, though he had every other quality under heaven, an—an Abolitionist. That Alice should have an affection for one *kills* me."

No more than that; but oh the tone in which it is said! Mrs. Bowles closes her eyes and lies as pale and cold as marble, as much beyond Dr. Warner's reach as if she were in Heaven.

He feels it, gives over rubbing his forehead, and steps quietly out of the room, as a wrecked mariner might crawl ashore out of the waves, the storm-beaten condition of the man altogether indescribable.

He finds Alice reclining on the sofa of the next room, which is the parlor, Mrs. Sorel sitting on a low stool at her head. Alice has been, is weeping, and at a glance Dr. Warner sees that these two, at least, are in fullest sympathy with each other.

Yes, he thinks Mrs. Bowles will sleep, perhaps, if left undisturbed. Nothing from Robby yet? For Robby has gone back to send the servants out in every direction to inquire—a labor of love with them—in regard to Mr. Arthur. Robby has not returned, has not had time as yet.

"A dozen of us will be off as soon as it is day," Dr. Warner remarks, and proceeds to prove that there is not the least possibility of any harm having befallen their friend. "Heaven has pressing need of just such a man in the new times before us, Mrs. Sorel," is the somewhat inconclusive argument, among others, which he urges, amidst much warm eulogium of Mr. Arthur. "He has been a living, powerful contrast to that man Barker, a sort of peaceful antidote to his virulent poison in Somerville for years now." Dr. Warner dwells much upon that. "There is no man living to whom I would as proudly and gladly give our 'Ria as a wife," the Doctor adds for Alice's especial benefit, drooping his head the instant after in self-reproach for having spoken the words.

Meanwhile Alice has stolen once or twice into her mother's room, and pronounces her to be resting quietly. She has just persuaded Mrs. Sorel to go to her room and lie down, when a step is heard upon the front porch and a knock follows at the door. With stealthy step, lest he should disturb the invalid, yet with beating heart, Dr. Warner hastens to the door. In deepest anxiety Alice and Mrs. Sorel hear him greeted in a voice they do not recognize. There is a low but rapid conversation upon the front porch. Then Dr. Warner introduces no less a person than Mr. Bob Withers into the room, says that gentleman will explain, and is himself gone, gone in such hurry as to forget his hat, and then, still more wonderful, his saddlebags, after each of which he has to return.

"You will forgive my intrusion, ladies, though I believe it is not yet nine o'clock," says Mr. Withers, declining a chair. "Thank you, no, I can stay but a moment. The fact is, I called at the Doctor's house and was told he was here. By-the-by, I should have told him to return by way of his own house. I fear his lady is in strong hysterics. The instant I told her Mr. Arthur was shot—I beg pardon," adds Mr. Withers, in dismay; for Mrs. Sorel, passing one arm around Alice, herself totters as she stands, while Alice rallies all her soul to her aid, and composes herself by desperate struggle.

"By George!" The exclamation bursts entirely of itself from Mr. Withers's lips. "He isn't killed, you know, on that account. I have been shot myself twice. I dare say you have heard the circumstances, in connection, I am sorry to say, with cards. There is hardly a man in all my acquaintance—in a certain circle, of course—but has been shot at some time during his life, badly cut at least. But it *is* a wonder in this case. Peel or Wright, whichever one of the two it was, evidently aimed at a coat-button on the left side; button shattered, by George!—excuse me—to shivers, only grazed his side, you see. His horse must have started at the shot, or his coat have hung off from his body, but it was enough to knock him off. He has bled, too, badly. You observe—"

Alice can now look steadily at their visitor.

She has often seen him before, knows his general character as a good-natured but dissipated man; generally esteemed, somehow, in spite of his wild courses. Mr. Withers has a frank, honest face, a little too highly colored, but he glows before Alice now, beautiful as Apollo—Bacchus rather.

"In one moment, if you please, Mr. Withers," she says, and glides quietly into her mother's room. Is detained there for several minutes. "I hoped my mother was sleeping," she says, "but I found her awake. She begs that you will please come into her room, she is anxious to hear."

Excessively awkward does Mr. Withers feel as he takes a seat in the sick chamber. He is startled at the appearance of Mrs. Bowles, whom he has not seen before for a long time. It reminds him of his mother, of promises made by him to just such a pale invalid in just such a darkened chamber; promises made with passionate weeping, but, alas! how poorly kept. Mrs. Sorel has told him in a whisper of the death of Rutledge Bowles. Very quiet is Mr. Withers in his manner, having vague ideas, in addition to all else, that those present have deeper interest in Mr. Arthur than he imagined when he first came.

"You see, ladies," he says, "I was returning about noon to-day from Colonel Juggins's—been out to buy corn for my bays—in my ambulance. About a mile this side of Mr. Wright's I saw some one lying in the road—Mr. Arthur. He was waving his hand to me to make haste as far as I could see him. 'For Heaven's sake make haste, Mr. Withers!' he said, 'haste, haste!' I supposed he was anxious to get to a doctor, and placed him, as fast as I could, in the ambulance. 'Now drive for Mr. Wright's as hard as you can,' he says; 'never mind me. I am weak from loss of blood, but I can see a physician afterward. Fast, Mr. Withers, fast, fast!' he kept saying, which was unnecessary, for my bays were young; they always go when I am behind them, very fast indeed. I don't perfectly understand the thing," remarks Mr. Withers, pausing for a while, "but I will tell it all to you as it happened. As we drove along he would not say one word how he was wounded, only this: 'The instant we get to Mr. Wright's house,' he said, 'Mr. Withers, leave the ambulance with me, run in and tell Mr. Wright as he loves his daughter to come out instantly, instantly! and see me one moment. You will find Dr. Peel there; don't mind him, any thing he says or does. You are a kind-hearted man, Mr. Withers, and a brave man, do as I tell you as you ever loved mother or sister,' he said; 'excuse my repeating it.'

"'Well, but what the mischief?' I began. 'I can not explain at all,' he says, 'can not, can not. Only do as I say, and that quick, for God's sake.'

"'But you may be in, by George! dying need of a doctor,' I began. 'On! on!' he only said; 'it's ten thousand times more important for me to get there in time than for me to live!'

"By that time we were at Wright's gate. There was a carriage before it. I began to suspect the thing. I dashed in and, by George! yes! There in the parlor they were! They must have gone in but that moment. Dr. Peel was on the floor, the most splendid-looking bridegroom I ever saw—broadcloth, ruffled shirt, gold chains, white satin vest, kid gloves, perfumes—in my life, big and magnificent as an emperor, handsomest fellow I ever came up with. By him was his bride, Miss Anne Wright, in a traveling dress. You know her, ladies; the least little bit of a lady, sweet and beautiful as a lily. Parson Barker had just begun when I dashed in. There was a tremendous to do, by George!" added Mr. Withers, with excitement; "it was all in a minute; I saw the couple standing there so beautiful and happy, saw Peel turn positively blue, knocked Parson Barker flat over in my hurry. I do not know how I managed it, but I had Mr. Wright out at the ambulance before he knew it. I was holding him there over Mr. Arthur lying pale as death in the bottom of the ambulance, his head on a cushion, when he seizes upon Mr. Wright's hand like a vice and waves me off, this way, with the other, serious as death.

"Wright was bewildered. Mr. Arthur drew him down and said a few quick words. Wright seemed actually frozen to the ground. I could see Mr. Arthur draw him down again and say something as rapidly and earnestly as a man could. Then he came tearing back past me, with the livid face of a devil. I never saw such a face as that before," remarked the speaker, with a shudder, "I never want to again. But Mr. Arthur beckoned me to get in. I did so. 'Now for a doctor as soon as we can, Mr. Withers, if you please,' he said; and then he added, 'I couldn't help it—he would have—God help him—what comes of it!' something like it, and fainted dead away. I put it to them bays I rather think, left him just getting out of his swoon on his bed at your house, Mrs. Sorel, came on for Dr. Warner, and that," adds Mr. Withers, passing his hand through his hair, "is all I know about it."

Without saying a word, Alice brought Mrs. Sorel her bonnet and shawl, and aided her to put them on, though with trembling hands. "I will take good care of mamma," she says, with a color in her face, a light in her eye, a tone in her voice such as sheds a new light upon Mr. Withers's mind.

First, indulging, as he eyes her, in a shrill whistle, strictly internal and inaudible, he remarks to himself: "But I don't see myself what business a preacher has with as pretty, by George! as splendid a girl as that. However, Arthur's a trump if he is a parson!" A little discontented, though.

"I am sure Mr. Withers will be kind enough to drive you home," says Alice, with beautiful eyes upon Mr. Withers.

"Oh, certainly, with pleasure. Ambulance standing over at Dr. Warner's gate," replies Mr. Withers, promptly. But he lingers, with his hand upon the back of the chair upon which he has been seated. "There is one thing—I know nothing, you observe—I hope you will pardon my attending to such a matter. The fact is," says Mr. Withers at last, as by a desperate effort, "No human being ever hears about this matter from my lips. You ladies, I am sure, will never allude to it to a soul. Mr. Arthur has fixed it so the very bride, poor, poor thing! will never know the truth if her father only manages right. Mind, ladies, Mr. Arthur has never whispered a syllable to me, by George! he has acted with the coolness as well as pluck of a Trojan, hasn't he? But I am satisfied, putting every thing together, perfectly satisfied that man Peel, Dr. Peel he was called, was, by George! — excuse me, it is almost impossible to believe it—was, after all, a—" The word sticks in Mr. Withers's throat. "I know the man that whispers it will be killed by Wright, as sure as I am standing here. But I am satisfied, by George! —excuse me—I *know* it now, it is the only thing that can explain it at all. Peel was a negro, a mulatto, I feel certain of it. Or *was*, I should say. If he is a living man this moment I am mistaken. At your service now, Madam." And Mr. Withers starts for the door, stands hesitating there a moment, and returns again.

"I hope you will be certain to excuse me, ladies, for mentioning such a matter before you —by far the most horrible thing I ever knew in, by George! *my* life. No other human beings besides yourselves will ever have a whisper of it from me. Fact is," continues Mr. Withers, with a furtive glance at Alice, "I thought there were those here to whom all I did know about Mr. Arthur was solemnly due. Only, mind, I don't pretend to be certain, that about Peel not positively, you know. Feel morally satisfied myself, putting all things together, but couldn't undertake to swear it, by George! Ah, excuse me. Good-evening!"

"When he come rushin' out ob de back-door," the very black Parson Orange, a sleek, rotund, exceedingly smooth-spoken and utterly unprincipled negro man, is saying, at that very moment, to Colonel Juggins's Jem, in the latter's cabin, "I thought de man was goin' to turn white, he was so pale! Dressed up!"—and Orange can only express the degree thereof by an exclamation often used by him in public prayer, and only suitable thereto. "Oh, yes, I had your Massa's blood-mare ready; it was my dream to do it, as I told you. Jest as it was in my dream—berry mare, berry spot, berry man rushin' out widout his hat, berry lips blue as I saw in my dream, Humph! Nebber laugh at my visions again, will you?—heh, heh, heh!" nodding his wise head over the memory of it with wonder on wonder.

"Well, what den?" Jem breaks in upon Orange's ruminations.

"I'll belieb in dreams from dis day out; always did. Oh, little more! 'Is dat you, Orange?' says he. 'All right'—jumps on dat mare and is gone. Jest like in a dream. Humph! I don't know but it all *was* a dream. Ef only your Massa can look at it in dat light 'bout his blood-mare," adds Orange, with a grin at his duller confederate. "Now see how much brighter I am dan you'd been, Jem. You would a hurried off. I didn't. No, Sir. Sot down flat on de ground; took off one shoe, and broke de string." With another grin.

"What dat for?" asks Jem, with respect.

"Listen, nigger: 'fore you could count one hundred, Mr. Wright he come tearing out after him, de white heat ob hell in his eyes, revolver cocked in his hands. Come upon me, happenin' dere fixin my shoes. 'Which way?' dat was all he said. 'Which way?' Man all dressed up, Massa? I asked. 'Which way?' dat is all he said, his pistol touchin' my nose, finger on de trigger, all de debbils in hell in his face. Dat way, Massa, dat way, I says, in a hurry, pinting dimetrically de wrong road. 'Tell Jack to follow me on Roan,' he says, and *he* is gone—exactly as in de dream."

"An' you told Jack," asks Jem, eagerly.

"Yes, Sar, de farder an' de faster *he* trabbel on dat road de better. Yes ; I went on de place an' told Jack. But wasn't dere a muss in de house? Jack told me 'bout it while he was saddlin' Roan. Peel was on de floor to be married—actu'ly to be *married*, nigger, to Miss Anne. Yah! Ambulance drove up to de door; man jumped out, run in, carried de father out to it like a child. De instant he do it, Peel took out de back-door, knockin' ober de niggers crowded dere to see de ceremony; didn't eben stop for his hat. Parson, he run up stairs an' shut himself up; got to prayin' up dar, Jack said."

"Miss Anne?" asks Jem, with intensest interest.

"Jack say, when her father was hurried out one door, Peel run out ob de udder, she stood frightened out ob her wits. Sudden' her father came rushin' back, wild! Then she rushes for him, all in her bonnet and trabbling clothes an' hold him in her arms. Jack say she kept hollerin', 'I knew it, pa, I knew it; he didn't hide it ; he told me he was a Union man. It was my fault ; he wanted me to let him off if I would. I loved him, pa ; don't kill him, don't kill him!' windin' herself about her pa like a snake, shrieking an' cryin'—her pa sayin' nothin', only cursin' an' tryin' to get away. 'If you kill him kill me,' she said, Jack told me, 'I'm a Union wo-

THE LOVERS.

man; I hate de Souf; I hate de Confederacy; kill me too, me too; I love the Yankees. I hate de Secession!' Jack said it was all her pa could do to break from her, she wrapped herself all 'round him so.

"But he broke away at last, leavin' her dar on de floor in her bonnet an' things in a dead faint, poor thing! like a flower struck by lightning. Dey all lubbed her mightily, dem niggers, dey was all cryin' over her, said it would kill her dead. I 'member," added Orange, reflectively, "one day 'bout two weeks before, she was at a prayer-meeting we had over at your Massa's, Jem, you mind it? she shook hands with me in de front porch. 'I hope you'll do dem some good. Orange,' she said. Yes; an' smiled so . . . . it. Yes," adds Orange, after far. . . . . n, "she was for certain de sweetest . . . . . a'est work of God I ebber see. 'Tis migo . . . . "

But time flies very fast, even though it accomplishes the greatest events as it flies. In the compass of two weeks after Mr. Arthur's wounding, the Confederacy, more like, now it has come and gone, some awful vision of inspired prophet than a reality, has, in the surrender of the last of its armies and in the capture of its Lucifer, expired from the face of the earth, only a terrible memory henceforth and forever. It is a pleasant June evening, and Mrs. Sorel and Alice are seated in Mr. Arthur's room. He is able to sit up now in an easy-chair, pale from loss of blood, but rapidly recovering. Her great affliction has left its traces upon Mrs. Sorel, if it were only in the fuller peace which has softened into a deeper, purer quiet the lines of her mouth, the light of her eyes. And Alice, seated by her lover's side as if they had been already long married, is serene of countenance, even though its paleness is heightened by the deep mourning in which she is clothed—double mourning—for at once brother and mother.

"Yes," Mrs. Sorel is saying, while Alice is silently sewing, with downcast eyes, "there is indeed the hand of a Father in it. That Mr. Withers should have been able to say all that to her, and just then, how providential it was! 'I had feared, before, Mr. Arthur entertained sentiments—was one of a class whom I have been trained from infancy to regard with horror unspeakable,' she said to me when I went back to her next day. 'I have given over endeavoring to understand matters, Lizzie. I am content to leave it all in the hands of Him who doeth all things well. I withdraw now all objection in regard to Mr. Arthur. Rutledge Bowles is gone. I once regarded Mr. Arthur next to him. Though I do not, can not, in this life at least, understand matters, he must have had powerful reason for the course he pursued. You, Lizzie, and he and Alice, too, were calm and quiet while I was feverish; but we will speak no more about it,' she said, and kept repeating— you remember, Alice?—even to the end, 'He doeth all things well, doeth all things well.' You ought to love Alice very dearly, Mr. Arthur," adds Mrs. Sorel, gravely; "her mother was the truest lady I ever knew in all my life."

"God knows that I do that only too well," Mr. Arthur adds, as gravely, looking with fondest affection at Alice; "and," as she lifts her loving eyes to his, "I have loved her from the first moment I saw her with an ever-increasing affection. I will not speak of that, because no words can at all express it. My gratitude to God for giving me back at once my country and you, Alice, is unspeakable. And, of all the world, it is Brother Barker shall marry us! If I had been in his case I might have been— probably would have been—worse than he. We have both endured, darling, long and terrible trial. I hope we are fitted for the new world upon which we are entering together—a new world, Alice, with new duties, new sufferings, perhaps—who knows? But we are entering upon it together. I ask no more, love, than that!" Unconsciously to both of them, their hands lie upon the arm of the easy-chair, clasped in one. But at this moment Robby comes into the room soberly as he can, yet in greatest excitement.

"Mr. Brooks, oh, Mr. Brooks!" he exclaims, and holds up a warning hand—"Listen!"

Sure enough. The distant music of a mili-

"HOME, SWEET HOME!"

y hand. Very faint, yet they can hear it as they sit with suspended breath. Nearer now and louder. What is the air? Wait. Still nearer. And the lover takes the other hand in his, one there already. Nearer. Their eyes meet inquiringly. Still nearer the music sounds music loud, clear, sweet exceedingly. Robby and his mother have turned, are looking the other way, attentive only in that direction, and the lips, too, of the lovers meet. For the tune is plain now. And it is not Hail Columbia. Nor the Star-Spangled Banner. Nor yet Yankee Doodle. It is—to these two of all tunes on earth!—Home, Sweet Home.

THE END.